The Sins of Empire
Unmasking American Imperialism

Jason Hirthler
Kindle Direct
New York

1

Published in the United States of America

First Published, June 2015

Published with Kindle Direct Publishing

Cover photo by David Mark

This book is for citizens of the planet wherever they are and under whichever flag they live. Together we share the fight to turn a ruthless and exclusionary imperial system into one that satisfies the needs of the majority, protects the rights of minorities, and offers prosperity to all.

Also for my parents, who introduced me to the love of reading and writing, to the anti-war values of the Sixties' Left, and to the great civil rights story of Martin Luther King, Jr. and the communities of Southern African-Americans who won their rights in the face of brutal oppression.

"Freedom of speech is the principal pillar of a free government; when this support is taken away, the constitution of a free society is dissolved, and tyranny is erected on its ruins."

Benjamin Franklin

"During times of universal deceit, telling the truth becomes a revolutionary act."

George Orwell

Table of Contents
Empire of Deceit

Preface

The United States is an empire. It may not look like the old colonial British Empire, but it colonizes nations and peoples much as the British did. We don't put boots on the ground as often because we've found more economical methods of domination. Subtler forms of violence. We foment coup d'états that swap out the leaders of a nation, typically replacing an independent-minded populist with a venal servant of the imperial system. Then we load up the country in question with onerous debts, the loan conditions of which demand social austerity and the selling off of national assets and resources to foreign concerns. Fancy words for looting. Should that nation's leadership find themselves waxing nostalgic for self-sustaining days of yore, we can easily threaten them with interest rate hikes and currency attacks to keep them subservient. There's nothing like runaway debt to quell the seething mob.

If choreographed color revolutions and midnight coups don't work, military action can be swiftly procured, often justified on the basis of falsehoods and usually legitimized by corrupted international institutions originally designed to keep the peace. Wars of aggression are the calling card of the imperial state. Sadly, most countries on earth can point to either the wreckage of a U.S. invasion or the nearest U.S. military base. We have some 800 bases around the world. We've bombed 14 Muslim countries since 1980. We've invaded around 50 since the end of World War II. In total, we've <u>invaded</u> some 70 nations since the founding of the republic. A notable study just released in 2014, *America Invades*, <u>claims</u> we've invaded 43 percent of the countries in the world, and have had "military involvement" in 98 percent of them.

The coups and the wars and the debt regimes all serve a single purpose: global power, which evidently is best earned at gunpoint or with an unpayable invoice. The elite capital formations that control the American empire are ever hungry for new markets in which to profitably invest billions of restless dollars. Dollars that, if they aren't re-invested, will lose value simply through the process of inflation. This capitalist impulse, an inexorable mandate, furnishes the economic incentives that drive us to war. Wars are always about wealth. Wealth that can then buy power and influence. The more the powerful influence government, the less restraints are placed on their powers of exploitation. It seems that without a vigilant and informed public to keep the political class—and their patrons—in check, the latter will resort to every manner of deceit in an effort to expand its power.

This is the system we should challenge and change. America's second president, John Adams, said that, "Liberty cannot be preserved without a general knowledge among the people." In the early Seventies, frightened by the liberal turn of the post-war era and the Sixties especially, the one percent launched a class war against the majority. It was designed to dismantle the checks on its already outsized influence over Washington, and hence its right to press for more unnecessary military violence abroad and the bitter pill of austerity at home. To that end, propaganda has been its most effective tactic in neutralizing popular dissent. Most of us don't even know what is being done in our name. Wars are always rationalized for us by the Mainstream Media (MSM) in ways that let us comfortably forget about politics and busy ourselves with our daily lives. They are humanitarian in nature. They reflect our responsibility to protect. They are sanctioned by the United Nations Security Council. No matter the aggression, you can be sure it is accompanied by a writ of assistance, as it were, permitting us to ransack the nation of our choice in pursuit of some phantom—and no doubt imminent—threat.

The people have to challenge this unchecked freedom to exploit. Judge Louis Brandeis said, "The most important political office is that of the private citizen." Because many of us don't bother with politics, we need a new political consciousness based on the solidarity of our class—the class of the 99 percent. Adams was right. We're losing our liberty because we don't know what our government is doing. Knowledge through education is thus an important piece of what we might call an anti-totalitarian project. Hopefully this book will be a small step in that direction.

J.H.
New York City, June 2015

Part One
Foreign Policy: License to Kill

"It's not radical Islam that worries the US—it's independence"

Noam Chomsky

A Neoliberal Field Guide
How to Bomb, Corner, and Bet Your Way to Riches

In author and editor Michel Chossudovsky's excellent book, "The Global
Economic Crisis," he quotes democracy's bête noire emeritus, Henry Kissinger,
who stated in that plain and bloodless manner, "Control oil and you control
nations; control food and you control people." This cynical insight could be the
mission statement of global corporate power bent on the total control of the
world's food and fossil fuel.

As Chossudovsky and writers including James Petras and Michael Hudson
variously illustrate, this goal is pursued largely through three techniques perfected
in the killing fields and bombed out urban craters of the developing world, in the
maquiladoras and sweatshops of the Third World, and in the borderless ether of
global finance. Sometimes characterized as a neoliberal class war by the rich on
the poor, elite policies are funded by Fortune 500s, implemented domestically by
bought governments, and abroad by a two-tiered alliance of military power and
perverted Bretton Woods institutions. Their proven strategies for success include
illegal wars of aggression, building commodity monopolies, and rampant
financial speculation. If there were ever a field manual made for neoliberal
exploitation, these three models, and their representative case studies, would
comprise its core chapters. Here are a few cases worth considering.

Blinded on the Road to Damascus
When Abby Martin interviewed dissident writer William Blum on her Russia
Today program, "Breaking the Set," she asked him why he focused so squarely on
foreign policy. With his inimitable frankness, Blum replied that it was because
that was where the most damage is done. So let's start there. Although engineered
famines compete with war, nothing seems to quite match warfare in its capacity to
extend its cruel hand into the past, present, and future. Like nothing else, war
obliterates the cultural heritage of the past, slaughters and displaces the living, and
deforms the unborn. Past, present, future—no generation untouched, no soil
uncontaminated.

While militaries get all the press, the defense corporations that supply their
arsenals too frequently skirt the media's roving eye. Corporations like Lockheed
Martin, Northrop Grunman, Boeing, and General Dynamics comprise the
American quarto of elite weapon makers. Generals at the Pentagon peruse their
brochures over apple balsamic salads, checking off their preferred items: Hellfire
missiles and military aircraft from Lockheed Martin, the latest in gun systems and
ammunition from Alliant Techsystems and ArmaLite, Predator and Reaper drones
from General Atomics, F-15 fighter jets from Boeing and Abrams tanks from
General Dynamics. The list goes on. We know little about it in the States.

But if you live in Damascus, for instance, you may find yourself an unwitting "early adopter" of some of this leading-edge technology, like a Raytheon Tomahawk missile blasting its way through Syria's antiquated missile-defense systems into your local hospital or perhaps into your living room. If you live in Waziristan, you may have already grown accustomed to the buzz of MQ-1 Predator drones in the high sky, surveilling your neighborhood for energetic youth bearing the hallmarks of terror. You are savvy enough to know, however, that should your neighbors be hit by a "signature strike," you shouldn't attempt to rescue any potential survivors lest you find yourself blown apart by a "double tap" strike, which targets first responders (or, friends of terrorists, according to Pentagon and CIA logic).

It's no coincidence that Raytheon's stock price hit a 52-week high on rumors of war with Syria. But aren't these arms makers seeing their remits reduced? Sequestration? Don't kid. Austerity? For whom? Northrup Grumman shares are up by 56 percent this year despite the theatrical claims of deficit reduction emanating from beltway bean counters. Northrup also enjoyed a tidy income spike of $38 million year over year. The message is clear: war is coming, one way or another, one place or another. For these corporations, war is good. War is bounty. War is a new guest wing on the CEO's Monticello-like mansion. And a fresh coup in some remote and abstracted nation.

Jilted in Java

Many needless nonmilitary crises are caused by financial speculation. The collapse of the U.S. housing market was perpetrated largely by greed-driven derivatives trading and speculation. Likewise, the unnecessary spikes in commodity prices before the 2008 crisis owed much to the same speculative frenzies. When the price of wheat and rice and corn and oil double overnight for no good reason other than futures and options trading, billions are negatively affected—from the billons living on $2 a day, who suddenly can't afford basic foodstuffs through no fault of their own, to the Western commuter who finds the rising price of gas unsustainable or sees his equity evaporate over a weekend.

Author Amy Chua, in her book *World on Fire*, pointed out several useful examples of the dangers of speculation, drawn from the finance-fueled collapse of the Asian Tigers in the late nineties. Let's say you're a tofu maker in Java. One day, unbeknownst to you, thanks to some clever price manipulations on the Chicago and London commodities exchanges, the price of soybeans triples. After some hand-wringing conversations with your wife, you pull your children out of school and put them to work so that you have enough money to buy the beans that you turn into tofu. Fortunately, the price of fuel is steady; you need about 100 liters a day of fuel to light your pressure cookers. Then the Indonesian government announces, with great fanfare and optimism, that it has rescinded its fuel subsidies based on the sage advice of the IMF, which promises that "free trade" will deliver an economic boom. Your wife walks in to the room. "Welcome to bankruptcy," she says.

Far from Indonesia, Goldman Sachs, Morgan Stanley, and Bank of America are all heavily invested in some or all of the various trading boards, from Chicago's CME to the NYSE to London's International Commodity's Exchange (ICE) and International Petroleum Exchange (IPE). Ever since the deregulation of futures under the Clinton administration, houses like Goldman have been able to stake huge commodity positions, even employing a derivative especially formulated for commodity indices. Over the last decade, money has poured into commodities futures, generating the price bubble that eventually wrecked small farmers and lined the pockets of banking behemoths like Goldman and JPMorgan.

Swindled in Addis Ababa
Instead of gun running or commodity swindling, some imperialists prefer the rather more serene methodology of agricultural dispossession. In market terms, this might be known as a monopoly, in that it dispossesses people of their market opportunities. Corporations like Monsanto, Archer Daniel Midlands (ADM), and ConAgra, use standing international institutions like the International Monetary Fund (IMF) and the World Bank to smuggle their products into developing markets. The IMF Structural Adjustment Programs (SAPs) have always conditioned loans on the "liberalization" of the local economy. This often meant not only the acquisition of domestic industry by foreign capital, but also the eradication of protectionist measures designed to shelter fledgling domestic businesses, like small farmers, from infusions of competitive foreign products with absolute advantage.

This opening up to "free trade" instances two fairly cruel events. First, the dumping of Western agribusiness commodity surpluses on poor countries. The laws of the WTO stipulate unfettered market access for global agribusiness under the principles of free trade. Naturally, there are no agribusiness titans in Kampala dying to penetrate the American peanut market, so this trade is usually a one-way highway from the overflowing grain silos of the West. Generally, this "food aid" paradoxically leads to a loss of food security in a once self-sufficient land. Instead of producing beans or maize for local consumption, farmers are either pushed out of business or find themselves producing Arabica coffee beans for export to trendy Western cafes (while the government takes loans to import corn and other essential foodstuffs).

Second, and this is even more invidious, say you are a small farmer in an African country. As Chossudovsky has outlined numerous times in relation to Ethiopian agriculture, perhaps you've just marginally survived a terrific drought (brought on in part by climate change owing to the outsized and indiscriminate consumption habits of the Western world). Suddenly, with all the serendipity of a Countrywide lender approaching a unwitting mark, an NGO or perhaps an agribusiness agent himself is standing at your door, arms extended, cupping a handful of seeds for which he requires no recompense. You gratefully accept, thinking God has granted you a fresh bounty for your suffering.

A year later things have changed. You discover that either the seeds are "terminator seeds" that go sterile after their first harvest; or you discover that replanting the seeds requires a sizeable outlay of cash to the true owner of the seed, Monsanto. You are told that Monsanto owns the intellectual property rights to the seed variety, which is conjured in a laboratory in Missouri, building a new genetic form based on several existing strains, some of them drawn from your own backyard, hewed over millennia of local hybridization, which cost nothing, and the benefits of which were shared throughout the community.

Not only that, but you've got to purchase costly pesticides to ensure you achieve the promised yields at harvest. You might need a pre-emergent herbicide to kill the weeds and a post-emergent fungicide to kill the mold, and significantly more water, since the seed, although touted as drought-resistant, may require more water at planting to achieve a healthy stand. You can't afford all this, your crop collapses, your farm fails, and you think—suicide or lifelong shame? 270,000 thousand Indian farmers chose the former. It should be an oft-repeated trope that once the IMF enters a developing economy, it ceases to develop.

Of course, I've failed to mention the external cost of agribusiness to the local population. As a report on Argentina recently noted, cancer rates in rural communities there spiked almost simultaneously with Monsanto's introduction of glyphosate, the infamous 'silver bullet' herbicide launched in 1996. While 'Round Up Ready' seeds have helped farmers make unproductive land arable, contamination of the water table and, subsequently, the local population, is frightening. In yawning self-defense, the global giant lamely rehearsed its warmed-over talking points about the safety of its toxins. They've probably had enough of the troublesome Argentines anyway, given that the government threw the IMF out of the country a decade ago. When it comes to smashing protectionist measures, there's nothing quite so helpful as the dangling carrot of a multi-billion dollar IMF loan. Not too dissimilar from the sight of Commodore Perry sailing into Tokyo Bay with a squadron of steaming gunships. One inspired avarice, the other fear, but the result was much the same.

Bamboozled in Baghdad
Of course, sometimes there's no need to involve international lending organizations or the World Trade Organization (WTO) at all. In Iraq, after blowing apart Saddam Hussein's vaunted Republican Guard, the Americans set up camp at Saddam's presidential palace in Baghdad, crafting their neoliberal utopia under the gilded domes and marble columns of the fallen dictatorship. As

13

Vice President Dick Cheney hustled no-bid reconstruction contracts into hands of his Halliburton friends, Viceroy Paul Bremer outlined 100 Orders designed to de-Bathify the government and neoliberalize the economy. Order 81 stipulated the use of "stable" plant varieties, a coded term for GMO seeds delivered on demand from Western agribusiness.

As a rough guide to the kind of money there is in agribusiness, Monsanto banks about a billion dollars a quarter—clean profit. They netted $1.48 billion in Q2 this year, coinciding with the infamous "Monsanto Protection Act", which protects GMO seed producers from litigation over health risks. (This legislation received the Midas-like imprimatur of President Obama in March.)

Under the Viceroy (or is that the vizier?), oil, too, was quickly opened to Western multinationals through Production Sharing Agreements (PSAs) that would apply to the dozens of unbuilt Iraqi oil fields. British Petroleum, ExxonMobil, and other oil conglomerates receive fresh oil exploration contracts when the U.S. occupies a country and shreds existing production arrangements (Often, it's the French or Russians who get screwed in this regard).

One of the unmentionable crimes of Saddam Hussein was the fact that he nationalized Iraqi oil fields in 1972. ExxonMobil, BP, and Shell all have billion dollar production arrangements to mine Iraqi oil fields—this despite the Iraqi government's unwillingness to sign the hydrocarbon law the Bush administration attempted to push through.

Of course, simply promising the local government a hefty slice of the pie also works. Shell has been wreaking havoc in Nigeria since the 1990s, mostly in the southern Niger Delta region. Various militant organizations have sprung up in largely vain attempts to wrestle control of their own resources away from the corrupt government and multinational alliance. Notably the Movement for the Emancipation of the Niger Delta and its telling acronym MEND. Nonplussed, Shell has offered scant compensation for its oil spills in the region and last year pocketed $25 billion, a small rise over 2011, which naturally unsettled greed-soaked shareholders (as opposed to oil-soaked but penniless Nigerian villagers).

As Shamus Cooke recently wrote, "The essence of neoliberalism can be reduced to the following: government should be used exclusively to help big business and the wealthy with tax cuts, subsidies, privatizations, anti-labor laws, etc., while all government programs that help working and poor people should be eliminated. It's really that simple." Sadly, Cooke's definition of the core of the neoliberal program is spot on—profits, by any means necessary.

(*CounterPunch*, November 8, 2013)

America's Unceasing Contempt for Venezuela
Fear of the domino effect will never subside

Some things never change. The petulant and undemocratic Venezuelan opposition is at it again, with the full backing and check-writing support of the U.S. government. Recent protests have inflamed the streets of Caracas, as opposition groups, as they have in the Ukraine, called for the ouster of the sitting president. I suppose it's needless to note that Nicolás Maduro is Venezuela's democratically elected president, and that he won by a higher victory margin in a cleaner election than did Barack Obama in 2012. Nor is it worth asking, one supposes, that if the entire country is engulfed by dissent, as *The New York Times* insidiously suggested by claiming the "The protests are expressing the widespread discontent with the government of President Nicolás Maduro, a socialist…", then why did Maduro's party, *Partido Socialista Unido de Venezuela* (PSUV), claim wide majorities in municipal elections in December? Or why are these "widespread" protests largely confined to middle-class or student areas of Caracas and not rife within much larger poor neighborhoods? Or if a government has the right to arrest opposition leaders (in this case Leopoldo Lopez, the latest rabid ideologue) for inciting violence?

Public Virtue, Private Vice
Secretary of State John Kerry has ratcheted up the drivel stateside, claiming to be "alarmed" by reports that Maduro has "detained scores of anti-government protesters" and that the crackdown would have a "chilling effect" on free expression. A bit rich coming from a man whose own government has been icing free speech since the Snowden revelations. Kerry failed to mention whether the millions of American taxpayer dollars being funneled to the opposition were behind the violence. The *Los Angeles Times* described Maduro's administration as an "autocratic government." Opposition leader Henrique Capriles, demolished by Maduro in last year's landslide election, rejected Maduro's invitation to talks and claimed one of the Latin America's most popular political parties was a "dying government."

For its part, Mercosur, the alliance of South America's southern cone countries, denounced the violence as an attempt to "destabilize" a democratic government. Of course, the behavior of Maduro's government in response to these street provocations ought to closely watched, as this is the new president's first real test coping on an international stage with the intrigues of a small but virulent neoliberal opposition.

There's plenty to suggest that this is, like Ukraine, another external attempt to uproot a democratically elected government through a volatile cocktail of in-country agitation and violence paired with global media defamation of the existing administration. It wouldn't come as a surprise. Like a frustrated and

15

petulant infant, the United States has repeatedly attempted to derail the Bolivarian Revolution launched by former President Hugo Chavez in the late nineties, as CEPR's Mark Weisbrot has noted. It backed an anti-democratic coup by business elites in 2002 that actually succeeded for a couple of days and happily dissolved parliament before Chavez regained power. It supported an oil strike in an attempt to destabilize the economy and perhaps bring down the government. It encouraged opposition members of parliament to push for recalls (failed) and boycott National Assembly elections (useless) and clamor incessantly that last year's national presidential election was rigged (false). Of course, despite being widely held to be a superior electoral process than that of the United States, Kerry was only shamed into recognizing the legitimacy of the election long after the rest of the world had.

The U.S. has poured millions into opposition activities on an annual basis since the failed coup in 2002. (NGOs are convenient destinations for this money since foreign contributions to political parties are illegal in both countries.) Just look at 2013 alone. Washington would hardly stand for interference of this kind from, say, China. Or, better, from Venezuela itself. Imagine if it was discovered that Chavez had been seeding major American metropolises with anti-capitalist pamphleteers. Obama wouldn't be able to hit the "signature strike" button fast enough. Nevertheless, Kerry, in his role as Secretary of State, has turned out to be a masterful mimic capable of registering a fusty outrage on short notice, especially over claimed violations of civil liberties. Curious, since the ceaseless trampling of civil liberties by his own Democratic party have elicited nothing from this flag-bearer for democratic values.

Dollars & Bolivars
This is not to say that Venezuela does not have protest-worthy problems. Inflation has been chronic since the pre-Chavez days. Now food shortages are trying the patience of the population. And in one sense, these shortages are self-inflicted. According to Gregory Wilpert of VenezuelAnalysis.org, the government's currency controls have been undermined by an all-too-predictable black market. While the government has placed strict criteria on the ability of citizens to purchase dollars with bolivars, the black market allows citizens to buy dollars without any criteria whatsoever. The government's exchange rate is likewise controlled, and has over time begun to distort the real value of the bolivar. The black market exchange rate, by contrast, reflects the external value of the currency. The gap between these exchange rates has grown rapidly, such that there is now exist huge incentives for citizens to play currency arbitrage. If they satisfy the federal criteria—such as needing dollars to travel or import goods— Venezuelans can buy dollars cheaply using the government exchange rate. They can then pay those dollars to import goods, then export those goods in exchange for the dollars they just spent on the imports. From there it is a simple step to the black market, where they can sell those dollars for many times what they paid at

the government's official rate, making a tidy profit for themselves. If they happen to be rabid anti-socialists, they can enjoy the companion thrill of generating food shortages that can be blamed on the government. Ah, the timeless magic of import/export.

These are legitimate grievances, however, as are crime figures, which top the regional table. Yet the question is, do they merit the overthrow of a legitimate government backed by a wide majority of the population at the behest of a small but fierce oppositional faction openly funded by an imperial power committed to its overthrow? To do so would risk the absurdity of gratifying the strident demands of a few at the expense of the many. Nor would it wouldn't be far removed from the recent episode in Watertown, New York, where the city council banned residents to have roommates based on the complaint of a single citizen. (This even more amusingly recalls the opposition of Ambrose Bierce to the concept of prayer, since to Bierce the devout were requesting that "the laws of the universe be annulled in behalf of a single petitioner confessedly unworthy.") The fact is, despite the inflation and shortages, the population continues to support the Bolivarian Revolution because of its accomplishments—massive reductions in poverty, extreme poverty, and illiteracy. Significant growth in per capita GDP and other important metrics.

A Doctrine in Decline
We're seeing in clear images the viciousness with which neoliberal factions resent the loss of power and seek to restore it by any means necessary. Democracy is the least of their concerns. But this has been the Latin American backstory for a couple of centuries. Much of the U.S. activity in Latin America feels like a frantic and desperate last-ditch effort to preserve the Monroe Doctrine, by which we essentially declared Latin America to be our own backyard, off-limits to European empires. What was ostensibly a call to respect independent development in the Southern hemisphere rather predictably evolved into an excusive for self-interested intervention. But now, for the first time in centuries, Latin America has struck out on its own, slipping from beneath the clutch of the eagle's claw to form organizations like Mercosur and CELEAC, PetroCaribe and Petrosur, the Bank of the South as well as the Bolivarian Alliance for the Americas (ALBA). Aside from Columbia, an implacable outpost of American influence, the region has shunned greater U.S. involvement, and begun to view its proffered trade agreements with far more suspicion, particularly in the long wake of NAFTA, the poster child for lopsided and economically destructive trade treaties.

Whether the U.S. will eventually succeed in a cynical ploy to unseat Maduro remains to be seen. If recent events in the Ukraine are any indication, that may have been a test run for Venezuela, as Peter Lee suggests. It hasn't helped that, as in practically every country that comes to mind, an elite class of neoliberal ideologues own the mainstream media. The tools of propaganda have rarely been more fiercely deployed than since Chavez launched his socialist revolution. And yet, since then, practically the entire continent has experimented with left-leaning leadership: Rafael Correa in Ecuador, Evo Morales in Bolivia, Nicanor Duarte in Paraguay, Tabare Vazquez in Uruguay, to some degree Luiz Inácio Lula da Silva in Brazil, and Maduro in Venezuela. Nor should exiled Honduran president Manuel Zalaya be forgotten. These figures have collectively stepped back from the brink of dubious integration with North America and sought stronger regional ties and continental autonomy.

The U.S. has replied with a predictable confection of threats, lies, and sacks of cash for ferociously anti-democratic elements. Perhaps it most fears the bad karma it generated for itself with Operation Condor, which on September 11, 1973 overthrew and murdered Chile's socialist leader Salvador Allende and replaced him with a gutless sadist, Augusto Pinochet. Pinochet—a repressive militarist—happily instituted the untested prescriptions of the Chicago School of Economics' sermonizing armchair guru Milton Freidman, with predictable results. Now, Maduro, carrying the mantle of Chavez and his Bolivarian manifesto, is arguably the spiritual vanguard of the socialist left in South America. Venezuela's efforts to continue to forge its own independence in the coming decade will surely influence the mood and courage of other leftists in the region. The stakes are obviously high. Hence the relentless American effort to destabilize and publically discredit the PSUV. The fate of the global left is in a very real sense being tested in the crucible of Caracas.

(*CounterPunch*, March 11, 2014)

Another Killer Deal for the Defense Industry
Human rights take a backseat to hegemony—again

The American public seems not to clearly recognize that since "troops on the ground" went out of fashion, its government has devoted itself to arming terrorists and tyrants to do its bidding by proxy. This is no accident. Since the majority of the population seems to disagree with Washington policy choices—such as impoverishing its citizenry to pay for imperial wars in far-flung lands—and since it often responds to poll queries with alarmingly socialist views, pains must taken to deceive it. This is an ever more sophisticated practice, now requiring banks of slick public relations professionals and a colossal media budget to ensure the "media saturation" called for by all good professors of propaganda. All channels—television, print, websites, a litany of social media platforms, m-sites and mobile apps—must all be inundated with what is sometimes called a "single overarching communications objective," namely that the United States actions are always either a form of self defense, pre-emptive humanitarian intervention, reluctant punitive measures taken against recalcitrant rogue states, or very occasionally pure altruism. The rights of the weak forever play upon the lips of the spokespersons of power.

Cash, Guns and Reassurances to Cairo
Nowhere is the abyss between America's hegemonic values and the universal ones it avers more transparent than in our latest weapons deal with Egypt. On Monday President Obama lifted holds on the sale and delivery of F-16s, Harpoon missiles, and M1A1 tank kits to Cairo. All this aside from the $1.3B in military aid we deliver annually to former General and current President Abdul Fattah al-Sisi. During a friendly trans-Atlantic call, Obama warmly assured al-Sisi that America's military largesse would continue indefinitely. One wonders whether how he phrased it. Perhaps, "Mr. President, in our inestimable wisdom we have decided to overlook several, shall we say, transgressions. Most recently, the 183 people you sentenced to death in a grotesque mass trial that violated nearly every standard of international justice. Many were tried in absentia. Nothing like getting a death sentence by mail, eh, Abdul? But because we like your repressive militant style of governance, we'll pretend that it never happened. Your weapons order is shipping out this afternoon. And the check is in the mail. Just do us a favor: cut down on the mass trials, tossing nonviolent activists in jail, and the slaughter of members of the Muslim Brotherhood. Otherwise we may have to send you aid on the hush-hush."

He might have added that the trial of former despot Hosni Mubarak was "dismissed." By that we mean to say that no government police were prosecuted for the slaughter of 1000 protestors during the Arab Spring uprisings in 2011. In 2013, al-Sisi's storm troopers nearly matched Mubarak's accomplishment by murdering hundreds of citizens protesting the military *coup d'état* that toppled

19

Mohammed Morsi, the first democratically elected president in Egyptian history. None of the killers have even been charged. In any event, it was a fairly short-lived experiment with democracy. Morsi celebrated his one-year anniversary in office one day, and found himself in a dank prison cell the next.

Morsi, of course, as a member of the Muslim Brotherhood, frightened the West for being sympathetic to the Palestinian cause, being thoroughly reviled by American ally Saudi Arabia, and being generally amenable to Islamic influence in the Egyptian state. He had notably loosened border restrictions at the Rafah crossing in Gaza, permitting abused Palestinians to temporarily leave their "open-air prison," a relief for Palestinians as Israel rationed out basic utilities, withheld tax monies, and conducted occasional "terrorist" cleansings of Gaza. It was clear to all that federal empathy for the plight of a stateless people simply wouldn't do. Much like Palestinians who naively elected Hamas to lead them in 2006, it was self-evident to any imperialist that Egyptians, unfamiliar with the implicit understanding that democracy is mere window dressing for plutocracy, had simply voted the wrong way.

Restoring Repression
Which is why the U.S. cash and support to Morsi's opposition through its notoriously transparent "democracy assistance" from the State Department, a tactic employed almost as often as an election goes awry. It is naturally unlawful to waste taxpayer monies fomenting coups in foreign lands, but this is of little consequence to the president, who told Americans that Washington had no preference in the outcome of the Morsi destabilization. It most assuredly did. It feared the retreat of its Western pawns from political influence in Egypt. (Saudi Arabia feared the Brotherhood itself and worked to undermine Morsi's government, cobbling together an post-coup aid package in the paltry sum of $12 billion, a gift from Riyadh and its fellow Gulf monarchies, which always enjoy the sight of a despotry regained.

They needn't have feared so much. Morsi proved ham-fisted as a domestic leader. He sought to redraft the constitution and preference sharia law, and exhibited enough autocratic tendencies and appointed enough Islamists to bring non-Islamist citizenry into the streets, prefacing the takeover of the Supreme Council of the Armed Forces (SCAF), and al-Sisi's subsequent election. SCAF subsequently appointed a new "Constituent Assembly" to vote on a revised constitution, but attempted to control it much as Morsi had. The current constitution evidently provides extraordinary license to police, intelligence and military groups. (Morsi proved effective, however, in foreign diplomacy, actually negotiating a ceasefire between Hamas and Israel in 2012.)

Al-Sisi didn't wait long to bloody his own slate. After crushing coup protests, he purged the Sinai in the fall of 2013 of "takfiri" militants (Muslims who kill wayward Muslims). The Muslim Brotherhood reported shortly thereafter that more than 2,000 of its supporters had been killed. The government engaged in something akin to an extermination campaign to eliminate the power of the Brotherhood, notably by outlawing its Freedom and Justice Party. It also reversed Morsi's sympathetic action on the Gaza border, ratcheting up the border controls back to a level more in keeping with a penal colony, where persistent shortages of food, electricity, water, classrooms, and employment ensured the closure is a mortal threat as well as a form of perverse discipline.

Setting these particular abuses aside, it might be noted that Egypt resumed state executions in 2014 once al-Sisi settled in. According to a new report from Amnesty International, only 15 citizens were executed in Egypt last year, paling in comparison with Iran's sanguinary 289. But the Cairo cabal was top of the table when it came to issuing death sentences—Field Marshal al-Sisi's specialty—where it pronounced at least 509, many in the mass trials that recall the farcical show trials Joseph Stalin arranged for the edification of his Soviet minions. None of the other nations researched issued even 100 death sentences.

Amnesty reiterated a point that we know all too well—that innumerable states in the region and worldwide are putting people to death on charges of "terrorism" on the "flawed premise of deterrence." While true, this phrasing implies that these states are simply misguided, a motley lot of well-intentioned despots who simply haven't recognized the fuzzy math at the heart of their domestic policies. Nothing could be further from the truth. These regimes, like Egypt's, know perfectly well what they are doing. A systematic elimination of one's main Islamic rival organization by branding them a terrorist organization and killing hundreds of them cannot be plausibly dismissed as a good faith national security initiative— the conflict of interest belies that judgment.

From Cairo to Riyadh to Tel Aviv
But Cairo is just the latest proxy to blush beneath the gaze of Washington's beneficence. We'd be remiss not to toss in the 60 billion in arms the United States sold to Saudi Arabia in 2010, its largest ever sale to the radically anti-democratic, Wahhabi-proselytizing monarchy. The haul included dozens of F-15 fighter jets and many more Apache attack helicopters. A year later the Saudis conducted their brutal takedown of the Bahrainian uprising during the Arab Spring. The Shias there had staged a revolt against the Sunni tyrant on the throne, had destabilized the country, until they were put down by the Gulf Cooperation Council's (GCC) two thousand soldier contingent, a majority of which were Saudi. As one might have expected, as the GCC took control, martial law was imposed, torture became routine, dissidents were routinely jailed, and hundreds were killed. The Shia majority just wanted to elect their leaders. Talk about radical. One wonders what percentage of the Saudi arsenal currently being deployed in Yemen—to put down

an indigenous uprising against another Western-backed stooge—is of American provenance.

Nor should we ignore the $10 billion deal the U.S. cut in 2013 with Israel, the Saudis, and the United Arab Emirates, including aircraft, missiles and transport vehicles. The deal was made on the inane pretext that these munitions would help these nations fend off attacks from Iran.

What all these arms deals tell us is that the U.S. has been executing a full-blown strategy to arm its Middle Eastern proxies to the hilt, the better to affect a hostile posture toward those regional rivals that might think to make their own decisions. Namely Iran, Russia, Syria, Lebanon and Hezbollah, and Palestine. How telling that with one hand the U.S. bestows incalculable destructive powers upon nations increasingly known for their savagery, domestically and on neighboring soil. With the other it is hectoring defensive-minded Tehran into an absurdly stringent agreement that will nearly dismantle the country's civilian nuclear energy program, to which it is entitled under the Non-Proliferation Treaty (NPT). In this, Washington affects the deepest concern—against all evidence—that Iran might race to a bomb and imperil the populations of its regional allies. Washington's only real concern is that an Iran with a nuclear weapons capacity would shift the dynamics of power in the Middle East. To prevent that it needlessly tramples on the rights of millions, those of Iran and those of the populations repressed by the despots we so freely arm. As all of these examples demonstrate, there are some forms of freedom that the U.S. simply can't abide, self-determination not least among them.

(*Dissident Voice*, April 4, 2015)

Barbarians at the Gate

"One thought alone preoccupies the submerged mind of Empire: how not to end, how not to die, how to prolong its era. By day it pursues its enemies. It is cunning and ruthless, it sends its bloodhounds everywhere. By night it feeds on images of disaster: the sack of cities, the rape of populations, pyramids of bones, acres of desolation."
— J.M. Coetzee, *Waiting for the Barbarians*

Nobody quite knows how it started. The etymology is traceable to the Ancient Greeks, but it probably began earlier, with spats between combative cave-dwellers or disgruntled nomads. The Greeks, who spawned such lofty rhetors as Socrates and Plato, distinguished between "*barbaros*" and "*polites*". The former, if not wholly pejorative, essentially meant non-Greek and more often than not "candidates for conquest and enslavement", as one scholar of antiquity put it. The other term—polites—indicated a Greek citizen and by definition someone properly urbane. We often deploy the term barbarian in jest now, sardonically, with implied mockery of the rather embarrassing condescension of our ancient forbears. As though we dispensed with such faulty mental filters long ago. But still they endure.

Just this month we were subjected to another round of fulminations against the temporary deal between the Western powers—the vaunted P5 + 1—and Iran. According to mainstream media pundits, the Obama administration was making a dangerously naïve foray into diplomacy with an untrustworthy partner. As the tempest over the Iranian temporary deal subsided, we aimed the arrows of our antipathy at Afghanistan, as Hamid Karzai toyed with rejecting the Status of Forces Agreement (SOFA) agreed to by a *loya jirga*.

From *The New York Times* to Charlie Rose, the jets of propaganda were opened full bore in the service of patriotic fearmongering. The American public was slimed in the amniotic afterbirth of whole-born mendacity. And as much as left-wing analysts credit the American government with creating the most sophisticated propaganda apparatus of all time, the thrust of the message bears us back to that original prejudice—the haunting notion of the barbarian.

Barbarians with Bombs—From Flights of Fancy to Full-Blown Fantasy
Take the terrorists, for example. We have variously been admonished by voices across the spectrum that the terrorist mind is incomprehensible. No enlightened Westerners can fathom the gothic savagery of the bootless and bomb-strapped Arab who would drive a car into a compound or a café. It is "apocalyptic nihilism." For years, we relied on Jack Bauer to rescue us from the deranged Arab bomb confectioner, their larval plots ever afoot in our flour-pure American cities.

Don't scoff—the mindset of a show like *24* minutely reflects that of the American public, no less steeped in fantasy and folly. How we fear the madman and his chemistry set. At the micro-level, the lone wolf with a grudge against freedom. At the macro, the menace of a trigger-happy mullah at the helm of a nuclear state. To that latter end, not a single mainstream outlet, to my knowledge, can stand to countenance the image of a nuclear Iran. The question is never permitted as to whether a nuclear weapon would provide a much-needed check on Israel and even American action in the region. In other words, would an Iranian nuclear deterrent help stabilize the Middle East? The notion is, quite figuratively, too much to bear. Yet this country we have demonized across the decades hasn't attacked anyone unprovoked in centuries, and has been subject to ceaseless American provocations, whether coups or clandestine assassinations or cruel sanctions that put basic foodstuffs at the far end of a Tehranian's budget. It is simply a regional Shia hegemon perched atop lakes of crude oil—the stuff imperialist dreams are made of.

Yet while men like Republican Representative Mike Rogers, Chairman of the Permanent Select Committee on Intelligence, rave—in dulcet tones—on Charlie Rose and other such weapons of mass distraction, buried beneath the avalanche of insincerity is a report that claims to reveal that Israel has 80 nuclear warheads with the capacity to "sprint" to hundreds more. This is lost on dignified and decorous men like Rogers and Rose, who gravely debate Iran's (factitious) capacity to weaponize uranium for even one bomb. The absurdity of this circumstance, castigating Iran's potential future capacity while ignoring the stockpile of the region's most hostile presence, belies the deeply insincere or xenophobic impetus of Western policies—and the ignorance and indifference of the public that support them.

As a quick aside, it would be remiss not to mention the *piece de resistance* of modern barbarian myths—the Israeli-Palestinian conflict. It is a common trope reiterated by pro-Israeli media that Israel simply doesn't have a partner to negotiate with in the pursuit of peace (such is the Palestinian's moral bankruptcy and incapacity to organize). On the RT Network's "Worlds Apart" program, anchor Oksana Boyko repeated pressed a Palestinian activist to admit that Hamas bore significant responsibility for the breakdown of peace negotiations. The stupefied activist might have hastily tabulated the actual death toll on each side since 2000, on the order of a six-to-one disparity. Also note Secretary of State John Kerry's remark on Saturday that Palestinian citizens of Israel represented a "demographic time bomb" to the integrity of the Jewish state.

Now, you might argue the root of American policy is self-interest—control or possession of fossil fuels—and that a prejudicial ideology has been crafted to cloak and justify naked aggression. Or, you might posit an authentic xenophobic prejudice—hatred of the strange—as the core of policy. Either is plausible, but neither is possible without invoking the barbarian myth.

We Don't Do Body Counts—Or Check IDs

Hamid Karzai is regularly savaged in the media as an insufficiently obsequious puppet, daring to speak up for the nameless dead in the Afghani killing fields, where drones circulate with impunity. Recently an interesting article appeared in the *Los Angeles Times*, penned by Sarah Chayes, former advisor to member of the Joint Chiefs of Staff Mike Mullen. Chayes wrote that, "...U.S. decision-makers should have expected such antics." Her description has to do with the unnecessary step of convening a *loya jirga* to provide a non-binding approval of the security agreement, rather than going to the National Assembly for binding ratification, as the constitution calls for. There is certainly some credence to this critique. Yet no column width is given to assessing Karzai's stated reasons for refusing to sign the agreement, which pivot on an errant war on terror, seeding corruption through bribes, and adopting a "colonial" attitude toward Afghanis. Defending your own is thus little more than "antics" in America's geopolitical worldview. Chayes then reproves U.S. leadership for being unwilling to flex its considerable muscle to mute Karzai's counterproductive "stunts". Such stunts, Chayes relates, are harmful to the Afghanis we are trying to help. The trope is obvious: we are on a noble mission to help those who can't help themselves. (Interestingly, in this country, the government reverses the rhetoric, claiming that every American can help himself, which is why they need no government assistance.)

While you might question Karzai's motives for his refusal to sign the accord—he is likely as self-interested a politician as any other—one can hardly dismiss the additional demands he has appended to the security agreement: the ending of house raids, the release of Afghanis illegally held in Guantanamo, and help jump-starting peace talks with Afghani Taliban. He has also been a vocal critic of civilian casualties of U.S. operations. Instead of vowing to address these grievances and demands, national security advisor Susan Rice told Karzai that the U.S. would have "no choice" but to execute a complete withdrawal of troops at the end of 2014. Secretary of State John Kerry echoed Rice's myopic response by suggesting that perhaps the Afghani defense secretary might sign the Bilateral Security Agreement (BSA) instead.

Jacob Hornberger recently noted that the names of innocents slaughtered by drone attacks in Afghanistan are rarely mentioned in the Western press, even as the numbers mount. Despite high costs, low popular support, and having to field plenty of bitter obloquies from Afghani leadership, the U.S. is pushing Afghanistan for a deal to extend its presence across nine military bases in the country, keeping thousands of troops in-country, and—crucially—insisting upon both total legal immunity for its forces and for the obviously unrelated right to enter Afghani households at will. This is terrific arrogance, especially as it comes amid a barrage of criticism for its slaughter of innocents in the pursuit of so-called terrorists—whose guilt has not been proven, whose arrests might be made through simple police work, and whose worth as terror suspects have never been weighted against the worth of the lives claimed in their assassination.

In death by drone, Afghanis lose their identity, blown to bits in a savage strike from the sky. But not just Afghanis. Pakistanis, Yemenis, and others in countries that sit close to coveted hydrocarbon fields. It is a kind of sad inversion of a spontaneous ritual in the film *Fight Club*. When a member of "Project Mayhem" died, he received a name. While living, he had no name. The death was thus sanctified as a worthy martyrdom. In the Middle East, the sacrifices are worthless, and the names buried in the memories of families, themselves under relentless predatory threat from above. And as if adding an irony of cliché to their work, drones function best in tribal regions where, as President Obama says, terrorists "hide in caves" and "train in empty deserts." Quite the fitting coda to this recent chapter in American perfidy, where the cliché of American nobility and the inadequacies of foreigners so nicely aligns with the polite/barbarian dichotomy.

Overtures of Peace, Promises of Peril
Although the U.S. military issues an occasional apology for civilian deaths, the victims vanish in nameless obscurity as the policies that precipitated their demise are amplified. Defense Secretary Chuck Hagel recently stood on the deck of the USS Ponce, just 120 miles off the coast of Iran. There, on the sun-blown deck of this amphibious transport dock full of aerial and underwater drones, Hagel was perhaps feeling jaunty and confident, poised at the helm of the most powerful military known to man. He was quick to remind the admiring crew of soldiers that although America had risked diplomacy with Iran, it would not alter its "force posture" in the region. The primitive image of the posturing warrior is ever at the ready, is it not? This was, of course, a message for Tehran, a reminder of the naval menace floating just beyond its nation's shores. Although Iran hasn't started a war in centuries, Hagel's tone, and that of official stenographers CBS News, was frightful. (Remember that, when engaged in negotiation, Iran is a "wolf in sheep's clothing" according to Israel.)

Hagel assured the assembled patriots that he "understand very clearly the dangers that Iran represents and has represented." Shivers down the collective starboard spine. Hagel usefully forgets to name any of the dangers Iran represents, particularly since it has been under perpetual assault from either the British Empire, the American empire, or occasionally its neighbors for the last century. Iran's future hardly looks brighter. In the last seven years, America has sold more than $80 billion in weapons to allies in the region. Not least among the intended targets of those guns is Iran. Rest assured, the Defense Secretary continued, "this is not an exercise based on folly." CBS News added to the collective hysteria by noting that the "military standoff continues alongside diplomacy." How exactly Iran is engaged in a military standoff is left unexplained.

In any case, the intended impression might be summarized as such: The people of the Middle East are clearly not to be trusted, their complaints are needless jeremiads to be ignored, and their warmongering natures require ceaseless vigilance from our military—a task within our never-ending noble mission to "make the world safe for democracy."

A Literature of Devaluation
At home, our postures of aggression are rarely recognized. Indeed, we take great care to craft artificial distinctions between our behavior and that of our enemies. If we suffer ceaseless political infighting, it is "partisan politics," always ready for some sensible patriot to "reach across the aisle" in good faith. If Syrians suffer the same, it is "sectarian strife," vulnerable to ineradicable blood enmities. Were the CIA an element of the Columbian or Lebanese government, American media wouldn't hesitate to label it a "paramilitary group." But as an American organization, it is simply a benign intelligence agency.

This use of vocabulary as an alembic that purifies our own actions, and as a virus that infects the behavior of the other, is not new. The sordid history of demonizing enemies is instructive in understanding our present propaganda. The religious notion of the sect and the related ethnic construct of the tribe are frequent historical allusions. Chinua Achebe, Nigerian author of *Things Fall Apart*, once wrote that he no longer referred to his Igbo people of southeastern Nigeria not as a "tribe," but as a "nation." Achebe defended his choice by consulting his Pocket Oxford Dictionary, where he found that "tribes" are "(esp. primitive) families or communities linked by social, religious or blood ties and usually having a common culture and dialect and a recognized leader." Achebe denied that the Igbo were primitive, linked by blood, tied to a single dialect, or organized under a common leader. Rather, he noted, they were closer to the dictionary definition of a nation: "a community of people of mainly common descent, history or language, etc., forming a state or inhabiting a territory."

Isn't there a kind of implied condescension in the language of Western media or leadership when it refers to tribal conflict? When it denies the political legitimacy of Hamas or Hezbollah? When we, in the unforgettable phrasing of assassinated Dutch politician Pim Fortuyn, remind ourselves that the peoples of the East haven't been through, "the Laundromat of the Enlightenment." Achebe referred to what Dorothy Hammond and Alta Jablow called, "a literature of devaluation" in their aptly named book, *The Africa That Never Was*. The authors studied British writing over a 400-year period covering the slave trade, exploration, and colonization in the African continent, documenting the invention of a barbarian other to mollify the creeping conscience of slavers and invaders and colonizers. What would a comparable study from 1776 to the present look like?

In his controversial work *Orientalism*, Edward Said forcefully argues that the Middle East has for hundreds of years been characterized in a way that allows it to fit neatly into the existing cosmology, as it were, of the West. One of the first major studies of Mohammed, in 17th century Britain, was called *The True Nature of Imposture*, by Humphrey Prideaux. The founder of Islam was defined against our truth—that Jesus was the Son of God—and fitted nicely into Western mental landscape. Said refers to a piece of state propaganda that typifies the technique: In the Seventies, a former member of the U.S. State Department, Harold Glidden, penned an essay in in the *American Journal of Psychiatry* called, "The Arab World." Glidden contrasted our peace-loving values ("Westerners consider peace to be high on the scale of values") with the warmongering cultures of the East. "In Arab tribal society, strife, not peace, was the normal state of affairs because raiding was one of the two main supports of the economy." The position of the P5 +1 Western powers, notably the U.S., Britain, France, and Germany, might be said to carry the same bias into its fatuous negotiations with Iran and Afghanistan: Iran is a volatile commodity in need of policing, and the West is there to do the job; Afghanistan needs the presence of an occupying power lest its society, left to its own devices, descend into chaos.

Said wrote that the "author imposes a disciplinary order upon the material he has worked," in order to accommodate it to Western ideology. This is very nearly exactly what CBS News accomplished in its article on Hegel's Persian Gulf speech: a raft of assumptions—that Iran is a grave threat "not to just the region, but the world," and that it is actively seeking a bomb, etc.—are used as guardrails to discipline the discussion. Any notions that venture beyond these bounds are elided from print.

But if the historical record of aggression is of any importance, then we have to face a much different conclusion. If anyone is behaving barbarically, or threatening to, it isn't the Afghanis or the Iranians or the Venezuelans. It is us, and we stand at their gates, not they at ours. Hagel rattled the saber in the Persian Gulf, the homeland of Arab petro wealth. There are no Iranian subs or transport ships floating in Long Island Sound. Iranian Defense Minister Hossein Dehghan isn't perched on the deck of a frigate fulminating about "force posture." We have projected onto others the very image of ourselves we fear to see. It's time for America to gaze at its own reflection, and quit painting pictures of some ghastly 'other' drawn from the fevers of a dream or, perhaps more accurately, the heat of material greed.

(*Dissident Voice*, December 20, 2013)

Big Capital's Collateral Damage
Imperial neoliberal capitalism is the root of terror, not Islam

The citizenry of the *La Ville Lumière* collectively re-affirmed the principles of "Liberté, égalité, fraternité" on Parisian streets last weekend. The heirs of Voltaire and Danton and Zola marched in solidarity and outrage over the killings at the editorial offices of *Charlie Hebdo*, at a kosher market and an industrial park. Seventeen dead, 22 wounded—one of the worst terrorist attacks in French history. Police are still on high alert. Four suspects were hauled before a Paris court on Tuesday, suspected of providing "logistical" support to the supermarket shooter. Monday five Chechens were arrested in the south of France for a suspected plot. The streets outside the *Charlie Hebdo* offices were strewn with flowers and wreaths and New York mayor Bill de Blasio flew in to express his empathy (partially rectifying the absence of any American officials at last weekend's march). Over the last weeks, the country has been shaken by a delicate mixture of sympathy and fear, bafflement and rage.

Consider the scene in Paris last weekend: From the Place de La République to the Place de La Nation, millions of Parisians and a flock of world leaders marched in solidarity to protest the terrorist attacks. Dignitaries and commoners appeared to be united in spirit, bound up in an unshakable commitment to Western liberties. Placards declared, "Je suis Charlie." Francois Hollande, the bland neoliberal president of France, declared, "Today Paris is capital of the world." His prime minister, Manuel Valls, declared that France were now at war with radical Islam, "with jihadism." Ex-president Nicolas Sarkozy thumpingly confirmed a "war of civilizations," however many decades late. *The Guardian* breathtakingly reported that, "The occasion was somber and heavy with symbolism. As the dignitaries left the Elysée, it rained. By the time they arrived, the grey clouds had parted, allowing a rare ray of winter sunshine."

The people and the plutocrats united in a just cause. Or so it seemed. Polls pretty consistently show that popular majorities—even in America—prefer negotiated solutions to conflicts and find most Middle Eastern wars not worth fighting. But unlike their constituents, this rank and file of notables and statesmen did not really represent the freedom of the press, or the liberties of Western democracy, or the promise of peace. In fact, it was later revealed in a wide-angle shot from an untutored French television crew that they were not even part of the main crowd, having been kept a suitable distance from the rabble itself. Instead, this contingent of dignitaries represented imperial capital and its proxies. They represented its policies of repression, its wars, and its avarice. They reminded us that empire brooks no challenge in its breathless race for dominion, be it independent nationalism, Islamic governance, or revelations of corruption from whistleblowers or an undisciplined press. They also told us everything we need to know about the *Charlie Hebdo* attacks and why they happened.

As Hollande led the diverse cohort, his country was prosecuting one war in Iraq, backing another in Syria, and clamoring for the revival of a third in Libya. As Benjamin Netanyahu linked arms, his lemmings were confiscating more lush territory in the Jordan valley, violating international law and the rights of the occupied. As Kiev's tepid technocrat Arseniy Yatsenyuk took his purposeful steps, the European Union was introducing his countrymen to EU-style austerity and NATO-style bombs—orchestrating the Western takeover of his nation. As David Cameron marched, his nation was training lawless jihadists while concluding an arms deal with the Saudis, unconcerned they were beating a <u>critic</u> into silence—a regular practice in the kingdom. Bahrain too sent a minister to join in the show of unity, even as its government worked to imprison a journalist for an unflattering tweet. While Egypt's Foreign Minister Sameh Shoukry paid fealty to press freedom alongside his cosmopolitan peers, his blood-stained coup government was equipping itself with the latest American military technology, preparing for more bloodshed, and prosecuting *Al-Jazeera* journalists for "spreading false news" and consorting with the now banned Muslim Brotherhood. As Jordan's King Abdullah shuffled forward, his thugs in Amman were sending another journalist to a labor camp. Another brushfire of *lese majesty* doused by absolutism.

Last but not least is the United States. The absence of American representation was curious. Normally, our leaders never miss an opportunity to beat the drum of liberty. Perhaps the White House sent no one since it recalled that we have targeted journalists fairly regularly, in Serbia and Iraq, for instance, as William Blum <u>notes.</u>

Yet some organizations noticed the hypocrisy of this crowd. Reporters Without Borders (RWB) decried the presence of so many serial human rights violators and enemies of the press, and the *Washington Post* dug up some of the <u>facts</u>. Others <u>recognized</u> it for what it was: a lineup of the compromised, the corrupt, and the merciless aligned in defiance of a terror incited by their own actions. In a sane world, this body of dignitaries would have been shamed from the streets for jeopardizing the safety of their own populations in the name of profits. But the march was an object lesson in Orwellian mystification: there were warmongers against war, human-rights violators defending human rights, and subverters of democracy rallying to its cause.

Roots and Causes
A female marcher told a reporter, "We are united – Muslims, Catholics, Jews, we want to live peacefully together." This was likely the true feeling of the million or so French citizens who came together to symbolically reject terror—as well as that of millions of Westerners who followed the event. A sentiment both just and fair. But as David Hearst of the *Middle East Eye* <u>said,</u> "History did not start in

Paris on Sunday." If you want to live peacefully together, you have first to be peaceable yourself. And the West is decidedly not peaceful.

The real provenance of these attacks on Westerners is not radical Islam—it is the persistent and relentless slaughter of Arabs by Western militaries. It is attacks on nations like Iraq and Afghanistan and Syria and Iran and Yemen and Pakistan and Libya. It is historic enmities over the colonial past when borders were carved like highways across tribal communities, when unsuitably Westernized nationalists like Mossadegh and Nasser were undermined or overthrown. The United States and its allies have committed acts of war against every one of the aforementioned nations, and have done it with an arsenal that is the envy of every fantasist with a grudge: an unending conveyor belt of drones, computer viruses, sanctions, troops, bullets and bombs. State terror at its finest.

Many of these wars wiped out modern secular states, leaving behind a festering wound over which the disfigured scar of terrorism grew. Not only that, but some 16.7 million Arabs have been displaced from their native nations thanks to recent conflicts in the Middle East. Double that have been internally displaced. The total dead is a fluid figure, but seems to be in the tens or hundreds of thousands. Civil societies have been wrecked, patrimonies blasted, resources expropriated, armies disbanded, sectarian enmities incited, radicalism nourished, and the nest of its purveyors feathered with petrodollars.

Added to this mix is the crime of propaganda. The false narrative that has duped most of the Western world into believing we are the civilized society batting down the flailing assaults of a medieval one. Orientalism by Orwellian means. We portray the Middle East in the colors of its radical fringe, but we see ourselves in the noblest words of our Founding Fathers. Both are caricatures of reality.

It is easy to cut and paste Salafist slogans across the banner of the Arab world. It is easy to cherry pick the bizarre and misogynist and tyrannical from the holy books of any monotheism. It is easy to pin the blame for all the violence on takfiri jihadism, close the file, shutter the shades, and lock up shop. No further reflection required. Weaponize the drones. Move the ships into firing position. Prepare the president's talking points.

But listen to the terrorists themselves. They spelled it out for us before they hurled themselves into the void. The Kouachi brothers and Ahmed Coulibaly left no doubt. These flailing amateurs that shot dead an entire office of writers and editors and designers—heinous as they are, their words shouldn't be ignored. Before committing their crimes, they pointed to the larger crimes that motivated their own. They spoke of the Western massacres in the Middle East. They spoke of a precise vengeance. They said they were representing al Qaeda in Yemen, a sub-sect of Al Qaeda in the Arab Peninsula (aqap). What they forgot were the names of the corporations that the machinery of Western terror represented.

This conflict isn't democracy versus radical jihad. The real conflict is imperial capitalism versus anything in its path. The path leads to "one of the greatest material prizes in history," the treasure of oil and natural gas that lay beneath Middle Eastern soil. Just think of the margins to be had. No shale to frack. No tar sands to purify. No seas to plunge. Just desert soil to ply.

It is this reality—the reality of capitalism's march of destruction—that is the taproot of a century of conflict with Arabs and Persians. Imperial neoliberal capitalism is a holy terror. Think of what it has wrought. It has <u>ravaged</u> America, savaged Europe, and fractured the Ukraine. It has <u>plundered</u> Iraq. It has <u>leveled</u> Libya. It has turned Afghanistan into a narco-state. It is <u>sundering</u> Syria for all the wrong reasons. And it is behaving with its predictable <u>belligerence</u> toward the one nation in the Middle East capable of resisting its advances—Iran. If you want to see whom Washington hates, just find out who is in its way. Tehran is. Caracas is. Moscow is. Tripoli was. Baghdad was. Kabul was.

A Slim Pretext

Imperial capitalism is especially potent because it has the American military acting as its vanguard, clearing the ground, opening the market, and safeguarding the relevant ministries for use by exploitive capital. Likewise it has commandeered global lending and trade institutions to ensure its extractive objectives are embedded in every loan and free trade agreement it creates. Yet when a terrorist attack occurs in the West, challenging the wisdom of a policy of continuous intervention, our leaders never ask what could drive men to such extremes. They take their prefabricated answer—radical Islam—and redouble their commitment to intervention. But Islamic terrorism supplies the West with a plausible pretext for its resource wars. Nobody in the Middle East, save the comprador bourgeoisie, buys this farcical justification. Just think: we invaded Iraq on manufactured evidence, resurrected the old British Trojan horse, the Iraqi Petroleum Company, which immediately cut no-bid deals with Exxon Mobil, BP, and Shell over solicitations from dozens of other companies, including Russian and Chinese energy firms. We made foreign direct investment the law of the land. Then we told the world we were there to fight terror. Why would anyone believe such a claim?

Those who commit terror on Western soil are rightly hunted down and brought to justice. We rightly honor the dead and defend the liberties that make us Westerners. But we should also root out and rectify the causes of terror, even if it requires reevaluation of our own policies. But instead of removing the cause, we multiply it. Which is to say, we <u>multiply</u> the likelihood of more terror, not less. But that is the villainy of unchained capital, that every objective is eventually

32

sacrificed to the singular goal of power and profit, no matter the means, however hurtful. But, as one senior officer on the Joint Staff reportedly told former Coordinator for Counterterrorism Michael Sheehan, colleagues not infrequently said that terrorist attacks were, "A small price to pay for being a superpower."

(*CounterPunch*, January 22, 2015)

Chavez vs. Obama – The Final Score
In the end, Chavez did far more for his people than Obama has done for his

The world got word on Tuesday evening that Hugo Chavez was dead. Felled by chronic cancer, the 58-year old transformed Venezuela in his 14 years at its helm. He lifted masses of his countrymen from the depths of poverty, the ignorance of illiteracy, and the penury of medical neglect. He reclaimed Venezuela's oil resources for the benefit of the majority, and rallied Latin nations under a banner of common interest, anti-imperialism, and self-determination.

Perhaps the best way to consider Chavez accomplishments is by contrasting them—head to head—with those of his American counterpart, Barack Obama. After all, they are each the most celebrated and reviled figures in their countries, and perhaps the hemisphere. Chavez has been in office for three terms; Obama only one. But the Obama administration is simply the latest caretaker of an ongoing neoliberal and imperial regime inherited from George Bush and his predecessors. Empire's game plan is continuous; details change with leadership.

Both Obama and Chavez were re-elected in the fall of 2012—one claiming a paltry mandate, the other swept unchallenged to a fourth term. Prior to Chavez' passing, analysts expected to see a widening abyss between the austerity-addicted North and the socialist-leaning South. But with the Venezuelan constitution requiring new elections within a month, that forecast is less certain. Future elections aside, the ideological—and social—gulf between the United States and Venezuela is as immense as any in the region, with the possible exception of perennial hemispheric pariah Cuba.

Authoritarianism: Vilification vs. Villainy

Chavez was routinely characterized as a tyrant or dictator in western media during his 14-year run as Venezuela's president. He provided little support for these claims, although he did exhibit a few authoritarian impulses in office. But he was so consistently vilified in western media principally because of his thankless role as a paladin of the underclass. He was demonized because he didn't follow Western prescriptions for economic development—or rather, economic dispossession. In point of fact, what he did was simply work in the interests of his own population, not on behalf of Western multinationals. He sought to shelter domestic industry, reviled extractive finance, and loosed global capital's grip on the federal till. Somehow, thanks to the dividend dementia of our autocratic elites, this was taken to be a radical position. A position consonant with the State Department's definition of a dictator. Forget the fact that Venezuela is now the most equal nation in Latin America, and that the opposition controls the majority of the domestic media, and that a recent comprehensive labor law was passed guaranteeing worker protections, social security, and gender equity. Only whole-cloth subservience to the Washington Consensus is acceptable behavior in the eyes of beltway plutocrats.

Perhaps one fact above all renders moot the tyrant label. In last October's election, Chavez won 55 percent of the vote in demolishing one-percent stooge Henrique Capriles. A record 97 percent of eligible Venezuelans registered and many millions voted, causing the normally unstinting election critic Jimmy Carter to say, "…of the 92 elections that we've monitored, I would say that the election process in Venezuela is the best in the world."

By contrast, the 2012 election in the United States reflected the general public's lack of enthusiasm for either candidate on offer. The president, claiming the mandate of the American people, was reelected with a paltry 29 percent of eligible voters in tow—in an election notable only in that 90 million eligible voters were too dispirited to vote or were barred from participation. Perhaps Obama's own autocratic behavior offers a partial explanation. A small sampling: Over Christmas 2012 Obama signed a five-year extension of H.R. 5949, better known by as the Foreign Intelligence Surveillance Act, or by its acronym FISA. This bill allows Homeland Security to spy on citizen communications with people abroad. On New Year's Eve last year, Obama signed the National Defense Authorization Act, better known by its acronym NDAA, which authorized the government to indefinitely detain Americans at sites like Guantanamo without trial. Laws like these, and the widely assailed drone assassination program, a failed surge in Afghanistan, and a destructive attack on Libya, have disillusioned a vast percentage of Americans, including progressives, who now question whether their Nobel Peace Prize winning savior has become the Anti-Christ—an authoritarian enthusiast of empire willing to set aside *habeas corpus* and due process to prosecute a metastasizing and ever remote "war on terror."

Poverty: Amelioration vs. Exacerbation

There's a reason why Hugo Chavez won his fourth consecutive term in office in 2012. A simple graph should suffice. In Venezuela over the last decade, Chavez cut poverty by half and deep poverty by 70 percent. Millions have been enrolled in a free healthcare system that is less than perfect, but better than the nothing 17 of 29 million Venezuelans were receiving before the Bolivarian Revolution took hold. Chavistas also launched a major literacy initiative, lifting hundreds of thousands out of intellectual indigence. As literacy surges, so does education— free education—from grade school through university. This means graduates won't be saddled with debts needlessly incurred while funding university endowments. This often drives college grads to move down career paths they'd rather not follow, but for the albatross invoice that lands in their mailbox with maddening regularity. Of course, debt-free Venezuelans are also signing up in droves for rapidly expanding pension programs that cover even taxi drivers and cosmeticians.

As of 2011, by contrast, 46 million Americans were mired in poverty. Six million have descended into poverty since 2008. Officially, 'poverty' means a family of four trying to make do on $23,000 a year. Good luck with that. Or, as CBS News reported the same year, 150 million Americans—half of us—are officially low income, according to the Census Bureau. So, the lower class metastasizes, larger in number and broader in distribution than the crumbling middle class, but our political leadership has taken a blood oath to deny the existence of the former as the latter evaporates, leaving a curious cipher at the soul of American politics— for whom are these shirt-sleeved liberals fighting? One class is nearly extinct, another non-existent. Is there a third unmentionably tiny slice of the citizenry that factors into the equation? Perhaps a parallel of Venezuela's vengeful investor class, so pleased their Presidente has finally slipped the surly bonds of earth?

Trade: Collaboration vs. Exploitation

In terms of trade, few nations do less to love their neighbors than the United States. The North American Free Trade Agreement (NAFTA) is an unimprovable example of how our trade agreements wreak havoc on hemispheric economies. Heavily subsidized agribusiness in the United States desperately needs to dump its surplus abroad. Local producers in countries like Mexico can't begin to compete when NAFTA shreds the protectionist measures that shielded them from American economies of scale. Hence a decimated domestic agricultural community in Mexico, not to mention NAFTA's other bequests, such as *maquiladoras* and slave wages.

Our venerable model for dispossessing the natives is to divide and conquer. For decades, the United States has divided the economies of the South, largely by forging discrete trade agreements with each, using aid as the carrot and debt payments and capital flight as the stick. For Chavez, accords like NAFTA and other bilateral agreements (CAFTA-DR, for example) represented attempts to impose unfair trade protocols on Southern nations teased into complicity with promises of access to lucrative American consumer markets.

The last thing the White House wants to see is more continental trade agreements among South Americans—a clarion call of its faltering regional sway. Of course, this is precisely what Chavez had been trying to effect. Recognizing that only a unified front stands the slightest chance of defying the hemispheric bully to the north, Chavez set out to expand Mercosur into a continental trade platform, not simply that of South America's southern cone. Then he worked to build additional inter-continental co-operatives including Telesur, PetroCaribe, and Petrosur, as well as the Bolivarian Alliance for the Americas (ALBA).

Chavez also threw the IMF and World Bank out of Venezuela and encouraged his neighbors to do the same; for him, they were simply empire's first responders, opportunists happy to exploit misfortune, and rushing into the breach to do with debt what had once been done by arms. As Latin growth figures show, Chavez' concept of continental self-reliance has its merits, but this stab at regional independence—a step outside Washington's sphere of influence—is the very policymaking that northern pundits are quick to undermine.

It sometimes seems as though United States' foreign policy models itself on Gore Vidal's memorable note of *schadenfreude*, "It isn't enough that I succeed; others must fail." If only the two were not so imbricated, as non-zero sum theorists tirelessly proclaim.

Economics: Equality vs. Austerity

Our politicians and their media parrots remorselessly remind us that there is no money available for lavish social programs that might correct our imbalances. Rather than irrigate the tree of liberty, we must chop it down to size. Instead of enshrining health care as a human right—as Chavistas did in Venezuela's 1999 constitution—we must imperil the security of seniors in order to reign in deficits that would drop naturally if we stimulated growth artificially—with a public jobs program, for instance.

What's more, we are told, corporations must be unshackled from onerous concepts like taxation, so that they might generate greater shareholder dividends through interest rate arbitrage on exciting international currency markets (keywords: global casino). And, of course, we must set aside half of our treasure for that great cause of noble men everywhere—war—while Venezuela practices the inexpensive but exotic concept of non-aggression. Even so, a trillion dollars a year is unlikely to stanch the flow of the global dispossessed into the sympathetic embrace of jihadists. At least not as long as we continue to lead the world in state terror—the leading cause of reciprocal terrorism.

As we yoke austerity to recession, thus ensuring deeper depression, Venezuela raises domestic spending. Real GDP in Venezuela has doubled since 2003, when Chavez made the unconscionable decision to seize the oil sector and funnel its profits into popular social programs, leaving in his wake a tranche of spoiled petro-executives clamoring for a coup. Legislating that at least 51 percent of your national resource be owned by your government—ostensibly the people's representative—hardly seems a radical notion. Of course, this is exactly the kind of policy IMF lenders seeks to subvert when they condition their loans on the privatization of public resources.

What's the immediate result of such a 'radical' policy? Government monies culled from oil sales have been rolled into the domestic economy; worker cooperatives, communal councils, diversified local media, and investment banks have delivered power into community coffers, decentralizing the means of production in a move that feels alternately Bolivarian and, dare we say it, Jeffersonian. Per capita GDP, according to the IMF, is up some 50 percent since the failed 2002 coup. Venezuela now has the least income inequality on any country in South America.

And while Capitol Hill rehearses its pantomime of horror at recession-fuelled deficits, debt levels in Venezuela stand just over 50 percent of GDP—leading no one outside of *The Washington Post* to declare an economic crisis. The European Union, by contrast, regularly carries debt at more than 80 percent of GDP.

Other metrics of the economy—used by Western media to paint a portrait of destabilization—are variable. After devaluing its currency in 2010, pundits predicted massive inflation. Instead, inflation declined for two years, while economic growth topped 4 percent both years. Nor do critics note Venezuela's spiraling rate of inflation before Chavez took office—or that he has actually significantly reduced it.

Food shortages are also present, another surprising condition in a country of declining poverty. Western critics naturally point to price controls as the cause, providing a typically ideological explanation for a problem that appears to have a more nuanced answer. Food consumption in Venezuela has exploded since Chavez took office in 1999. The population consumed 26 million tons of food in 2012, double the 13 million tons they consumed in 1999. The government claims the shortages are simply a consequence of consumption. Food production is up 71 percent since Chavez took office, but consumption is up 94 percent.

One related metric that isn't encouraging is crime. In stark contrast to improving economic numbers, Venezuela's murder rate increased threefold during Chavez' three terms in office, now third highest in the Americas. Analysts find these figures baffling since most had assumed crime would decline with inequality.

The Wolf at the Door

As Naomi Klein pointed out in her book *Shock Doctrine*, neoliberals salivate at an opportunity to exploit calamity. What Klein didn't mention was that disaster capitalism applies as much to individuals as to global events. A tsunami sweeps through a sleepy fishing village in South Asia, and the vultures of laissez faire swoop down to claim valuable coastline. A tranquil fishing trade is papered over by the errant ecology of a five-star resort that twice dispossesses natives: it bars them from their own land and sea, and it vacuums profits out of the country that might usefully be made on the now-confiscated soil. But unquenchable capitalists know they can achieve the same effect when they unseat nascent nationalists who don't toe the line. Cue the people's "tyrant", Hugo Chavez. His death opens a door for American foreign policymakers that desperately want to eliminate the threat of a good example, to borrow a phrase from our glorious Vietnam era. With Chavez gone, a new election will be scheduled to take place within 30 days. Will Chavez' Vice President Nicolas Maduro claim the presidency? Will opposition forces, backed by major national media and fueled by American dollars, be able to wrest the government from the socialist majority?

Instead of squandering taxpayer dollars trying to undermine of popular social movement on another continent, the Obama administration could do something truly constructive. It could finally concede it has something to learn from socialism, from other peoples' constitutions, from the Fifth Republic, and from the defiant brown faces of political revolutionaries across the Caribbean, Atlantic, Pacific, and Indian Oceans. There's plenty on offer from Chavistas, Naxalites, Adivasis, indigenous Bolivians, Spanish *indignado*s and other off-the-imperial-path communities. The world is full of solutions. Not all of ours have to originate in the chicken scratch of a Founding Father or the madcap scribble of an Austrian economist. But all this may be a tall order for a speechifying elitist that has been so comprehensively outdone by a melody making, poetry reciting, Lincoln-quoting man of the people.

(*CounterPunch*, March 12, 2013)

Chemical Weapons Abuser Deplores Use of Chemical Weapons
The administration's behavior on chemical weapons is morally absurd

Sometimes obvious duplicity can be hard to fathom. Why would someone tell a bald-faced lie when everyone knows it's a lie? Perhaps because not everyone does know it's a lie. This must be the case with our venerable White House, from which we hear daily pronouncements that are swiftly undermined by a tranche of WikiLeaks cables, a closer look at the Excel spreadsheet, or a cursory inspection of recent history. And yet the difference is simply that President Obama's bully pulpit is incomparable in scope and reach, while the riposte from truthdiggers usually has the auditory power of a whisper, reaching a sliver of the voluminous masses that have already ingested the official narrative. We can only hope that by continuing to beat the drum in ever-greater numbers, we can bring the beast into the light, and expose it.

In that spirit, let's consider President Obama's famed "red line" across which Syria would face dire consequences, ostensibly from the global community, but in actuality from the United States and a diminutive contingent of allies it drags into the fray kicking and screaming. The red line is chemical weapons use. Should the Syrian government engage in this unspeakably barbarian behavior—as it surely is—the U.S. would be compelled by its newfound Responsibility to Protect (RTP) to annihilate the Assad government, sweeping into power a rogue assemblage of disaffected Islamists with western assault rifles slung over their shoulders and a dog-eared copy of Sharia law in their back pockets. Hopefully for the White House and Pentagon, this loose confederation of militant terrorist cells would be mostly Sunni and thus predisposed to despise Iran and its Shiite 'hordes'. A divide and conquer strategy worthy of the British Empire, that infamous hegemon with a gift for social amputation.

The Benefit of the Doubt—Experiments in Credulity
But for a moment let's suspend our collective disbelief at the idea of creating a power vacuum and then filling it with mercenaries. Could it be that the president really cannot countenance the use of chemical weapons anywhere in the civilized world? Does this position stand the test of investigation? Let's look.

The first stumbling block on the path to credulity is Fallujah. American forces used radioactive depleted uranium, white phosphorous 'shake-n-bake' bombs, as well as napalm and "mark 77 firebombs," a mix of kerosene and polystyrene similar to napalm. Thanks to this almost indiscriminate deployment of chemical weaponry, the Fallujah population has suffered an irruption of congenital malformations that *Al Jazeera* reporter Dahr Jamail suggests exceeds even those seen among the nuked survivors of Japanese cities Hiroshima and Nagasaki.

Afghanistan isn't much different. Researchers have discovered evidence of uranium isotopes in the bodies of Afghans (compositionally slightly different from depleted uranium). They've witnessed alarming conditions—sudden death, cancers, skin lesions, deformities—especially in Pashtun villages, consistent with the use of depleted uranium weapons. The curse of chemical weaponry, and a significant reason there are international conventions against their use, is that unlike conventional arms, which might kill you, chemical weapons threaten to kill your unborn children, too. Genetic deformities can result from the ingestion of uranium particulate matter. Some might arguably call this a kind of slow-motion genocide, aimed at a particular ethnicity, but spaced over generations.

Most recently, and in the most absurd contradiction of Obama's professed concern for the population of Syria, the Israelis bombed a weapons depot with depleted uranium shells. Here is America's closest ally, regional proxy, and the fourth largest military on earth—using chemical weapons to weaken a rogue state it suspects of using chemical weapons. In other words, we'll annihilate you by the very acts for which we condemn you.

If depleted or non-depleted uranium is such a common feature of the U.S. arsenal, it is no surprise that America voted against a 2007 United Nations General Assembly resolution to debate the effects of depleted uranium armaments. A year later it again voted against a resolution for three UN agencies to update their research on the effects of the chemical—this despite an overwhelming plurality of states that voted in favor of more research on the subject.

Purveyor of Chaos and Deceit
If this brief outline of hypocrisy doesn't rattle your faith in America's goodwill abroad, perhaps the horrifying consequences of its recent military invasions will. The U.S. track record in the twentieth century is dismal. In twenty instances—one per decade—of attempting to install prefabricated democracies in foreign nations, it failed seventeen times. But forget democracy, what about simply avoiding mass slaughter? Iraq is rapidly threatening to unwind itself into three ethnic enclaves, each one intensely hostile to the other two. Likewise, Libya's collapse has left hundreds of towns presided over by virulent militias, with the nominal federal authority in a permanently defensive posture. Afghanistan, a pot-boiling stew of graft and frayed alliances is neither consolidating nor democratizing. All this begs the question: how can the State Department conceivably justify its position on Syria?

Sadly, one can imagine the Department of Justice (DOJ) cobbling together some wickedly disingenuous defense of its behavior. Beginning with the bizarre fact that the Chemical Weapons Convention (CWC) outlaws neither depleted uranium nor white phosphorus. Phosphorous, despite its deadly effect on the human body, is legal as an effective smoke screen that can scramble radar. Depleted uranium, also <u>deadly</u> and with the potential to generate genetic deformities, is highly valued for its armor-piercing capacities, being heavier than steel. Once these jaw-dropping nuances are instanced, the DOJ might then note that Syria itself is one of the few non-signatories to the CWC. Various suppositions about the use of sarin gas by the Assad regime can be tabled, seeding further doubt in the minds of the half-attentive American public and within important ideological segments of the global elite. Thus, having extracted itself from notional culpability and heaped further calumny on Syria's international standing, the administration could move swiftly into action—aggressive, brutal, and destabilizing—under the auspices of NATO and beneath the casuist legal cover of the DOJ. In the modern imperial model, just two tools are needed: a cache of guns and a battery of lawyers. Which is more lethal is up for debate.

(*Countercurrents*, May 21, 2013)

Defending Ukraine from Russian Imperialism
The Russian bear emerges from hibernation

In Bertrand Russell's *A History of Western Philosophy*, the philosopher delivered his summarization of the writings of Catholic theologian Thomas Aquinas thusly, "Before he begins to philosophize, he already knows the truth; it is declared in the Catholic faith. If he can find apparently rational arguments for some parts of the faith, so much the better; if he cannot, he need only fall back on revelation. The finding of arguments for a conclusion given in advance is not philosophy, but special pleading."

American foreign policy is determined in much the same fashion. Valuable objects are desired. Noble justifications are manufactured. Trusting populations are deceived. War is made. Empires do their special pleading on a global scale. For instance, the U.S. and its allies know precisely how they want to portray the Ukrainian conflict to their deluded Western populations. They need only apply the false flags and fashion the nefarious motives—like so many brush strokes—to the canvas of geopolitics.

Both the government and their corporate media vassals know their conclusions in advance. They are simple: Russia is the aggressor; America is the defender of freedom; and NATO is gallant security force that must counter Moscow's bellicosity. As the chief pleader in the construction of this fable, the Obama administration has compiled a litany of lies about the conflict that it disseminates almost daily to its press flacks.

One lie is that Putin has a feverishly expansionist foreign policy. No evidence exists for this claim, repeated *ad nauseum* in the West. The annexation of Crimea hardly seems like an example of such a policy. Crimeans voted overwhelmingly to secede from Ukraine. Russia was quite content with its long-term agreements with Kiev over the stationing of its Black Sea fleet at Sevastopol. It was the Kiev putsch that forced its hand.

There are plenty of signals that Putin has sent a stream of conscripts across the border to battle alongside the besieged "rebel separatists" in the East of Ukraine. But is this a crime of imperialism, sending soldiers to defend communities of ethnic peers under attack? Seems a difficult argument to make.

Moreover, Moscow has long stated that it wouldn't permit NATO bases on its border—a purely defensive stance. The West knows this, but that is precisely its plan. It also surely knew that by capsizing Kiev and installing a few Westernized technocrats, it would provoke Russia into taking Crimea rather than sacrifice its Black Sea outpost. This cynical baiting permitted Washington to frame its aggression as self-defense, and Moscow's self-defense as aggression. For context, consider how the U.S. might react if China suddenly toppled Mexico City using local drug lords with the aim of stationing hypersonic glide missiles in Tijuana. For once, Washington's contempt for diplomacy would be justified.

Another lie is that we know Russia was behind the downing of MH17. Obama repeated this outlandish claim in the pulpit of the United Nations, no less. No proof exists, but plenty of circumstantial evidence seriously undermines the charge—missing air traffic controller (ATC) transcripts, the absence of satellite evidence of Buk anti-aircraft missile launchers in rebel territory, shelling traces on cockpit material, and Ukrainian ATC worker tweets pointing the finger at Kiev, and so on. Yet within hours of the crash, Barack Obama had told the world that Russian-backed separatists were responsible, and that Moscow must be punished. Nobody owns the narrative better than the USA.

A third lie is that the toppling of Viktor Yanukovych was a democratic uprising. Interesting how these always seem to occur wherever America has "strategic interests" in peril. Only then does the fever for representative government seize upon the minds of the rabble. Setting fantasy aside, the most reasonable conclusion, judging not least by admissions from Victoria Nuland and Obama himself, is that the U.S. engineered a coup using fascist thugs in the vanguard, and false flag shootings to drive Yanukovych into hurried exile. Odd how it all occurred when Yanukovych, after prevaricating for a time, discarded his association agreement with the EU for a better Russian offer. (Note likewise how Syria erupted in violence immediately following Bashar al-Assad's decision to reject a Western-backed Qatari pipeline deal in favor of an Iranian one. In both cases, the inciting incidents were examples of an imperial province defying the diktats of Rome.)

A fourth lie is that Western sanctions against Russia are merited, since they are based on Russian aggression. However, a State Department run by his rhetorical eminence, Secretary of State John Kerry, would never phrase it so bluntly. Instead, we were informed that Russia was being chastened for "violating the sovereignty and territorial integrity of Ukraine," and because it had worked to, "undermine democratic processes and institutions in Ukraine; threaten its peace, security, stability, sovereignty, and territorial integrity; and contribute to the misappropriation of its assets." One can just imagine the media flacks in speechless submission as this decree was sonorously recited from on high. None of this puffery removes the fact that the coup was a contemptuous move to bring NATO to the edges of Russia.

Bootlickers Anonymous
My, how the media lemmings fall in line with the official rhetoric. Dutiful to a fault, Western corporate media have performed their servile tasks with aplomb this month. A Thursday *Times* edition earlier in the month led with the headline,

"U.S. and Europe working to end Ukraine fighting." Saturday morning's edition led with "U.S. faults Russia as combat spikes in East Ukraine." A lead in the *Economist* put it rather more bluntly, "Putin's war on the West." Beneath the headline was a Photoshopped image of the Russian President, looking resolute, hand extended with puppet strings dangling from each digit. The op-ed pages of the *Washington Post* teemed with vitriol, continuing efforts to portray Obama as a latter-day Neville Chamberlain, arch appeaser of transparent tyrants. The "alarmingly passive" White House should be more concerned about how "to keep Vladimir Putin in line."

This isn't nuanced propaganda. It isn't hedging or garden variety bias. It's flat-out mendacity. Surely these publications have, as none of the rest of us does, the resources to know that the United States, trailed by its milquetoast EU lackeys, is trying to provoke a conflict between nuclear powers in eastern Ukraine. It either wants Russia to quit backing eastern rebels and permit NATO to establish bases on its border, or allow itself to be drawn into a resource-sapping proxy war. The end goal of the former is to divide Moscow from Europe. The goal of the latter is to vastly diminish the federation's capacity to support its Shiite and Alawite allies in the Middle East, all of who stand in the way of Washington's feverish dream of regional hegemony. Neither option holds much hope for residents of Donetsk, Luhansk and the surrounding *oblasts*, or provinces.

Yet the *Times* leads the Western world in disseminating, in every Starbuck's in America, the folderol that our high-minded, hand-wringing, and munificent leaders are pursuing peace. This despite the unquenchable imperial ambitions of Russian President Vladimir Putin, who will not cease his provocations until he has resurrected the former glory of the Soviet Union, circa the Stalin era. How soon before the term "Hun" starts circulating? We've already got warmongering Senators releasing fake photos and cantankerously arguing that Obama is weak in the face of a world-historical threat.

Howitzers for Peace
Despite hysterical claims that Obama is a dove and tremulous fears that Putin will roll unopposed across the European mainland, the U.S. Congress approved new sanctions on Russia just before Christmas. The Orwellian, "Ukraine Freedom and Support Act" was intended to make Vladimir Putin, "pays for his assault on freedom and security in Europe," according to co-author of the bill, Senator Larry Corker, the Republican who will soon chair the Senate Foreign Relations Committee.

But what are sanctions without a little lethal aid thrown in? The bill also provided $350 million in such aid to Kiev. That means "anti-tank and anti-armor weapons, crew weapons and ammunition, counter-artillery radars to identify and target artillery batteries, fire control, range finder, and optical and guidance and control equipment, tactical troop-operated surveillance drones, and secure command and communications equipment."

Now President Obama, tired of the pretense of diplomacy, is said to be weighing a recommendation from the always-helpful Brookings Institute to speed some $3 billion more in military aid to Kiev, including missiles, drones and armored Humvees. Look at this stern-faced collection of the pale and pious, spines erect as they advocate more slaughter in East Ukraine, where the U.N. has condemn both sides of the conflict—Western-backed Ukrainian government *and* the Russian-supported Novorossiya Army in the East—of indiscriminate shelling, which no doubt accounts for the hundreds of civilian death in just the last few weeks. A million have already fled to Russia as shelling from their own nation's army has destroyed power and medical infrastructure, one of the first steps toward the impoverishment of a region. Couple that physical distress with the economic stress being implemented through Kiev's agreement with the European Union.

The U.S. has also promised energy aid to Kiev to counter—as the media generally puts it—Russian threats to cut gas supplies. It is rarely noted that Kiev has refused to pay or even schedule payments on its $2 billion past-due invoice on previous deliveries. This is no doubt a Western prescription or precondition of assistance.

Note the staggering disparities here. Kiev owes Russia $2 billion in back payments. Vice President Joe Biden promises $50 million in energy relief, none of which will make it to Moscow. Then the president weighs in with $350 million in military aid and contemplates a staggering $3 billion more. He also offers a piddling $7 million for humanitarian purposes alongside some 46 million in the same bill for border security and the like.

That's some $3.35 billion to further destroy a fractured Ukrainian society and $57 million to help repair it. Forgive me for being obtuse, but how is this peacemaking? Yet Secretary of State Kerry, Senator John McCain and others in Congress have continuously cast the conflict in defensive terms, producing all manner of fabrication to support the conceit. In the next sound byte, NATO's Secretary-General Jens Stoltenberg says the alliance wants to double its Response Force to some 30,000 troops. France's Hollande has called for Ukrainian entry into NATO.

Peace Before the Thaw?
Amid all this belligerent posturing, cameras crisply flashed when Angela Merkel and Francoise Hollande, Vladimir Putin and Petro Poroshenko concluded a second Minsk ceasefire agreement last week, implemented Sunday. It was perhaps a last ditch effort by a temporizing EU to prevent a vicious proxy war, or possibly more insincere diplomatic posturing to provide cover for Western aggression. In any event, Washington was notably absent, but surely it loomed

large over the meetings. The core points of the accord include a withdrawal of heavy weapons behind the nominal buffer zone; amnesty for prisoners; withdrawal of foreign militias and disarming of illegal groups; decentralization of areas controlled by Novorossiya Armed Forces, supposedly in the form of constitutional reform; but also Ukrainian control of the Russian border by year's end. Despite the agreement, the battle for city of Debaltseve continued, with the rebels—or "terrorists" in Kiev parlance—finally emerging victorious yesterday and driving the Ukrainian Army into retreat.

Betting on peace isn't a smart call in this circumstance. Already radical voices have flared up in Kiev and also in rebel circles declaring their contempt for the agreement. None of the contracting parties in Minsk seem to have control over these groups. Poroshenko himself said he agreed to the first Minsk agreement to let his troops regroup, and he has evidently refused the stipulation of constitutional reform this time around. Nor has Washington shown any serious interest in implementing a peace plan. In fact, the financial outlay by the White House suggests this is no token conflict, but part of a larger imperial strategy that many pundits claim doesn't exist.

But it does. Look at Carter administration National Security Advisor Zbigniew Brzezinski's strategic master plan, laid out in his book *The Grand Chessboard*, among others. Then see how that plan found its apostles in the neoconservative movement, re-articulated in Paul Wolfowitz's 1992 Defense Planning Guidance for the Clinton administration, and later in the Bush administration's madcap blueprint for reshaping the Middle East. As ever, the objective is full-spectrum dominance, an arcadia or nightmare, depending on which side of the imperial fence you find yourself.

(*CounterPunch*, February 20, 2015)

Empire of Deceit
William Blum's latest book unmasks imperial America. It's not a pretty sight.

If you took all the uncomfortable truths omitted from mainstream media over the past half century, compiled and indexed them, and added a dash of withering sarcasm, you might end up with a book a lot like, *America's Deadliest Export: Democracy* [Zed Books, 2013] the latest offering from serial dissident William Blum. Like his better-known peers Noam Chomsky and Howard Zinn and Gore Vidal, Blum is a perennial gadfly on the imperial hide, puncturing falsehood and punctuating hypocrisy with an implacable zeal. On the back cover of Blum's book *Rogue State*—and repeated in the current volume—is the following paragraph, probably the finest he has or may put to paper:

If I were the president, I could stop terrorist attacks against the United States in a few days. Permanently. I would first apologize – very publically and very sincerely –to all the widows and orphans, the impoverished and the tortured, and all the many millions of other victims of American imperialism. I would then announce that America's global interventions – including the awful bombings – have come to an end. And I would inform Israel that it is no longer the 51st state of the union but – oddly enough – a foreign country. I would then reduce the military budget by at least 90% and use the savings to pay reparations to the victims. There would be more than enough money. One year's military budget of $330 billion is equal to more than $18,000 an hour for every hour since Jesus Christ was born. That's what I'd do on my first three days in the White House. On the fourth day, I'd be assassinated.

This paragraph was famously quoted by Osama Bin Laden in one of his grainy video homilies to the world in 2006. A minor media storm followed, hovering over Blum like a drone over a Waziristan hamlet. Once the furor subsided, however, Blum's connection to OBL contaminated his reputation as a public figure. In the half dozen years since, Blum has received scant few speaking invitations from universities after enjoying a steady diet of engagements in the years prior. One can just envision the blandly decorous university administrator, seated in his mahogany office, dismissing out of hand a proposed invite to Blum, admonishing naïve student advocates to use a bit more discretion in their choice of speakers. But it was their loss.

Blum's latest offering confirms that his exile from the college circuit has done nothing to dim his fury. The new book is a compilation of essays and articles dating from the middle of the Bush years through 2011, and covering a vast range of foreign policy issues. Blum writes with disarming informality, a writer with little time for the artful turns of the poet or novelist. His mission feels too urgent for anything but blank candor. In contrast to a more measured analyst like Chomsky, Blum holds nothing back. He launches salvo after salvo at the edifice of imperial falsification, a veritable babel of cloaked belligerence. Yet his indignation is leavened by healthy doses of humor, including a late chapter that envisions a global police state of comical extremes.

Blum's central objective, it seems, is to expose the American mythology of good intentions. He states in the introduction, writing about the American public, "No matter how many times they're lied to, they still often underestimate the government's capacity for deceit, clinging to the belief that their leaders somehow mean well. As long as people believe that their elected leaders are well intentioned, the leaders can, and do, get away with murder. Literally."

From this premise, Blum quickly establishes the central goal of U.S. foreign policy: world domination. The concept, so infrequently phrased like this—even on the left—may sound like something out of a Bond novel—the sinister plot of SPECTRE, hatched in some underwater command center. But as Blum begins to lay the foundation for his claim, the ostensibly fictive begins to feel factual. He asserts that the American military is the vanguard of American business, bent on corporate globalization by any means available to it, which happen to include state terror, undermining elections, bombing, assassination, support of autocratic mass-murderers, and a general suppression of populist movements. In fact any means by which it can vanquish the threat of economic democracy—a model that would needlessly tax and encumber corporations in their efforts to advance the bottom line.

Our Bipolar Worldview
Blum then walks us through a litany of foreign policy issues, throwing aside the façade of official doublespeak and subterfuge, and revealing the honest face of American foreign policy—and it is almost never a pretty or admirable or defendable reality. Reading through the cases, a disturbing polarity emerges. On one hand, the Noble American, whose civilizing missions abroad are always necessary interventions, conditioned by a desire to ennoble benighted peoples. On the other, the Terrorist, a shockingly savage barbarian frothing with fundamentalist ire at the profligate and infidel freedoms of the West. The Terrorist would reduce the western hemisphere to dust, given the chance. Hence the forward positions of our military—purely a defensive measure against a foe with whom negotiation is a fool's errand.

According to received orthodoxy, U.S. foreign policy is at best an almost messianic force for global good, and at worst capable of blundering mistakes that misread the cultural character of the developing world. Note here the preclusion of even the capacity for immoral behavior. Misguided, yes. Unethical, never. Think of Barack Obama's oft-cited claim that the Iraq war was the "wrong" war, a "dumb" war, and poorly managed. Not once in his 2008 campaign, or prior to it, did our future president even hint that the Iraq war was deeply immoral. If it wasn't, it follows that none of the war's prosecutors should themselves be prosecuted for war crimes. Hence Obama's swift decision to "look forward" and permit criminals like George Bush, Dick Cheney, and Donald Rumsfeld to stroll leisurely into the history books. It likewise follows that violations of our civil liberties can be effected with a clean conscience, since the government means only to protect its citizenry. What this perspective requires of the average citizen is the unstinting faith of childhood, an increasingly risible notion in the age of WikiLeaks.

At the far polarity of the moral spectrum is the terrorist. Those we dislike— redistributive Marxists, agrarian reformers, big-government socialists, anti-totalitarians—are cavalierly labeled terrorists by our government, thanks to the magical euphemism of "material support." Simply add a heavy dose of fearmongering and the general consent is induced. Thus, your freedom fighter becomes my insurgent. My indigenous resistance becomes your Maoist army. The terrorist is characterized as a moral degenerate, impossible to understand because fundamentally depraved—unlike us. As exemplified by state rhetoric, the terrorists always strike first. History begins with a car bomb and ends with a humanitarian intervention.

Blum exposes this perverted reading of history in scenario after scenario: Iraq and Iran; the Bush White House; the demonization of WikiLeaks; the catastrophes of the former Yugoslavia; the bombing of Libya and the support of state terror in Latin America. In a chapter on the Cold War, Blum revises what is perhaps the 20th Century's most serviceable fable by making the startling claim that the Cold War was not a back-channel battle between capitalism and communism, but was rather an American effort to crush populism in the Third World. Even the establishment has sometimes conceded this claim. No less than influential Harvard political scientist Samuel Huntington, said in a recorded private conversation in 1981, "You may have to sell intervention or other military action in such a way as to create the misimpression that it is the Soviet Union that you're fighting. That's what the United States has been doing ever since the Truman doctrine."

Necessary Illusions
There are plenty of forays into related terrain, including social ideology, environmentalism, the contradictions of capitalism, the effectiveness of government, religion, dissent, the mainstream media's proclivity for deceit through omission. The chapter on media is smartly followed by a takedown of Barack Obama, who Blum's strips of his public-relations façade as a progressive reformer. The president is revealed as a rhetorically vacuous warmonger, an ally of big finance, and a committed imperialist. To underscore the power of rhetoric to cloak not only venality but villainy, Blum closes the chapter with a stunning passage from a speech by Adolf Hitler in 1935, which sounds a chorus of pacifist

platitudes and internationalism that might have been mouthed by any neoliberal elect in any developed economy. Among other statements of perfect liberal pragmatism, Hitler states,

Our love of peace perhaps is greater than in the case of others, for we have suffered most from war...The German Reich...has no other wish except to live on terms of peace and friendship with all the neighboring states. Germany has nothing to gain from a European war. What we want is liberty and independence.

Blum is a perfect portrait of candor when contending with rabid patriots and reflexive nationalists. When asked by one if he loves America, he bluntly replies, "No, I don't love any country. I'm a citizen of the world. I love certain principles, like human rights, civil liberties, meaningful democracy, an economy which puts people before profits." This characteristic and unadorned honesty shimmers throughout the book. On page after page, Blum translates the complexities of doublespeak into layman's language, unpacking the malevolent aims of American militarism.

Outflanking Big Brother
As with most left screeds and polemics, there comes a final chapter in which much of the force and momentum of the preceding text is lost, and when the elephantine question is finally voiced, "So what do we do about it?" Fortunately, Blum's answers are as simple and sensible as the rest of his work. For the author, the "sine qua non" for any real political change is clear: the removal of money from politics. To summon the kind of political pressure required to force such a systemic overhaul, we need an educated populace. Blum notes that the best we can do is educate ourselves on the imperial project. By unmasking the subtle and not-so-subtle deceits of state-sanctioned media, we can inform ourselves and others until we reach a critical mass of dissent, at which point change might be effected.

In a late chapter on resistance, Blum offers a measure of hope from a report from the Defense Science Board, a Federal outfit created to give independent advice to the Secretary of Defense. In 2004, the group critiqued global Muslim attitudes toward America. After debunking the myth of the Middle East's irrational hatred of American freedoms, the report came to this lapidary conclusion: "No public relations campaign can save America from flawed policies."

True enough abroad, but you would have to be asleep to miss the effectiveness of public relations on public opinion in the United States. We are presided over by the P.R. President, by whose invisible hand our reality is sanitized of its sanguinary character. We find ourselves seduced by the soothing platitudes of state-sanctioned media—putting people first, compassionate conservatism, change we can believe in, Camelot, a shining city on a hill, morning in America. Gustave

51

Le Bon, a pioneer of mass psychology, once noted that the masses are especially susceptible to comforting fantasies, and that, "Whoever can supply them with illusions is easily their master; whoever attempts to destroy their illusions is always their victim."

Blum cites some illusion-shattering work of the sixties counterculture, notably activist and musician Gil Scott-Heron, whose song, "The Revolution Will Not Be Televised", warns America that a revolution is coming. Scott-Heron sings that people, in Blum's paraphrase, "would no longer be able to live their normal daily life," and—more incisively—that they, "should no longer *want* to live their normal daily life." But in today's tranquilized social climate, this last line feels at once terrifically apposite and sadly naïve. How many of us simply want to leave work, repair to our couch, sufficient alcoholic sedatives at hand, televisual narcotics coloring the living room, and slip into a state of unthinking reprieve? Creature comforts may be the opiate of the American people. Deflating this bubble of banalities, via the expanding tools of information, seems to be one of the few viable paths forward.

And so long as lonely prophets like Blum soldier on, a handful of excavated truths may threaten to capsize the artfully constructed narrative of empire. A note of injustice may sound in the thought stream of a blandly acquiescent middle manager or tongue-clipped service worker. As Mao Zedong once intoned, "A single spark can start a prairie fire." Without that tremulous hope, the fact that Blum's central premise of malign intent has been proved right so often is of little consolation. A Cassandra acquitted is little more than a salve to the ego of the gadfly. But given the damage done to democracy and its prospects here and abroad, which of us can safely say that this is not his fight?

(*CounterPunch*, April 1, 2013)

From Gaza to the Hindu Kush
An exercise in cultural empathy

Slip into their shoes for a minute. No, not into a traditional Iranian *galesh* or Pakistani *khussa* or Palestinian sheepskins. Step into the western sneakers they wear today: Nike and Adidas and Converse. Then run for cover as you hear the whistling warning of an incoming missile, drone, or helicopter.

First, you are a Gazan, wondering why your Mediterranean stretch of land hasn't been turned into the seaside paradise it could be—with a vigorous fishing trade, sustainable agriculture, holiday tourists frolicking on the beautiful beaches, and a healthy Palestinian state partly funded by abundant natural gas supplies beneath the Gazan soil. Why instead it feels like a high-security prison camp, garroted by Arab-hating Israelis to the North and disinterested Egyptians to the South? Fulminant crews of IDF praetorians are prepared to confiscate your water and food and electricity at the slightest offense. Your people are a perpetual pariah on the global stage, like a troublesome relative at the holiday dinner, prone to revealing family secrets nobody wants to hear. And now this. The leader of Hamas, <u>negotiating an extended ceasefire with Israel,</u> is assassinated by…Israel. You find the level of hypocrisy staggering. Then you hear that supposed friend of the Middle East, Barack Obama, tell the world that he supports <u>Israel's right to defend itself</u>. Evidently your people have no such right. Palestinians barely cross the President's lips, except to imply that they should stop firing pointless rockets over the border.

Were you were a Gazan, would you abandon violence as a means of resistance? Would you renounce retaliatory attacks? Would you concede Israel's illegal settlements are here to stay and forfeit your right to pre-1967 borders, despite your legal right to them? Would you simply bow your head and ask the fierce-eyed hawks atop Israel's militarized state to show a little mercy?

Next, you are an Iranian, a member of the country's expansive pro-Western middle class, once hopeful that Washington and Tehran might forge a bond of mutual understanding and shelve the animosity that has animated the relationship for years. After all, wasn't it Iran that helped pave America's path into Afghanistan by mediating with the Northern Alliance? Wasn't it Iran who helped stabilize the Iraqi government on America's behalf? Wasn't it Iran who has been reasonably disposed to negotiating its nuclear goals with the West?

All of this despite the history of American aggression within your borders and on your doorstep. First there was the <u>American-supported coup</u> in Tehran in 1953, setting up a corrupt American puppet regime which plausibly led to the fanaticism of the Islamic revolution. Then U.S. support for Saddam Hussein's brutal war with Iran in the eighties, followed by America's own attacks on Iraq in 1991,

Afghanistan in 2001, and Iraq again in 2003—wars that must have completely unnerved the mullahs. And now, here is America again, brandishing the leash that restrains a rabid Netanyahu while rattling its own saber at Tehran.

But all that is non-history. The historical plotline is clear: You must abandon nuclear power for the safety of the free world. Your Islamic leadership can't be trusted with a bomb. They may be terrorists like other radicalized Muslims in the Middle East. They may be intent on global jihad and anxious for self-immolation (a certainty if they were to fire a nuke at the Holy Land). Each time you refuse to end your program of civilian nuclear power, you move further up that long list of rogue states.

You wish you could remind the West that Iran is fully within its Non-Proliferation Treaty rights. Within its IAEA rights. You would remind them there isn't a shred of evidence that you are enriching uranium in an effort to confect a bomb. Despite having not attacked a country in decades, you are the unstable threat in the Middle East. Not hyper-aggressive Israel. Not India and Pakistan, whose Kashmir competition is an odds on favorite to spark the first nuclear war. No, the real threat sits, curiously, at the chokepoint of Middle Eastern oil. But, you ask, what makes a man like Netanyahu fit to oversee hundreds of nuclear weapons and an Iranian leader like Ahmadinejad not fit to oversee one? You stare in wonder at Americans on television reflexively defending Israel's right to hold a monopoly of nuclear violence in the Middle East.

If you were Iranian, would you want a bomb? Would you be skittish at the prospect of an avaricious imperial superpower sitting on your doorstep—with a giant militarized fortress in Baghdad, destroyer patrols crisscrossing the Strait of Hormuz, and drones selectively zapping shadowy figures Obama picks from a PowerPoint show? You gaze up at the blue sky above you and wonder if this is what it's really come to: your fate determined by a stiff in a suit in some distant corporate conference room.

Finally, you are a humble Pakistani living in the Northwest Frontier Province of Pakistan, on the edges of the now-infamous Federally Administered Tribal Area (FATA) and the cloud-capped Hindu Kush mountains. When you read a dog-eared copy of George Orwell's 1984 in your teens, you thought the story was a piece of clever fiction, a warning of the perils of propaganda. Now you feel like you are living it. The random bombs that blitzed the "proles" in 1984 are now reigned down on your village by American drones. You can hear them buzzing in the sky, heard but unseen, a kinetic threat that occasionally delivers a lethal payload against an unsuspecting neighbor. You understand your government's hesitance to attack its own people at America's behest. You understand the comic futility of trying to police the Afpak border, despite U.S. insistence that your country do so. And you wonder, now that they've got bin Laden, why don't they just go away?

If you were a Pakistani, would you condone the drone? Would you support the War on Terror, that state-led violence against stateless actors hiding in remote hamlets? Shouldn't this be police work, you wonder. Isn't there a more effective means of capturing civilian criminals than aerial assaults managed remotely by brainwashed conscripts in air-conditioned bunkers deep in the American desert—the gamification of warfare has finally arrived. But you recognize the political dynamic in play: To the West, the lives of American soldiers have higher value than the lives of anonymous Arabs and Persians in some far-flung dystopia. The American President must limit American casualties even as he corrals the metastasizing army of madman in yet another failed state.

These questions are surprisingly easy to answer when you put yourself in their shoes. You discover that, quite possibly, these people are lot like you. They want peace, they want prosperity, they want to feed their families and have weekends free. One characteristic of people everywhere is a desire not to be bombed. Another is and that, pushed into a corner, they will defend their own. Shouldn't these basic observations be central to our understanding of the world, instead of the incessant drone of media punditry that tries to dehumanize the weak and poor and voiceless?

(*CounterPunch*, November 27, 2012)

Greenbacks for Bloodbaths
How to get maximum return on taxpayer dollars

In these times of pinched budgets and reduced expectations, do you every sit back and wonder where 30-40 percent of your income goes every year? Or perhaps you are contented by the glistening images projected by your new debt-financed flat screen. Surely, that slender fellow in the tailored suit has put our tax dollars to good use. Well, perhaps you should turn off the mute button.

Over the last year or so, some very interesting uses for our tax money have surfaced, notably Syria and the Ukraine. Most of our money, it seems, appears to flow either into the cloistered coffers of defense contractors, or otherwise disappears overseas—into the pockets of despots, deranged psychopaths, amateur regime-changers, Nazi sympathizers, Saudi-backed thugs, Al-Qaeda allies, and a vanishingly small number of normal people with humane objectives (I won't discount the possibility).

The lion's share of our cash goes to the military. This is no surprise. Ever ready to hyperventilate over a new threat, the Pentagon generals can spin a pretty convincing campfire story, the better to wrest $549 billion from the coffers of our discretionary funds. Of course, not everyone can be efficiently bombed and invaded. Sometimes clandestine activities are preferable when the goal is regime change, as opposed to simply sending a lesson to a profligate nation-state that may have caught the independent nationalism virus. In the former case, much of that money flows out under the guise of humanitarian aid or "democracy assistance". Note Robert Parry's assessment that, "Hundreds of millions of taxpayer dollars is channeled through the Bureau for Democracy, Human Rights and Labor (DRL), The Middle East Partnership Initiative (MEPI), USAID, as well as the Washington-based, quasi-governmental organisation the National Endowment for Democracy (NED)."

Remember how it used to be, when we took the words of Human Rights Watch and Amnesty International and Greenpeace on faith? When it was as good as gospel? Surely these were honest brokers of the peace, we thought. With their tireless altruism and shoestring budgets. Their purpose-built business models uninfected by the profits virus. The images flitted across the tube: boats banging across big waves to challenge heartless whalers; images of jailed artists and stirring calls to defend free expression; the faces of desperate children, flies buzzing their heads, driven into tent communities in parlous conflict zones.

Things have changed. Whether to faux NGOs or faux rebel armies or faux protestors, countless American tax dollars tend to migrate abroad into the hands of a dubious confection of ne'er-do-wells. When you add military spending and the international affairs allocation from the 2014 budget, it accounts for 60% of our discretionary spend, or 18% of our total 2014 budget. Consider this brief hit list of deceits bought and paid for by our innocent contribution to the public weal:

- **Fact-Free Advertising:** The National Endowment for Democracy (NED), the NGO of the U.S. State Department, evidently funded the infamous "I Am Ukraine" video, supposedly a triumphant expression of the human spirit expressed—how propitiously!—by a beautiful young woman. A trumped up PR vehicle to sway public opinion in advance of premeditated destabilization. Again we fell for that magic verbal elixir: "grassroots!" Just drop that gold-plated adjective into your byline and watch the Facebook likes pile up.

The NED is thirty years old and is the bête noir of the NGO industry's good name: it was developed by the myopic Reagan administration expressly for the purposes of subversion. It is a funnel through which the government passes cash to minor NGOs on the ground in all manner of places hostile to the imperial will. Hence, under the pristine blanket of American 'democracy promotion', we can dismantle nationalist projects the world over. The NED now pulls upwards of $100 million from the federal government for dubious work in more than 100 nations. It financed 65 projects in Ukraine alone.

- **Friends of Al-Qaeda:** America's clandestine intervention on behalf of non-Syrian Salafists was sanctioned in part by the endless stream of supposedly "grassroots" videos that surfaced on YouTube, most by nominally helpless and endearingly innocent Syrian locals being hammered by the fist of state. How quickly the press seized on these files to justify the demonization of Bashar Al-Assad and clamor for his instant removal—democratic process be damned. (Picture a reverse scenario in which China, say, leaked a fake video showing American troops committing some nefarious act. Imagine the scrutiny that would be given that video, the tireless efforts to discredit it. Now consider the near thoughtlessness with which American and European media rushed these videos into the news cycle.)

Likewise, last year's chemical weapons claim against Bashar Al-Assad's government. Look up the phrase "rush to judgment" and you should see an image of Secretary of State John Kerry wielding his farcical report on the Syrian government's supposed use of chemical weapons against its own people at a time when the West was contemplating a bombing blitz. A perfect pretext for violent intervention—provided by a besieged president desperately trying to dodge a hail of American bombs. Although the storyline lacked evidence and motive, it was trumpeted as a near certainty. Kerry assured the assembled media that no more thought need be given to who perpetrated the crime (all in attendance nodding in grave acquiescence).

Alas, the 'surgical' strikes were averted. Relieved of having to air its violence on the world stage, the Obama administration returned to the more comfortable confines of subversion. Evidently most of the 'non-lethal' goods and 'light arms' sent to 'moderate' rebels are CIA-funded, not to mention the fact that the U.S. likely isn't just equipping jihadists with small arms—and perhaps chems through its Saudi proxies—but is paying their salaries to attack the Al-Assad regime. Last year the administration earmarked an extra $123 million for the Syrian rebels, for a non-lethal total of $250 million since the war erupted. American monies helped foment the civil unrest with perhaps $12 million since 2005, including a special gift: a London-based TV station beaming in Western propaganda for the edification of benighted Syrians.

- **NGOs for Coup D'Etats:** Next comes what the chairman of the NED called, "the big prize", the Ukraine. The brown revolution was supposedly a stirring display of democratic independence protesting the vile corrupt autocrat Victor Yanukovych. Yet while there may have been a smattering of genuine protest, just as in Syria it was quickly hijacked, funded, and amplified by monies passed through the State Department to the NED to dozens of NGOs. USAID has also poured $1.8 billion into Ukraine over the last 20 years, where much of it has evidently helped Ukrainians "experience increased political freedoms." One off-the-books participant may be CANVAS, a nefarious clandestine tool of the U.S. state, according to journalist William Engdahl, among others. Given the CANVAS track record, dating back to the 2004 Orange Revolution in Ukraine, were it and other so-called NGOs involved in the deployment of fascist bullies and rooftop snipers that precipitated and rationalized the coup d'état? CANVAS isn't listed in the NED's massive number of Ukrainian recipients, but its methodologies seem to have made their way onto the Maidan. (Useful templates for fake unrest include Indonesia circa 1965 and Venezuela circa 2002.)

- **Persecuted Neoliberals:** Speaking of Venezuela, this Latin petro-giant is next on the Obama hit list (the regime change hit list, not the drone hit list, or the whistleblower hit list, lest you find yourself confused). Since the onset of the Bolivarian Revolution in the late nineties, the U.S. has airdropped cash into the swarming vortex of Venezuelan politics, helping petulant neoliberal capitalists to conduct all manner of anti-democratic activities. Venezuelan journalist Eva Golinger has estimated the U.S. has spent $100 million trying to undermine the socialist project all-told, including recent budgetary requests from President Obama, money funneled through USAID and the NED, not to mention suspiciously high operating costs for the American Embassy in Caracas. Who needs $24 million to maintain an office with 81 employees? Failed coups, Parliamentary boycotts, efforts to debilitate the oil economy—just a few of the elaborate techniques facilitated with your tax donations. Perhaps this is Undersecretary of State Victoria Nuland's next stop. Maybe she can engineer rolling regime change across the northern tips of the southern hemisphere, from Caracas to Havana to Quito. Surely, the treasury already has the checkbook in hand. Perhaps Obama can coordinate his latest humanitarian actions to coincide with the June World Cup, as suitable a smoke screen as the Sochi Olympics.

- **Bribes for Puppets:** Best to pass quickly over the crown jewels of U.S. idiocy since 9/11, lest the venerable reader find him or herself short of breath. Afghanistan is a blood-money pit, where until recently sacks of cash were regularly deposited at Hamid Karzai's slippered feet. This 'ghost money' evidently produced or dramatically abetted a mercenary culture of bribery that has resulted in little good, mostly vanishing into networks of warlords tied to opium and the Taliban. And Iraq? Well, our troops seem to have been either happily evacuated or quietly slipped inside the American Embassy in Baghdad, which suspiciously swallows nearly $5 billion a year to feed its 16,000-person staff and conduct hazy police and military operations inside or outside the 104-acre plot of banks-of-the-Tigris real estate.

Provisional Conclusions
We can draw a few tentative conclusions as we observe the results of all this judicious spending. First, as always, is the still surprising realization that the U.S. government, in the incendiary words of former Reagan Assistant Secretary of the Treasury Paul Craig Roberts, is "a malevolent force with no sense of justice or respect for truth, law, or human life. Just ask the residents of Iraq, Afghanistan, Libya, Syria, Palestine, Pakistan, Yemen, Somalia, Lebanon, Honduras, Venezuela, Cuba, Iran. Even the deluded western Ukrainians will soon catch on."

Secondly, we've learned that American power doesn't seem to give a damn whether their lies are eventually exposed, as they inevitably are. So long as they work long enough to justify an invasion, subvert an election, shotgun a fusillade of sanctions across the bow of state, or just drop another veto on a censure of Israel's illegalities in the West Bank and Gaza. (Israel drops anchor in one occupied territory, missiles in the other.) Lies are the means that serve the ends, and once the ends are had, the means are discarded. Disowned as blithely as a shoddy jobs report. Leave it for the pundits to clean up the mess. Leave it for the paid politicos to rationalize the mayhem. Which they dutifully do. Recall all the reasons Bush went to war in Babylon? First, WMDs. Then Al-Qaeda contacts.

Then the forgotten genocide of 1988. Then tyranny. And on and on it went. But by that time nobody in the White House cared what the justification was. The bombs had already fallen.

The important thing is that the means suit the situation—the method is determined on a case-by-case basis. So long as, when the fog of war has cleared, the President can don a flight jacket and declare, "Mission Accomplished." So long as John Kerry can claim that our foreign policy investments are returned to us in the form of "security, stability, prosperity, jobs, opportunity, and the value in and of itself of backing up our ideals and values with actions." And as long as Assistant Secretary of State Victoria Nuland can tell us that the fascists rioting on the Maidan were actually "doing so peacefully, with great courage, and with enormous personal restraint as they sang hymns, and prayed for peace." Then, as former Secretary of State Madeleine Albright famously intoned, "the price is worth it."

(*State of Nature*, Spring 2014)

Hypocrite in Chief
Living in a Counterfactual Epoch

A hypocrite's work is never done. Thus the need for our Nobel Prize bearing Commander in Chief to execute a needless and devastating war of aggression on a country preoccupied by its own civil war. He should pin that prize to his lapel when he announces his surgical strike on Syria. Let's be clear: wars of aggression are, by the standards we set at the Nuremburg Nazi trials, the "supreme international crime." Crimes for which Nazis were put to death. Anyone who pulls the trigger on a war of aggression is, by our own measure, a war criminal. But President Barack Obama needn't worry about being isolated by his action— the annals of the American presidency are chock full of war criminals. He'll have good company in the pantheon of imperial lore.

Of the numberless hypocrisies of the administration, this one is particularly crude. The White House claims *to need* to punish Syria's Bashar al-Assad regime for the unproven use of chemical weapons (sarin) in Ghouta. Not only does this atrocity, committed by unidentified actors in a civil, ethnic, sectarian, and proxy conflict within Syria, somehow make Syria a national security threat to the United States, but it also suggests we deplore the use of chemical weapons. Neither is remotely true. I think the former could be true if we do bomb Syria, as it may incite Syrians to plot against the empire that slaughtered its men, women and children. The latter cannot be true by virtue of the fact that chemical weapons are a primary element in our military arsenal, and have been repeatedly handed over to unreliable allies or deployed ourselves, against Vietnam most notably, but recently against Iraq, Afghanistan, and Libya.

The author of the August 21st attack has yet to be identified. Suspects include Syria, one of the rebel groups, Saudi Arabia, and Israel. The White House report offered plenty of unverified claims said to be drawn from "streams of intelligence." Nobody outside the beltway bubble is convinced. We can, however, have "high confidence" in our assessment that the U.S. will use chemical weapons itself if it attacks Syria. At least three sources of American firepower potentially threaten to deposit a destructive payload of depleted uranium on Syrian society and soil should we attack. Destroyers in the Eastern Mediterranean are likely to fire Tomahawk missiles, which have long been rumored to contain depleted uranium, either in their tip or wing. However, this has been disputed by the International Coalition to Ban Uranium Weapons (ICBUW). At the very least, Naval combat crafts are equipped with anti-missile Gatling guns that use shells with tungsten or depleted uranium. This has been conceded by the military itself. Likewise, A-10 anti-tank aircraft are known to use depleted uranium bullets.

Depleted uranium, although not outlawed by the International Convention of Chemical Weapons (ICCW), are uranium wastes, the leftovers from the uranium that can be usefully enriched (as Iran is prudently, or feverishly, doing this very moment, depending of who you believe). According to Global Research, depleted uranium found its way into the American arsenal thanks to the fact that there are enormous amounts of it leftover from the enrichment process, and that it is cheap to produce. (There is something deeply ironic here, although I'm not sure just what.) But the primary feature of DU is its armor-piercing capability. Not only is it the heaviest of elements, DU bullets keep their shape on impact, thanks to their hideous "self-sharpening ability", and the fact that they burst into flame on impact, generating radioactive dust. This naturally finds its way into the lungs of those nearby (who are perhaps lending "material support" to rebels, instantly nominating themselves for a double-tap drone strike should the DU not do its lethal work fast enough). Depleted uranium often produces radioactive poisoning, and potentially cancer, as former workers at a U.S. arms plant unhappily discovered. It is also likely to generate deformities in the DNA of the local birth population, as Fallujah has lately experienced. This cruel fate is often referred to by the lovely phrase, "mutagenic potential."

In any case, we've left enough in the ground in Iraq, Libya, and elsewhere for some viable case studies. Naturally, the development of leukemia in 76% of mice injected with DU, a study conducted by our own Armed Forces Radiobiology Institute, has been yawningly ignored by the Pentagon, although there is some suggestion that the upper echelons of international power have suppressed the growing movement to ban depleted uranium. The courageous claimant here is former WHO scientist Keith Baverstock, who eloquently concluded that, "politics has poisoned the well from which democracy must drink." The wells from which multitudes of Arabs must drink, too.

But DU is only the leading villain in an ensemble cast of malign characters. Alongside it one can observe the flesh-eating effects of white phosphorous 'shake-n-bake' bombs, napalm and "mark 77 firebombs," a mix of kerosene and polystyrene similar to napalm, all used to great effect in Iraq. American-made cluster bombs are an Israeli favorite, such as when it wants to blow up unsuspecting Arab farmers in southern Lebanon. Yet there they sit, our leaders Obama and Kerry, the urbane sophist and his zombie accomplice, mirroring our nation in miniature: a country whose signal conflicts seemed to carry the mantle of liberty, against the British then the Nazis, but which has since devolved, to borrow anthropologist F.G. Bailey's phrase, into "a babel of inconsistent moralities."

Largely owing to our commitment to chemical weapons, internationalist efforts to ban WMDs in the Middle East have met with typical disinterest. U.N. Security Council Resolution 687 twists in the wind. Agreed to in 1991 to provide a legal umbrella for the U.S. attack on Iraq, it calls for a WMD-free zone in the Middle East and the banning of chemical and biological weapons. Naturally, the looming regional hegemon Israel is the obvious roadblock to the realization of this initiative. In a forgotten instance of considerable irony, Syria proposed the same concept to the Security Council with a draft resolution in 2003, but then U.N. ambassador John Negroponte noted that we might consider it, but then hysterically added—as if snapping to his senses—that this didn't mean we would "adopt it, embrace it or endorse it in any way, shape or form." In other words, best to shelve it with all the other useful ideas the U.S. has nixed since the founding of the U.N.

If you're looking for a link between our degraded civil rights and our depleted uranium, look no further. There it is, in the White House report and its dearth of actual evidence. If only they had added an addendum with the dozens of YouTube videos that factor heavily in their portfolio of supposition. But what reason is there, truly, for yours or my indefinite detention, for the continuous invasion of our privacy, the usurpation of legislative power (the people's tribune) by that of the executive (the ghost of monarchy), and the evisceration of the sovereignty of other nations like Iraq, Libya, Afghanistan, and soon Syria? Whether shot from ships or fired from jets, depleted uranium bullets and shells will strike innocent targets with the same fact-less impunity with which our rights are denied. We live in a counterfactual epoch, where the shrill presence of conjecture disguises the voluminous absence of evidence. Hypocrites lie, victims die.

(*CounterPunch*, September 6, 2013)

Imperial Lockstep
The bipartisan assault on the Middle East

Imperial adventures are nothing new in the Middle East. Neither is their glorification, as Peter O'Toole's pained *Lawrence of Arabia* eternally reminds us. But for a decade or so now, things have been heating up, as if to coincide with climate change and fears of declining petroleum reserves. Fuelled by 9/11 and inspired by material avarice, the West has been proudly shouldering its "White Man's Burden" across the Middle East and has now dipped into the Maghreb. Under the rippling flag of "democracy promotion," the West has attempted to install prefabricated democracies in regional populations already steeped in decades of interventions—mostly at the hands of noble Anglo-Saxon tribes. So anxious is the West to impart its "values" to demented Asian nomads, it is apt to shrug off diplomacy, international law, global consensus, and other minor impediments that might slow its efforts to give thankless Arabs a crash course in enlightenment values.

The Belly for Belligerence?
In the post-election haze, as smoke from liberal fireworks settled over our metastasizing urban ghettos, we were entertained by erudite speculation among the punditry whether President re-elect Obama had the "stomach" for more "humanitarian interventions" abroad. The question loomed over beltway intelligentsia like an ephemeral Gordian knot. Then two weeks ago, threatening to violate the War Powers Act all by himself, our stalwart Secretary of Defense Leon Panetta posted two Patriot missile batteries and 400 soldiers to Turkey. This nicely complements the 150-member "task force" Obama quietly dispatched to Jordan in October, supposedly to help "process" the flow of immigrants streaming out of Syria. Amman must have been clamoring for assistance from our world-renowned border control experts. Perhaps it would have been wiser to simply hire IDF construction crews to build a replica of the West Bank apartheid wall? In either case, we've actually been busy in Jordan since the summer, when we staged a training "mission" – note the ecumenical undertone – suitably entitled "Eager Lion."

We have now bookended Syria, that fearsome new addition to a revanchist Axis of Evil. Panetta noted the cause for these postings: the grave threat of chemical weapons use posed by the Assad government. Secretary of State Hillary Clinton, still baffled by the Benghazi bombing, has lately been worried that the "increasingly desperate" Assad might deploy chemical stores against rebel forces. A serious threat, as any of the thousands of U.S. soldiers indiscriminately exposed to our own radioactive depleted uranium bombs in Iraq and Afghanistan could attest.

Still, the presence of our troops on Syrian borders should answer the beltway question of Obama's ability to stomach another war. If that question wasn't already answered by the clandestine arms support we've provided to the Free Syrian Army and its Islamist fanatics—a worrisome confection of genuine Syrian rebels and flanks of disgruntled Islamists from around the region.

We're All Hawks Now

What disturbs the distant observer is the memory of Wesley Clark's revelatory aside in a speech last December when he distinctly recalled Donald Rumsfeld mapping out multiple regime changes across the Middle East—seven countries in five years. Nominated "regimes" included those of Iraq, Lebanon, Somalia, Sudan, Libya, Syria, and Iran. (Afghanistan was a side project.) Notice the last three on the list? Our Democratic administration has already toppled Gaddafi and left a humanitarian catastrophe to sort itself out in Libya. We are now banging the drums for a confrontation with the Syrians. And, as always, the imaginary specter of an Iranian bomb looms menacingly on the horizon.

Is Obama executing the neoconservative's original plan? After making a fuss about the foolishness of the Iraq war during his inaugural Presidential campaign? After depositing a small river of American blood into Afghan soil and a mountain of American treasure into the pockets of corrupt "government" functionaries?

If true, then the Democrats have only made a couple of tweaks to the plan. One being semantic—the substitution of the liberal incantation, "humanitarian intervention" for the conservative mantra of "regime change." The former is no improvement on the latter. The Libyan intervention generated social chaos, when instead of enforcing the no-fly zone the UN had mandated it to ensure, NATO bombed government forces to tip the civil conflict in favor of the rebels. This precipitated the turmoil that UN resolution 1973 was intended to prevent. It also produced the epiphenomenon—unremarkable to American hawks—of a multi-party civil conflict in neighboring Mali. Thugs from al-Qaeda-linked Ansar Dine—passing easily across the nations' shared Saharan border after the Libyan war— have effectively taken control of Northern Mali, instituting Sharia law and enforcing it with such popular tactics as stoning adulterers, chopping off the hands of thieves, and imposing the usual raft of misogynistic restrictions on females. Tens of thousands have been displaced. The UN just this weekend green-lighted an African expeditionary force to reclaim the territory.

Mostly because of the Libyan adventure, which was a clear regime change action. Troublingly for the U.S., the nationalist-minded Gaddafi had been acting like a born-again socialist in recent years, persuading the African Union to reject American bases and doing his best Hugo Chavez impersonation by establishing an African Investment Bank to elide IMF influence on the continent. This kind of behavior is precisely what the U.S. detests—attempts at regional independence. Hence the need to unseat the crazed terrorist fanatic.

The second modification to the Rumsfeld plan is military in nature—the substitution of conventional ground warfare (code word "quagmire") with heavy aerial bombardments, a temporary deviation from the 'always on' tactic of drone warfare. While George W. Bush mired troops and mercenaries in Iraq and Afghanistan, Obama only briefly explored an expanded ground presence in the latter. His Afghan "surge" failed; elsewhere he has opted for aerial attacks. Any Democrat will tell you that fighting from the sky is more manageable, safer for American soldiers, and, unlike the complicated issue of prisoners of war, dodges the entire legal challenge of detainment through the alembic of assassination. It seems America has finally settled on a strategy of addressing asymmetrical terror.

Neither adjustment alters the general plan—to reshape the Middle East. Still, on the face of it, Syria seems an unlikely candidate for America's military attention. It produces less than one percent of global oil production, and Assad hasn't been adverse to American regional activity. But with the Arab Spring geopolitical hope springs eternal in the breasts of Defense Department hawks. Syria has long been an ally of Iran, a funder of Hezbollah in Lebanon and Hamas in the Levant. Toppling Assad and installing a favorable client regime would help isolate these parties and particularly Iran, the heresiarch of the Rumsfeld cabal.

Our Civilizing Mission
Yet these are not the reasons given to the public. We are told stories about America's noble mandate to protect helpless republics abroad. But as Center for Economic and Policy Research (CEPR) co-director Mark Weisbrot pointed out last week, Arabs can depose their own dictators, as the Tunisian and Egyptian revolutions amply demonstrated. What's more, they did it with little bloodshed and no breach of their national sovereignty. But the White House already knows this. The reformation of the Middle East was never about our vaunted "responsibility to protect." It was about our responsibility to the shareholders of the American government—Lockheed Martin, GE, Goldman Sachs, Raytheon, and so on (corporations are human beings, too).

Moreover, what will American interventions produce? If Assad falls, what pot-boiling alchemy of Salafists and other Islamists will slip on the emperor's clothes? Perhaps a bland coalition government modeled on enervated European models? Funny. Perhaps an aspiring autocrat like Mohammad Morsi will emerge? More likely. In any case, stability is a dubious prospect in Syria, as it now is in Libya, Mali, Iraq, and Afghanistan. And our sanctions on the Iranian people are not doing any favors for Persian peace, either.

History hasn't been kind to the evangelists of enlightenment of any stripe. Massachusetts was settled in part on the premise that Christian colonists needed to save the natives from paganism, an early version of the responsibility to protect. Some people don't need saving; some countries are better left unsaved. Nations from the tip of Africa to the Arabian Peninsula have managed change more bloodlessly and with more civility than "humanitarian interventions" from the world's top beat cop.

Given the predictably chaotic results of hawkish interference abroad—and the fact that even Obamacare had to be debated by the Supreme Court before it was marginally affirmed—maybe it's time for the Democrats to stop cribbing their policy ideas from neocon think tanks. Not everyone has to be a Clintonite.

(*CounterPunch*, December 27, 2012)

Iran's Familiar Destiny
U.S. position on Iran hamstrung by history

In the waning stages of his career, Gore Vidal nicknamed America the "United States of Amnesia." Although he was much derided for speculating on U.S. involvement in 9/11, and in interviews was prone to exchange factual analysis for comic mimicry of George W. Bush, his play on words was precise and accurate. There are few more salient examples of this self-imposed forgetfulness than America's attitude toward Iran. Without delving into the sordid history of our relationship with the Persian giant at the heart of the Middle East, a glance is enough to confirm that we've trespassed ceaselessly in a country both blessed and cursed by its geographic patrimony. Sitting atop a wealth of petroleum and natural gas, positioned at the delta of the Caspian Sea and the Persian Gulf—that great liquid highway by which ravenous Western powers have extracted black gold for decades—the Iranian people must be exhausted by the hectoring and rebarbative attentions paid them by our colonial legates. Nor is it any consolation for Iranians that their nearest neighbors are also tirelessly plagued by imperial interventions.

Where Emperors Love to Tread
Historical images can be instructive. In 1943, a tripartite conference among the WWII Allies was held in Tehran. The press picture from the proceedings is famous: At center sits Franklin Delano Roosevelt, suited like a Wall Street scion, gazing in the middle distance with the sanguine disposition of the world's emergent superpower; to FDR's left slouches Winston Churchill, gazing glumly down, perhaps reflecting on an alliance that would salvage his nation, but see it spent, deposed, and being fitted for epitaphs by history's versifiers; to Roosevelt's right sits Joseph Stalin, one of the century's most odious criminals, back erect, military cap crowning his head, his face a bemused mixture of self-regard and intrigue. Never the trusting type, Uncle Joe.

How curious then, that these three figures, whose countries would soon divide the developing world into areas of influence, would meet in Iran, a nation upon whose resources the global economy would soon turn. After agreeing to support Iran's reformulated Pahlavi dynasty, America with Britain's anxious assistance would in a decade's time overthrow Prime Minister Mohammad Mossadegh's democratic government and shuffle Reza Shah Pahlavi from his rather benign role as constitutional monarch into a malignant new capacity as authoritarian defender of Western interests. Mossadegh's crime had been to nationalize the oil industry, naively supposing that a country's natural resources were its own. Before his doomed bid to reclaim the petro industry, Iranian oil was safely in the hands of British Petroleum, then under the moniker, the Anglo-Iranian Oil Company. Of course, before resorting to a coup d'état, the Americans had tried the always-popular tactic of economic strangulation.

68

Sixty years later we've learned little save for a single prosaic maxim—that might makes right. The bully's creed prevails, and we must again rally our international lackeys in efforts to choke the Iranian economy, assassinate its scientists, and launch cyber-warfare—all with the express intent of preventing Iran from achieving the capacity to build a bomb. Bombs like England and America and Israel happily shelter in clandestine caves throughout their depopulated countryside. Instead, the sanctions simply make it harder for Iranian cancer patients to receive chemotherapy, HIV patients to receive anti-retroviral therapy, and hemophiliacs to find anti-clotting medication. But no matter, as that great humanitarian Bill Clinton outlined in his defense strategy in 1997, it is quite legitimate to do what we must to ensure unfettered access to "key markets, energy supplies, and strategic resources."

Polaroids from the Scrapbook

It was that same Reza Shah—the one we restored to autocracy when we upended parliamentary democracy in '53—that we encouraged and abetted in his attempts to establish 23 nuclear power stations across the country, a program initiated with the United States under President Eisenhower's Atoms for Peace project. An amusing American ad was run in the seventies by a consortium of northeastern power companies. Emblazoned with the headline, "Guess Who's Building Nuclear Power Plants?" the full-page advertisement showed the grey-templed Shah in full regalia, an anodyne partner in our Persian plunder. But for the raven brows, he might have been a white man. This curious historical artifact is memorable because it actively promotes Iranian nuclear energy, the very idea of which now sends the White House into spasms of derelict fearmongering.

Modern media references to Iran are indeed slightly more menacing: a giant billboard looms over Times Square with the galled visage of Iranian President Mahmoud Ahmadinejad and a hectoring sub line that proclaims, "Should Not Be In N.Y. Should Not Be In The U.N." The billboard is sponsored by United Against Nuclear Iran (UANI). This organization promotes the removal of Iran from the U.N. based on the premise, "The U.N. Charter provides for the expulsion of any member which has persistently violated its principles." By this logic, there would be a worldwide exodus from the body, with Uncle Sam, shrouded in perfidy, in the vanguard. The U.N. would then float away on the wind, like the emptied husk of a molting cicada, its former inhabitants too busy with humanitarian interventions to save it.

Evidence of Naught

Peter Jenkins, former British diplomat and one-time member of the IAEA Board of Governors in charge of policing Iran's nuclear activities, noted that the organization's late 2011 report contained zero evidence that Iran had diverted any nuclear material toward the production of a nuclear weapon. Evidently, then, our attitude toward civilian nuclear power in the region is conditioned by our attitude toward those in power: are they secular puppets happy to do our bidding in the oil-slick salt marshes of Khuzestan? Or are they surnamed Khamenei, committed to theocratic Islam, and indisposed to foreign obtrusions? This makes all the difference.

Media bias against Iran, nicely chronicled by Kevin Young, is now an alarming replica of our histrionic build-up to the Iraq war, where journalistic best practices were discarded, and heedlessly counterfactual ideologies leveraged to help catapult public opinion—and a healthy tranche of bunker busting bombs—into Mesopotamia. The International Atomic Energy Commission (IAEA), has even become something of a pulpit for America's frenetic attempts to dodge dialogue and steer armaments to vantage in the Gulf—the better to hurry liberty to benighted peoples.

One of the hastily interred facts of the Iranian situation is that it is in full compliance with its comprehensive safeguards agreement (CSA) with the IAEA. That means it has fulfilled requirements to demonstrate that it hasn't "diverted" nuclear material for weapons making. The IAEA, perhaps under the Mephistophelean urgings of an unnamed Western hegemon, has added two peculiar postscripts to its demands, called, "additional protocols." These protocols have not, to my knowledge, been agreed to by Iran, which would be necessary for them to be appended to the CSA, which in point of fact is a treaty between nations; both must agree to revisions. Iran is likely unwilling to admit the additional protocols because they call for verification of "the absence of undeclared nuclear material and activities in Iran."

Sound familiar? Remember the bespectacled Donald Rumsfeld, veering into his dotage, but still clothed in the lineaments of power, gripping a particleboard lectern before a blazing White House crest, and admonishing a bewitched press corps that, "Absence of evidence is not evidence of absence." Therein, the generalissimo of Abu Ghraib noted, lay the necessity of invading and scouring Iraq, inch by inch, in order to confirm the irrefutable—the absence of WMDs. The movie Green Zone nicely captures the crackpot peregrinations of Matt Damon's American soldier around Iraq looking for the phantom arsenals. When finally frustrated at uncovering nothing but "absence," he confronts his superiors, suggesting that perhaps the intelligence is flawed. Comes the boorish reply, "The intel is solid, it's good to go!" In the end, as Mehdi Hasan of the New Statesman notes, "The greatest weapon of mass destruction turned out to be the invasion itself."

Now, in an Orwellian evolution worthy of the finest thought crime, we would now criminalize Iran's unintended intent, as opposed to Iraq's unfound stocks, insisting that the Iranians prove the absence of something they never avowed in the first place. We're back to ruling out figments. Easily done, assays the IAEA.

70

Simply allow the United States and its noble allies, unfettered, immediate, and interminable access to all and every inch of Iranian soil—every suspicious shed unbolted, every hard drive examined. After all, our satellites are seeing things. Don't make us dispatch Colin Powell to bamboozle the U.N. again. It's amazing what Photoshop can do with a school bus.

Déjà Vu, One More Time

It seems Vidal was right on the money, as he so often was. We forget our past even as it returns to us recrudescent on television screens and tablets and tiny mobile devices. It's easy to forget history when it happens somewhere else. Our government, though, remembers its past all too well—hence its ability to reproduce historical blunders with such perfect facility. But then, oppressors always remember. Victims, too. Only bystanders forget.

History will likely remember our time as the Age of Oil, and perhaps one day our thesaurus will conflate petrol with freedom, as our government does now. Having sated our westward appetites, the jackals of Manifest Destiny have seen fit to extend the currencies of freedom to the Middle East, Africa, and Asia—as often as not denominated in tribal partitions, mass displacement, regional diasporas, and, crucially, hospitable business climates favorable to the extraction of precious resources—all under the imprimatur of harsh autocracies. Of the 18 governments the United States overthrew in the 20th Century, five resulted in democracies. Why should we expect an Iranian intervention to produce a higher probability of representative and pro-Western government? Should we not rather anticipate the more familiar outcome, the seething internecine quarrels of a failed state? Of course, that would require remembering what we've already sent down the memory hole.

(*CounterPunch*, February 25, 2013)

Istanbul Dispatch
A rightward shift in the Muslim world's model of moderation

It was Karl Marx, in his essay on the Eighteenth Brumaire of Louis Napoleon, who said, "They must not represent themselves; they must be represented." Marx was writing about Louis Napoleon Bonaparte's 1851 *coup d'etat* of the French state, dissolution of the French parliament and eventual assumption of the role of emperor. Among the events that led to the coup were Bonaparte's efforts to change the constitution so that he might be re-elected President. After his efforts were frustrated, he staged a successful coup, and rewrote the constitution to consolidate and extend the powers of the presidency (although a year later he declared himself emperor).

One could draw a few parallels between the Eighteenth Brumaire and unfolding events in modern Turkey. Not representing themselves, the natives here are represented by Turkish Prime Minister Recep Tayyip Erdogan and his AK party (AKP). Coincidentally, Erdogan has launched a new constitutional convention in part to consolidate powers in the office of the president, a post he is thought to crave once his current term as PM ends next year. Not only that, but Erdogan— once a cosmopolitan figure with an eye on Europe and the backing of secular Turks—has lately moved to boldly realize his personal vision of Turkey as a regional Islamist heavyweight ruled by a robust executive. Whether the Turkish people desire the same is increasingly immaterial. Erdogan's once liberal veneer has faded with his recent attempts to regulate alcohol <u>consumption</u> after ten o'clock, crimp sales licenses, <u>separate</u> male and female students, implement conservative educational reforms, and offer slices Istanbul's majestic commons for private profit (see July's Gezi Park protests). Ironically, Erdogan once posed as the Ataturk-minded cosmopolitan who would take Turkey into the European Union, liberalizing the nation's economy and society. Liberalization, of course, meant a parliamentary system and a move away from sharia law to Mustafa Kemal Ataturk, the nation's founder. For Erdogan, it had more to do with the deregulation of Turkish protectionism and financialization of the economy. Now, with the Eurozone a shambolic burlesque of fiscal health, and the prime minister growing neglectful of his country's partly secular psychographic, one wonders whether Turks consider Europe's temporizing behavior regarding EU membership as serendipitous.

For some, Erdogan has accomplished a neat trick of subterfuge: he preached democratic reform to Europe, and under the guise of liberalizing Turkey's legal framework he unshackled Islam from some of the more burdensome restraints emplaced by secularists—notably the ban on head scarves, now removed. What was thought to be a liberalizing tendency in Erdogan is now seen as an attempt to simply liberate Islamism to reassert itself in the country—this perhaps as a requisite step in Erdogan's vision of Turkey as a political centerpiece of the

Middle East. How different a view this is from that of Ataturk, who sought to bring Turkey firmly and forever into the 'modernist' camp of Europe. It is no small piece of history that in 1924 Ataturk abolished the Islamic Caliphate, closing sharia courts, and shuttering Islamic madrasas. It has not been viably reestablished since. The frequent calls we hear from radicalized Muslims for the establishment of a global caliphate reflect Ataturk's decision 89 years ago. If Ataturk faced West, Erdogan presents a more nuanced picture, happily adopting Western neoliberal prescriptions for the Turkish economy, however discredited, while taking slow but deliberate steps toward an Eastern-facing conservatism. Call it *laissez faire* hidden in a hijab. Although Turkey's economy has tripled since the early 2000s, the numbers again belie the unreliability of GDP as a measure of broad social prosperity. Nearly half of Turkey's population live near, at, or beneath the poverty line. Unemployment is up, prices are up, stocks are down, and the economy has slowed. OECD figures note Turkish laborers work exceptionally long hours, and under Erdogan's AKP party, union membership has become a desiccated feature of a frayed solidarity. Sounds a lot like America—or Columbia when you see that the government jails union activists with an impunity normally reserved for suspected terrorists. (Part of the global shift to conflate protest of any kind with internal security threats, dissenting journalists are also jailed with terrific regularity.) In Turkey, bank deposits also indicate the wealth gap. A sliver of account holders own most of the depositor funds. What the knock-off handbag touts and teacart vendors and simit salesmen have left is public space. Which is where protests flared in June.

The demonstrations were roughly handled by police during the summer, when millions across Turkey protested the planned redevelopment of Gezi Park—at the center of the city alongside Taksim Square. The plan, a recreation of Ottoman artillery barracks, was taken in a private with no public input. For Erdogan's AKP, this was a clear instance of overreach, attempting to seize most conspicuous park in the largest city in Turkey and transform it into a needless ode to the Ottoman Empire (and, nearly as obviously, to Erdogan's own legacy). To their great credit, Turkish citizens acted to shut it down. The redevelopment plan, or plot, should we say, was shelved by a court ruling in July, and then reauthorized by a higher court, behind a number of belligerent statements from Erdogan, who expertly inhabited the perennial role of the myopic prime minister, caught flat-footed by an explosion of public frustration, responding with characteristic defiance, condescension, and heavy handed police actions. Across Istanbul, one is exposed to images of Ergodan, his placid gaze sitting atop a thick mustache, now grayed with age as he sails through his twelfth year in power. His efforts to crimp alcohol sales added kindling to the protests, which rapidly broadened beyond Gezi Park to encompass perceived threats to secularism. Erdogan's subtle and not so subtle shift into authoritarian habits has many Turks worried that the secular foundation of the state is being steadily eroded. As of last year, Turkey had more journalists in detention than either China or Iran. Under its terrorism law, the state has convicted 13,000 citizens of terrorism offenses— just another innocuous number without context, but consider that, according to the Associated Press, between 9/11 and 2011 more than 35,000 people worldwide have been convicted as terrorists. A full third of that number have been convicted in Turkey. The government also launched an attack on Dogyan Holding, the largest media conglomerate in the country (including *Hurriyet*), fining it half a billion dollars in a tax evasion case that appeared to be politically motivated, after the company's outlets began investigating improprieties in Erdogan's AKP.

Together, the zealous use of the pretext of terrorism and the evident social encroachments have many Turks worried Erdogan has shifted into full autocrat mode. The new constitutional convention has as one of its chief aims the expansion the powers of the presidency. Pundits suggest Erdogan and current President, Abdullah Gul, may simply switch roles in next year's election. Or Erdogan could modify AKP party rules to permit him a run for a third term as PM (there is no constitutional barrier). The administration also has put considerable muscle in recent years into uprooting Turkey's phantom "deep state", long thought to be an underground coterie of militarists devoted to defending the secularist character of the state, and believed to be behind the country's several coups since its founding. It is then no coincidence that the constitutional convention aims to replace the current constitution, which was written under military rule decades ago and which unsurprisingly invested considerable powers in the military. Yet much of Erdogan's pursuit of deep-state groups have the character of show trials, suggesting an ulterior effort to weaken a secularist military rather than unwind its clandestine sect. And since a healthy chunk of the more than 5,000 pending criminal cases against journalists are related to this political purge, one might add a desire to vitiate civil liberties to the programmatic shortlist. Indeed, the focus of the government's crackdown is on a group called Ergenekon (consult your tradecraft bible for the etymology) that supposedly includes military and parliamentary leaders, as well as journalists and academics.

Given the abuse of free speech, the creeping conservatism, and efforts to defang military leadership, one could be forgiven for thinking that Erdogan is doing his best to throttle the very soul of secularism, all under the guise of liberalization. Nor would it be adventitious to conclude that Western-style democracy is neither a sufficient condition for general prosperity, nor a reliable guarantor of the commons—although, to be sure, those aims are often denied under the very banner of their promotion. The late Edward Said, referencing Marx's "representation" line, added that representation was ever a theatrical art. Thus, when one thing plays at being another, it's theater, but not less frequently, politics.

(*CounterPunch*, November 26, 2013)

Kerry's Last Stand

A one-time anti-war activist agitates for war

One can easily summon the image of him from memory, arrayed in a bisque-colored pheasant hunting jacket, doing his best impression of a rural hayseed, the better to sway Midwest voters likely to stump for illiterate gunslinger George Bush in the 2004 elections. That's when many of us gave up on John Kerry. He was outed as a man who would do practically anything to be popular. A man bereft of consistent convictions. A Senatorial rogue who had traded on his slightly raffish New Englander mien to accrue his undeserved credibility. That, and a genuinely affecting appearance before the Senate back in the seventies, when he questioned the Vietnam War—hardly a novel posture at the time, but one that helped launched his fledgling political career as a man of some conscience.

But people change. A lot has changed for Kerry since he appeared before the Fulbright Hearings in decorated fatigues, taking a stand against the war, leading to several years of high-profile anti-war activism. For instance, there he was as a Democratic Senator in 2002, authorizing his demented Commander in Chief to use military force against Saddam Hussein. There he was, after being appointed Secretary of State, saying he would forge an Israeli-Palestinian accord in nine months. There he was, saying the Egyptian military was restoring democracy by overthrowing Mohammad Morsi. There he was, claiming the perpetrator of Syria's "moral obscenity" was quite obviously Bashar al-Assad. Has this man, one wonders, ever been on the right side of an issue since 1969?

The man who once seemed a plausibly reasonable alternative to the warmongering Quixote nine years ago—is now a globetrotting deputy of the latest violent imperialist to inhabit the White House. *This is no joke. The threat of force is real. We're facing a Munich moment. We're talking about an incredibly small number of strikes. The President is not asking you to go to war.* And so on, Kerry blathers into the blathersphere on the upcoming conflict with Syria, his each and every quip inscribed into the national conscience by our supine media. Rather than showcasing this stilted buffoon for what he is, *The New York Times* has done its best to craft the persona of an astute, judicious man of principle practicing the most rarefied kinds of statecraft. *Au contraire, mes amis.*

In this weekend's *New York Times*, Kerry stood alongside the world's foremost fearmonger, Israeli Prime Minister Benjamin Netanyahu. Bibi, as he is known, was looking decidedly glum as he listened to Kerry drone on in belabored tones about the need to hold this savage regime (Syria's, not Israel's) to account for its unproven use of chemical weapons. He was depressed by the meddlesome Russian proposal that staved off a vicious offensive. Bibi surely wanted fireworks—the flash of uranium-tipped shells making the Arab sky luminous with

American wrath. He longed to hear the creaking sounds of another teetering Arab potentate. And why not? Neither Gaza, Lebanon, nor Iraq have proven to be particularly troublesome for the West from a security standpoint. Evidently, sectarian and tribal and warlord conflict can be fairly well contained, much like the urban slums in America's once feted capitals. At least, Kerry and Bibi seem to think, this would be easier to manage than another wanton strongman with a flair for independence and a taste for Tehran. But then, divide and conquer is not a new strategy.

Lest anyone forget the long-term vision of the administration, Kerry was swift to remind the world that stripping Syria of its chemical weapons was intended to "set a marker for the standard of behavior with respect to Iran and with respect to North Korea." Neither Kerry or Netanyahu blinked at this statement, which was delivered in full cognizance of the fact that neither Israel nor America have conceded, publicized, or otherwise offered to dismantle their own chemical stores, including depleted uranium, napalm, white phosphorous, not to mention their burgeoning cluster bomb and nuclear arsenals.

"The threat of force remains," Kerry then intoned, which instantly set off a chain reaction of mirror clichés across the region. French President Francois Hollande, once the false hope of Europe's dying left, declared that military means must "remain on the table." The Turkish government, the scourge of Kurdish minorities, warned that the agreement should not be manipulated by Syria to "commit more massacres." Israel's former chief of military intelligence and now think-tank propagandist, welcomed the accord but was sure to punctuate his lack of faith that Syrian President Bashar al-Assad would keep to the deal. (Israeli voices always make sure to drive home their ever-implicit point: Arabs can't be trusted.) Hollande added that the disarmament deal was not "an end point," a not-so-subtle message to Assad that regime change was still "on the table."

Behind the scenes, while the front men work to keep violence top of mind, deputies are working feverishly to craft a Security Council resolution that will apply impossibly strict protocols on the Syrians, allowing ample opportunity for the Americans to discard the accord and step into a "material breach" with guns ablaze. The resolution will be produced under Chapter VII of the United Nations Charter, which will make it militarily enforceable. French Foreign Minister Laurent Fabius, anxious to move beyond the bromides of negotiation to the crack of gunshot, noted that "we need a stronger position" to unseat Assad, which would entail "supporting" the "moderate opposition" in Syria. As Musa al-Gharbi relates, there is no real moderate opposition fighting in Syria. Moreover, the majority of the people reject intervention. They reject arming foreign zealots. The reject regime change. They want to deal with Assad peacefully. Even at the misty outset of the supposed civil uprising, pro-government counter-protests outnumbered the minor demonstrations by citizens who wanted, not regime

76

change, but for Assad to more swiftly negotiate their social demands. In other words, Fabius is simply parroting the equivocations of the Obama administration.

Kerry leads them all—Fabius, Netanyahu, British foreign secretary William Hague, Turkish foreign minister Ahmet Davutoglu, and Saudi foreign minister Saud al-Faisal—his counterparts in a wayward march of mendacity. Each publically professes humanitarian sympathies. Each does the private calculus of geostrategic power. These men are the lost souls of geopolitics, deputized to do the bidding of implacably venal nation-states jostling for finite resources in a market of diminishing returns. And so we are left with the image of Kerry, once a nominal tribune eliciting the despair of a war-weary nation, now functioning as empire's evocator. He is modernity's Macbeth, "a poor player that struts and frets his hour upon the stage," bloody handed, bloody minded, his brave and original promise long forgotten.

(*Dissident Voice*, September 18, 2014)

Law of the Strong
Every imperial power needs a storyline that successfully perverts the historical record

How curious that those who live by the adage "might makes right" are often so unwilling to say so. In fact, they go to great lengths to say the opposite—that they are abiding by international norms of civility and decency. The Crimean situation provides another stellar example; U.S. power never tires of furnishing the history books with ever fresher case studies in unwarranted aggression. Despite the uncovered and too predictable role of U.S. cash and employs, we find Secretary of State Hillary Clinton issuing proclamations on Russian President Vladimir Putin's astonishing criminality in accepting Crimea back into Russia or—if you prefer, as *The New York Times* put it, his "lightening annexation" of the former Soviet territory. Perhaps tired of repeating the same farcical bromides to blank-faced media zombies, Clinton finally declared that although neither she—nor any right-thinking peoples—wants another Cold War, that fate is "up to Putin." Clinton's fear-mongering is rushed into print by our lapdog media, which hastily confects a couple of cookie-cutter op-eds designed to bring John Le Carre fans bolting out of their armchairs. This week's freshet of fantasy invective included a piece of notable hand wringing in the *Wall Street Journal* on the rapidly fading strength of NATO and another model of histrionic chest-thumping in *The Times*, begging the West to "Stand Up to Russia Now" with a series of provocative moves that would certainly reboot Cold War antagonism, but before the irredentist Russian bear achieves "absolute hegemony" in the region. It's enough to make the average reader assume the apocalypse is nigh. With repeated calls for this kind of myopic posturing, it may well be.

Shift the scene slightly (although never leaving the confines of the blinkered beltway) to the rollicking burlesque of the House of Representatives and you'll find House Intelligence Committee Chair Mike Rogers' theatrical references to Russia's "brutality and expansionism" while waxing nonsensical on his particular obsession—the likelihood of world-historical snitch Edward Snowden being a Russian spy, most certainly under the direction of the Kremlin.

But this is standard fare, although Russian scaremongering has been largely decommissioned since the collapse of the Berlin Wall. But these scripts can be hastily reproduced, as recent weeks have shown. The general storyline is and has always been to characterize Russia as violent imperial hegemon wielding nukes in one hand and a tattered copy of international law in the other. As usual, reality is very nearly the opposite of what the White House says.

President Obama ostensibly lectured Mr. Putin, and presumably the world, on the value of international legal frameworks, etc. (Given Obama's soaring credibility, this was about impactful as his rambling oral history of surveillance.) Had only

Putin responded with a "speck and plank" parable. Alas, he did point out that the "West" abides only by the "law of the strong" by which it pursues its own savage hegemony. Putin also noted the exceptionalism that seems to form the basis of America's moral blindness. Of course, the sense of exceptionalism might be said to follow directly from might; the concepts are probably interdependent, although a heavy dose of "chosen people" claptrap might free the presumption of the former from the actuality of the latter.

Likewise, a political science professor from Barnard College was thumping the bully pulpit on NPR's popular Fresh Air program this week. Again the narrative was a risible hash of the facts. Barnard's Kimberly Marten characterized Putin a rising threat: "The leader of a state that wields a massive strategic nuclear arsenal, controls a significant portion of the world's petroleum and other raw materials, and holds a veto in the U.N. Security Council, has just revealed his willingness to use force on behalf of ethnic nationalism. This was the nightmare that Western policymakers hoped to avoid when the Soviet Union collapsed." Marten also noted that, "There's no question he's stirring it up," meaning ethnic strife. She fails to mention, as her ilk always do, the context. That America certainly "stirred it up" by funneling billions of dollars into Kiev, backing far-right elements such as the Ukrainian Svoboda party. A recent European Parliament report highlighted the party's xenophobia and racist proclivities. (Note their leader Oleh Tyahnybok claiming that "organized Jewry" controlled Ukrainian government.) It was the U.S.-backed putsch by these Nazi sympathizers that led to the Crimean vote to secede and join the Russian federation. The motif of an expansionist Russian threat can only be adequately sustained out of context—by removing both the contemporary chronology of events, but also historical regional dynamics.

The West's Original Backyard
In fact, history reflects the accuracy of Putin's words. Noam Chomsky has written—along with numerous historians—on the idea that the North-South dynamic in global economics, with the North using the South as its raw materials depot, was modeled on the traditional East-West model, in which Eastern European countries were supposed to serve as the natural resources hub of Western enterprise. Ever since the Bolshevik Revolution, Russia has thornily defied this objective. Hence the post-revolutionary interventions from the West, the Cold War and the West's repeated rejection of Russian efforts to thaw military buildups, from Khrushchev to Gorbachev.

Once the Berlin Wall fell, the world got a taste of what the West had in mind for the East. Numerous former Soviet satellite republics were integrated into the Western economic system, set on a path to deindustrialization, debt, and collapsing standards of living, while protectionist measures were eviscerated, even as they were strengthened in the western countries. The threat of competition was muted, the raw materials grab stepped up. The Russian people, too, saw much of their national wealth fall into the hands of a handful of "oligarchs," the Jamie Dimons of yesteryear. Men like Boris Berezovsky guided former Russian President Boris Yeltsin in the privatization of state assets—essentially handing over public resources to private interests, the better to loot the nation's wealth. (It was Berezovsky who once said, "Privatization in Russia goes through three stages. The first stage is privatization of profits. The second is privatization of property. The third is privatization of debt.")

External to Russia, since *glasnost* and against the promises of George H.W. Bush that NATO had no interest in moving an "inch" in easterly directions, nearly all of the Eastern European nations freed from Soviet dominion have been rapidly shuffled inside NATO. The Ukraine is just the latest effort in that long-term strategy of building hyper-threats all along Russia's western borders. The U.S. use of fascists as *agents provocateurs* to unsettle and overthrow popular governments surely called to mind the Nazi attacks of the Second World War, which bled the Soviet Union of millions of men.

Yet despite their history of being attacked by fascist regimes as well as Western democratic nations, President Obama and Secretary Clinton expect Russia to stand aside and permit a neo-Nazi putsch in Kiev that seems to have the obvious objectives of a) bringing Ukraine into NATO and positioning ABMs on the Russian border; b) introducing IMF prescriptions to plunder and loot the Ukrainian economy; and c) eject the Russian Black Sea fleet from its post in Sevastopol. Given the historical record of anti-Russian aggression, not to mention criminal activities in Libya, Venezuela, Honduras, Syria, Iraq, Afghanistan and elsewhere, American hypocrisy is, as they say, "breathtaking." But then, it seems that for a healthy majority of the world's population—at least outside America— to say so is simply to rehearse common knowledge.

A Hesitancy to Embrace the Narrative
I hesitate to characterize Obama's statements on Wednesday as a positive development, but the President said at The Hague that Russia was simply a "regional power" that had acted in Crimea "not out of strength, but out of weakness." The President at once insulted his rival and handed himself a suitable pretext for doing nothing about the annexation of Crimea, aside from a smattering of ineffectual sanctions. With two years left in the Oval Office, Obama clearly has little appetite for an open-ended proxy war with Russia that could bleed into the next decade, much like the Iraq War, his criticisms of which help launch Obama into the presidency.

Aside from Obama's legacy considerations, terrorism may be experiencing a resurgence. American interference in Iraq, Syria, Yemen and elsewhere has helped reinvigorate Al-Qaeda as myriad rag-tag militias and rebel groups begin to blend together, perhaps the incipient stages of a global jihad. Successive

80

administrations have created a self-fulfilling prophecy, generating monsters where there were few, and hatred were there was once indifference.

Seemingly in an effort to recapture the chilling note of 9/11, the President added that his far greater fear was a "nuclear weapon going off in Manhattan." This was likely an attempt to shift the media focus away from Eastern Europe, with its Cold War dynamics, and back to the vaguer and thus more manipulable war on terror. Secondly, though, Obama's was simply rehearsing the same scare tactic George W. Bush had absurdly invoked with his "mushroom cloud" imagery.

The last person that needs to paint dire pictures of the apocalypse is Obama. Yet neoconservative elements within the administration may still convince him that resuscitating the Soviet poltergeist may be a necessary step if the terror narrative becomes increasingly threadbare from overuse. In terms of its appeal as a technique used to disquiet a population and surface latent societal anxieties—and in so doing enable the closure of civil liberties and intellectual resistance—the "Red Scare" has a long, sordid but eminently useful track record. Perhaps Obama is this very minute weighing the two narratives in the balance alongside his imperial storytellers. In either case, the tale told will prove some distance removed from reality.

(*Dissident Voice*, March 28, 2014)

Mike Rogers and the Prophets of Doom
Our intelligence community lives inside a beltway bubble of alarming hysteria

In his 7,000-word State of the Union speech last month, President Obama waited 5,700 words before stintingly devoting a single sentence to the subject of surveillance. He didn't mention the rogue NSA, didn't name specific reforms, adding only that the important thing was that "public confidence" in the "vital work" of the intelligence community was maintained. This cavalier approach to the topic of the year belies the administration's essential disinterest in the public interest. This perspective was reified in the last two weeks by the voices of the American intelligence community. On Tuesday the House Intelligence Committee staged its annual "worldwide threat briefing" only a week after the Senate Intelligence Committee's briefing on the same subject.

It is no small cause for alarm that, among his colleagues, the President is perhaps the least condemnatory of Edward Snowden. The President recently diminished the value of the Snowden files by claiming they had caused more harm than good, but grudgingly conceded that they had raised a "policy debate." He has, however, condemned Snowden for not following prescribed NSA protocols to red flagging questionable activities, protocols that themselves include every possible opportunity to silence disclosure of the activities being flagged. Protocols invented by the offending party, as it were. That is whole point of whistleblowing, a nuance evidently lost on the Surveiller-in-Chief.

There would be no such calm demurrals from our threat-obsessed intelligence hawks at the recent summits, however. Hyperbole was the order of the day. We must of course concede the penchant for crowds, such as that of the intelligence community of Capitol Hill, to devolve into the mass hysteria of groupthink. How much more so when the principals arrive already seized by frenzies of fear. Which among them doesn't see a suitcase bomb at every baggage claim or, to use Himmler collaborator Reinhard Heydrich's phrase, doesn't see "carriers of tendencies" in every email exchange that might critique state policy? (In a sinister note from a 2012 British intelligence document on the extraction of data from mobile applications, the author noted the ability to plot a user's "political alignment.")

A Theater of the Absurd
Tuesday's House Intelligence Committee hearing seemed to serve as much as a PR op than an informed review of threat levels. Presided over by Republican Representative Mike Rogers, Chairman of the Permanent Select Committee, some of the exchanges were as disingenuous as they were cretinous.

Rogers surfaced—not for the first time—Cold War-era suppositions about links between Edward Snowden and Russian intelligence. The Sunday following the

President's lame January surveillance speech, Rogers and Democratic Senator Diane Feinstein joined *Meet the Press*, hosted by the feckless David Gregory, to peddle the fiction that Russia aided Snowden in capturing NSA files.

The New York Times, never one to shirk its responsibility as official stenographer of the state, quickly amplified this false accusation with an article entitled, "Lawmakers Suggest Snowden Link To Russia Before He Leaked Data," a piece of defamatory piffle that the *Times* needlessly popularized without a shred of evidence to support it (the article's questioning of the claim in fine print notwithstanding). Rogers seems to be sourcing his antiquarian Soviet paranoia from his favorite John Le Carre novels.

As if this echo chamber of mendacity were not sufficient to discredit the entire proceedings, Rogers then hectored FBI Director James Comey to concede that journalists profiting off the sale of stolen property, i.e., the Snowden files, were vile lawbreakers. Comey, himself terrorized by Rogers' seething presence, stuttered a few words about "First Amendment implications," after conceding that the sale of top secret files might be akin to "hocking stolen jewelry."

During the Senate Intelligence Committee briefing on worldwide threats last week, Director of National Intelligence James Clapper claimed that journalists that supported or helped Edward Snowden were his "accomplices," a catch-all term with which Clapper perhaps hoped to jointly implicate both phantom Russian spies and real journalists. British Parliament was at least a bit more specific, claiming Guardian journalists aided terrorists in their support of Snowden. Sadly enough, each of these instances represent alarming attempts to widen the circle of culpability and create legal pretexts by which citizens can be silenced for dissent.

Clapper added to his growing legacy of harebrained sound bytes on Tuesday by noting, without a trace of humor, that he had never in fifty years of government work, "experienced a time when we have been beset by more crises and threats around the globe." Of course, there is a modicum of truth in this, given that gun-wielding Americans are now arrayed across 700 plus military bases around the world, "protecting" the kind of angry ingrates that so typify imperial subjects.

The Prince of Piffle
Not wanting his organization to be excluded from the festival of ignorance, CIA Director John Brennan then weighed in. In an effort perhaps to explain why America was being slung beneath a dragnet of surveillance, Brennan dramatized the ability of al-Qaeda camps to operate in destabilized nations like Iraq and Syria, neglecting of course to note the American role in destabilizing these countries. In this Brennan was only seconding the insuperable alarmist Rogers, whose opening remarks noted that, "al-Qaeda has morphed and spread throughout

Yemen, Syria, the Levant, and Africa, this Administration has piled on even more bureaucracy in Washington, D.C." Rogers failed to note the wondrous efficacy of the U.S. drone program in radicalizing the families of slain "suspects" in these regions. Instead, he savaged the Obama administration for piling on more "bureaucracy," a strange claim given the swiftness with which FISA authorizes intelligence agencies to hoover the data of millions of Americans. (Rogers, bereft of novel ideas—so obvious in his Soviet spiel—was simply re-commissioning the tired trope of government red tape as another of the numberless causes of our terrifying insecurity.)

After the festivities ended, Rogers told assembled stenographers that "a thief selling stolen goods is a thief," an obvious reference to former *Guardian* journalist Glenn Greenwald. Note how Rogers smuggles his conclusion into his premise. A "thief selling stolen goods" is all we need hear of this sentence to see he has already concluded Greenwald and journalists of his civil liberties ilk are thieves, a conclusion reached sans evidence or, evidently, a desire to find any.

Rogers is one of the most enthusiastic fear-mongering propagandists inside the beltway. You may recall him from a recent appearance on Charlie Rose, where he reiterated a number of farcical lies about Iran, while Rose massaged his jowls in consternation. This is the same Rogers who infuriated England by suggesting that if Parliament invited Edward Snowden to speak, it could jeopardize its participation in the developing Transatlantic Trade and Investment Partnership (TTIP). He also claimed last fall—in a stellar summation of his views on privacy—that, "You can't have your privacy violated if you don't know it." Rogers exposes here the twisted logic by which he justifies violations of the Fourth Amendment, or perhaps how he absolves himself of defending the public against such violations. If there is a sitting representative that most shoulders the responsibility to defend the public interest against surveillance scope creep, it is the Chairman of the Permanent Select Committee. Yet Rogers has ingested the poisonous myth that nothing is forbidden in the name of national security. And as we now know, the NSA metadata program hasn't foiled crimes, just exhausted more of the federal budget on paranoid military initiatives.

If You See Something, Say Nothing

How ironic that our evolving war on terror asks eternal vigilance from citizens—in New York, we are exhorted, "If you see something, say something!" (I was personally exhorted to do this very thing last year after questioning a congeries of cops as to why they had summoned an army of police vans to surround a pitiful assemblage of vestigial Occupiers attending a meeting in Zuccotti Park.) Yet when one of us summons the courage to step forward, he or she is hit with the hammer of the state. One is shuttled into a decades-long prison sentence, another hounded into permanent flight and what will likely be a life of itinerant exile. Likewise the glaring hypocrisy of the intelligence community's furious indignation at having their lies and illegalities exposed, while delivering only the most blasé assurances to Americans that their privacy isn't being hacked. So although the terror narrative now more than ever seems a splintering ship on an ocean of cynicism, the government shows no signs of relinquishing the pathological insincerity by which it reconciles its claims.

Martin Amis once provocatively suggested, in his book *Visiting Mrs. Nabokov*, something to the effect that the best way to rid ourselves of our obsession with nuclear weaponry was to treat pro-nuke proponents as lepers. To use peer pressure, in other words, to shame nuke lovers into conformity with nonproliferation. The technique has yet to be tried, as best I know. But I sometimes think we should apply it with our war on terror propagandists. The moment the least of them begins a mindless peroration about national security, we ought to instantly denounce him or her as a coward, incapable of living in an uncertain world without resort to hysteria. And perhaps accuse them too of a lack of patriotism, as though the armed forces were not already keeping us safe. Surely, these peddlers of fear are shameless in their conflation of surveillance with security. Ought they not to feel a little discomfort for their deceits?

(*Media Roots*, February 8, 2014)

Obama's Narrative of Deceits
Shaping the official history of empire

If the American public knew what was being perpetrated in its name, it might put an end to the slow-motion coup d'état of the United States by corporate wealth. But it is kept in the shadows, pinioned by a harness of half-truths that underwrite its ignorance and enable its indifference. The public will likely remain in this state until it hears the whole truth, and not the abridged version peddled by an unscrupulous administration, its Pavlovian Cabinet, our obsequious Congress, and the sycophant media (those dutiful court stenographers of state power). Until this confederacy of knaves is exposed at scale, the Janus-faced narrative streaming from the lips of the Commander-in-Chief—whomever he or she may be—will neither change nor falter. Ringing in a new year will not matter.

Let's take a look at a few of the key storylines in foreign policy. Note how each is fundamentally incomplete. Key facts are elided. Context is erased. Ulterior motives buried. American action is thus cast in the lambent light of good intentions. From the administration's standpoint, the fundamental goal of selective storytelling is to portray offensive acts of aggression as defensive acts of nobility, the backbone of the myth of American exceptionalism.

Defending Ukrainian Sovereignty
Perhaps the story of the year in 2014 was Ukraine. The president has roamed the world declaiming on the sacred rights of our dear Ukrainian friends in Kiev. As Obama has it, these freedom-loving patriots have suffered multiple injustices this year. When their former Crimean province endured the indignity of annexation by the Russian bear. When they were forced to bravely face down a savage uprising in the East—where Moscow infected the people with failed ideas and false hopes. These poor Kiev allies, who overturned a corrupt government and instilled the leaders it wanted, still hopes in the humblest of terms to integrate with Europe. We must stand beside it, support its dreams, and defend its fledgling liberty from those who would usurp it.

Most of this is fog-addled dissembling from the estimable firm of Balder and Dash, recently retained by the White House. But a few facts persist. There was a coup—but America facilitated it. A new government did take office—but it was comprised not of democrats but <u>fascist</u> sympathizers and neoliberal technocrats. There was an uprising in the East—but it was led by ethnic Russians who rejected the Kiev putsch. There was a plebiscite—in which Crimeans overwhelming opted to join the Russian Federation rather than sign up for ECB-style austerity and a phalanx of NATO bases.

Notice how Obama's version casts the conflict as a defensive one. It employs the threadbare rationale that America is the noble enforcer of democratic values the world over. Here it is defending defenseless borderland Slavs from unquenchable imperialist thirst of Moscow. In truth, Russia has always indicated that interventions in its border states would be considered provocations, just as the U.S. nearly went nuclear when the Soviets deployed missiles in Cuba. Despite promises from the first Bush administration, successive administrations have moved shamelessly to the east, absorbing new states into NATO and slowly working to marginalize Russian influence from its eastern border to the Atlantic. An aggressive posture if there ever was one.

Iran and the Persian Threat
The President has told us that the "international community" has made tremendous progress in eliminating Iran's capacity to "breakout" and "sprint" to a nuclear weapon, as it most assuredly hopes to do in its endless quest for apocalypse. But while he warns that nations with honest intentions must be wary of scheming nations, the supporting evidence for the madness of the mullahs is sketchy and ignores Tehran's IAEA right to pursue civilian nuclear energy. But the president won't mention the Ayatollah's *fatwa* against nuclear devices. Nor will he remind you that our dangerous sanctions—notoriously killing 500,000 Iraqi children in the 1990s—have significantly damaged the Iranian medical industry and restricted healthcare for the gravely ill.

He might tell you—quite rightly—how naïve Iranian President Hassan Rouhani was to think that making nuclear concessions, softening Mahmoud Ahmadinejad's provocative language, and glad-handing a few dignitaries would make the slightest difference to the U.S. perception of Tehran. But he won't ask you any hypotheticals either, such as how you might feel were you watching a hyper-nuclear aggressor run roughshod over your largely defenseless neighbors? If the U.S. really believes Iran is chasing a nuke, then why not quit giving them a reason to?

ISIS and the Long War
President Obama quite rightly expressed his contempt for ISIS and their unconscionable acts of decapitation and discriminatory slaughter of Shiites. The revolting behavior of ISIS is plain to see. But the president will not summon the image of our own allies, Wahhabi autocrats that savagely behead their own for the sin of sorcery and other fiendish behaviors.

What Obama will also not do is move to end the brutal actions of the U.S. military. He does not mention the drone strikes that slaughter suspected plotters and their families, drawing diabolical schemes in the dirt behind their village hovels. The evidence against them, mind you, is buried in clandestine bureaucratic enclaves—unfit for untrained eyes. And still, village Arabs are nothing more than illuminated targets on a heat map.

Obama will not mention our own sordid history of malevolence. For instance, what we backed in Central America throughout the presidency of his political hero, Ronald Reagan, including brutality through our proxy forces in Nicaragua and El Salvador, which the Council on Hemispheric Affairs (COHA) found to be unique in the hemisphere because they "abducted, killed, and tortured political opponents on a systematic and widespread basis." Torture techniques were said to have been learnt at American counter-insurgency schools and overseen by the CIA. And yes, these atrocities included decapitations.

If you're looking for evidence that American troops performed these deeds themselves, look no further than Iraq. Or into the annals of American history. During the Wilson administration, for example, marines invaded the Dominican Republic and leading a criminal and savage repression in order to secure a profitable market for U.S. sugar concerns. At the time, the advantages of outsourcing were little known.

False Flags and a Paranoid Pyongyang
The president will publically affect a grandiose outrage and claim that invidious rogue state North Korea has hacked Sony Corporation and leaked millions of files, an act of war under international law. What kind of barbaric society would think to conduct such outlandish cyber attacks on a harmless corporation, our flabbergasted White House spokesmen and press flacks ask us in disbelief?

But what our great leader will not tell you is that we have no firm evidence that North Korea is behind the attack. Much like the United States affected certainty when assessing the Damascus chemical attack in 2013, the degree of certainty rises in inverse proportion to the paucity of proof. The FBI released a bantamweight statement suggesting codes, IP addresses, and other surface indictors pointed to North Korea. These claims have been met with derision by those familiar with digital hacking.

Nor has the president bothered to note that his administration has largely pioneered the art of the cyber-attack by smuggling sinister viruses into the Iranian grid hoping to infect and destroy its nuclear capacities and undermine its feverish obsession with a bomb (again, sans evidence). This is not to mention the heroic efforts of the NSA to hack into and imbed trackers in millions of domestic computers.

A Tortured Exception
At all times, the president poses as a man who cherishes justice, peace, and the sovereignty of nations. He will tell you as much. He claims Iraq was a "strategic blunder"; he plaintively concedes that "we tortured some folks" and behaved in a manner not in keeping with "who we really are."

88

But perhaps the best way to prevent future torture is first, to quit practicing it, and second, to punish those that did it in the past, even if they are members of your own clan. Neither has been comprehensively achieved.

The president claims to have banned torture. But he hasn't banned the practice of outsourcing it via rendition. And he has <u>evidently</u> only banned it for the interrogation of prisoners ("detainees") captured in "armed conflict," which leaves a broad loophole concerning noncombatant detainees. As for the authors of our elaborate <u>torture</u> of Arabs across the Muslim world in infamous Bagram and Abu Ghraib and Guantanamo and in anonymous black sites where the gloves truly come off, well, let's put that behind us. He has also decided that to <u>prosecute</u> the war crimes of administrations past would simply be unhelpful, and that we ought to look forward and not into the (unhelpful) past.

Yet his elegies to lawfulness include his steadfast <u>defense</u> of CIA Director John Brennan, who himself had the audacity to <u>defend</u> CIA war crimes before the press from Langley, in which he repeatedly claimed—once more without evidence— that torture works. Not surprising from a CIA director. But Obama will always take a more nuanced view, insisting that these minor missteps are not in keeping with "our values."

Turning a Blind Eye to Tel Aviv
Whenever an exchange of fire occurs between Palestine and Israel, Obama is swift to commandeer the nearest microphone, only to remind us that Israel has a right to defend itself. This is not only a prejudiced view, but it isn't actually true. Under international law, occupying powers don't have the right to attack the populations they occupy, let alone to collectively punish them for the crimes of its leadership, which in this case are resistance to occupation.

Obama will also forget to mention that the Palestinian occupied territories represent the world's most salient example of persistent state terror. He will instead authorize yet more money and munitions and gunships to be quietly shipped to Tel Aviv, trumpeting Israeli democracy. Before the ink dries on these forms of Israeli welfare, the president will reject U.N. resolutions that acknowledge Palestinians' right to be free. To live unoccupied. To escape the grinding gears of racism that have transformed Israel into the South Africa of its day, a nation purblind to its own fascism.

The Energy Subtext
Of course, Obama has never acknowledged that the rise of ISIS, Iranian fundamentalism, Palestinian oppression, and North Korean isolationism is partially creditable to U.S. policies and interventions. We exacerbate the things we claim to deplore. We commit the behaviors we hope to curtail. The reason

why is the nasty little secret at the heart of the American empire: the profits of the few trump the prosperity of the many. The fact is that Russia, Syria, and Iran are the West's three great nemeses in the contest for control of the earth's resources. All three have variously conspired to build pipelines across their nations and others—such as Ukraine—that lead to Europe, where these Slav and Shiite alliances hope to supply oil and gas to the lucrative EU market. But this cannot happen.

This is the silent meta-narrative lurking beneath Obama's patriotic vagaries—that these are proactive resource wars. Pipeline conflict that will benefit defense contractors (Raytheon) and energy companies (Exxon). They are also wars over market access through "free trade" agreements that will privilege Western industry (agribusiness) and finance (IMF). Victory in these conflicts will keep America's dollar hegemony in tact, forcing energy purchases to be denominated in dollars, which will be used to buy U.S. debt and thus help fund the next energy conflict. But these delicate facts are left out of the final draft of the president's talking points. Nobody in the government believes Americans would back wars perpetrated for control of fossil fuels, guaranteed markets for GMO seeds, and globalized serfdom via compound-interest debt regimes.

Paul Wolfowitz had made it plain enough in his 1992 defense policy paper for the Clinton administration: in the post-Soviet world America would permit no rivals to materialize on any front, the better to achieve 'full spectrum superiority,' that dreamy Elysium that sends chills down the spines of the habitués of the Bilderberg Group. Military superiority as a guarantor of market dominance and profit optimization. Simple as that. As William Hartung, Director for the Center for International Policy, has said, "War is good business for those in the business of war." If these are the businesses that put candidates in the White House, does it not stand to reason that administration policy reflect their interests? Energy conflicts obviously do.

By lining the Eastern front with NATO troops and the peripheries of the Persian Gulf with U.S. bases; and by controlling all government concessions in Kiev and Damascus, the United States can ensure that no Slavic Islamic pipelines will cross either nation, and that Europe will be nearly severed from its umbilical dependence on Russian energy. But this is not part of the story. Our dutiful press assures us that Vlad the Conqueror now rabidly seeks regional hegemony and unchecked sway over befuddled but peaceable Europeans. Again we are forced into the fray.

Promoting the Ideal, Demoting the Reality
In his book *The Purpose of American Politics*, author and authority on the realist school of foreign policy Hans Morgenthau claimed America had "a transcendent purpose to uphold equality and freedom." As Noam Chomsky has said,

90

Morgenthau believed that to deny the validity of our national purpose was to "confound the abuse of reality with reality itself." Thus the ideal is more real than the reality of history. It seems President Obama is of the same mind as Morgenthau.

It is time someone informed our arch idealist that values are distilled from actions, not homilies. In the arena of action, we are an empire created by genocide, built on slavery, and maintained by violence. As Abraham Lincoln once said, America is "a nation dedicated to a proposition," that all men are created equal. But the wattage of that lovely conceit has dimmed with time. If there is anything exceptional about America, it is the abyss that yawns between the eloquent phrases of the Constitution and the barbaric actions that defy its every word. Maybe our values were once noble, and perhaps those of the average American still are, but the government has long veered off on a path of its own, its habitués corrupted by the clichés of power, empowering cronies for all manner of criminality. For peace, they've substituted violence. For transparency, intrigue. For economic equality, lawful pillage. For consensus, conclave. For participation, exclusion. For representation, a price tag. Our flight path may once have aimed at popular rule, but that was a long time ago.

(*Consortium News*, January 9, 2015)

Piketty, Odessa, and the March of Profit
Despite more damning insights, capitalist-fueled imperial violence marches on.

Thomas Piketty's <u>book</u> *Capitalism in the Twenty First Century* is all the rage, notably for its 700-page rationale of a very simple formulation: r >g. In this formula, "r" stands for return on capital and "g" stands for general economic growth. Having read a few fairly painless selections from the celebrated tome, and a host of reviews, here's what I have gathered: the idea seems to be that capital gains, rents, and other forms of moneymaking in which you don't have to break a sweat, all grow faster than the general economy. We are thus condemned, should the status quo prevail, to a world in which the rich get richer and the poor get only marginally less poor. Hmmm. Sounds oddly familiar. Almost like reality itself. Nevertheless, bourgeoisie liberals are simply stunned, absolutely gob-smacked, by the revelation of the apparent inequality of the capitalist model. Who'd have thunk it? Reformist liberals across the political spectrum are hurrying back to their greatest-model-of-wealth-creation handbooks for reassurance.

But does any sensible person really doubt that capitalism is a battle between labor and capital, where the enrichment of one is had by the dispossession of the other? Or perhaps this is underground knowledge, known only to deranged leftists and free-range libertarians. (At this point in our story a Lilliputian academic in oxford-cloth cornflower blue materializes to claim that economics is a nonzero sum game, brandishing *Wealth of Nations* and *The Road to Serfdom*, but never bothering to note the declining-rate-of-profit mechanism that instances dispossession in the first place. A philosophical "externality", perhaps.)

No matter. It appears Piketty has produced a post-hoc data-set for what Citigroup announced back in 2005 when its brightly titled report, "Plutonomy" and the much-anticipated sequel, "Revisiting Plutonomy" were unfortunately leaked to the rabble. These signal <u>reports</u> essentially divided the world into "the Plutonomy and the rest," the rest later adopting the more dramatic moniker, "the Precariat." Unfortunately, Citigroup hastily attempted to suppress its reports when it was discovered their authors had been so dreadfully honest about everything. Nor did Citigroup provide any colorful illustrations of its two-tiered world, as it might have done. Perhaps some Raphaelite vision of a high cloud populated by mincing dandies in horse-drawn carriages, while far, far below a burning wasteland of scavengers, tramps, and thieves collected the crumbs that overspilt the cloud of plenty. Such a rendering might have popularized the reality Citi was describing. Instead, nobody read the text-heavy communiqués from on high. Thus poor Piketty was left to labor away trying to transform his awe-inspiring mountains of data into an exceedingly simple three-symbol formula, the better to demonstrate to the myopic ivory tower and the huddled masses just how our destinies diverge. (John Calvin has already usefully explained *why* they diverge.)

But, of course, ivory towered academia already knows all this, too. What are the words "market efficiency" but a description of a good scenario for capital and a bad one for labor? What is the word "liberalization" or "labor flexibility" but descriptions of a good scenario for capital and a bad one for labor? What is the suspicious absence of the word "externality" from the logic of the invisible hand but an absent-minded oversight for capital and a life-debilitating elision for labor?

So, is Piketty preaching to the choir? The rich know it. Academia knows it. The people know it. But at least the people don't respond with shock and awe when the findings are released. "Same old, same old," they might reply. (I recall a former Obama canvasser relating how hard it was to convince rural African-Americans in the Deep South that Obama represented *real* change.) Needless to say, those who perpetuate the system trade despairing glances over bottles of Pinot Noir and fret about "such a troubling book", before ordering a second bottle and laying the whole problem at the foot of those insufferable Republicans. Some well-intentioned reformers will weigh in. Perhaps a little tinkering on the periphery of the system is in order? Might we innovate a few public-private partnerships to ameliorate the general misery? Possibly charter a new NGO to replace our collapsing institutions? Or might we simply rely on the largesse of billionaire philanthropists? In any case, we can all agree it is possible to "do well by doing good", can't we? Cheers to that.

Probably Piketty's book soon will die a painless death as it is swept into the great dustbin of progressive causes. Obama might mention it in passing, decrying the inequalities that keep him awake nights. He'll then announce that, using his incrementalist approach, we should achieve full employment by 2250. A hasty Republican rebuttal will claim this is far too ambitious a plan and would dampen small business initiative, *thereby harming the very people he had hoped to help*! (Note to filmmakers: These Republican monologues are best filmed in the Russell Rotunda, which lends an air of gravitas to the proceedings with its columned grandeur and marbled decorum. Nicely contrasts the sophistic blather of whatever rep you've shoved in front of the camera. Also, aides can be seen scurrying in the background, providing a false sense that something is actually being accomplished.)

Meanwhile, Odessa burns. The pivot to Asia is on, boys. First prize—Ukraine. And you thought it was just another throwaway Slavic backwater on the edge of the Black Sea? Anything but. Just ask George H.W. Bush's Defense Secretary, snarling Dick Cheney. Just ask the doyen of geopolitical statecraft, Zbigniew Brzezinski. Ask former President of the World Bank itself, Paul Wolfowitz.

First, we slow-drip five billion dollars into the country, fomenting unnecessary unrest. Then the Wicked Witch of the West Victoria Nuland descends on Kiev reciting various odes to democracy. Cue the midnight putsch, which forces Viktor

Yanukovych to flee for his life as Parliament empties. (Through the flames some glimpse Nuland's private jet soaring in the direction of Versailles.) Then CIA Director John Brennan visits Kiev for a friendly chat with the new Nazi-sympathizing government. Then Vice President Joe Biden visits Kiev for a friendly chat with the new Nazi-sympathizing government. Cue the fascist thug brigade, which promptly wrecks a tent city of pro-Russian protestors in Odessa, harrows them into a nearby building, and sets it aflame (while diligently executing those inside who don't catch fire). A few dive to their death. A few try to make a run for it, but soon succumb to the Louisville Sluggers on the sidewalk. Afterward, Obama gravely affirms Kiev's right to calm any civil disturbances in the eastern Ukraine, and then mutters something about Russia being "just a regional power."

Just as he finishes his speech on the White House lawn, Secretary of State Kerry touches down in Helicopter Gunship One. Bedraggled and sleepless, Kerry informs the President that Israel-Palestine negotiations didn't exactly work out. He staggers into the White House still clutching David Ben-Gurion's lofty memoirs. An aide flails after him, exclaiming, "Secretary Kerry, I've finally discovered what a 'Bantustan' is!" Obama follows them in, shaking his head with a wry grin, "John Kerry, reporting for duty."

Somewhere on the Grand Place in Brussels, Thomas Piketty is flogging his 700-page behemoth to EU bureaucrats, but they are too busy consorting with visiting IMF cohorts—over growlers of Chimay and Orval—loosening their ties and putting the finishing touches on the newest loan installment for Ukraine, to be dispatched once a hefty list of "prior actions" are set in motion by the neoliberal-fascist cabal merrily ruling the roost in Mariyinsky Palace. Eventually, Piketty piles his remaindered lot into a wheelbarrow and quietly moves off into the crepuscular night. The bureaucrats order another round, and continue to parley the fate of nations with their clever data-sets. After all, they know what we know: what's ours is ours and what's yours is negotiable.

(*Dissident Voice*, May 13, 2014)

Return of the Evil Empire
The U.S. owns the narrative on Ukraine

You have to hand it to them. The United States media machine is unequaled at producing and disseminating misinformation. It begins in the bowels of the State Department or White House or Pentagon and is filtered out through the government's front organizations, otherwise known as Mainstream Media (MSM).

In 2014 the U.S. has succeeded in demonizing Vladimir Putin and Russia, precipitating a New Cold War that may yet become a hot one. The evil empire is back. The White House has made proficient use of mass media propaganda to get the job done. First, they've controlled the narrative. This is critical for two reasons: one, because it permits the White House to sweep the February coup in Kiev into the dustbin of American memory, never to be seen again. Second, it has allowed it to swiftly assert its claim that Russia is a dangerously expansionist power on the edges of a serene and peace-loving Europe. In other words, the omission of one fact and commission of another.

On the former front, by the State Department's own concession, it spent some $5 billion in Ukraine, fomenting dissent under the standard guise of democracy promotion. The myriad NGOs beneath the nefarious cloud of the National Endowment for Democracy are little more than Trojan horses through which the State Department can launch subversive activities on foreign turf. We don't know all the surely insidious details of the putsch, but there are suggestions that the violence was staged by and on behalf of the groups that now sit in power, including bickering neofascists that were foolishly handed the nation's security portfolio.

On the latter end, a frightful portrait of a revanchist Russia will be presented for public consumption. But consider the context before you consign Putin to the sordid annals of imperial tyrants. A belligerent superpower arrives on your doorstep by fostering a violent coup in a neighboring nation with the obvious intent of ensuring Kiev accepts an IMF deal rather than a better Russian one, and further that Ukraine become the newest and perhaps decisive outpost of NATO. Had you been in his shoes, would you have permitted an illegitimate, Western-infiltrated government to challenge the integrity of your Black Sea naval base at Sevastopol? Doubtful.

Crimeans swiftly organized a secession vote—swiftly denounced as fraud by Western media (with some credence, it should be added). Given their Russian ethnic profile and quite credible fears of oppression from Kiev, whose nationalist bully boys were already posturing about eviscerating Russian citizens rights,

Russia's annexation of Crimea is certainly understandable to minds not saturated in Western propaganda.

And yet the majority of the West, meaning the U.S. and Europe, seem content with this narrative of a recrudescent Russian empire with imperial designs on Europe. The White House has successfully characterized Russia as the Slavic aggressor while sweeping NATO's undeniably hostile behavior beneath the rug of its false rectitude. Claims of the need to defend another nation's "sovereignty" are always a bit rich coming from the White House. Yet the rhetoric of outrage streams forth from Washington, and it sometimes seems the principal qualification for a high-level appointment in an American administration is the capacity for a blithe hypocrisy that brooks no irony.

This is no surprise. A sophisticated doctrinal system adept at manufacturing consent will succeed less by what it asserts than by what it leaves out. The facts omitted are always inconvenient ones. Among other missing pieces of the story currently being peddled by the MSM, is the issue of NATO's *raison d'être*, which vanished with the collapse of the Warsaw Pact and the dissolution of the USSR. No matter, it has swiftly refashioned its mandate into a rapid-reaction force ready to descend on flashpoints around the globe, like Serbia and Libya and Afghanistan. Despite promises to the contrary, it has essentially worked to bring all the former Warsaw Pact countries into its U.S.-dominated embrace. The goal is self-evident: put missiles on Russia's doorstep, the better to alienate Moscow from Berlin and ensure that Washington isn't left out in the cold by its rivals.

If recent history weren't sufficient to lay plain NATO's blueprint of aggression, consider the behavior of its chief spokesman, NATO Secretary-General Anders Fogh Rasmussen, a frothing hawk who yesterday announced plans for a large and permanent military presence in Poland and the Baltics. Ready with prefabricated war motifs, Rasmussen said the plan was to deploy, "…what I would call a spearhead within [a] response force at very, very, high readiness." He generously conceded that such a rapid response unit would require "supplies, equipment, preparation of infrastructure, bases, headquarters. The bottom line is you will in the future see a more visible NATO presence in the east."

Sounds like war footing. Sounds like chest-thumping, drum-beating posturing. Sounds like NATO baiting the Russia Bear. No doubt it hopes to lure Moscow into aggressive actions with which it can a) quickly smear Putin in the MSM, and b) use to rationalize a massive arsenal in eastern Europe.

Note that Rasmussen's pronouncement was no doubt timed to coincide with a
tête-à-tête
between Putin and Ukrainian President Petro Poroshenko in Minsk, Belarus. What purpose exactly did the stillborn summit serve, given the bellicosity emanating

from Brussels by one of Ukraine's leading backers? One supposes the idea was to gain negotiating leverage, as if Russia hasn't been observing NATO's covetous moves for the last twenty years.

In a domestic context, this scenario might be described as entrapment. The West seems intent on manufacturing a conflict, if not a war, where none existed. Peace, described as elusive in the press, could be achieved in a matter of days if the White House were so inclined. Instead, it prefers escalation. And sooner or later, Russia will move more visibly to defend the eastern rebellion, stepping squarely into the trap. In fact, it may already have.

Yesterday NATO released U.S.-supplied satellite imagery supposedly showing Russian troops "establishing firing positions" inside eastern Ukraine, a claim instantly ridiculed by Moscow. Naturally, the imagery was obscure. Impossible to verify, but not hard to believe. Despite its own flood of propaganda, it would be credulous not to imagine the Russians supplying arms and tactical support to the so-called "pro-Russian insurgents" in the east. Nor would it be astonishing to see Russian troops cross the border. Again, the question arises: what would you do? Particularly given the Kiev-led brutality aimed at eastern "rebels"? Would you respond like Putin has, or rather more recklessly, perhaps like John F. Kennedy when he heard of Russian missiles in Cuba? Or imagine a pro-Russian Mexican government, installed by a Moscow coup, shelling pro-American citizens near the U.S. border. In imagining how Washington might respond, the words 'restraint' and 'judicious' don't come readily to mind.

Little if any coverage is given to another critical piece of real story, namely the obvious economic rivalry underlying the conflict. Ukraine is a major chip in the tussle for access to Black Sea resources, and for primacy in the provision of those resources to European homes. Likewise, the importance of channeling that access and supply through IMF-engineered loans, naturally denominated in dollars and central to the dollar's now-threatened role as the world's reserve currency.

Next, the false historical narrative will be distanced from the White House through internationalist channels which, although they are fronts for American power, will be perceived by many as independent judgments that happen to agree with the American assessment. U.S.-controlled NATO, the U.S.-dominated United Nations, and the U.S.-submissive EU will convene to censure Russia, ignore Kiev crimes against its own population, and clamor for more sanctions and a provocative NATO build-up in eastern Europe. Short shrift has been given to the news that the BRICS nations—representing some 40 percent of the world's population—have declined to join the West in its sanctions regime.

But such history—distant or near—is trampled underfoot, beneath the crushing weight of MSM misinformation, thanks to which we can expect millions of

Americans to dutifully wave their star-spangled totems as our ships and drones and battalions reluctantly set off to defend our freedoms once more.

(*CounterPunch*, September 1, 2014)

Secretary Kerry Weighs In
Peddling myths to a credulous public

Just last week, the pagliacci at the head of America's Department of State, John Kerry, gave an interview on the much-esteemed house organ of domestic propaganda, the "PBS NewsHour". The entire interview was a farce of human reason, yet was mindlessly absorbed by millions of armchair Americans, 41 percent of whom cannot name the Vice President of the United States. If they cannot perform this simple act of civic sentience, how can they be expected to cut through the thick fog of propaganda that blankets American consciousness on a nightly basis?

They can't. They can't be expected to laugh uproariously when Secretary Kerry points a condemnatory finger at Tehran, blaming them for the mysterious instability in Yemen, and saying, with not the slightest trace of irony, that, "...*the United States is not going to stand by while the region is destabilized* (italics mine)." Nor can they be expected to choke with incredulity when, in his next breath, Kerry says, "...or while people engage in overt warfare across lines — international boundaries of other countries."

No, this is all too much to digest. We are blind to the irony. Blinkered by the hypocrisy. After all, the CIA has been arming al-Qaeda thugs in plain sight for several years now in Syria and Iraq, under the myopic eye of the American public, with hardly a murmur of protest. How compelling must be the White House spokespersons that tell us we are only arming "moderates." We nod sagely from our couches: it is far better to be deposed and slaughtered by moderates than genuine radicals.

No, our blank faces register nary a twitch when Kerry accuses Iran of destabilizing its own neighborhood when it is the United States that has turned the entire region into a confused pastiche of tattered borders, despoiled sovereignties, roving refugees, makeshift graves, and tribal compounds. Evidently, in Kerry's twisted beltway perspective, only the U.S. is authorized to ruin the region—a region where it doesn't belong but has refused to vacate since the collapse of the Ottoman Empire. From the arrogant diktats of British imperialists to the cynical coups and free-market experiments of imperial America, the Middle East has suffered ceaseless depredations at the hands of the West. One wonders how countries like Iran are even capable of sitting at the negotiating table and facing our cabal of inveterate cheats. Maybe they don't read history. We certainly don't.

History As Myth
For Kerry and his State Department lemmings, history is a blank slate on which future historians will pen a chronicle of plaudits to American power. We will be

lauded as peacekeepers or, as President Obama noted in 2009, the exceptional nation that "…has underwritten global security for over six decades."

Presently, the U.S. is stepping up weapons shipments to Saudi Arabia and establishing a "joint coordination planning cell" with Riyadh to help in the destruction of Yemeni rebels seeking redress for religious oppression and other injustices inflicted upon Yemenis by pro-Western governments in the capital of Sana (such as idly permitting unrelenting drone attacks by the U.S.). This is Obama's, and by default, Kerry's, idea of global security. To hurry arms to a brutal authoritarian dictatorship that wishes to violate the sovereignty of a neighboring nation in order to install a pro-Western government that mirrors its own regime. Thus far it has met with little success, destroying only civilian infrastructure, murdering just 500 civilians and uncounted Houthi rebels (soldiers are unpeople, duly fit for slaughter), but doing little to impede radiating Houthi control over the country.

This is quite surprising considering that Nobel Peace Prize winner Obama awarded the protest-crushing, female-silencing, citizen-beheading Saudi royals the largest weapons deal in the sordid history of U.S arms sales in 2010. Not to mention a colossal shipment of banned cluster munitions two years ago. Why exactly, one wants to ask, do the Saudis need more guns? Haven't we supplied a sufficient arsenal with which to thwart populist uprisings and annihilate Shia calls for justice in the flashpoints of self-determination that dot the peninsula? One would think. But then there is always the possibility that the Kingdom might unspool itself back into the array of fiefdoms from which it first emerged.

The NPT Community
Later, deeply concerned interlocutor Judy Woodruff (a modest improvement on unblinking zombie Jim Lehrer) suggested the Iran deal was really about just delaying Tehran's acquisition of a nuclear weapon. This question itself is so profuse with false assumptions that it would require an entire seminar to unpack. But Kerry breezily dismissed the query with his own priceless riposte, claiming that the deal represents "…a guarantee that for the next 15 to 20 years [Iran] won't possibly be able to advance that program and then, *when they become a more legitimate member of the non-proliferation community and subject to lifetime inspections* and investigation, we will have accountability (italics mine)."

As a member of the Non-Proliferation Treaty (NPT), Iran was determined to have concluded its nuclear weapons program in 2003, subsequently subjecting itself to the most rigorous and unnecessary inspection regime in the history of the IAEA. It was hectored and harrowed into this regime by the two leading nuclear threats to world peace: the United States and Israel. The former has openly violated the NPT by distributing nuclear formulas to India, both a non-signatory and serial provocateur in Kashmir, the lush territory it disputes with arch-rival Pakistan, another nuclear power that has the U.S. to thank for its status. The latter, America's deputized aggressor Israel, is another non-signatory of the NPT and currently holds the dubious honor of being the single member of the Middle East opposed to the creation of a Nuclear Weapons-Free Zone, such as exists in Latin America and other saner parts of the planet.

Woodruff, masterfully emulating a paranoid neoconservative, continued to ask misinformed questions, one of which prompted the pagliacci to reply, "They have agreed to abide by what is called the additional protocol of the nonproliferation treaty. That protocol requires participating states to adhere to a higher standard and if they don't, Judy, then the sanctions can, and will, come back."

Interesting that the aforementioned U.S., violator of the NPT and the only country to actually use nuclear weapons, has refused to abide by the additional protocols it desperately wants applied to any nation it deems a regional rival.

In 2004 the U.S. adopted the Model Additional Protocol in a good-faith attempt to bring other NPT members on board. But they were of little consequence to the U.S. as it is a Nuclear Weapons State (NWS) and thus held to less stringent standards than Non-Nuclear Weapons States (NNWS). Nuclear states don't have to comprehensively apply the safeguards to all of their sites. They can even except sites for reasons of national security. Non-Nuclear states have to make practically all of their facilities—even non-nuclear energy sites with the additional protocol—eligible for NPT safeguards.

But that's not all. As soon as it pretended to adopt the protocols, the U.S. added two addendums to its adoption, a corollary of the NPT's exemption for NWS members, called by the U.S. a National Security Exemption (NSE). The NSE lets the U.S. permit access to sites, activities, information, and additional locations, *at its own discretion*. A second addition limits the use of environmental sampling and the number of inspectors who can access a site.

Before Congress ratified this feckless edition of the additional protocol, it added a letter from the Senate Foreign Relations Committee that stipulated that the NSE would be used with, ahem, some regularity. It also insisted that the President ensure that security and counterintelligence training will have been completed by the time any sites are declared to the IAEA.

Were Iran to attempt anything of the sort, the Lausanne negotiations would have instantly collapsed, additional sanctions would have been hysterically imposed, and both the U.S. and Israel would have begun issuing veiled threats (violating, in the process, both the NPT and the UN Charter). As it is, Iran has dealt with demands to "anytime, anywhere" access, air reconnaissance, access to military bases, and other invasive measures. Remember, when the U.S. was turning the vice grip on Iraq before attacking it more than a decade ago, it even requested unfettered access to Saddam Hussein's presidential palace, which it later inhabited. Most of this while Hussein was frantically trying to negotiate a peace via any go-between he could find—including Syria, France, Egypt, Russia, and Germany. Aside from Iraq, it is also useful to contrast U.S. hyper-vigilant posture toward Iran with its laissez faire attitude toward Israel's absurd "policy of deliberate ambiguity" regarding its WMD stockpile. Of course, it isn't as though the Israeli arsenal is manned by some rabid paranoiac.

Buying Friends, Abetting Allies
Woodruff, at this point, has descended into a frothing neocon huff. She announces that cutting a deal to limit Iran's nuclear program is fraught with concerns (as opposed to the alternative, perhaps, of annihilating Iran's nuclear sites and rendering swathes of Persia uninhabitable thanks to the not-so sanitary act of dropping thousand pound bombs on nuclear reactors). She clamors, "The U.S. is going to have to increasingly show its support for those in the region who fear Iran." Kerry attempted a dignified and fulsome response, mumbling some well-rehearsed stock clichés about defending "friends and allies." He might have simply shouted into Woodruff's ear that the United States delivers $3B annually to Tel Aviv for its bi-annual slaughter of defenseless Palestinians. He might have hammered the table and reminded the world that he personally mails Egypt's criminal President Abdul Fattah al-Sisi some $1.3B a year to fund mass trials of dissidents, fulfill numberless death sentences, and slaughter protestors. He might have flung his hands in the air and recalled the bombastic $10B deal the U.S. cut in 2013 with Israel, the Saudis, and the United Arab Emirates, providing even more aircraft, missiles and transport vehicles to these terribly fraught apartheid states and fanatical theocracies teetering on the edge of civilization. Finally, calming himself, he might have softly reiterated the $60B record-setting deal with the Saudis, the munitions of which are proving themselves admirably in their ability to liquidate both human quarry and entire municipalities across Yemen.

Finally, our lantern-jawed secretary closed the interview with a fatuity, claiming that Iran was flying supplies to the Houthis "every single week", despite the fact that the Saudis have imposed a no-fly zone over the country that would have prevented this. No matter, there is little time to resolve contradictions when there are so many raging fires to extinguish on the ground across the oil-rich Middle East.

Perhaps Kerry should have ended the show by stating the obvious: we are executing a global campaign to disarm every potential rival via the effete and infinitely manipulable constructs of international law. As part of this campaign, Iraq was combed by inspectors and bombed by Western aircraft on a regular basis for more than a decade before having its defense systems torpedoed and its entire army disbanded. All this as a deliberate prelude to permitting the artificial nation-

102

state to sink into anarchy. Syria had its chemical weapons stockpile destroyed on the farcical premise that it used them against citizens just as international observers entered the country. Libya had to have its air force vaporized, its government toppled, and its left-leaning president brutally murdered. And then—the coup de grace—Iran has had its 20 percent enriched uranium destroyed, its civilian nuclear program rolled back, and its nation set to by IAEA inspectors eyeballing every nuclear facility in search of the slightest discrepancy. Clearly, that 1979 revolution still burns brightly in the minds of Pentagon hardliners.

Fear not, Mrs. Woodruff, for it won't be long before there aren't any countries left in the Middle East capable of defending themselves. That is, aside from the vitiated autocrats and trigger-happy settlement builders we have authorized to arbitrate the bloodletting in the world's most brutalized region.

(*CounterPunch*, April 15, 2015)

Sharon and the Art of Self-Deception
The American media response to the Israeli leader's death exposes the flawed narrative of U.S. leadership

In the 1970s, evolutionary biologist Robert Trivers pioneered the biological roots of self-deception and theorized that self-deceit may confer a survival advantage on humans. Mostly because lying is more effective when you believe your own lies. With nothing to hide, the telltale physical signs of deceit—flared nostrils, higher vocal register, a distracted gaze—are diminished. When peddling a false product, sincerity sells. Nowhere is this daunting proposition better exemplified than in politics.

In her tome on the origins of totalitarian politics, Hannah Arendt notes that the structural design of totalitarian systems are intended to shield the masses—but notably its leadership—from reality. In fact, totalitarian politics are marked by the insularity of the ruling regime. The effect is to reinforce the fictional narrative the inner circle has embraced, ingested, and declared allegiance to. In Nazi Germany, it was the bizarre vision of a purified Aryan species. In Stalinist Russia, it was a perverted vision of class struggle. And although America hasn't yet achieved full-blown totalitarian status, there are enough heralds of its coming to draw parallels between its practical blueprint and ours.

Media as Front Organization
One popular totalitarian method by which to insulate leadership from the potentially painful realism of the outside world is through the use of front organizations. These are associations and support groups that are not technically part of the organizing regime but share its narrative and ethical assumptions. These groups serve as buffers designed to shield power from the censure of its minions. Sheltered Nazi leaders never caught a whiff of dissent or counterargument in their fascist hermitage, since counterpoint could never penetrate the wall of zealotry and reaffirmation that enveloped them.

Bill Maher used to mock Republicans by suggesting they lived in a giant bubble in which reality was inverted; there's plenty of truth in the bubble idea. Today the media plays the role of the front organization, feeding a factitious storyline to the inner circle but also to the supporting intelligentsia that furnishes its ostensible legitimacy, be it academic or clinical. By contrast, the light pelting on the outer walls of power—stones flung from leftist or rightist media like *CounterPunch* and *ZNet*—likely never receive the slightest attention from the brokers of federal power.

An exemplary storyline of this kind appeared with the death of Ariel Sharon. On word of Sharon's demise after years in a blessedly harmless coma, the mainstream media leapt into action, penning and presenting a thoroughly counterfactual narrative to the public, a story invented in the inner sanctum of American and Israeli power and perpetuated through the mediasphere—not simply to the masses, but crucially back to the believing crowd of liberal and conservative leadership. Like a positive feedback loop, convictions are confirmed each morning when Barack Obama or Joe Biden or John McCain leafs through *The New York Times* or are briefed on media activity. The air of sensible deliberation and cautious judgment is the narrative tool by which the "paper of record" legitimizes its fatuities.

Butcher, Bulldozer, or Man of Peace?
After Sharon's death, both the *Times* and *Washington Post*, the liberal intelligentsia's go-to resources for groupthink, soft-pedaled Sharon's legacy. The *Times* even headlined the paper with the line, "The Israeli Hawk Who Sought Peace on His Terms." It's subheads were suitably benign: "Pragmatism and Resilience", "A Zionist Vision", and "A Reputation for Boldness", a "Turn to Politics", and "Lebanon and Beyond". This cleansed presentation shelters government leaders and the educated classes from which they are drawn from troubling questions about America's support for a reputed war criminal. It's hard to ferret out a resume of war crimes from such a tepid portrayal. Doubtless it never crossed Vice President Joe Biden's mind, as he represented the American government at Sharon's funeral, that he was delivering a paean to a terrorist.

But the crimes are confirmed, evinced succinctly by Sharon's bloodthirsty nicknames, "The Bulldozer" and "The Butcher of Beirut." The former refers to the fact that Sharon, as relentlessly rehearsed on leftist media channels, made his reputation with the butchery of Arabs both Lebanese and Palestinian in Qibya village in the West Bank in 1953, Lebanon in1982, and Gaza and the West Bank in 2002, but also for pioneering the now familiar practice of bulldozing Arab homes, occupied or not. Some 27,000 Palestinian homes have been leveled since 1967. In that same span, zero Israeli homes have been destroyed by Palestinian bulldozers. Yet the victimization narrative, the narrative of oppression, danger, and imminent threats—indeed, existential threats—is so powerful as to invert the facts.

Sharon also sparked the second Palestinian intifada with his visit to a contested holy site, Jerusalem's Al-Aqsa mosque. The subsequent crackdowns were criminal and vindictive, the slaughter of refugees—Sharon's specialty—in the West Bank's Jenin being a much-popularized and much disputed instance of, at the very least, significant human rights violations if not a full-fledged massacre (a claim later rejected by the United Nations, despite eyewitness accounts). The "separation wall," quickly dubbed the "apartheid wall," was another Sharon maneuver, giving the lie to the hope that Israel might one day re-establish the legal borders specified by United Nations Security Council Resolution 242.

The *Post* whitewashed Sharon's culpability in the massacre of Palestinian refugees in the 1982 invasion of Lebanon, even falsely presenting a libel suit against *Time* magazine as evidence that he had been exonerated of the crime. Another example of the softening of a profile so that it is easily absorbed into the delusory normalized world of the fanatic. Even war criminals are "good guys" in this counterfeit history, which reduces the world to its basest black-and-white, us-and-them formulae.

That he was sometimes said to want peace, was in actuality another inversion of reality, (unless one confines oneself to the notion of 'peace on my terms', as indeed the *Times* did; one could say the same of any jihadist—they want a peaceful caliphate). Israeli historian Avi Shlaim called Sharon "the father of the settlement movement". Shlaim might have added that the settlements are not only illegal but as such have perpetually derailed the so-called peace process with Palestine. Just last week, as a fitting coda to the Sharon legacy, Israel announced the development of new settlements in Jerusalem, perhaps the most valuable piece of real estate in the occupied territories and would-be capitol of Palestine. This announcement was made as John Kerry played the perennial role of the spineless American diplomat consigned to the thankless task of facilitating Israel's slow-motion takeover of Jerusalem and the West Bank, but somehow representing it as a peace process.

Sharon was likewise a virulent adherent of the Zionist vision of a Greater Israel, once described by Zionism founder Theodore Herzl as stretching from Egypt to the Euphrates. Later concepts envisioned pauperizing surrounding Arab states and transforming them into satellites under Israeli purview. To that end, Sharon who continually supported the absorption of the contested Palestinian lands that the United Nations has long condemned Israel for occupying. He later reversed himself with the cynical ploy to voluntarily abandon the hellhole of Gaza, illegally resettling already illegally settled Gazan Israelis in the much-preferable and illegally occupied West Bank as part of his plan to completely annex the latter territory. Gaza was then fully transformed into an open-air prison suited for stateless Arabs fighting vainly for their dignity and historical legitimacy. Yet despite the death knell these actions signaled for an Israeli-Palestinian accord, both mainstream papers reinforce George W. Bush's ludicrous statement that Sharon was "a man of peace." The facts say otherwise, but American leaders won't hear the truth, buried as they are beneath this avalanche of disinformation.

Polishing the Headstone
Noam Chomsky opened his *Democracy Now!* discussion of Sharon's legacy by noting that the convention of not speaking ill of the recently deceased would consign us to a "vow of silence" regarding Sharon. No truer words were spoken about the man, but who in the American administration will hear Chomsky's estimation of the Bulldozer? Rather, they'll be treated to takeaway images of an

avuncular Sharon, with his "large paunch and a soft, gentle smile that gave him a grandfatherly image." In the *Times*, the final word was given to his aide Raanan Gissin, surely an objective observer, who claimed that Sharon, "was not an ideologue, but a political architect." Only a deeply deceived propagandist could produce a statement at such odds with reality. In fact, all of Sharon's aforementioned behaviors reflect an odious and all-too-common ideology among Zionists and American militarists—that force is all Arabs understand. (Shlaim noted this position was referred to as an "iron-wall strategy".) This concept is part of the psychological underpinning of Western ideology that justifies Israel's and America's litany of criminal violence in the region over the decades.

This, though, is all part of the media's role, to act as a salve on the conscience of American leadership, a congeries of violent, radicalized imperialists who must nevertheless conceive themselves as reasoned and judicious arbiters of global justice. Israel, of course, is a pivot of the American imperial strategy, and thus must be perceived in the corridors of power as aligned with the confected value system of elite American rule. The historical atrocities and legacy of the Holocaust provides an ideal "moral high ground" from which to justify Israeli security activities. As such, leaders such as Joe Biden, who spoke at Sharon's interment, can envision his pro-Israeli stance as a humble service to human rights and the protection of persecuted peoples. Fellow speaker and British Prime Minister David Cameron can likewise, without a trace of irony, credit the deceased leader with "brave and controversial decisions in pursuit of peace," permitting himself and his liberal supporters to interpret "controversial" as a benign signifier of nothing more than well-intentioned disagreements between reasonable parties with a shared commitment to conciliation.

The media perpetually reifies these statements about Sharon and the ideological fictions they represent, such that the rank and file American, Israeli, and British politicians can ingest them with their morning coffee, quack nostrums that nevertheless help immunize the conscience from fact. The evolutionist Trivers referred to a form of collective self-deceit that he termed "false historical narratives," a chilling concept not least because nearly anyone can immediately point to historical examples. The American interpretation of the Israel-Palestine conflict is a sad case study of one such narrative. Likewise, the American corporate media, in its role as official stenographer and rationalizer of state policy, is as comprehensive a front organization as ever existed, buffeting U.S. leadership from the sordid realities its imperial policies create. Instead, the occupiers of the White House, Capitol Hill, and the Pentagon, can all relax in the knowledge that their chimerical vision of themselves as champions of democracy is shared by all right-thinking people.

(*Asia Times*, January 23, 2014)

Something Very Like Aggression
America's posture toward Russia is nothing if not consistent—and consistently misrepresented

During frantic post-Second World War planning sessions in the West, the British Foreign Office noted its fears of "ideological infiltration" from the Soviet Union, a terrifying possibility it described as "something very like aggression." This near-hysterical fear of independent nationalism has been the hallmark of Western foreign policy ever since. Lately it has been restored to its natural fever pitch by the crisis in the Ukraine. Last week the venerable *Economist*, that heady rag that all financial fledglings and crusty mandarins fold beneath their arm on the way to lunch, headlined its April 19th issue with a map of Russia and Ukraine with the header, "Insatiable". All that was missing was a series of social media-esque exclamations points to ram home the clamorous message.

The lead did much to amplify the histrionic tone struck by the cover image. As the presiding house organ of neoliberalism, *The Economist* is ever anxious to decry any threat to the supremacy of its ideology. Here it sounds the alarmist note at once: the "cost of stopping the Russian bear now is high" but it will only be worse if we (all right-thinking inheritors of the Magna Carta) fail to face our fears at once. After all, the trembling byline proceeds, Vladimir Putin has "mauled" Georgia, "gobbled up" Crimea, and "infiltrated eastern Ukraine." Clearly, if the West does not face down the frothing Siberian menace, "it may find him at its door." (Cue house chills.)

Alas, we are "feeble and divided" before the drooling visage of the beast. Here the byline runs out of breath, and in the panting pause that follows, it recalls that it has provided no hard evidence for its suggestion that Russia plans to overrun the western world (although, devoid of context, the capture of Crimea seems a nice start.) The author or authors—and it probably took a battery of zealots to craft this masterpiece—first claims the amateur takeovers in the eastern Ukraine were designed in the Kremlin because "the attacks were coordinated, in strategically useful places." A few sentences later it recalls that in one of these professionally coordinated attacks, a phalanx of "'local people' stormed what they thought was the regional administrative headquarters in Kharkiv only to find that they had taken control of the opera house."

Amid all this, the authors breezily note that the Kremlin has "much to fear from the pro-European demonstrations that toppled Ukraine's president, Viktor Yanukovych. It appears determined to see the new Ukraine fail." Pity that. Especially since the "new Ukraine" is a model of democratic legitimacy ruled by admirable, even-tempered progressives. Or not. The article then produces a line equally desirous of irony as this last: "Mr. Putin has shown that truth and the law are whatever happens to suit him at the time."

Nowhere do the authors, blinkered by their own propaganda, betray the slightest awareness that they are blaming Russia for the exact kind of illegal interference of which their own Western governments are the undisputed masters. Could they be unwittingly projecting their own side's global ambitions onto the ever-useful foil of Russia?

A subtitle in the "Insatiable" piece said, "Hope for the best, prepare for the worst". This is a nice illustration of the standard profile deployed by Western propaganda agencies like *The Economist*, *The New York Times*, and the *Washington Post*, among others. Namely, the 'innocent bystander' motif. The purpose of this persona, as it were, is to characterize the United States and its lessers east of Kiev as mild-mannered defenders of liberty, constitutionally disinterested in anything but the happiness of its own minions (still huddled at Lady Liberty's feet, but that's another matter). Foreign intrigues? No thanks. Murderous occupations? Why, we would never! A midnight putsch? Not for us, thank you very much. The West is simply the innocent bystander of history, being forced to intervene by pressure from weaker nations and, dare it be said, by the goodness of its heart. We are, after all, as President Obama tirelessly repeats, an "exceptional" people, alone among nations, with both the wisdom to know what to do and the might to actually do it. (At some point, shouldn't the sons of Abraham garner some royalties for this blatant rip-off the "chosen race" narrative?)

Is It True?
But are we history's innocent bystander? Do we gape in horror at the latest bloodbath, appalled at the behavior of (lately) Slavic degenerates whom we have so painstakingly tried to shepherd into the light of neoliberal finance capitalism? Do we flex our considerable muscle only after hand-wringing deliberations with the community of nations?

I hope you've already answered the question. If you haven't, you may be a victim of the greatest propaganda machine in human history—the U.S. government. Thankfully, there are reliable remedies for such conditions. Looking at the facts can be a useful prescription for mental health. To that end, in our quest to discover whether America is freedom's reluctant defender, the planet's mild-mannered policeman, we should look at its strategic thinking over the years.

It might be useful to refer to a document penned 64 years ago this month. That would be NSC68 from April 1950. This founding document of the Cold War lays out the American estimate of Soviet strength and the plan to resist it. Inherent to the document was the belief that the Soviet Union was bent on "absolute power" and "the dynamic extension of their authority and ultimate elimination of any effective opposition to their authority." This included the "domination of the

Eurasian landmass," a threat that "whether achieved by armed aggression or by political and subversive means, would be strategically and politically unacceptable to the United States." Estimations of Soviet resources and nuclear strength were reviewed, along with several potential responses, before finally recommending a build-up of weapons and active efforts to place "maximum strain on the Soviet structure of power and particularly on the relationships between Moscow and the satellite countries."

Move to the end of the century. The Berlin Wall has fallen, Russian satellite states are being happily looted by Western interests. But the Russian threat still remains, at least in the minds of U.S. planners. As have many others in recent weeks, Arnie Mayer has unearthed the mad ravings of President Obama's foreign policy advisor, Zbigniew Brzezinski. Like a poor man's Rasputin, Brzezinski has exerted a hypnotic effect on John F. Kennedy, Jimmy Carter, and now the pitiful Barack. In his 1997 book *The Great Chessboard*, It was Brzezinski that foresaw, in his crystal of global domination, the importance of Eurasia, rather than the Middle East, in future geopolitics: "America is now the only global superpower, and Eurasia is the globe's central arena." Note how the reemergence of Eurasia as the central prize of the geostrategic game recommissions the former Soviet Union as a primary threat. Here's Mayer's recap of Brzezinski's thinking:

Brzezinski argued that "the struggle for global primacy [would] continue to be played" on the Eurasian "chessboard," and that as a "new and important space on [this] chessboard . . . Ukraine was a geopolitical pivot because its very existence as an independent country helps to transform Russia." Indeed, "if Moscow regains control over Ukraine, with its [then] 52 million people and major resources, as well as access to the Black Sea," Russia would "automatically again regain the wherewithal to become a powerful imperial state, spanning Europe and Asia." The unwritten script of Brzezinski, one of Obama's foreign policy advisors: intensify the West's—America's—efforts, by means fair and foul, to detach Ukraine from the Russian sphere of influence, including especially the Black Sea Peninsula with its access to the Eastern Mediterranean via the Aegean Sea.

In this context, with the Ukraine playing such a pivotal role in the plan for Eurasian hegemony, the U.S.-backed coup d'état might have been predicted the moment deposed president Viktor Yanukoyvch vacillated over the onerous conditions of the IMF loan he was offered and turned a welcoming eye to the East. Likewise, Mike Whitney recently pulled out a dog-eared copy of the scribbling of that great progressive, former Deputy Secretary of Defense Paul Wolfowitz, which naturally found their way into our US National Defense Strategy. Note how Wolfowitz prizes liberty and self-determination for all: "Our first objective is to prevent the re-emergence of a new rival, either on the territory of the former Soviet Union or elsewhere, that poses a threat on the order of that posed formerly by the Soviet Union. This is a dominant consideration underlying the new regional defense strategy and requires that we endeavor to prevent any hostile power from dominating a region whose resources would, under consolidated control, be sufficient to generate global power."

"...convincing potential competitors that they need not aspire to a greater role or pursue a more aggressive posture to protect their legitimate interests. In non-defense areas, we must account sufficiently for the interests of the advanced industrial nations to discourage them from challenging our leadership or seeking to overturn the established political and economic order. We must maintain the mechanism for deterring potential competitors from even aspiring to a larger regional or global role."

Here, the emphasis is not simply controlling Eurasian resources, but aggressively checking the ambitions of any regional power.

Think Globally, Act Locally

If these documents suggest generalized world dominance at a planetary level, they suggest rather clear strategic goals at the local level. Namely, the dismemberment of Russia in an effort to return it to the subservient status held by the rest of Eastern Europe. Russia has been the black sheep of Eurasia since the Bolshevik revolution, at first providing the world with a horrifying example of non-capitalist industrialization, and then annoyingly preaching communism even as it launched its manic purges.

Weakening Russia always began with uncoupling Soviet satellites from Russian influence. Ukraine is seen as the central bridge between Russia and Europe, particularly since most of Europe's Russia-sourced gas, flows through it. Likewise, Crimea has long served as Russia's Black Sea outpost, from which it exerts influence over the resource-rich body of water. By severing the umbilical cord of the Ukraine, Russia can be detached from Europe and its Black Sea dominion and reduced to the role Wolfowitz foresaw for it, with a modest regional mandate, restored to its servant role cowering in the shadow of American power.

NATO is the most useful tool in this regard. It can hardly be said that Russia is more aggressive than NATO. Just recall Mikhail Gorbachev's unrequited gestures in the late eighties, when he let go of the Warsaw Pact and agreed to the reunification of Germany, taking home a promise from the U.S. that NATO wouldn't move an inch eastward. Ever the amnesiac, NATO forgot its promise and "gobbled up" a dozen Eastern European states, moving its heavy weaponry ever closer to the Russian heartland. Outstripping its original mandate to launch itself into far-flung locations like Libya and Afghanistan, it had to fashion a new mission statement for itself, even as it swallowed the majority of former Soviet satellites, including Albania, Bulgaria, Romania, and Slovakia, but also Estonia,

Lithuania, Latvia, Croatia, and Slovenia. Georgia, Montenegro, and Bosnia and Herzegovina are short-listed for membership.

And it was of course the West that instigated the faux uprising in Ukraine; fomenting a coup d'état of Ukraine's democratically elected government by a confection of paid snipers and unhinged ultra-nationalists with fascist sympathies. The historic context in which this coup happened shouldn't be forgotten. In the 20th century, Russia was very nearly destroyed by German fascists twice in 30 years.

No matter, the imperial drumbeats drone on. Obama is moving destroyers in the Black Sea, flying NATO patrol missions close to the Russian border, rushing an uncertain contingent of U.S. troops to Poland, hundreds more to the Baltic states, and dispersing F-15s and F-16s to complement this hasty display of power.

If the five billion dollars spent clandestinely undermining democracy in Ukraine wasn't enough, there's also the "hard power" military budget. We spend most of our discretionary funds on guns. America accounts for close to 40 percent of global military spending, and its military budget has grown by 35 percent since 9/11, dwarfing expenditures of Russia and China. Given the gross inequality in military spending, it's not surprise that since the dissolution of the Soviet Union, the United States alone has invaded six nations (officially), and the Russians two.

None of this adds up to the portrait depicted by *The Economist*, that of a cautious, peace-loving West unhappily shouldering the burdens of history, battling to preserve the light of liberty in a world of barbarians and degenerates. But it was ever thus, one story peddled to the world, another inscribed in the history books. Usually in blood.

Fear of the Alternative
Simon Bolivar, the Latin American revolutionary who inspired Hugo Chavez to launch his Bolivarian revolution, once described the United States, saying, "There is at the head of this great continent a very powerful country, very rich, very warlike, and capable of anything." It was Bolivar's Pan Americanism that had to be crushed by the United States, preserving its dominion over the South, as mandated by the Monroe Doctrine.

Bolivar's ideas were but one variation on the theme of independent nationalism. It's characteristics are varied but well known: state managed economies, regulation of industry, capital controls, import-substitution development strategies, strong social safety nets, import tariffs and other measures to protect fledgling domestic industry, etc. How can a ruthless capitalist ever dispossess the masses when the state keeps intervening on their behalf? It's damned nigh impossible.

112

A cursory glance at recent history may be enough to persuade you of the threat that Henry Kissinger tremblingly referred to as the "domino effect". Troubling socialist experiments were variously achieved in Cuba, Venezuela, China, and pre-WWII Russia—until they were brutally undermined by the West. As well the protectionist measure successfully employed by nations like Holland, Germany, and Korea in the last century—against the better wisdom of Washington. And perhaps most terrifyingly, the successes of socialist state interventions in our most burgeoning industries—military procurement, biotechnology and Big Pharma. Evidently there's no industry that a trough of taxpayer funding and a government-guaranteed market can't fix.

Indeed, as Mayer notes, we've had to forcefully intervene across the hemisphere just to stave off the nightmare scenario of leaving a foreign population to its own devices. One can only imagine what the rabble might do, left unchained. Mayer provides a cursory list including, "Guatemala (1954), Cuba (1962), Dominican Republic (1965), Chile (1973), Nicaragua (1980s), Grenada (1983), Bolivia (1986), Panama (1989), and Haiti (2004)", each intervention conducted, "almost invariably without enthroning and empowering more democratic and socially progressive" governments. Gore Vidal has provided a more comprehensive list in his *Dreaming War* screed (some 200 interventions between Pearl Harbor and 9/11).

What with all the indictments of laissez-faire capitalism flying about—notably Thomas Piketty's *Capital in the Twenty-first Century*—a hidebound capitalist extremist could be forgiven for feeling nervy and anxious to secure his power. Indeed, that's precisely what elite capital is doing through its benign front organization, the IMF, according the European Network on Debt and Development (EURODAD). Likewise, the lapdogs of elite money in Washington have dusted off the old Cold War phrase book in a concerted campaign to demonize Russia and any other threat to the neoliberal program of pillage and plunder. For this Russia is delightfully suitable—a distant nuclear power, ruled an ex-KGB autocrat, and with a blood-soaked legacy of misguided communism, brutal purges and fatuous show trials. Behold the Russian bear. On both fronts, whether enslaving nations with debt or encircling them with missiles, it has the feel of something very like aggression.

(*Dissident Voice*, May 1, 2014)

The Banality of Empire
Oil, Politics and the road to Damascus

You have to ask: does Syrian President Bashar al-Assad have a death wish, launching a chemical attack within miles of a U.N. chemical inspection team? He must. Like those cloistered mullahs in Qom, whom Zionist sage Benjamin Netanyahu claims would fire a nuclear warhead at Tel Aviv the moment one fell into their hands, a mere *fait accompli*. Even though Iran would be instantly vaporized by American WMDs. Even though all those coiling spires would turn to dust. Because, as Bibi makes clear, you have to set aside the survival instinct when you're dealing with madmen.

Framing the Enemy
Assad, of that nefarious Alawite sect, must have similar dementia, since according to the Obama administration he launched a chemical weapons attack on Syrian "rebels" in Ghouta, a suburb of Damascus, at perhaps the most ill-advised moment in the two-year conflict. A moment when Assad had just welcomed United Nations chemical weapons inspectors into his country to see whether accusations of a May chemical attack were true. The latest attack has generated a freshet of rhetorical fraud we haven't seen since the lofty height of the Bush administration, when Dick Cheney was touring the Sunday talk shows waving his imminent-threat manifesto and sneering uncontrollably at spineless pacifists. It's Iraq all over again. Just like the fabricated charges against a fangless Saddam Hussein, Assad awaits the verdict of history—a false accusation, a war fever in the West, and then the falling skies. There's no preventing it. Nobody mainstream has bothered to point out that Assad would have to be suicidal to launch an attack with inspectors in-country, and with the use of chemical weapons being President Barack Obama's vaunted "red line" across which no sovereign Shi'ite government can cross.

Rebels in Desperate Straits
On the other hand, there are plenty of perfectly reasonable pretexts by which the so-called "Free Syrian Army" might have launched a chemical weapons attack, as they likely did in May, according to Carla Del Ponte of the U.N. and the Independent International Commission of Inquiry on Syria. She has now suggested the latest attack may have again been launched by the rebels. Despite the support of al-Qaeda and their al-Nusra Front affiliates, who each want Assad gone for very different reasons, this mercenary melting pot has been ceding territory to Syrian government forces at an alarming rate in recent months. It would behoove them to stage a chemical attack that the Americans could quickly attribute to the Assad regime, and begin fueling the drones and launching destroyers. Otherwise, the government might subdue all the factions ranged against it, consolidate its power, and be that much more difficult to unseat. Better to conjure a crossed line from the dust of civil, sectarian, and proxy strife.

Baseless accusations can then issue from the White House lawn, being loudly seconded in Tel Aviv, where lawmakers have just rubberstamped another bank of illegal settlements for prime West Bank real estate, while Palestinians refugees in Ramallah are shot in murky dust-ups with the IDF. Illegal interventions. Outlawed occupations. Suspect crackdowns. World conflicts in miniature are always afoot in the Knesset.

The Bi-Partisan Blueprint

Regardless of the trigger mechanism, the administration seems intent on pushing through Donald Rumsfeld's old madcap <u>blueprint</u> for the Middle East, which involved toppling the governments of seven consecutive countries on the way to unchallenged dominion over Arab and Persian fossil fuels. Their eyes are on the prize. The rest is detail. It seems to make little difference to the Americans what becomes of Syria, only that Assad is overthrown, and the warlord that plants his flag atop the wreckage is hostile to Tehran and is willing to viciously put down any foolhardy bids for self-determination that might emerge from the populace. After all, the U.S. has left a trash bin of fallen monuments and blown infrastructures in Afghanistan, Iraq, and Libya. If the entire Arab world is a flaming midden whose only functional entities are oil derricks, what cause for concern is that to our imperial chieftains? Let the Islamists slaughter each other on the peripheries of the bonfire while we vacuum every ounce of natural gas and petroleum from the core of the earth. (One conjures visions of Daniel Day-Lewis in *There Will Be Blood*, mocking his young evangelical rival and shouting, "I drink your milkshake!")

Revving Up the Propaganda Machine

The more controversial actions of state always require a heavy dose of cheerleading from the press, the better to manufacture the consent of the general population, or at least seed enough doubt to prevent a riot. To that end, *The New York Times* is <u>back</u> in the organ well, lifting its <u>chorus</u> of fearmongering to new heights. *The Washington Post* is cranking up the shrill <u>calls</u> for intervention. The 'Situation Room' is firing on all cylinders. Fox News is <u>delivering</u> thumping polemics on how slow-footed Obama is on foreign policy. Liberals stare blankly from the sidelines while their "lesser evil" does another expert impression of the "greater evil". Obama channels Clinton. Kerry channels Cheney. But this is par for the course; justification cometh before the sword. It feels like 2003 again. All we need is Judith Miller to surface with a source in the chthonian depths of the Assad administration. Or Colin Powell to crack open PowerPoint and lift a few hollow tube photos from Google. And for someone to climb into the bully pulpit and tell us in mournful tones that yes, yes, we must once again wage war on those nomadic savages pitching their tents above our God-given bounty.

Four Steps to War

What can you expect in the coming day\s and weeks? Here's a sneak preview. It's none too surprising, since the formula has been refined over decades. Its architects have their names inscribed on the walls of the White House, infamy emeritus. The model calls for Obama to undertake a series of anti-democratic and pro-war actions that will be reformulated as pro-democratic and anti-war:

- First, he'll ignore the people that elected him. He'll cite some moral platitude from a posture of deep anxiety—the man of peace forced to confront the need for noble violence. His wrinkled brow will slowly morph into the steely eyed gaze of determination—the defender of liberty come to rescue the hapless Syrian proles. He'll wave a flag of universal human rights, declare that actions have consequences, and point a heavy finger at Bashar al-Assad. Just nine percent of the American population want this. But Obama will be too transfixed by his moral crusade to take notice.

- Next, he'll ignore Congress. This is the formal equivalent of ignoring the people. But unlike laughing off a Reuters poll, disregarding the entire legislative branch of government will require some nuanced prose from the Department of Justice (DOJ). No problem. For the Libyan war, the DOJ asserted that the provision of guns, drone strikes, missile launchers, and other weaponry didn't collectively amount to "hostilities." Hence there was no war. Hence no need to bother with Congressional approvals.

- Feeling more confident by the day, Obama will then ignore the United Nations. He and deputy John Kerry have already said it is too late for U.N. weapons inspectors in Damascus to investigate the new claim of chemical weapons abuse. They offered a smattering of nonsense about "corrupted" evidence, despite the fact that sarin can sit in the soil for months. In any case, the U.N. could normally be relied upon to roll over in the General Assembly and Security Council on war authorization, but for the annoying presence of Russia, finger poised above the veto button, awaiting for the Obama administration to ask the Security Council legitimate its belligerence. Russia, of course, is itself hiding behind a façade of shocked innocence, saying it was fooled by America on Iraq in 2003 and won't be fooled again. This, too, is sophistry.

- Then he'll bomb. Missiles will be fired from the safety of the Mediterranean or the comparative calm of high clouds. The missiles will target heavily populated areas in Damascus, much to our great leader's great regret. Images of wailing Muslims will dot the airwaves. NGOs will assemble lists of the collateral dead. The refugee count—already at

116

one million—will climb toward two. And Syria, part of the cradle of civilization, will begin to resemble Iraq and Afghanistan and Libya in its kaleidoscopic mix of blasted infrastructures, sectarian slaughter, rampant abuse of women, genetic deformities in the birth population, and the steady buzz of Predators and Reapers policing the carnage from the sky.

But, in the end, the oil and gas will be ours, and in Washington, that's all that matters.

(*CounterPunch*, August 30, 2013)

The Best of Intentions
What's behind the president's ISIS campaign?

Listening to President Obama <u>describe</u> his intention to "degrade and destroy" ISIS, he named a number of reasons for launching yet another war in Iraq. Gazing out at the nation through the eye of a camera lens, he intoned, "In a region that has known so much bloodshed, these terrorists are unique in their brutality. They execute captured prisoners. They kill children. They enslave, rape, and force women into marriage. They threatened a religious minority with genocide. In acts of barbarism, they took the lives of two American journalists - Jim Foley and Steven Sotloff."

Forgive me for saying so, but moral indignity usually rings hollow in the mouth of an American president. Unfortunately, ISIS is not unique in its brutality. Saudi Arabia <u>beheaded</u> at least eight people in August, for "crimes" as absurd to the Western mind as the ISIS crime of being an "infidel." Saudi Arabia's puritanical Wahhabi legal apparatus ends lives in the same brutal fashion for such offenses as adultery and, by my troth, sorcery. Yet the Saudis are a permanent American ally, and seem nearly incapable of offending Washington.

Even some of the so-called moderates that the U.S. plans to arm and train—*once more*—have also beheaded many of their ISIS enemies of late. But that's just the highlight reel. Since the inception of their rebellion, they've evidently been shelling Damascus neighborhoods without regard for who lives there. It doesn't matter. What matters is that the citizens of Syria are punished for their errant ways. For bothering to show up at the polls in June. For stupidly choosing to overwhelmingly re-elect Bashar al-Assad. Mortars packed with nails and shards of glass rattle through their cafes and thoroughfares. A proper discipline for a people that don't pick the right candidate. Just ask the Palestinians that voted for Hamas. Here's a first-hand <u>look</u> at some of the non-ISIS "moderates" we're thinking of arming.

That covers Obama's claim about ISIS' "unique" form of brutality and the charge of executing prisoners. And this is setting aside the military <u>regime</u> the U.S. backs in Egypt that snuffed out the dying embers of the Arab Spring in Cairo and banned the Muslim Brotherhood with a severity to match the Mubarak regime of which it is a remnant.

The president also noted that, "We cannot allow these communities to be driven from their ancient homelands," referring to Christians and Yazidis, both religious minorities that are said to have been threatened with genocide. In fact, the Catholic Church has called, "slow motion genocide." This is a fair statement and ISIS cruelty against infidel minorities is awful enough, but one can't help but notice the parallel in U.S. support for what Israeli historian Illan Pappe calls the "incremental genocide" of the Palestinian people by the Israeli state. The monopoly of media support for that conflict seemed to finally exhibit cracks of dissent in the margins of the latest IDF savagery in Gaza, in which dozens of families were extinguished entire, and more than 2,000 people died, including women and children, in a chilling display of indiscriminate brutality.

You couldn't say the U.S. is especially vexed by torture, bombings and extrajudicial killings, or other vile assaults on defenseless populations. After all, we have, in the president's words, "tortured some folks." And although this is surely deeply regrettable to the president, it isn't enough of a crime in his view to prosecute the perpetrators. It may have then come as no surprise when we learned that this is what former Iraqi Prime Minister Nuri al-Maliki practiced his entire time in office, backed with little reservation by America. The American insistence on his removal and the formation of the kind of inclusive government Maliki was supposed to form is likely too little, too late to hold the country together, not that a European construct should be forcibly preserved in any event.

And this is not even to mention the general failure of the administration's much ballyhooed plan to arm and train the Free Syrian Army—even if via the Gulf states—which at one point was said to include a shabby alliance of some 1200 "moderate" groups (swiftly steamrolled by ISIS). It was—and still is—practically impossible for the White House to guarantee that these groups were moderate Muslims, and many are ideologically similar to ISIS or the radical Wahabbism exported from Saudi Arabia. According to sources within Jordan, the U.S. trained dozens of Syrian rebels there that already were or later joined ISIS, thinking they were moderates anxious to unseat the Assad regime and usher in some sort of secular, Western-guided government. Think again.

In the end, freshly minted U.S. arms wound up in ISIS inventories, either sold to them by the moderates themselves, or captured in conquests of Syrian rebels and Iraqi Armies. So why reboot a strategy that proved so utterly bootless in its first iteration? Is it because this time the Pentagon will directly train and arm the rebels? Twenty five billion dollars worth of best practices did little to stanch ISIS's roll through northern Iraq, where the soldiers who absorbed all that training abandoned their weapons, shed their uniforms, and fled for the hills. The CIA has actually been training rebels in Jordan for some time, apparently to no avail.

However, the White House claims that it has some 40 nations willing to participate to one degree or another in rolling back ISIS. This is a far larger Rolodex of participants than George Bush's shoddy "coalition of the willing" more than a decade ago. The coalition of the willing that Obama has cobbled together, however robust, may be little more than a headcount of obsequious foreign ministers. Turkey doesn't want to see dozens of its diplomats slaughtered on YouTube. Sunnis may interpret U.S. intervention as just more support for Shia causes. Qatar and the Kingdom will likely see a degraded ISIS as a boon to the reviled Assad regime. Yet properly ending the ISIS threat would require Turkey to close its border to them, coordinating air strikes with Tehranian foot soldiers in Iraq, and communicating with Assad on countering ISIS in eastern Syria. And convincing Gulf monarchies to quit their Wahhabi evangelism. None of these things is likely to happen, largely because we've so dramatically demonized both Iranian and Syrian governments, and seem so beholden to Saudi oil. Such an about face would require more than a series of blandishments from Obama.

In short, the president's stated reason for renewing American interventionism in the Middle East is what it has always been—terrorism. But surely Obama has observed that terrorist jihadism has metastasized by several orders of magnitude since 9/11, owing not least to American interventions—from Kabul to Baghdad to arming raiders of Aleppo—which have destabilized strong if corrupt governments, unearthed simmering sectarian enmities, and even unwittingly trained and armed the very jihadists that became ISIS.

The United States has other objectives. Terrorism is a useful cover story that posits a righteous cause for American action. To be sure, ISIS is infected by an ideology of puritanical intolerance and hatred, but they are hardly a threat to the might and power of the U.S. What threat there is likely stems from the citizens of some 74 nations that now populate ISIS, many of them American. Repatriating— or not—these radicals will require serious vetting by Homeland Security, but not missiles by the Pentagon. A better, if flawed, argument for war can be made on pure ROI grounds—that the U.S. ought not to stand idly by and watch the dismemberment of a nation it spent the better half of a trillion dollars attempt to cleanse of "insurgents" and usher into a free-market fantasyland.

Not So Ulterior Motives
So, then, what is the president's underlying motive for another intervention in Iraq? He actually told us in his speech. His reasons were contained in the often-overlooked promise, "to use force against anyone who threatens America's core interests." This has been publically stated at least since the Clinton administration wrote it into its defense policy. It is surprisingly that more scrutiny hasn't been given to this regular concession, since it openly implies that we may be fighting for access to natural resources, if not simply to secure the homeland. But it has been privately the guiding light of American foreign policy since its inception, not the "security of the American people", which Obama disingenuously claims is his first priority as Commander in Chief. Were this his priority, he would have long ago seriously addressed two of the leading instigators of jihadism mentioned above.

To clarify key drivers of U.S. foreign policy, dissidents like Noam Chomsky have repeatedly pointed out that one need only look at post-war planning documents, notably the "Petroleum Policy of the United States." Drafted in 1944, the barely veiled imperial license which characterizes this policy paper insists on "the preservation of the absolute position presently obtaining, and therefore vigilant protection of existing concessions in United States hands *coupled with insistence upon the Open Door principle of equal opportunity for United States companies in new areas*" (italics mine).

You could hardly say it more plainly, although Woodrow Wilson did just that a few decades earlier when he articulated the all-encompassing policy of which the petroleum credo is but an article: "Since trade ignores national boundaries and the manufacturer insists on having the world as a market, the flag of his nation must follow him, and the doors of the nations which are closed against him must be battered down. Concessions obtained by financiers must be safeguarded by ministers of state, *even if the sovereignty of unwilling nations be outraged in the process.* Colonies must be obtained or planted, in order that no useful corner of the world may be overlooked or left unused" (italics mine). One might merely add that now the tendency is rather for the flag to precede the manufacturer, not follow him.

Moving from strategy to tactics, the administration's plan may be to use an attempt to blunt the ISIS advance as cover for the overthrow of Assad, an long-lived objective of the U.S. blueprint for the region, memorably shown to a stunned Wesley Clark, who later leaked the plan to the press. Seven countries in five years. You could never fault a neocon for lack of ambition. Obama's cold feet, Kerry's gaffe, and Sergey Lavrov's quick thinking prevented Syrian regime change about a year ago. No matter. The timeline was adjusted. A new pretext would soon emerge. Indeed it has.

All this is not to say that Barack Obama lacks a soul. Unless he is a sociopath of special dimensions, he probably recoils tamely at the sight of a beheading, like the rest of Westerners well trained in stomaching scenes and descriptions of far-flung violence. He probably believes ISIS is an even more lethal incarnation of jihad than al-Qaeda. And he'd be right. But the reasons he, or any U.S. president, for that matter, give for our actions are not the real reasons for those actions. They may be secondary considerations at best. In a democratic society, or one premised on an assumption of democracy, the cynical self-interest of the state must always be cloaked in some noble purpose. Otherwise, the population, not itself thinking in geo-strategic terms, would clamor for peace. Even if the population doesn't wholly digest the proffered cause, it must be handed that moral palliative by which it might rationalize actions taken in its name. In this sense, the interplay between president and people is a tango, a two-step in which each partner plays a part. And Obama, for his part, is pinioned by forces far greater than himself. Perhaps having seen this political eventuality from afar, he developed his incrementalism early in his career, the perfect rationale for placating vested interests while attempting modest reforms that change little but indicate intent. That tired look in the president's eyes? He's tired of being played for the pawn that he is and has agreed to be, and he hasn't the courage to defy the powers that elected him. Corporate. Networked. Disguised. Ubiquitous. Unsentimental.

Beware the military-industrial complex, cried a post-war Cassandra. But that prophecy came too late. The di was already cast. Now every president feels the pinch of private power. Those of a liberal frame of mind may believe we are much advanced in our sensibilities since the era of shameless colonialism. Yes, our rhetoric has been revised. We now conduct "humanitarian interventions" and are compelled to violence by our high-flown "Responsibility to Protect," (which may indeed have their proper use in a liberal internationalist policy). Yet, as Patrick Cockburn noted, " intervention in Iraq in 2003 and Libya in 2011 turned out to be very similar to imperial takeover in the 19th century." The priorities haven't changed, just their wording. And we have subtly turned the Bretton Woods institutions on their heads, refashioning them as mechanism of control and extraction, rather than the stepladders of independence they were invented to be. This meant the need for boots on the ground was no longer of pre-requisite of colonialism. Debt disciplines a nation better than rifles.

Socialists might suggest that the Wilson quote makes clear the primacy of capitalist priorities in American foreign policy. Doors must be flung open to American capital. And capitalism, if anything, has become even more radicalized since Wilson's day. We live in an age of extremes, ISIS at one pole and Collateralized Debt Obligations at the other. My money's on the CDOs. They have better weapons. Financial WMDs. And this radicalism, borne in part by the emergence of Asian rivals—the kind neocon Paul Wolfowitz warned we could not permit—is why well-intentioned calls for diplomacy—and globally broadcast proclamations, like the Pope's avowal that "war is madness"—will finally fall on dear ears, rendered mute by the din of an approaching delta of drones. If you live in the Levant, cover your ears. You're in the path of empire.

Post Script: Neither Syria or Iran will attend Monday's meeting of world leaders in Paris to discuss rolling back ISIS.

(*Dissident Voice*, September 15, 2014)

The Black Gold Brigade
Environmental destruction isn't just a consequence of capitalism, it's a prerequisite.

You might imagine that a dystopian <u>report</u> from the United Nations or <u>one</u> led by a Princeton University would give the global capitalist machine a moment of pause. You'd be wrong. A disinterested media largely ignored the July report from the UN and a November report led by the illustrious college. Not to mention the latest dire climate <u>summary</u> from the International Panel on Climate Change (IPCC). The discouraging UN study examined the first decade of the 21st century from a meteorological perspective. It found some troubling trends. Just to name a few: a more rapid thawing of Arctic sea ice, accelerated melting of glaciers, more extreme floods and droughts, more tropical cyclones, and the hottest decade on record. Surely there's a big story there? Evidently not. But even if there was, it would make little difference. The sad fact is that the leading culprit of our ecocide happens to be the fulcrum of the American empire—the American military.

Fueling the Machine
The U.S. military is the world's largest buyer of oil, dropping about $20 billion a year on black gold and other energy types. Our military needs oil even more than our economy does. Even more than Exxon and BP and oil giants do. Our military consumes more gallons of gasoline a day than all but 35 nations on earth. Without oil, our ships can't sail, our jets can't fly, our helicopters can't hover, and our tanks can't roll. As of 2009, the Department of Defense emptied <u>360,000 barrels</u> of oil a day. And that number skyrockets during a war. For every one of our occupations a vast range of fuel imperatives arise: high-octane jet fuel, auto diesel, marine diesel, electricity, natural gas, and so on.

The increasingly prevalent drone program lends a particular currency to this insight: drones literally sit in the air for hours on end, some up to 40 hours at a time, their low-level buzz audible on the ground and in the small villages that are being surveilled for targets. To do that, to hang stationary in the sky and monitor—like a giant mechanical predator—the livelihoods of mostly poor Muslim populations, enormous stores of diesel fuel are required. The Predator Unmanned Aerial Vehicle (UAV) can store <u>600 pounds</u> of high-octane jet fuel. The military has been testing <u>in-air refueling</u>, which would create floating gas stations capable of refueling swarms of drones that gathered around its octane-rich hub in unvarying, buzzing formation. As you might imagine, the per-gallon costs of this in-air replenishment are extravagant. The goal, of course, is to keep drones in the air longer, perhaps permanently. Keep in mind, we had 50 drones in 2001, and nearly 8,000 now. In keeping with humanity's imitative character, seventy countries around the world now <u>own</u> drones.

Thankfully for the odd conservationist, the Air Force has been testing drones powered by more economical <u>fuel cells</u>. The Navy, too, wants to convert to <u>biofuels</u>, like the Nazis did when their supply chains were crippled during the Second World War. At least then, when aerial assassinations are carried out against mere suspects, we won't be saddled with the companion guilt of having murdered at the environment's expense.

Protecting the Stash
But the squandering of oil isn't the military's only ecologically indifferent activity. There's also the oil protection racket. A Princeton-produced report from two years ago suggested that from 1976-2007, the U.S. military spent $7.3 trillion guarding oil resources in the Middle East with fleets of destroyers and aircraft carriers, not to note the inevitable chains of supply vessels. The General Accounting Office (GAO) estimated that from 1980-1990, America expended <u>$366 billion</u> safeguarding oil supplies in the Middle East. Note this year's dispatch of warships to the Straight of Hormuz to guard petrol transport routes. In our pathological pursuit of oil, we burn oil to protect what's left of the oil, while we readying the troops for an assault on another nation that has more oil. The only thing we recycle is the business model. Repeat after me: invasion, extraction, exhaustion.

Extract or Die
But it isn't just oil. Oil is simply the energy byword of the modern age. It used to be coal and will soon be natural gas. Resource extraction has a ruby red history that surges in parallel with the rise of industrial capitalism. From the earliest days of the Manchester coal mines, industrial capitalism has depended on massive resource extraction: French rubber plantations in Southeast Asia that were desperately defended when faced with potential nationalization; destructive oil exploration in the Ecuadorian Orientale on the edges of the Amazon rain forest; the government-led ejection of indigenous Naxalite populations from the Indian interior so multinationals can mine the mineral-rich hill country; Nigerian natives battling in vain to stave off the corporate piracy of their hydrocarbon wealth; coltan mines in the Congo flinging aside local communities just to speed new smart phones to store shelves. Note the presence of conflict at each of these resource hubs.

And now that we know about Pentagon plans for a larger global footprint, what can be done to stem the tide of ecological destruction? Down to its last card, the American empire is doubling down on war. It's the only remaining advantage we can claim over our rivals. China has a better economy, Brazil a better democracy, and India has cheaper labor. But we are superior warmongers. And we hope that force of arms can rejuvenate our terminal capitalist enterprise, keep the dollar in reserve, and the hydrocarbons under our thumb. Either it will, or we'll die trying. Resources are the ulterior motive that actuate imperial violence. Not democracy.

124

Not peace. Not self-defense. Not humanitarian empathies. Resources can be hawked for money and then money can be used to make money on money. (See the financialization of everything and the history of IMF loans for more on the latter.) So when it comes to fossil fuels, the character of our demise reveals itself—capitalist in origin, extractive in character, and violent in execution.

(*CounterPunch*, December 16, 2013)

The Dilemma of Empire
Which will impale you—humanitarian intervention or deficit reduction?

The word dilemma springs from the Greek for *di* and *lemma,* basically a "double proposition." The idea is that you have found yourself in a situation in which your only choice is between two 'horns', and your only question is which horn you would prefer to be gored by? As Americans, we may look abroad to avoid the calamity of Congress, but there we find war. We may look homeward to avoid the horror of industrial warfare, but here we find gangs of elitists jockeying for position in the great race to privatize the commons. We are left to ask ourselves, which is the greater betrayal of our nation's ethos: our seven decades proclaiming to secure the world for liberty while wrapping its innocents in chains, or the feverish work of capital, over the last four decades, to starve and desiccate and finally inter the American economy in the name of economic freedom? (In terms of violence or environmental destruction there is no contest—there the answer is clearly our commitment to global peace. But our faithlessness on either front is worth a look, if not a judgment.)

Resource Wars Abroad
On the one hand, the profession of peacekeeping. Here we are, several weeks after Obama disgraced the pulpit of international law at the U.N., claiming America has for "seven decades" served as the "anchor of global security." That effrontery was rich enough, leading anyone with a modicum of nonmainstream education to double over with sudden nausea. As Noam Chomsky recently noted, with his wonderfully toneless derision, that America is "the world leader in spreading destruction and misery." To that end, last week a handful of Syrian rebel factions banded together, these blood-stained parties of God, rejected American-backed secular rebels, whom they outnumber, and declared themselves for an Islamic state. Surely, the U.S. government will claim it had no hand in the furnishing of weapons or intelligence or training to seething Islamist mercenaries, but likely it has, whether through its Turkish or Jordan-based training sites, or via Gulf allies who have supplied weapons and arms of American provenance.

All of this against a supposedly sovereign state, all for the purpose of isolating Iran as part of our Sunday stroll through the Middle East. Having left Iraq, Afghanistan, and Libya in tatters, weakened by internecine bloodbaths, we will now topple the Assad regime before moving onto the more complicated showdown with the regional anchor in Tehran. All of this within the few short years of the new century, and all more or less designed to encircle the font of fossil fuels that comprise the Arab-Persian world.

Nile Bowie has usefully explored the progress of American Asia "pivot" designed to envelop China in the warm embrace of its ceaseless belligerence. Likewise, a proxy war between America and China has enflamed Africa, with recent Kenyan mall violence attributable in part to U.S. Somalian intervention. On continent after continent, we have brazenly swept aside the fragile conventions of peace to which we are more often than not the principal signatory.

Our Syrian involvement resembles our Cold War modus operandi of undermining Soviet interventions, as in Afghanistan, by supporting anyone with a simmering sense of injustice and a comparably meager fear of death. But elsewhere our evolving drone fleets and special forces apparatus has nicely calibrated our faux humanitarian interventions to match the American public's war fatigue. The emphasis is decidedly on marketing our wars now—we must produce a frisson of horror in the population, selecting from a cache of media-ready caricatures. There's the rogue dictator feverishly pursuing a mushroom cloud with mobile labs crisscrossing Mesopotamia. There's are the turbaned warlords of the Maghreb, capable of the most unspeakable savageries (much like our regional proxies). Now there is the autocratic nepotist in bespoke suit with his thin Arab mustache, coolly dispatching civilians with airy chems. One can summon similar archetypes from our blood-stained past: Gamal Nasser, Jonas Savimbi, Hugo Chavez. The details vary, but the broadly adumbrated image is what counts.

Yet our slimmed arsenal of humanitarian destruction has also produced a slightly more novel effect: Empire creep has become more blatant and unapologetic in the age of Obama. Last week we violated two more sovereign borders with total impunity, capturing an al-Qaeda operative in Tunisia and attempting the same in Somalia, although the operation was rebuffed with American covert forces fleeing from a firefight. Secretary of State John Kerry, with the witless aplomb that has become the hallmark of a once-bright career now veering toward an ignominious grave, said that the Tunisian operation was legal since it was sanctioned under the Authorization of Military Force Act (AUMF) of 2002. This comment should be the subject of a week's worth of national introspection, but it barely imparted a ripple on the smooth waters of the mainstream media, which daily absorbs a freshet of Congressional and Executive claptrap without the slightest impulse to self reflection.

After all, Kerry had essentially mistaken American law for international law, or traded the latter for the former. If Congress denies the sovereignty of another nation, invading that nation is legal. This notion fails to reflect the most rudimentary grasp of international law. Lacking this sensibility, America will act with complete temerity absent the presence of a military counterweight able to give it pause. The glacial but steady pace of Sino-Russian integration may one day provide this, if it isn't then too late. (Not that those whose fate it is to fall under the shadow of that hegemon will find life any more pleasant.)

Class War at Home

But what about our commitments to life, liberty, and the pursuit of happiness within our own borders? Here we are, a couple of weeks of government quietude in our furloughed wake, still more to come, with rightwing zealots gloating at the prospect. Obama and Boehner issue grave apothegms and assume the posture of petulant school kids, awaiting some deity of justice to strike the other down. Meanwhile, delusional liberals, as far-fetched with their ideological assumptions as the Tea Party, furiously expend their energies heaping defamation on the Republican Party, itself one half venal sycophants of capital, the other a fetid swamp of anti-federalists. These two noise factories provide enough fodder to fill the airwaves and preclude informed debate.

Waving their pamphlets of DNC talking points through the brisk air, liberals forget, or overlook, or never learned, that the Affordable Care Act (ACA) commands increasingly poor or near-poverty Americans to purchase healthcare policies that <u>cost too much</u> per month to maintain, and cost too much at the doctor's office to use. Whether it's a high premium, stupendous deductibles, or prohibitive co-pays, the ACA is a servile effort to prop up a broken system and preserve the sacred profits of insurance and Big Pharma. <u>Meanwhile</u>, the burden of health will be shifted from the shoulders of business into the hands of the young, who are a trillion dollars in the red to their institutions of higher learning, of whom only 48 percent are employed, of which only half work full time, and for whom median net worth continues to slide.

Fulminating about the socialist outrages of the Obama administration, Republican right-wingers are beholden to the self-defeating ideology of Ayn Rand, which prescribes total selfishness as an elaborately rationalized altruism, the bounty of self-interest delivered through the invisible hand of the free market (all externalities aside). In this context, government is a feckless and misguided arbiter of morality, interfering in the free pursuit of self-interest. The fact that roads are paved, poor are fed, borders defended, and scientific innovation funded by the government does nothing to stem the tide of their ire for the municipal stamp and seal. Behind this obsession with unabridged individualism lies the people's government-protected trove of national resources, which have been valued at more than a hundred trillion dollars. Whether Tea Party activists realize it, this is the final goal of the think-tank rhetoric that has shaped its ideology.

Little from either camp bears the signature of objectivity, as both work tirelessly to undermine their own objectives. And now the debt ceiling looms. Easily sidestepped through an Executive Order, Obama will employ the faux debt debate to gaze gravely into the cameras and maintain that Medicare and Social Security must be cut, part of the bi-partisan blueprint to 'starve the beast'. This despite the facts that:

1) America has borrowed profligately from Social Security, leaving its coffers filled with <u>tattered IOUs</u>;
2) The outsourcing of American jobs has decimated both consumer incomes and the tax base, leaving us more in need of free heath care than ever before;
3) Ceaseless wars across the last "seven decades" have spent billions whisked from the higher purpose of social good.

Each of these challenges offers its own solution: stop borrowing from social trust funds; quit offshoring jobs and bring them back; end needless wars and interventions. But each is rejected in its turn. War matters more, since war promises the orgasmic boon of global hegemony. Outsourcing matter more, since offshoring the American economy will line the calfskin wallets of the Robber Barons. Worthless IOUs matter more, since the one percent must be freed from the onerous burden of contributing to the general welfare—and because a desiccated federal system will free corporate America to loot our mineral, gas, and petro wealth.

The debt ceiling will inevitably be raised. The government will inevitably reboot. And the social tragedy of both American economic suicide and foreign slaughter will proceed apace. Nothing of substance will change. Except perhaps the complexion of the swindler in the White House, and the nomenclature of the wealth transfers and humanitarian wars we disguise as altruistic policy—both of which are part and parcel of the imperial project, since war is the vanguard of elite capital; they are no less yoked than the horns of the same bull. If Obama was right about anything at the U.N., it was that America is indeed exceptional. We lead the world in the slaughter of innocents and are the only nation to have voluntarily destroyed our own economy. In the end, though, we can't even pick the horn that would impale us. If we live abroad, we get one. At home, another. Even our vaunted consumer choice has been swept aside.

(*Dissident Voice*, October 12, 2013)

The Fifth Freedom
Making the world safe for a different kind of liberty

In the mid-1980s Noam Chomsky gave a series of lectures in Managua, Nicaragua. At the time, Managua was the epicenter of the Iran Contra scandal, which itself was the pinhead of widespread American intervention in Central America. As he was dispassionately outlining serial abuses across the Dominican Republic, Haiti, Honduras, Guatemala, Nicaragua, Cuba, and elsewhere, he made reference to Franklin Delano Roosevelt's famed "Four Freedoms," now enshrined on a slim jut of Roosevelt Island, in the East River between Manhattan and Brooklyn.

Plus One
Roosevelt named the four freedoms in his 1941 State of the Union speech. They are the freedom of speech, freedom of worship, freedom from want, and freedom from fear. The freedom of speech is a cornerstone of democratic governance; the freedom of worship is a bulwark against religious intolerance, and especially the totalitarian tendencies of monotheism; freedom from want is instantly recognizable as an economic freedom, in which the state's role may be to generate work or welfare for the disadvantaged; and freedom from fear conjures the terrors of empire that imperial conquerors have visited on native populations from the dawn of time. By articulating four simple rights, FDR illuminated the central human issues of liberty, faith, poverty, and power. Safeguard the first, protect against the remaining three, and you might have a peaceful world.

To this list of archetypal human concerns, Chomsky darkly added a fifth: the freedom to rob and exploit. Peering out over his Managua audience, he recognized that Central Americans, perhaps more than anyone in the '80s, understood the fifth freedom. Cynical U.S. imperialism had led the Reagan administration to fund a "contra" army to overthrow the socialist Sandinistas who promised popular participation for all Nicaraguans. One could have easily predicted—based solely on the Vietnam experience—that the administration would be seized by fears of the dread "domino effect," in which populism in one country would produce its likeness in the next, and so on down the entire peninsula of the Americas. One can imagine Reagan's Secretary of State Alexander Haig hyperventilating in his office, envisioning a thousand Castros staking socialist flags into the fertile turf of Latin America, as constituencies such as the United Fruit Company fled in immigrant boats bound for Miami.

Before then, and ever since, the United States has consistently demonstrated that the fifth freedom is the one that matters. But the freedoms are interrelated, as fear and want are generally increased in order to secure the fifth. Americans are made to believe that their liberties must be curtailed in order to keep them safe. Occupied and bombed populations abroad are made to understand their liberties

130

must be curtailed in order to keep the occupiers safe. The surveillance net that blankets the country and much of the world flouts the fourth amendment and undermines the first. Surveillance produces self-censorship, as the PEN organization found. As for want, there have rarely been more Americans in poverty, deep poverty, or dependent on food stamps, although that last is thankfully beginning to decline. Real wages have flat-lined in the decades since neoliberal economics took hold, and lag far behind inflation. A mere 95% of gains since the recession have gone to the top one percent of Americans—the de facto statistic if you want to neatly summarize the domestic scene during the Obama years. Freedom from fear has perhaps suffered the worst fate in recent years, as ferocious American interventionism has become near continuous policy, particularly throughout the Middle East, as tensions mount around the dwindling supply of global energy resources, and the U.S. economy is caught and passed by China's. In addition to dozens of military missions in the neoliberal era, there are some 800 military bases around the world—often staging platforms for new interventions and surveillance models that hope to rationalize them.

Regarding religious freedom, more Americans feel freed from the sometimes-pernicious grip of Christianity, in part thanks to a more vocal atheist community. A climbing percentage of citizens claim to be unaffiliated to any religion. Will this mark the advent of a century of American Gnosticism, as literature critic Harold Bloom has suggested, or something equally benign? Of course, religious tolerance is a dicey proposition for Muslims, who have been shamelessly profiled, entrapped, and denied due process. There are some good signs of resistance at least to social abuse of Muslims, at least abroad. In the aftermath of the recent Sydney siege, tens of thousands of Australians countered a vitriolic #SydneySeige Twitter hashtag by supporting another one: #IllRideWithYou. The hashtag offered ride-along companionship to Muslims on public transportation if they feared abuse.

Freedom to Exploit
By contrast, the fifth freedom is galloping along with few impediments. But how is it asserted in practice? Consider a few edifying examples. First, recall the notorious Order 81 from the Coalition Provisional Authority (CPA) that modified Iraqi patent law, with the effect of extending American agricultural patents to Iraq, meaning farmers can't save genetically modified seeds from year to year. Instead, they have to license them from companies like Monsanto. Essentially, Monsanto's "terminator" seeds are single-harvest seeds. After one harvest, they don't germinate again, so farmers can't save them, forcing them to license new seeds from Monsanto.

A slightly more ingenious strategy has been hatched in Afghanistan. USAID and Nutrition and Education International (NEI), an NGO backed by agribusiness giants like Monsanto and Cargill, have launched a plan to ensnare Afghanis in

131

their patent monopoly scheme. As part of the global war on drugs, they'll use RoundUp™ glyphosate, the silver bullet herbicide, to eradicate poppy fields, and then dump massive RoundUp Ready™ soybean seeds on the fields. The seeds are resistant to the herbicide, while weeds and other flora are not. The seed design, of course, is the intellectual property of Monsanto. Those seeds, too, will go sterile after a single season and require new payments from the serfs to their the agribusiness overlords.

Most recently, the new U.S.-backed Ukrainian government has been slashing tariffs as part of its E.U. deal, enabling American ag firms to enter Ukraine, produce cheap subsidized commodities, then peddle them to the E.U. well above cost.

The Western-led economic attack on Russia, provocative NATO action, and the U.S. coalition of Sunni fundamentalists' war against Syria provide other instances of the fifth freedom at work. These are pipeline conflicts. Syria and Russia are America's competitors for lucrative European oil and gas markets. Russia had hoped to channel energy through Ukraine to the EU. Nixed by a proxy putsch. Then Moscow hoped to construct a "South Stream" route into the EU across the Black Sea. Nixed again by American arm-twisting of its obsequious European subalterns. Now Russia has turned to Turkey to salvage some European revenue.

Bashar al-Assad scripted his own demise in 2011 when he bailed on a Qatari pipeline proposal to channel liquid gas to the EU. Then he spun on a dime and penned the "Islamic gas pipeline" plan with Iran and Iraq. Not long afterward the Syrian hinterlands were aflame with revolution, happily supported by Assad's American nemesis.

But that's what happens when you defy empire. Just ask Manuel Zelaya or Muammar Gaddafi, one discarded, the other entombed. As the people's judge asks the convicted in *The Dark Knight Rises*, "Death or exile?" Quite often it's death *by* exile.

The Rifle and the Fruit
This sick coalition of militarism and corporatism was popularized in the same Central America where Chomsky gave his Managua lectures. Just have a look at the logo of the notorious United Fruit Company (UFC). A rifle and a banana against a backdrop of gold. A perfect symbol of the banana republic, which Afghanistan, Iraq, Ukraine and Syria are all destined to become. Either hydrocarbon theocracies like Saudi Arabia or lawless sectarian abattoirs like Libya.

When the UFC's Guatemalan concessions were threatened by the ascension of populist Jacobo Arbenz in the 1950s, they turned to the U.S. government with an array of public relations efforts to enlist the CIA in restoring its profit-rich arrangement with Guatemala. The CIA sponsored a coup in 1954 that did just that.

Some years later, the UFC got itself a media makeover at the hands of Sigmund Freud's nephew, fabled public relations guru Edward Bernays. He created a cartoon character called, "Chiquita," which helped restore the company's image and soften the contempt in which its name had come to be held (Much like brand Obama did for the U.S. plutonomy). Chiquita Brands International later conceded its financial support—in the millions—to right-wing death squads in Colombia, generally used for the suppression of labor rights.

The formula seems to work like this: when you mix capitalism and democracy, capital immediately buys the democracy, subverts it, and globally deploys both the military and the treasury as a vanguard tasked with prying open new markets for capital in a ruthless game of absolute advantage and labor arbitrage. Since it owns the government, capital wins its domestic war with labor, which it slowly marginalizes—boa constrictor style—through the long arm of the law. Conditions deteriorate for the many, but dramatically improve for the few (as noted with our Obama statistic). A vast abyss opens between the vassals and the corporate mandarins. The former is legion and disposable, the latter Lilliputian but indispensible. The crucial point is that the fifth freedom be preserved. Thankfully, its godless practitioners—increasingly opposed by the armies of Allah—are safe and prosperous in their D.C. annexes and corporate lairs, putting the finishing touches on their Asian pivot and a new decade of resource wars.

(*CounterPunch*, January 1, 2015)

The Pain in Ukraine
Two nuclear heavyweights jostle for position on the banks of the Black Sea

So Russia has moved to secure Crimea, where it's prized Black Sea fleet resides. No surprise there, although Secretary of State John Kerry, the lantern-jawed buffoon that President Obama trots out to justify the indefensible, comically affected indignant outrage and declared Russian behavior to be, "an incredible act of aggression." Yet neither the swift Russian reply, nor any of the other events in this latest deposing of a democratically-elected leader come as much of a surprise. At least not if history is a useful guide.

Obviously Not a Team Player
What were the causes behind the latest 'democratic revolution' in Ukraine? Best to view the scenario through the unvarnished lens of "straight power concepts," as post-war U.S. planner George Kennan once put it. Essentially, now-deposed Ukrainian leader Viktor Yanukovych seemed to have hoped to perform a Houdini-like balancing act between East and West, solidifying Ukrainian sovereignty, enacting enough 'business friendly' reforms to assure IMF loans and enough populist measures to keep him in office, all while holding imperial wolves at bay. As usual, apart from the self-enrichment, this strategy was a spectacular failure.

(Yanukovych has proven to be an easy target for pro-Western opponents. While he casts a fair profile of Westernized professionalism, has been dogged by criminal charges throughout his career. Despite felonies from his youth and questions about his academic degrees, he won the 2004 Ukrainian presidential election, but stepped down in the wake of the Orange Revolution and calls of electoral fraud. Opponents have scrupulously documented his expanding asset portfolio and labyrinthine financial connections since his 2010 election. In the wake of his exodus, everyday Ukrainians are now touring his former mansion, "Mezhyhirya", a stunning estate of otherworldly opulence, particularly given Yanukovych's modest $100,000 salary.)

Faced with making a distinct choice between the European Union and Russia, Yanukovych seemed poised to deliver his nation further into the clutches of IMF debt peonage and enable regular looting by Western multinationals through an "EU association and trade agreement" (facilitated by trunkloads of IMF cash). At the last minute, Yanukovych declined this devil's pact and opted for a Russian $15 billion dollar loan. This fatal misstep appears to have triggered American efforts to unseat Yanukovych and replace him with a Western-friendly face. Having likely witnessed the state of the European Union in the last few years, Yanukovych made a not so surprising about-face.

134

Of course, Yanukovych was already on thin ice with the West. He had been behaving in troubling fashion since his election, enacting various social programs that threatened to undermine the spending controls the IMF had stipulated, as well as refusing to lift utility prices to IMF-recommended levels—knowing that either could jeopardize his or his party's popularity. In any event, it's likely the West found him an unreliable partner in—and eventually an obstacle to—their hoped-for 'liberalization' of the Ukrainian economy.

Why Does This Former Soviet Republic Matter So Much?

But given all of this wrangling over economic policy, why does the U.S. care so much about the Ukraine? For a couple of reasons. First, the Ukraine is perched on the edge of the resource-rich Black Sea, a geostrategic prize for any fossil-fuel hungry empire. Russia's cyclopean Gazprom has traditionally led mining efforts, but Western multinationals like Exxon are shouldering their way in, particularly after finding a massive natural gas field on the Black Sea floor last year. Exxon subsequently inked a $735 million deal with the Ukraine to drill deep-water wells off its coast. The long-term interest of the European Union would be to diminish Russia's ability to wield political influence by virtue of the volume of its gas exports to the EU.

Second, the Ukraine also sits on the Russian border. What better place for NATO to set up camp and aim some ballistic deterrents at the Kremlin? From there NATO could reasonably hoist large megaphones aimed at Moscow with the booming voice of President Obama confirming that "all options are on the table." One shudders to think. It isn't enough that NATO now includes Romania, Hungary, Slovakia, and Poland. This after George H.W. Bush cut a deal with Russia's world-historical dupe Mikhail Gorbachev that, in exchange for unlocking East Germany, NATO wouldn't move "one inch eastward." It has expanded eastward three times since, including the aforementioned nations. So much for trusting the West.

It Worked in 1953!

All of this is par for the course. During the Cold War, the CIA normally performed the rabble-rousing subversion in countries that had been infected by the "nationalism" disease. Henry Kissinger once referred to such countries as a "virus" that threatened to spread "contagion" through the region. Kermit Roosevelt (one images a frog smoking a Camel from an ivory cigarette holder) helped execute the subversive activities that led to the overthrow of Iranian Prime Minister Mohammad Mosaddegh in 1953. Mosaddegh had himself made the foolish misstep of attempt to nationalize Iranian oil, much to the consternation of petro concerns in Britain and the United States. He was duly deposed and replaced with a military government led by a repressive monarch, Mohammad Reza Shah of the Pahlavi dynasty.

Yes, But Let's Use an NGO This Time

Some things have changed slightly, however. Now the U.S. prefers to destabilize democratically-elected governments using faux non-governmental organizations (NGOs). This has the twofold advantage of evading laws against directly funding opposition parties in foreign countries, but more importantly creates the appearance of supporting the promotion of democratic institutions in benighted nations that for whatever reason—backward religions, endemic corruption, latent influence of communism, etc.—have yet to glimpse the splendor of Western-style free-market neoliberalism.

The National Endowment for Democracy (NED) is the poster child for the modern say-one-thing-do-another NGO. It has funded 65 projects in the Ukraine, all of them naturally designed to help these boorish Eastern Europeans grasp the core concepts of our capitalist demos. Consider This from Consortium News:

The National Endowment for Democracy, a central part of Ronald Reagan's propaganda war against the Soviet Union three decades ago, has evolved into a $100 million U.S. government-financed slush fund that generally supports a neocon agenda often at cross-purposes with the Obama administration's foreign policy.

Some of the non-government organizations (or NGOs) supporting these [Ukrainian] rebellions trace back to NED and its U.S. government money.

For NED and American neocons, Yanukovych's electoral legitimacy lasted only as long as he accepted European demands for new "trade agreements" and stern economic "reforms" required by the International Monetary Fund.

NED's longtime president, Carl Gershman, took to the op-ed page of the neocon-flagship Washington Post to urge the U.S. government to push European "free trade" agreements on Ukraine and other former Soviet states and thus counter Moscow's efforts to maintain close relations with those countries. The ultimate goal, according to Gershman, was isolating and possibly toppling Putin in Russia with Ukraine the key piece on this global chessboard.

So much for NGOs being politically neutral.

Be Sure to Hire Some Street Thugs Like Kermit Did

Other things have stayed the same, such as funding violent opposition elements in an attempt to stir up street-level dissent that can then be broadcast worldwide. This causes conscientious European pensioners to put down their café and read in consternation reports emanating from the scene of the (clandestine) crime. And like American flag-wavers who fall into a frothing fury at the notion of revanchist Russian state, both conclude that democracy—its delicate flame dwindling by the day—is nobly struggling for its life against the arrayed forces of a fearsome fascism.

It is in fact the West that is employing the fascists and neo-Nazis to further its own ends. Like it used SUMKA in the Iranian coup, in the Ukraine, it has backed a motley confection of deranged fascists, Goebbels-reciting neo-Nazis, and various other unsavory types who all appear to have two characteristics in common: they celebrate violence and detest democracy. The Svoboda ("Freedom") Party in particular has a treacherous history of collusion with the Nazis during WWII. Several have slipped into the nascent governing group, despite a desire by Assistant Secretary of State Victoria Nuland's desire to marginalize them once they served their thug purpose. Nor should we forget that the specter of Nazism continues to haunt the Russian nation. It lost a generation of men—some 20 to 25 million—in its heroic battle against the Germans. The last thing it wants to see as it peers across its Western borders is fascist uprising.

If Ukrainians thought life was onerous under a democratically-elected Yanukovych (did they?), wait until they get a taste of IMF medicine, soon to be paternally administered by the new West-leaning government. You'll have noticed the first words out of the mouth of freshly minted Prime Minister Arseniy Yatsenyuk were that the Ukrainian people would quite naturally have to suffer deprivations on the hard path to free-market democracy. A cursory glance at Greece and Italy might be sufficient to give the average Kiev resident nightmares. Just consider what the IMF asked of Ukraine last October, according to Global Research:

In negotiations last October, the IMF demanded that Ukraine double prices for gas and electricity to industry and homes, that they lift a ban on private sale of Ukraine's rich agriculture lands, make a major overhaul of their economic holdings, devalue the currency, slash state funds for school children and the elderly to "balance the budget." In return Ukraine would get a paltry $4 billion.

On the other hand, the Kremlin was dangling a rather more attractive offer:

Before the ouster of the Moscow-leaning Yanukovych government last week, Moscow was prepared to buy some $15 billion of Ukraine debt and to slash its gas prices by fully one-third. Now, understandably, Russia is unlikely to give that support. The economic cooperation between Ukraine and Moscow was something Washington was determined to sabotage at all costs.

The City of Woe
It all adds up, doesn't it? Throw in Honduras, Egypt, Libya, and ongoing intrigues in Syria and Venezuela, and the Obama administration has fashioned for itself an impressive track record for regime change, normally associated with Republican

neoconservatives. Now we can watch events unfold as the U.S. and Russia perform alarming chest-thumping military maneuvers reminiscent of Cold War posturing. Perhaps it will lead to a donnybrook of heavyweights, or more likely, just the brutal division of another sovereign state into two not-so-sovereign dependencies. A giant new World Bank loan will be approved with much fanfare and sighs of relief among Western liberals. Austerity will be imposed. Kiev technocrats will claim they are shouldering the burden of making 'difficult' decisions for the benefit of all. The population will suffer untold deprivations, and another fledgling state will be buried in the charred aftermath of its own self-determination.

Rather strikingly, each Ukrainian that wishes to tour the palace of the exiled Yanukovych and its mind-boggling layout of baroque architecture, medieval armor, and Sumatran pheasants, must pass beneath a sign above the entrance that proclaims, "People, do not destroy this evidence of thieving arrogance." Interestingly, it was Yanukovych himself who must have seen—at the very last moment—the forbidding crest above the European Union that reads, as do the gates to hell in Dante's *Inferno*, "Abandon All Hope Ye Who Enter." Sadly, the Ukrainian people are now destined for that hopeless bourn, and are being marshaled onto mythic Charon's leaky raft to ferry them to fates unknown.

(*CounterPunch*, March 4, 2014)

138

The Permanent Paranoia of Empire
The U.S. empire fears any nation that thinks for itself

"Blind belief in authority is the greatest enemy of truth."
— Albert Einstein

The unmitigated effrontery of the Senate this month is hard to excel, but President Obama is doing his best to do just that. Over the past week the President has issued a couple of indictments from the Oval Office, both of which involve traditional rivals, Venezuela and Iran. Their sin? Thinking for themselves, a rare condition that must be instantly condemned with the most inflammatory rhetoric available, before steps are taken to eliminate the condition altogether. There's nothing so inimical to the freedoms of empire as the freedoms of others.

Crackdown on the Chavistas
First, Obama produced a breathtakingly daft Executive Order (E.O.) declaring Venezuela "an unusual and extraordinary threat to the national security and foreign policy of the United States, and I hereby declare a national emergency to deal with that threat." The cause? A confused pastiche of unproven items including the "erosion" of "human rights," "arbitrary arrest and detention," and "public corruption." Does anyone believe this farrago of libel actually expresses an actual threat to the United States?

Sadly, many of the brainwashed disciples of the *New York Times*, *Washington Post*, CNN and FOX NEWS mostly probably do. But can anyone not so heavily propagandized take the President seriously? One need merely summon the records of our faithful aid to such beacons of human rights as Colombia, a world-class slaughterhouse for unionized citizenry; Nicaragua, still scarred by the legacy of Regan's attempts to destroy populism there; Egypt, where President and former General Sisi has shamelessly conducted his sanguinary violations in the public square; Mexico, where we rely on corruption to keep our candidates in office; and Honduras, where the coup government we have supported since 2009 has turned the country into the bloodiest and most lawless nation in Central America. Still the money flows.

So this isn't at all about the causes Obama mentions. Perhaps the President misspoke. There is really only one way in which Venezuela presents a threat to the U.S. That is the threat that the stunningly successful Bolivarian Revolution poses to the neoliberal fascism practiced in America and Europe. After all, just compare the statistics. Across the board, the Bolivarian model is unquestionably superior to the neoliberal model when it comes to lifting the quality of life for the majority. It has liberated the Venezuelan people in numberless ways. Jobs, incomes, health, political participation, all surged while poverty plummeted under Hugo Chavez and his beleaguered successor Nicolas Maduro. Employment,

139

incomes, political participation, all headed south under George W. Bush and Obama, just to limit one's gaze to this century.

Did the President rather mean to say that no single country has larger crude reserves than Venezuela, and that American access to it has been limited since Hugo Chavez skyrocketed into the presidency on the backs of massive popular support and immediately nationalized the oil industry? A real black eye for the Exxons and BPs of the world.

Interesting that the order targets seven individuals in particular, members of Venezuela's armed forces, its national intelligence services, its department of homeland security (yes, it has one, too), a former member of its national guard, its national police, and its justice department. Looks like another "divide and ruin" strategy, as progressive political author Dan Glazebrook puts it. Sow division, seed turf wars, and splinter the Chavistas with the hammer and chisel of frozen assets. Seems similar to the sanctions imposed on Russia, which targeted members of the military, the security forces, and parliament.

Forget that the United States is openly violating Venezuelan sovereignty, sponsoring coups in 2002 and just last month, and aiding the rabidly anti-democratic opposition behind both failed coups as well as last year's outbreak of violence. Returning the opposition to power would likely return the country to 80 percent poverty, which is where it stood before Chavez. Forget that 33 nations from the Community of Latin American and Caribbean states (CELAC) announced their support for Venezuela and condemned U.S. interference. Forget that a majority of Venezuelans vociferously reject U.S. intervention of any kind. Forget that Maduro's government has produced some pretty damning evidence against the thwarted coup d'état planned by members of the Venezuelan right, including links to U.S. front organizations (all dismissed by U.S. State Department spokesperson Jen Psaki).

Crackdown on the Mullahs
Not satisfied with one transparent fatuity for the week, the President produced another. This time he was confirming and extending the cruel E.O. against Iran. This second "national emergency" in seven days is for the supposedly grave problem posed by Iran's efforts to produce civilian nuclear energy. This effort represents, in the administration's paranoiac mind, another "unusual and extraordinary threat to the national security, foreign policy, and economy of the United States constituted by the actions and policies of the Government of Iran."

It makes the average observer wonder why anyone has attempted diplomacy at all, given the hysteria produced by Israeli Prime Minister Benjamin Netanyahu's nose-thumbing speech to Congress, the subversive letter from Republican freshman Senator Tom Cotton, and now the President's own ruinous theatricality.

Why bother? One supposes Obama sees this deal as another piece of his legacy, and this E.O. as an attempt to push it through. Add this nuclear agreement to the rancid TPP (part of the Asian pivot), and the Affordable Care Act (ACA) and you can begin to mouth the words of fake progressives when they insist that Obama had major achievements in foreign policy, healthcare, and free trade. This before they enjoin you to vote (again) for the exceedingly venal Clinton dynasty.

Forget that Iran would be doing nothing illegal by enriching uranium to 20 percent. Under the Non Proliferation Treaty (NPT), it is free to do as it likes in this regard. Forget that, despite this, it is being massively sanctioned on the basis of claims with no evidence to support it (namely, that it wants a bomb). Forget that it has already made generous concessions to the P5+1 on its nuclear capabilities, and made plenty of acceptable offers before that (all rejected by the West). Forget that 16 U.S. intelligence agencies confirmed that it quit its nuclear weapons program in 2003, that the Ayatollah has issued a fatwa against nuclear weapons. Even the leading right-wing think tanks agree. And above all forget that the United States and Israel together have thousands of nuclear bombs at the ready, and that both have attacked Iranian neighbors and allies on fallacious premises, and that both have openly threatened and clandestinely attacked Iran, murdering scientists or launching cyberattacks. Both of which are acts of war by the U.N. standard. Or even, to challenge the received view that Iran is the seminal profligate of the NPT, the United States, though having reduced its nuclear arsenal tremendously since the Sixties, by some 83 percent, a notable achievement, it is still openly modernizing its arsenal. This suggests what we all instinctively know to be true: the U.S. will never fully eradicate its nuclear arsenal, or even permit its nuclear stock to fall behind that of any other nation. None of this matters, because in the U.S.-manipulated IAEA language ("the absence of undeclared activities"), Iran must effectively demonstrate not the absence of evidence, but the "evidence of absence," the impossible criteria former Secretary of Defense Donald Rumsfeld once laid upon Baghdad.

Regime Change Best Practices
The standard tactic for "taking out" the various unsavory democratic and socialist governments around the globe pivots on three principals: first, conduct clandestine subversion inside the country's borders, dutifully carried out by that most admirable of organizations, the CIA. Think here of dead scientists, vicious computer viruses and shadowy coup d'états. Second, sanction the country, a tactic best combined with some form of currency attack. Think here of shortages of medical supplies, secret deals to collapse the price of oil, and massive currency sell offs. If covert sabotage doesn't destabilize the government, and if sanctions don't "make the economy scream," then take the last step, invade the country. Think here of Colin Powell's U.N. theatrics and Netanyahu's adolescent time bomb sketches. What this axis of evil tactics reveals is that a WMD can be a financial tool as much as an MQ-9 Reaper drone. Neither is ever "off the table"

wherever Washington's hegemony-happy neoconservatives need to uproot democratic flashpoints. These exigencies usually occur in the most delicate of places, atop lakes of underground petrol or pipeline crossroads.

Iran and Venezuela are being subjected to this strategy, but they aren't alone. In the case of Russia, the economy has suffered a triple attack: sanctions applied by the U.S., EU, Japan, Australia and other allies; a U.S.-engineered price collapse in the oil market, driving prices below what nations like Russia, Iran, and Venezuela need to recoup to cover their production costs; and, just as the Russian economy was stung by both sanctions and the price drop in petroleum, the financial markets responded by attacking the currency, turning big profits by dumping rubles, watching their value crash, then picking them back up for a nifty profit.

Of course, all of this must be preceded by a pontifical decree. Before prescribing sanctions or intervention, the President must declare a nominally dire threat to national security. (Clandestine actions, by virtue of their blanket of anonymity, can happily dispense with such legal casuistry.) Hence the two memorandums of the last week.

Lessons from History
Yet Venezuela and Iran shouldn't be surprised at the ongoing demonization of their nations. Had they studied the history of empire, they would know that if there's one lesson for leaders of independent-minded nations, it's this: never utter the word "nationalization" and never prescribe any system of governance other than "free-market capitalism." There's nothing imperial power fears more than a country with an independent streak. If you have one, expect a nasty shock. Just ask the Guatemala's Jacobo Arbenz, Honduras' Manuel Zelaya, Iraq's Saddam Hussein, Libya's Muammar Gaddafi, Egypt's Gamal Abdel Nasser, Nicaragua's Daniel Ortega, Haiti's Jean Bertrand Aristide, not to mention Venezuela's own Hugo Chavez and Iran's Mohammad Mossadegh.

All of these deposed leaders took the brave but fatal step of nationalizing—or attempting to nationalize—their own resources with the aim of developing their domestic economy. This is a bad idea when the hegemon that owns the biggest guns, controls the biggest banks, and intimidates its biggest rivals, isn't keen on the idea. Much better to open your economy to commodity dumping, foreign takeovers, and imperial military bases. Your people may revile you, but you'll probably survive, succeed in embezzling state funds, and perhaps arrange an amiable retirement in coastal Florida.

If "don't think for yourself" is the central lesson for the subjects of empire, then "self-defense" is the dominant description of that empire's behavior. If there is a single overriding lie that permeates Western propaganda over the last century, it is the fable of self-defense. In this country, it began when we were compelled to demonize the native Americans, declaring them an enemy that we must eradicate to save ourselves. Woodrow Wilson's Red Scare ratcheted up the fear of the "Hun" such that a largely pacific populace was brought into a frothing fury, ready to defends its unthreatened freedoms. Hitler succeeded in invading numerous nations in a desperate effort to protect the vulnerable German people from the mad hordes lurking on its every border. Ronald Reagan told America that the little nation of Nicaragua, consisting mostly of forest guerillas armed by the U.S., was a mere 48 hours from Texas. This was perhaps inspiration for Tony Blair's "45 minutes" fabrication from which Saddam Hussein never recovered. And now President Obama is continuing this tradition by telling us that we must be vigilant against the inscrutable deceits of two rogue nations. Countries that—at least when it comes to eradicating poverty or not starting wars—do pose a threat to the United States: the threat of a good example.

(*CounterPunch*, March 19, 2015)

The Persian Bomb Squad
Some people just can't be trusted

A recent *New York Times* article offered another textbook example of the spectacular bias the U.S. employs to undermine those that might pose a challenge to its global hegemony. It also nicely illustrated the willingness of the media to serve as little more than a relay station for state propaganda. Yet it was but the latest in the glossary of deceits that characterize America's relationship with Iran.

The front-page article from two Saturdays covered the Iranian nuclear program negotiations between Iran and the so-called P5+1, which includes the United States, United Kingdom, France, Germany, China, and Russia. It was titled, "In Iran Talks, U.S. Seeks to Prevent a Covert Weapon." The subhead reads, "A 'Sneakout' Feared." The article then intones, with its vacuous air of impartiality and even-handed reserve, that the West (naturally acting with the best interests of all people at heart) is wrestling with "how to design an agreement to maximize the chances that Western intelligence agencies would catch any effort to develop an atomic bomb at a covert site." Concern is obviously, then, "over a future Iranian covert program."

The authors repeatedly emphasize Iran's "declared" nuclear facilities. The authors at least concede that the declared facilities are "crawling with inspectors and cameras." The goal, it is said, is to stretch the "breakout" timeline by which Iran could 'sprint' to a bomb. But the real problem for the U.S. and its allies is not only a "breakout," but also a "sneakout," which is the nonexistent covert program that it believes may one day exist "deep in the Iranian mountains."

Note that all of this talk of breakouts and sneakouts and covert programs is conjecture, speculation perhaps calibrated to produce distrust in Iranian aims, which to this point, seem to be in line with its right to pursue civilian nuclear energy—something the U.S. happily supported when its brutal stooge, the Shah of Iran, held the reigns of the country. But America has never forgiven the 1979 Islamic revolution.

This entire narrative smacks of the Iraq invasion of 2003, when the Bush administration's unquenchable thirst for regional dominion led it to fabricate a covert Iraqi WMD program. Though UNSCOM had found no evidence of WMD programs, and no radar or satellite detections of nuclear activity were ever reported, Secretary of Defense Donald Rumsfeld declared that, "absence of evidence is not evidence of absence."

Keep this quote in mind as we review five critical steps to bringing your rivals to heel.

144

1. Demonize and penalize…

The game plan for Iran is largely drawn from the Iraqi playbook, with a few modifications. For instance, it is important to establish an unreachable standard of compliance by which you can cast a considerable shadow over your enemy's motivations. Though the IAEA has repeatedly found that Iran has not diverted nuclear power toward a weapons program, the U.S. still seeks confirmation of "the absence of undeclared activities." This is, logically speaking, impossible to verify. To do so would require omniscience—knowledge of everything—to verify the absence of the imagined. It is under the rubric of this intellectual fatuity that the West has pressed for further inspections than members are required to provide under their NPT Safeguards agreement.

This is how it worked with Iraq. The White House knows if it pushes far enough, eventually the oppressed country will balk and resist. At that moment, the White House and State Department will leap into action, declaring that Iraq or Iran isn't negotiating in good faith, has failed its obligations, and so on. It will point to "hard-liners" in the target government, characterizing them as myopic fundamentalists that cannot cope with modernity.

In Iraq, absurd demands included a dire need to inspect Hussein's own palace for evidence of WMD subterfuge. The same is being proposed for Iran. Imagine Iran insisting that it be permitted to inspect the Knesset for possible plots to attack Natanz facility. How might our mild-mannered Zionist allies react?

A key sticking point are the "additional protocols" pushed by the U.S. as new measures to verify NPT compliance back in the late nineties, largely in response to successful Iraqi efforts to disguise nuclear work, which appear to have eluded the IAEA less from deficiencies in the NPT Safeguards but negligence in applying the full authority they accord inspection teams. They call for the member states to declare more activity related to nuclear energy and to permit more expansive access for IAEA inspectors.

Naturally, the U.S. was behind the push for more extensive access above and beyond the NPT. This process stretches back into the nineties when the additional protocols were being formed, ostensibly based on insights from the Iraq invasion earlier in the decade. The U.S. led the push for more access: "U.S. leadership in negotiating the Model Additional Protocol was instrumental in its acceptance by the IAEA Board of Governors. Countries with extensive nuclear civilian energy programs…opposed U.S. efforts to strengthen the draft protocol, citing its inapplicability to the United States."

Early in the 2000s, an IAEA report found that Iran was not pursuing nuclear weapons but that it had concealed the extent of its enrichment activities—a direct violation of the NPT. In an attempt to ease Western concerns, Iran signed on to the additional protocols (but didn't ratify them) and voluntarily suspended enrichment activity for a couple of years, hoping that by so doing it would gain EU promise to accept its uranium enrichment for civilian energy. The EU agreed that proviso in the Paris Agreements of 2004. A few months later it reneged on its promise. In response, Iran began enriching uranium again and dropped the additional protocols.

(Note during this long period of bickering, Iran had quietly offered complete transparency of its program, quitting its support for Hamas and Hezbollah, in exchange for security guarantees from the U.S. The West instantly rejected this idea. It also suggested its enrichment being managed by an international consortium. Again, dismissed.)

Despite its legal right under the NPT to enrich uranium to 20 percent, the IAEA tossed the Iranian dossier to the UN Security Council, which pretended to extend a new offer to Iran after requesting it halt the exercise of its legal right to enrichment. The new offer of negotiations, in a predictable tactic familiar to U.S. foreign policy observers, included a request that the purpose of negotiations—Iran's enrichment program—be halted before the negotiations began.

The Security Council imposed sanctions on Iran. The U.S. pressed the IAEA to declare Iran in violation of the NPT. Iran, by contrast, claimed he sanctions were illegal. By 2007, the West was demanding satisfaction beyond even the additional protocols, according to IAEA Deputy Director general of safeguards Olli Heinonen.

2. Falsely accuse...
Aside from demanding the impossible, one should produce a steady stream of false accusations to further undercut whatever credibility your rival may have in international circles. As evidence of Iranian duplicity, the U.S. points to the "hidden" Fordo plant, which it says was "uncovered" in 2009, before the site was finished. In actuality, Iran announced the facility to the IAEA. The "additional protocols" spearheaded by the West that Iran had initially agreed to then refused to ratify stipulated it needlessly inform the IAEA the moment it put spade to earth on a proposed nuclear facility. The old "Safeguards" that it still abides by require all members to give notice of a new facility 180 days prior to its going online. Iran did the latter, but not the former, in keeping with its original agreement.

Iran plausibly said the facility was a contingency facility it built after public threats from Israel (the latest here) and the U.S. to militarily destroy its Natanz program. In 2013 Iran granted additional access to facilities "including mines and mills" beyond even the superfluous extra protocol. But the West wants to account for "the location of every (centrifuge)." It wants to regularly interview Iranian

146

scientists, which Tehran has thus far resisted since a number of them have been assassinated, reportedly by Israeli clandestine agency Mossad.

The Europeans regularly chime in to call negotiations an "endless game of hide-and-seek." Unnamed "intelligence officials" and "experts" (the usual suspects the *Times* relies on) claim that Iran is riddled with "bunkers and tunnels." The *Times* article concludes that the "past lurks over the sneakout problem," and that, according to an American 'hard-liner', it needs to, "'guard against the hidden program.'" Notice here how the definite article is used twice in succession. This implies the existence of a thing unknown to exist. The entire article is based on a suspicion in Washington. But better to assume now than be fooled later, as the beltway hawks would have it. Left aside is the reality that despite myriad inspections and unprecedented access, no inspector has ever found weapons-grade uranium in Iran, or a program to quickly develop it.

3. Negotiate in bad faith...
Negotiations are often a preliminary means of posing as a dutiful and peace-loving member of the international community before you resort to force against your enemy. It is important not to be fooled by your own pretext of good faith. You must remember that negotiations are not about solutions, but about convincing onlookers that you have exhausted diplomacy in an effort to make the peace. This will nonetheless require extraordinary hypocrisy in order to properly vilify your rival.

How interesting it is that the West will take at face value the Hamas declaration that it wants to eliminate the state of Israel. In good faith, we say, we are taking them at their word. Yet when Iran's Ayatollah Khamenei issues a *fatwa* against the development and use of nuclear weapons, his sincerity is dismissed as transparent posturing. Likewise, when calls for policies of ethnic cleansing in Palestine appear, they too are brushed aside by Western nations, and their pliant press flacks.

Nor should it be forgotten that the U.S. violated the NPT by openly selling uranium to India, a non-signatory of the treaty. It also claimed Iraq was buying yellowcake uranium in Africa. Multiple efforts were made to discredit Iran during the Bush years. Not just that, but it is widely known that the Obama administration, having made peaceful overtures to Tehran, surreptitiously launched cyberattacks against it. But it is the mullahs who are not to be trusted, but perhaps rightly so, since their negotiating partner has acted so aggressively toward them.

Likewise, the West's double standards must be a grave insult to Iran. America happily obliges Israel's aberrant behavior. Tel Aviv can defy international accords and cloak its WMDs behind a "policy of deliberate ambiguity." It can

147

permanently derail efforts to create a nuclear-free Middle East. It can be the most violent and aggressive nation in the entire region. It can do all this and more, and no one in Washington will hold it to account because Israel can be trusted.

The arguments America makes against Tehran are transparently racist as well. Whether or not policymakers in Washington truly believe the Iranians are insane theocrats who wouldn't hesitate to start a nuclear war, we don't know. But we do know the tactic of claiming a people aren't ready for self-rule is by now a threadbare cliché of American history. After the Spanish-American War, the U.S. decided that Cuba was unfit for democracy. Haiti and Guatemala were similarly oppressed by maintaining the flimsy pretext that such unenlightened tribes must first benefit from our benevolent oversight before being permitted a modicum of self-rule.

When 16 American intelligence agencies hold no active nuclear weapons program, and that its foreign policy was "a posture of deterrence," why is it that Iran cannot be trusted with civilian nuclear power? Why is the trustworthy country the only one that has used nuclear weapons? Why is it Iran cannot be trusted when it hasn't launched a war in centuries? Why is the West to be trusted when it has not only attacked Iran on the sly, but openly invaded its eastern and western neighbors as well? When it is openly conceded that U.S. ally Israel has threatened its program and murdered its scientists, no doubt with Washington's approval? Why must the West be trusted when it has indicated on numerous occasions it is developing new and better nuclear weapons, and alarming rivals into action through aggressive military posturing? To be sure, the U.S. has admirably reduced its arsenal from 31,000 weapons in the late 1960s to fewer than 5,000 weapons today. However, more than a thousand are actually deployed. There is little talk internationally about whether these new plans violate or undermine NPT agreements.

The relationship between disarmament and nonproliferation is important. As the Women's International League for Peace and Freedom (WILPF) has insightfully noted, these are the bedrock principles of the NPT. They are interrelated in that the successful application of one will likely promote the success of the other. Likewise, a loose and negligent application of one will likely ensure the same in the other.

4. Be opaque but insist on transparency…
Part of your job as an international dissimulator will be to claim your rival is dangerously unhinged while simultaneously disguising instances when you behaved in precisely the same manner. A cursory glance at the NPT itself will be helpful in this regard.

148

What is rarely mentioned in western media is the bizarre discrepancy between the obligations of nuclear states and non-nuclear states under the NPT. Nuclear states don't have to comprehensively apply the safeguards to all of their sites. They can even except sites for reasons of national security. Non-Nuclear states have to make practically all of their facilities—even non-nuclear energy sites with the additional protocol—eligible for NPT safeguards.

In 2004 the U.S. adopted the Model Additional Protocol in a good-faith attempt to bring other NPT members on board. But they were of little consequence to the U.S. as it is a Nuclear Weapons State (NWS) and must adhere to less stringent protocols than Non-Nuclear Weapons States (NNWS).

Not only that, but the U.S. has, per its usual legalese, added two addendums to its adoption of the protocol, a corollary of the NPT's exemption for NWS members, called by the U.S. a National Security Exemption (NSE). It lets the U.S. permit access to sites, activities, information, and additional locations, at its own discretion. A second addition limits the use of environmental sampling and the number of inspectors who can access a site.

Before Congress ratified it, the additional protocol was tagged with a letter from the Senate Foreign Relations Committee (SFRC) that stipulated, among other notes, that the NSE would be used regularly and repeatedly. It also, in an almost comical provision, insisted that the President ensure security and counterintelligence training will have been completed for any sites it plans to declare to the IAEA. Hirsch, in his excellent reading, questions whether these extra conditions amount to "reservations" that would indicate that the U.S. was not accepting the same provisos as NNWS members.

Compare that with the incredible access required under the additional and comprehensive protocols. Imagine America being asked, as one Iranian government official complained, for concessions that included "permissions for reconnaissance flights over our country and that their inspectors can enter anywhere, even the presidential palace." (Note that an 'undeclared' American drone has already crashed in Iran.)

To date, some 72 members of the NPT have yet to adopt the additional protocols.

5. Never forget the big picture...
Finally, one must always remember the big picture. If you lose faith, and ask yourself why you are behaving like a boorish tyrant, just recall the treasures that lay just over the horizon. Keep your eyes on the prize; it's the geopolitical game that matters.

As regards the Middle East, there are long-term strategies afoot to divide and defang the Shiite Crescent that includes Lebanese, Syrian, and Iranian Shiite allies. Control over oil and gas fields in the Persian Gulf and Black and Caspian Seas are at stake, as is the fate of various competing pipeline projects of either Shiite or Sunni provenance. Dominion over energy will allow the U.S. and it's global partners to force most of the world to denominate their fuel purchases in dollars. This will sustain the buck's role as global reserve currency, which ensures that countries will buy up American debt, inadvertently funding its imperialist projects. And after all, nobody buys more oil than the U.S. military.

America will do all it can to assure that their Sunni proxies win these contests rather than the Moscow-backed Shiite coalition. In that regard, job one is preventing Iran from acquiring a nuclear weapon. The idea is pure anathema to Washington. Everyone knows a bomb buys leverage. And a Shiite Crescent with leverage deeply undercuts American hegemony in the region. Hence the fairly continuous project to demonize Tehran. In this game, controlling the media narrative is critical, and all forms of slander and calumny are fair game.

In any event, the talks have been extended until next July. It wouldn't require an extreme cynic to speculate that the seven-month extension serves U.S. interests by providing time for the ISIS debacle to play out, particularly in relation to Syria. Once the dust settles and the weather warms on that front, the West will be in a better position to decide whether it wants to opt for a military solution to its fabricated crisis with the Persians. To be sure, the international community—comprised of elites in Washington, New York, London, Paris and perhaps Riyadh—will affect the consternation of trusting but troubled Westerners, going to great lengths to persuade another rash and intemperate Muslim society to 'join the international community.' Once the media lapdogs paint a convincingly terrifying portrait of Iran for the edification of the masses, the wheels of war will begin to turn, legitimized by international sanction, prosecuted by the peacemakers.

(*Dissident Voice*, December 2, 2014)

First Causes, Last Rites
Nothing radicalizes like unprovoked violence

You may have noticed that nearly every essay or article emerging from the underfunded ghettos of leftist thinking in this country in the wake of a terrorist atrocity immediately offers a firm and frequently hysterical disclaimer that the author does not approve of the terrorist atrocity he will now discuss. This is necessary because the intelligentsia has conflated any form of self-criticism with condoning terror. It may be perfectly apt to reflect on "how good we are," as George W. Bush once mumbled. It may be admirable to haughtily meditate on the liberties enshrined in that hallowed scroll hidden in one of D.C.'s many tombs of culture. After all, "they hate us for our freedoms."

Yet we must not offer serious critique since it has not penetrated the propagandized skull that to condemn Hiroshima is not to condone Pearl Harbor. So we must all caveat our critiques lest we find our names in permanent exile along with arch whistleblowers Edward Snowden and Julian Assange. (A lesson from Assange: there's no better place to evade the long arm of empire than nestled inside one of its major capitals of financial fraud. Even Obama dare not sail a Predator over central London.)

The Hundred Years' War + Why They Hate Us
But were one to attempt some self-criticism, what would it look like? Perhaps something like this: Having uprooted one civil society after another in the Middle East, and having left roving caravans of jihadists in place of modern secular states, it shouldn't come as a surprise that Arab Muslims might be radicalized, might turn to Islam for theocratic justification, and might begin plotting terror attacks. Note the conclusion of just one victim. Afghan Mohammed Bismil, after his two brothers were killed by drone, said, "The only option I have is to pick up a Kalashnikov, RPG [rocket-propelled grenade] or a suicide vest to fight."

The terrorists who attack the West, such as in New York and Madrid and London and this year in Paris, are not doing so because they are wanton Islamic fanatics. It is because the West is at war with the Middle East—and they are fighting back.

The West has been at war with the Middle East for decades, if not quite a full century. It has been intensely interested in the region since shortly after oil was discovered in Persia in 1908. Since the British chopped up what was left of the

Ottoman Empire after World War I in British and French "mandates." (There was considerable Iraqi resistance to a United Nations mandate that seemed to them colonization by another name.) Since Henry Ford helped turn America into a automobile culture instead of public transportation society.

As America usurped Britain as the meddling superpower, it's thirst for petroleum grew. Fortunately for the States, Arab kings were a pliable clan, and were happy to lease off concessions on oil production to Western firms, who began draining the huge pools of black gold beneath the desert sands. The Middle East has 56 percent of the world's oil reserves and 40 percent of the world's gas reserves. During the Cold War, the Middle East a proving ground for the disparate ideologies East and West. Arab nationalism, embodied by Egypt's Gamal Abdel Nasser, was ultimately defeated by the West's model of enriching, arming and coddling desiccated Hashemite despots.

But forget ancient history. Let's just look at recent history.

Author and Islam critic extraordinaire Sam Harris suggests that Islam is the *ne plus ultra* of religious radicalizers. But what radicalizes far more easily than byzantine monotheism is unprovoked violence. A man whose family is droned out of existence by a missile from beyond the clouds doesn't need religion to make him thirst for vengeance. However, religion may often the ideological vehicle by which a sense of injustice, legitimate or not, is sublimated into a coherent worldview. By which an eye-for-an-eye attitude is consecrated.

Which perverted ideology has put more people in the ground this century, imperialism or Jihadism? Are there more makeshift tombstones for Christian soldiers or Muslim villagers? How many countries—all of them Muslim—has the U.S. bombed, invaded or occupied since just 1980? Here's Columbia University's Andrew Bacevich's list: "Iran (1980, 1987-1988), Libya (1981, 1986, 1989, 2011), Lebanon (1983), Kuwait (1991), Iraq (1991-2011, 2014-), Somalia (1992-1993, 2007-), Bosnia (1995), Saudi Arabia (1991, 1996), Afghanistan (1998, 2001-), Sudan (1998), Kosovo (1999), Yemen (2000, 2002-), Pakistan (2004-) and now Syria."

Many recent radical Islamic movements were born from the rubble of bungled Western intervention. Al-Qaeda, the Taliban, Hezbollah, and ISIS have all flourished in the shadow of American interventionism, whether direct or by proxy. The extremism of neoliberal capitalism, as Naomi Klein masterfully illuminated in *The Shock Doctrine*, uses moments of crisis and chaos to dispossess the defenseless and expand its power. It seems something similar happens in the bloody wake of U.S. invasions. Amid the collapsing scenery of civil society, extremists emerge to seize whatever territory and political power they can. Yet, for Middle Easterners, it is the original crime of Western intervention that, in the words of the Nuremberg judge Robert Jackson, wars of aggression are "the supreme international crime, in that they contain within them the evil of the whole."

Hezbollah leader Hassan Nasrallah expressed his views on American interventionism in the requisite maternal metaphor, "America, is in our view, the mother of terrorism and the origin of terrorism."

Osama bin Laden told us point blank: al Qaeda attacked us because we had troops in Islamic holy land, a major affront to fundamentalist Muslims, and because we backed Israel's brutal occupation of the Palestinian territories.

The Kouachi brothers and Ahmed Coulibaly said much the same thing before they shot dead an entire office of writers and editors and designers at Charlie Hebdo in Paris. Before authoring their own atrocities, they pointed to the larger crimes that motivated their own. They spoke of the Western massacres in the Middle East. They spoke of a precise vengeance. They said they were representing al Qaeda in Yemen, a sub-sect of Al Qaeda in the Arab Peninsula (aqap).

Not that it takes a radical Arab to oppose violence. Just look at a poll conducted by the Arab America Institute on the ISIS conflict, which found that:

"Strong majorities in every country favor U.S. policies that support a negotiated solution to the conflict, coupled with more support for Syrian refugees. Majorities in all countries oppose any form of U.S. military engagement (i.e., "no-fly zone," air strikes, or supplying advanced weapons to the opposition)."

After the U.S. reignited war in Iraq with its tawdry gallery of avaricious allies, Iranian moderate President Rouhani told the press corps at the U.N., "These bombings do not have any legal standing, so we can interpret them as an attack."

Exhausted from acting as the West's supplicant, the Palestinian Authority's Mahmoud Abbas finally relinquished the ridiculous pretext that Israel is interested in peace and that the U.S. is a neutral arbiter. He took the Palestinian cause to both the United Nations General Assembly and the International Criminal Court (ICC) at The Hague, groping for some avenue of relief from the prison camp of Gaza and Bantustan reality of the West Bank.

All of these facts are flung into the dustbin of history unexamined. We are instead offered a series of feckless platitudes to spare us the trouble of self-reflection. They hate us for our freedoms, we are told. There is surely a fundamentalist tendency in Muslim communities that find our self-indulgent consumerism repellent. That is a theme that runs beneath the banner of Occidentalism, the concept that the East reviles the West largely for its infidelism—its shameless rejection of Allah's diktats. There is plenty of this attitude festering in jihadist conclaves, but that isn't why they attacked us in 2001, or in Paris last month.

(*Dissident Voice*, February 12, 2015)

Tyranny's Toolkit
Torture, aid, and 'development' go hand in hand in hand

Citigroup concedes we live in an age of "plutonomy" and "the rest." During the mortgage meltdown, the free market apostles of Wall Street beseech the state to intervene. No less than Princeton University declares the United States to be an oligarchy. And French economist Thomas Piketty publishes 700 pages of data sets claiming that capitalism systematically exacerbates inequality. What was once a trickle of evidence has morphed from a freshet into a flood. Every month, it seems, new reports surface condemning the capitalist system and the fraudulent models of democracy that disguise its excesses. Disguise what Marxist professor Vijay Prashad has called the "Davos mentality" of elite capital, a reference to the annual World Economic Forum held in the rarefied air of a Swiss ski resort; presided over by global elites, the setting itself betraying the elitism of its program. One needn't look much farther than a hotel address to divine the obvious nature of the sessions.

Earlier this year, Daniel Wickham of *Left Foot Forward* <u>analyzed</u> President Obama's 2014 <u>budget</u> and discovered that the United States privileges aid to countries that practice torture. Among this confection of noxious governments are Israel, Egypt, Pakistan and Uganda. Some would no doubt argue that correlation is not causality, or that in fact our aid to these serial violators of the United Nations Convention Against Torture is intended to foster the very democratic reforms that will surely stem the tide of such abuses. This was essentially the argument made by the Clinton administration when it awarded China Most Favored Nation status as a trading partner despite its myriad human rights violations. Mere interaction with the West would be ennobling enough to transform all of Asia, the argument seemed to say.

This kind of self-interested casuistry has its roots in American exceptionalism— the notion that we alone are enlightened by democratic values and, as such, are obliged to impart our values to the world—whether they want them or not (and perhaps with a zeal bordering on the messianic). We don't always sail into Tokyo harbor with cannonade tilted landward, as Commodore Perry did in 1854 bearing a list of grievances from President Fillmore. Today the preferred method is economic policy. Now the WTO and the IMF are the battering rams we employ to bring down the walls of emerging Jerichoes, of ambitious young nations hoping to forge some kind of industrial self-sufficiency. Much easier, if more nuanced, to co-opt venal leadership—and there's always a Judas tucked away in the presidential cabinet—and persuade them to accept the supply-side economic program on which every IMF loan is conditioned and toward which every WTO expedient is aimed. (Note the "partners" of Open Ukraine, the foundation established by Ukraine's new puppet Prime Minister Arseniy Yatsenyk. They include NATO, the U.S. Department of State, the National Endowment for Democracy, and the rest of the usual suspects.)

Historical Groupthink

To inoculate oneself against this rather insidious line of reasoning, it's helpful to have a look at some of the critical U.S. post-war planning documents. Noam Chomsky has done the necessary shovel work, unearthing a documentary record that illuminates the common—in both senses of the word—ambitions that figure so obliquely in the state-sanctioned history, and so grossly in actuality. Namely, the wish for empire. And once attained, forever more empire, world without end.

To judge from actions rather than the odd rhetorical flourish, the purpose of U.S. foreign policy has always been power and profits, namely employing the considerable military and economic might of the nation as a revolutionary vanguard for U.S. capital. As Marx and others have long recognized, capitalists are ever in need of fresh and lucrative markets in order to boost profits. If, through endless donations and influence peddling, capital has come to control the democratic apparatus of our nominally republican state, why not use the might of the state to produce the markets you need?

President Woodrow Wilson put it plainly in his private journal, "Since trade ignores national boundaries and the manufacturer insists on having the world as a market, the flag of his nation must follow him, and the doors of the nations which are closed against him must be battered down." Likewise, "Concessions obtained by financiers must be safeguarded by ministers of state, even if the sovereignty of unwilling nations be outraged in the process."

To that end, former Secretary of State George Kennan outlined in a Policy Planning Study of 1948 how we must shift our attitude away from compassionate or empathic mentalities toward, "dealing in straight power concepts," and dispense with "unreal objectives such as human rights, the raising of the living standards, and democratization...The less we are hampered by idealistic slogans, the better."
Kennan was perhaps naïve in overlooking the essential value of "idealistic slogans" in a pseudo-democratic state, the better to dupe and distract a poorly educated populace and quiet the sometimes restive conscience of the rabble. Clinton didn't overlook this when he hailed "humanitarian intervention" in justifying wars of aggression, as well the edifying influence of trade in imparting Western values to benighted Asian nations. The Carter administration was perhaps a precedent setter for Clinton, authorizing aid to "gross violators" of human rights in Latin America on the premise that such aid would help ennoble savage South American tyrannies.

156

The most relevant statement by Kennan in relation to Wickham's article comes from a briefing for Latin American ambassadors in 1950, when he acknowledged that, "we should not hesitate before police repression by the local government...It is better to have a strong regime in power than a liberal government..." Notably one that might instance a regional outbreak of independence, the worst-case scenario for Western capital seeking absolute advantage in defenseless industrial backwaters.

Foreign Aid—Abetting Rogue Behavior

In light of these policy prescriptions, is it any wonder that we privilege aid to undemocratic governments that torture their citizens? That crush unions and savagely repress democratic protest? See Colombia for a model example of the former and Bahrain for the latter. Forget that we signed onto the U.N. Convention Against Torture in 1994. We pay nominal acquiescence to international law on the best of days, and actively undermine mine typically. We only supported the establishment of the World Criminal Court with the caveat that U.S. would be exempt from any of its prosecutions, a position that essentially delegitimized the institution and ensured that war criminals (convicted *in absentia*) like George H.W. Bush and George W. Bush are left to live in lavish comfort, ignorant of the plight of the desolate families and mutilated peoples their policies gifted to the Middle East.

The list of aid recipients is a gag-worthy collection of pirates and thieves. Heading the list is none other than Israel, the country that ejected 750,000 Palestinians from their homes, wiped out some 500 villages—as recent Nakba Day protests reminded discomfited Israeli hawks—and has established an apartheid state that economically strangles Gaza by denying basic needs and goods to besieged Palestinians there, and has built—in fits of fanaticism hard to fathom—more than 400 miles of apartheid walls separating precious Israeli settlers from displaced, dispossessed, and dehumanized Palestinian families. The latest farcical attempt at peace talks, this version presided over by court jester John Kerry, collapsed when it was discovered that Israel, just as negotiations got underway, authorized some 13,000 new settlements in the West Bank, on land legally but in on other sense possessed by Palestine. Meanwhile, President Benjamin Netanyahu intones on American television that, "Israelis *desperately* want peace." In a different kind of desperation, the Palestinian Authority successfully pressed for a degree of recognition in the United Nations and threatened to bring charges against Israel in the World Court. President Barack Obama, abiding by the Israeli sycophancy required of all U.S. leaders, decries this development, claiming that the issues must be settled between "Israelis and Palestinians." In the last year, both the U.N. and the Public Committee against Torture in Israel reported that Israeli military regularly subject Palestinian children to torture, sexual assault, and the delightful habit of imprisoning Palestinian youth in cages during winter. Later the report from the PCTI was

157

amended to note that those it kept in cages were not necessarily Palestinians, a useful revision lest Israeli be perceived as having an ethnic bias. Better to be indiscriminately cruel.

A Nefarious Model of Development
Torture is the tip of the spear of repression. Unrepressed, most informed populations would resist the imposition of Israeli-style oppression or U.S.-style capitalism, the latter of which privileges Western business interests over emerging domestic industries—indeed insists on replacing domestic development with "foreign direct investment", or FDI. Instead of producing, say, soybeans and maize for domestic consumption, cheaply grown and inexpensively consumed, Western interests, usually as a loan or trade condition, insist on the erasure of agricultural tariffs that then result in replacing domestic crops with a) a suitable export crop like Arabica coffee beans or cotton or rice, to be shipped to tony First World markets and cafes; and often b) insisting on the introduction of "sustainable" seed varieties, such as those only produced by American agribusiness like Monsanto, causing subsistence farmers to sink into debt in an effort to license those varieties—and all the weed and pest management inputs required to sustain a harvest. In the former instance, the government must take out expensive loans to import Western foodstuffs it once produced for itself. These goods are dumped on the country by Western agribusiness since they were unsalable domestically, thereby allowing Western agribusiness to collect a tidy profit from the sale, and for Western finance to collect on the compound interest from the loan extended to the developing nation in order for it to purchase the food.

Thus, while the West profits on both sides of the import-export equation, the developing country loses on both fronts. Internal development is crushed and external debts soar. Michael Chossudovsky of Global Research has excellently illustrated this model in relation to Ethiopia.

What emerging nation would accept such conditions? None but one that has been bought off at the highest levels. Add to that dire agricultural prescription a raft of additional austerities on the manner of reduced domestic subsidies and import tariffs, heightened utility costs, currency devaluation, and higher interest rates. These are recipes for misery.

Taming the Rabble
To implement the process, the IMF must find suitable quislings within the local government. They in turn must implement austerity but also move to repress the popular outrage those policies are sure to inspire. "Stability" is the byword of popular repression, and why President Obama supports a regressive military coup d'état in Egypt, as well the coup that deposed independent-minded Manuel Zelaya of Honduras. Zelaya had instituted a 60-percent minimum-wage increase in a

nation with 70-percent poverty. Naturally, the business class was outraged. Not long afterward, Zelaya joined the Bolivarian Alternative for the Americas (ALBA), a fatal move that presaged his U.S.-backed removal. Just this week Zelaya was chased from the Honduran Parliament with tear gas after he and a group of supporters had entered unwelcome. There's nothing quite so unsettling for an illegitimate government than to glimpse the ghost of the populist it deposed. According to the United Nations, Hondurans are now enduring a wave of repression, and the country has now become the "murder capital of the world".

Neither of these coups evoked even a word of protest from the noble mandarins on Pennsylvania Avenue. Nor is the White House affronted by the recent putsch in Ukraine. Quite the opposite—the White House initiated it, infamously fomenting rebellion with Victoria Nuland's "$5 billion" investment. It got what it paid for—a fascist-inflected coup that emplaced right-wing nationalists with Nazi sympathies nation's cabinet, notably in charge of the security apparatus, among other sinecures. Yet when a self-professed socialist like Hugo Chavez is legitimized by the ballot, ejects the IMF and declares his nation's independence from international finance, and tackles poverty as though it were a serious issue— every alarm in the Presidio sounds. Cue the Kennedy-esque psy-ops and CIA subversion, *modus operandi* of Washington subterfuge.

This is all perfectly coincident with the Cold War policy of considering the establishment of a communist government in Latin America as an act of aggression. Neither communism nor terrorism is the target—it is independence that shivers the imperial spine. Point being, we ought to register astonishment only if our leading recipients of aid are not serial torturers. The time when America could be plausibly credited with good intentions is long past. The best interests of Third-World peasants are antithetical to those of corporate multinationals—at least according to the latter's neoliberal creed. Hence aid flows to the fascist rather than the democrat, the better to line the coffers of capital through the repression of popular will, anywhere and everywhere it rears its medusan head. Indeed, this is one of the central reasons Israel receives three billion dollars annually: because the soul of Palestinian solidarity cannot be maimed, tamed, eradicated, or otherwise disappeared. And that is the eternal dilemma of neoliberalism—how to best shatter the human spirit. These are the night sweats of capital, or to borrow a phrase from Graham Greene, one of the Cold War's best chroniclers, they are rather "…the anxieties beyond the reach of a tranquilizer."

(*CounterPunch*, May 22, 2014)

Part Two
Domestic Policy: Empty Gestures

"We must make our choice. We may have democracy, or we may have wealth
concentrated in the hands of a few, but we can't
have both."

Judge Louis Brandeis

American Twilight
America faces the emergence of a multipolar world—and a check on its self-delusion

Few nations better embody the sense of humorless infallibility than the United States and Israel. Righteous. Infallible. Heedless. It's no surprise these two practitioners of state terror (a concept they both deny) are held to be the world's greatest threats to peace. Indeed, thanks in part to those two military juggernauts, our new century has been little more than a chronicle of extremism—imperial, Islamist, neoliberal. And all the strains seem to have converged after the atrocity of the twin towers.

Social geographer David Harvey has noted how, after September 11th, George Bush made numberless speeches about America's unexampled role in the world. He could have launched an Interpol-style police investigation into the atrocity. That would have meant bringing criminals to justice without resort to the heavy weaponry and their inevitable corollary, the slaughter of innocents. How banal. He could have recognized Al Qaeda wasn't a country, but a militant gang of religious ultras. How unimaginative. Instead Bush and his grotesque cabal of ideologues converted their victim status into a mandate to broaden the scope of American imperialism. Notice here how Bush interpreted 9/11 as an assault on our freedoms rather than what it was—a brutal riposte to our foreign policy.

Bush rhetoricalized it then as an "opportunity to further freedom's triumph over its age-old foes." He intoned, with his absurd gravitas, that "the United States welcomes its responsibility to lead in this great mission." Note the hubris. A mission to expand freedoms—self-declared. The "responsibility" to lead the mission—self-appointed. Napoleon crowning himself emperor. The world is left to observe and applaud and approve. After all, these were the "universal values of the human spirit," or so said the emperor as he was issuing his holy writ.

Bush's pomposity naturally included the supernatural. Where else did he unearth the notion of infallibility but from the pulpit of fundamentalism? Like plenty of presidents before him, he invoked Yahweh. This clues us to the origin of American exceptionalism. Is it anything other than a secularized version of the chosen people narrative of Judaism? Draw a direct line from the Torah to the New Testament, transmuted through the seductive prose of the King James Bible, ingested like "daily bread" by millions of Americans for two centuries. There's the bloodline. The lineal path.

As a mouthpiece of exceptionalism, Obama is no less committed than Bush. He may even invoke our special status more frequently. He mentions the deity less. But he shares with his predecessor the belief that, "millions in the Middle East plead in silence for their liberty." If that is your belief, and you are emboldened by a sense of your own eminence, then why not occupy Iraq, invade Afghanistan, obliterate Libya? Why not destabilize Syria and Ukraine? Why not drone bomb Yemen and Pakistan and Somalia? Why not permit a little housekeeping in Gaza?

Uprising in the Districts

But the world is tired of this world-historical insolence. This needless contempt for cooperation. The portents of change are all there. Witness the 30-year fossil fuel deal cut between Russia and China, to be denominated perhaps in petro-rubles. Watch BNP Paribas call for de-dollarization. Note Europe's distaste for sanctions against its Slavic fuel provider. See the surprise electoral wins of anti-austerity parties such as Podemos in Spain and Syriza in Greece. Then look at the latest news: Unable or unwilling to pose a military challenge to the almighty American behemoth, the formidable economic block known as the BRICS (Brazil, Russia, India, China, South Africa) have chosen a different tack: the launch of the BRICS bank, an end-run around the U.S.-dominated Bretton Woods institutions. The BRICS represent some 41 percent of the people on earth, but comprise 11 percent of IMF votes. No wonder Brazil's Dilma Rousseff chides them.

The BRICS will loan for third-world development and economic stabilization. They will lend in their own currencies—rubles, rupees, renminbi. They may invite the other luckless victims of Western imperialism to join the party. Mexico, Argentina, Indonesia. Hopefully the BRICS will attach fewer and less extractive conditionalities to their loans. Otherwise, the world will simply be exchanging one jailer for another.

If left economists can be believed, this is a serious challenge to the cornerstone of American empire—its fiat currency. As owner of the global reserve currency, the U.S. can print money, flog bonds, and finance its holy wars. Yet in the wake of this obvious threat to the dollar hegemony, the West is comically blind to its own frailty. Indeed the IMF, according to a recent study, has been *adding* conditions to its loan facilities, despite the PR whitewashing about a lending rethink.

But this is no surprise. Like an aging thief in a B-movie telling his girl, "Just one more job. Then I'm out!" the IMF bankers are conducting a last-ditch smash-and-grab amid the collapsing scenery of global economics. Under cover of recession. Reminiscent of the ethnic cleansing carried out under cover of the NATO bombing of Kosovo in the late nineties. Seventy-eight straight days of purification. Now the bankers' cutpurse spree draws to a close. At least the solidarity of the BRICS suggests as much. Such a simple thing—solidarity. If only American workers would acquaint themselves with the concept.

This is good news. A multipolar world is better than the unipolar one we've been living in. Counterweights are a hedge against extremism. Without them—watch out. Look at America run amok even as the Soviet rubble still smoked. Look at Israel, militarily unopposed in the Middle East. No one dare attack it for fear of nuclear extermination. How does it behave in light of this unspoken sanction? With total impunity, from total extremism. Naturally.

Perhaps a BRICS wall will provide the same kind of cautionary check that the Berlin Wall used to and reign in the frothing imperialism of the world's self-proclaimed policeman. Perhaps it will slow the rabid extremism of the U.S. deputies in Tel Aviv. Force the West back to the table of rational discourse. We need that check. Not a new empire, but a counterpoint to ours. Like Wall Street finance, we've proven ourselves incapable of self-policing. Capitalism seems to encourage indiscipline. We must be somehow made to respect our boundaries. Our recent history is nearly a personification of Christopher Hitchens statement that, "There's always some mediocre jerk who knows what's best for you." Just think. Free market neoliberalism in Mesopotamia. A reconstituted Baathist-free army in Baghdad. Puppet kleptocracy in Kabul. A police state in the Sinai. An unelected human-rights trampling cabal in Honduras. A rabidly anti-poor capital class in Caracas. Nazi sympathizers in Kiev. Where haven't we subtly offered our unsolicited advice and then provided the funds and guns to bring it to be? But times have changed. A specter is rising on the peripheries of empire. The call rings out: BRICS of the world, unite!

(*Countercurrents*, July 29, 2014)

Bonfire of the Liberties

For a second year in a row, Obama's stealth legislation unhands our claims to liberty

Walter Lippmann, one of the godfathers of public relations, once noted that in a totalitarian state you could control the populace by force, but in a democracy force wasn't an option—you had to control them through opinion. You had to "manufacture opinion." While the role of forcibly controlling the demos has been insidiously extended by Washington, opinion continues to be the primary means by which we are soothed and cajoled, frightened and enflamed, and sometimes bludgeoned into believing Washington behaves on our behalf, a paragon of selfless service.

Fewer and fewer believe this sinister imposture. Originally a government-funded project, the Internet has dramatically expanded access to dissident literatures, texts by radical leftists and musket-wielding right-wingers among them, as well as the burgeoning industry of conspiracy theory. All of these novel opinions flooding unchecked into the public consciousness have destabilized Lippmann's concept of manufactured opinion. Slowly, our tightly knit groupthink is coming unraveled, even as our enervated liberal class finally concedes that their conquering Hawaiian hero has not, in the end, been all that heroic—oh, how the house of cards crumbles. And so, just as conventional warfare no longer provides clear-cut victories, neither do the blandishments of the State Department necessarily produce media consensus, however much they are robotically repeated by *The New York Times* and *Washington Post*. But, as we are rapidly learning, the mere existence of available alternatives does not guarantee they will be sought, found, and utilized by the greater majority.

Stealth Legislation

Case in point: the constriction of our rights continues unabated. The only difference now is that greater stealth must be employed to dodge the telescope of those in the know. That's why on the final holiday weekend of the year, when the public's political interest was at a low ebb, President Obama signed a five-year extension of H.R. 5949, better known by as the Foreign Intelligence Surveillance Act, or by its inimical acronym FISA.

As viewers of CNN and Fox News were being regaled with last-ditch efforts to dodge the farcical fiscal cliff, another violation of our civil liberties was slipping its invisible net over a dozing population. For those who question the bill, such as Senator Ron Wyden (D-Ore.), national security and state secrets are instantly invoked as an unanswerable response. Craven flag-wavers tremble in fright at the grainy footage of machete jihadists in distant lands.

Bon Voyage, Fourth Amendment

Now with continued and unregulated access to all of our international communications—imagine bays of Homeland Security lackeys combing through our blathering emails and inane cell phone transcripts under flickering lights in giant data-mining factories—we have effectively buried the fourth amendment beneath our slavish surrender to fear of the foreign. No longer must the government provide "probable cause" to ransack our "papers and effects," at least when it comes to talking to people beyond our sacred borders.

Adios, Habeas Corpus

The timing of the signing is no coincidence. On December 31st of last year, Obama signed the horrid National Defense Authorization Act, better known by its insidious acronym NDAA, which authorized the government to indefinitely detain Americans at sites like Guantanamo without trial. On that night *habeas corpus* became a habeas corpse. This New Year's Eve we were all rendered suspect by our government. Instead of employing the singular zealotry of a McCarthy to forage through our effects in search of Marxist sympathies, we now employ invisible armies of data analysts to separate the patriotic wheat from the dissident chaff, suspicious Arab sympathizers from sycophant regime-change hawks. Again, the abandonment of privacy is said to be our only recourse if we want to be safe.

Manufactured Distraction

Instead of creating the roiling public protests it ought to, the FISA extension—just like its cousin the NDAA—is lost in the media clamor over the cliff and Obama's trumpeting very slightly higher tax rates on just over 0.6 percent of the population and solemnly confirming the "bitter pill" of billions in cuts to social programs. Some victory.

But fatuous distractions like the fiscal cliff are necessary to distract the populace from doing its due diligence—digging through Internet caches in search of non-imperial newspeak. But before we have the chance to unearth the stray leftist blog, we are bombarded with news of an impending debt ceiling, a madhouse of intransigent Republicans clamoring for political blood, and our gentle defender, President Obama, summoned to the scene to shepherd the nation past the threat of a work stoppage and into the clutches of deficit hawks who would savage their own to salvage their principles—namely that the rusting planks of the New Deal must be chopped apart in order to impose 'necessary' hardship on those who might turn to government in time of need.

Paternalism Decried, Big Brother Applied

The irony of the alternating techniques of stealth and distraction is that they uproot with one hand what they implant with the other. Political theatrics decry the paternalistic impulses of a caretaker government, even as a clandestine government embeds paternalistic surveillance programs they insist are required to save us from jihadists. So which is it? Are we adult enough to fend for ourselves, or are we eternal dependents on the benevolence of a stranger state?

Perhaps a conservative response might be, "But these two are not the same. On the one hand, we cannot possibly protect ourselves from terror without the overarching umbrella of state protection. However, we can guard against poverty, debt, unemployment, and malnutrition simply by taking responsibility for ourselves."

While the former has a grain of merit, it falters in the detail: while strong borders controls are essential, neither wiretapping nor indefinite detention have been shown to be bulwarks against terror, and in fact they can be argued to have invoked the psychological terror of perpetual surveillance.

The latter, however—the idea that we need no social safety net—is thoroughly without merit—the notion that we can all feasibly overcome the circumstances of our birth, the inconstancy of justice, our unequal genetic patrimony, and the hazards of chance to achieve our dearest dreams. This is a simple fatuity, unproven and unserious. The unlucky need help; the lucky should provide it. Is there a human morality that dispenses with this basic proviso? Unlikely, although the acolytes of the Ayn Rand cult of personal responsibility are doing their damndest to test its baseless hypothesis.

It was Benjamin Franklin who railed that, "those who would give up essential liberty to purchase a little temporary safety, deserve neither…" To that I would add 'illusory safety.' As we are interminably distracted by fears for our security, we forget the freedoms that those distractions are so often designed to remove. As the national pulse fails again to beat a drum of protest at their removal, we have only ourselves to blame. When we are one day cuffed for some untoward remark or glib gesture, we might then recall with nostalgia a time when speech was free, debate was civil, and the enemy was not so near.

(*Dissident Voice*, January 16, 2013)

Commiserator in Chief
Obama delivers more heartfelt words, but promises nothing concrete

So much for the radicalized Obama that liberals fantasized about before the election. As that comical fiction had it, a triumphant President, seizing upon a second popular mandate (that thunderous 29% of the vote) and no longer besieged by fears of being a "one-termer," would morph into a reincarnation of FDR, flinging progressive policy initiatives left and right, overwhelming bewildered, musket-wielding Tea Partiers, brandishing the executive order like a pre-flood Nixon, and finally, like a moulting cicada on the tree of liberty, would emerge as that paladin of progressive values we always knew he was.

I think we can now declare that chimera DOA. Sunday night, delivering a moving homily to residents of Newtown, Connecticut, Obama wrapped the tragedy of last week's senseless school shooting in the prose poetry of the King James Bible, imparting a sense of personal angst and concern that neither George Bush or Mitt Romney could summon in their finest hours. Heartfelt, stirring, unfeigned.

As he unfolded his narrative of parenthood, speaking of the anxiety parents feel as their children move into a fearsome and uncertain world, you could sense the building anticipation—this was a sea change moment. A tangible federal initiative was imminent. A policy worthy of the pain of the Newtown families. The momentous moment arrived: "Over the next few weeks..."

And then—nothing. A tepid promise to work with Washington to address the problem. No clarion call for an assault weapons ban. No angry declaration that the massacres on his watch would stop—this was the fourth. In fact, he quite deliberately shied away from uttering the dreaded term 'gun control.' Nothing, it seems, not the shooting of Gabrielle Giffords in Tucson, not the cinema slaughter in Aurora, Colorado, not the murder of twenty children in Newtown, is enough to stimulate Obama to challenge the NRA and handcuff our runaway gun culture.

Everyone else was up in arms. Even New York mayor Michael Bloomberg angrily declared on "Meet the Press," "It's time for the president to stand up and lead." Governor Daniel Malloy of Connecticut cast a spotlight on the hundreds of rounds of ammunition the killer still had in hand as police closed in. Some Democrats called for the renewal of the assault weapons ban. The gun lobby was notably silent in the din of calls for stronger. If there was ever a time to seize the bully pulpit, it was now. Instead, administration officials counseled caution, reminding the public of the fatuous "fiscal cliff" negotiations that are consuming all of the president's time and energy. Expecting quick and decisive action was simply setting oneself up for disappointment.

This is par for the course. After promising to renew the assault weapons ban during his first presidential run, Obama dropped the issue once installed in the palace of power. He signed legislation that allowed guns to be carried in national parks and avoided using his presidential authority to end imports of semi-automatic weapons. Obama even turned down stiffer rules on background checks put forward by the Justice Department in the wake of the Giffords shooting. Evidently, he was worried the issue would weaken his re-election odds. The list goes on.

Better to expend one's political capital fighting for a tepid tax increase on the obscenely rich, and through sleight of hand deliver up the core planks of the New Deal to the altar of deficit reduction. Better this then to respond to relentless appeals for stronger safety measures. Words, it seems, come cheap, even if lives do not.

Thankfully, there is a rising chorus of voices on both sides of the aisles—in the Senate, two pro-gun Democrats and a Florida Republican agreed—demanding a legislative answer to the most recent tragedy. Hopefully, it will be these voices that prod the laconic president into action. One would at least expect a bi-partisan ban on extended ammunition clips—an important but woefully inadequate step by a political class perpetually afraid of offending well-funded lobbies, however demented their demands.

For venal politicians, preserving power is vital—much more so than the loss of life. Rhetoric will cover the tracks of their cupidity, but losing an election is hard to hide. For gun lobbyists, retaining the right to the implements of slaughter is a far more exigent cause than public safety. Better to be well armed in the Wild West than disarmed in a pacified society.

(*Open Democracy*, December 19, 2012)

Crumbs from the Table
A fresh spate of wealthy summits promises to change…very little

If you've been reading the financial news lately, you may have noticed that two much-celebrated summits have taken place on either side of the Atlantic. A California conference organized by the Koch brothers was held in the secured enclave of St. Regis Monarch Bay luxury resort. The conference was called, "American Courage: Our Commitment to a Free Society," featured a half-dozen Congressmen and an overtly political agenda, namely taking Congress for the right and stonewalling another Clinton presidency. One comical session was entitled, "Over-Criminalization: Removing Legal Barriers to Opportunity." One doubts this was about the numberless minorities collared in our metastasizing prison system growth industry, and rather about the further decriminalization of white-collar crime of the Wall Street variety. Other panels and breakout sessions included themes on shifting the energy narrative (a tried and true right-wing skill set applied to a topic of planetary import), and defending free speech, i.e., ensuring political donations are legally synonymous with individual oral utterances.

Interesting that the event instituted a no cell-phone policy, such was the delicate nature of the discussions on offer. The Koch brothers correctly understand that public knowledge of their high-level planning sessions would provoke outrage from across the liberal spectrum. Liberals, on the other hand, seem to prefer the spotlight. That's because their task in the doctrinal system of extreme capitalism to the convince populations that there are well-intentioned plutocrats willing to defend the little guy against the rabid machinations of the Koch clan. Classic good cop/bad cop. That's why—when liberals come together to enthuse about empowerment—they do it in the most visible of places.

Their rendezvous was held in London, where the prestigious conference called, "Inclusive Capitalism" included the likes of notable outsiders such as Bill Clinton, the mayor of London, Christine Lagarde of the International Monetary Fund (IMF), Prince Charles, and someone called, "Lady de Rothschild." In other words, this was a conference produced, hosted, and attended by insiders—those who've already been included in a global system of dispossession that takes from populations that cannot defend their wealth and gives to small communities of the already-rich who can afford to raid that wealth. Hence the paradigm of the enriched rich and impoverished poor. Marxist geographer David Harvey, among others, calls the process, "accumulation by dispossession." Others, conditioned to avoid Marx like the plague and unthinkingly accept any adage from Adam Smith, call it "capitalism."

As Carol Hanisch notes, the "What We Believe" section of the conference agenda states that the group is nobly pursuing ways to, "improve capitalism so that it creates long-term value that sustains human endeavour without harming the stakeholders and broader environment critical to its success." Herein we see one of the contradictions of capitalism writ small. Stakeholders directly benefit by excluding the majority of people from the club of super-wealth that was generated by that very exclusion. Likewise they prosper from the exploitation of the natural environment free of restrictions on the degree of degradation they can inflict on the environment. One country combines both forms of exploitation in a single vile case study: the Congo. Are the coltan mines of the Congo being responsibly mined or, better yet, responsibly not mined? The entire nation is engulfed in a civil war sustained by the mobile phone market, for which the coltan is essential.

Yet sophists like Clinton and philanthropists like Rothschild would have us believe these system that produces these inequities can be modestly reformed and thereby create a general prosperity open to all. Inclusive of even the Congolese. Yet as Hanisch perfectly put it, "if capitalism (ownership of the means of the production and distribution by the few) were "inclusive" it would be communism (ownership of the means of production and distribution by those who actually do the work of producing and distributing)."

In other words, the inclusion of economically disenfranchised workers in a more equitable marketplace is dependent on the generosity of the capitalists. Hence the conference is little more than a call for greater philanthropy by sympathetic elites. Yet their sympathy has a limit—the threshold at which capitalism itself is challenged. That is a line elite wealth won't cross. The conference organizers cleverly concede the flaw in the ointment, Milton Freedman's astonishingly honest admission that the "social responsibility" of business is to grow profits. Business guru Peter Drucker was of much the same mind. Against this embarrassingly unsympathetic view of capital's role, the attendees thus suggest that, "in light of growing public resentment toward finance and business, many argue that business should actively assume a much broader role in society that addresses the demands of other key stakeholders, alongside their duty to create shareholder value." This suggests that the shareholder value—created by exploiting externalized populations—can be protected and enhanced even as that exploitation is reduced. How, exactly?

Notably, the solutions are to come from within. The conference examines how, "…companies are tackling the challenge of establishing corporate cultures and good business practices at all levels of their organisations." This is a typical nod to the discredited notion that corporations can police themselves. Was not the predatory lending and derivative-driven mortgage collapse of 2008 a sufficient case study in the perils of deregulation, of trusting companies to practice self-discipline? It was attendee Bill Clinton whose deregulatory legislation (including the Glass-Steagall Act and the Commodity Futures Modernization Act of 2000, as well as relaxed lending standards for economically disadvantaged communities)

170

helped precipitate the collapse. His henchman and fellow attendee, Lawrence Summers, revealingly delivered a lecture on, "Which type of capitalism" best builds social value. Note, much like the public option was slid under the table during the healthcare reform debates five years ago, alternative to capitalism itself are not broached by Summers.

Notice, too, how the conference emphasizes vagaries including "economic value", "solve economic problems" and "create social value." The groups appear to stop short of the quick solution—much higher wages—and the long term one—worker owned companies. Probably because that is tantamount to socialism.

The solution is evidently to convince CEOs, investors, and asset managers to ignore short-term profits in favor on long-term profits. In other words, brainwash hedge funds, academic and foundation endowments, mutual funds, pension funds, and other institutional investors to tell their shareholders that they'll now have to wait a lot longer for their profits. Why? Presumably so that the jobless vagrants increasingly inhabiting our city streets don't decide to riot.

Again, back to relying on the benevolence of wealthy strangers. Is this the best we can do? It probably is within the capitalist system, barring a massively mobilized and eternally vigilant public—a prospect that appears vanishingly small given the apathy of Americans. But perhaps Europe, where protest movements are stronger, perduring, educated, and radicalized, can lead the way not simply to temporary reforms in capitalism like those of the 1930s which were rolled back over time by the social ancestors of the attendees of this conference, but of alternative economic systems altogether. Comically, and as a fitting coda to the conference's feckless ambitions, it was sponsored by the Rockefeller Foundation, a paragon of philanthropist action, and a group called, "Gatsby" that works to create agricultural markets for the private sector in Third World communities. Perhaps as a result of "Inclusive Capitalism," the next time Gatsby and Rockefeller clink glasses on New Year's Eve, you might be happily employed to carry away their empties.

(*Dissident Voice*, June 29, 2014)

Divided We Fall—A Tale of Two Realities
The American economy continues to slide, but there's plenty of optimism at the top

"Teach these boys and girls nothing but Facts. Facts alone are wanted in life."
These lines from schoolmaster Thomas Gradgrind open Charles Dickens' *Hard Times*, which satirized the quantitative ethics of 19th century utilitarians. The simple premise of utilitarianism pioneered by Jeremy Bentham was that an action or policy should be judged by a single criterion: whether or not it contributed to the greatest happiness of the greatest number. It can feel, living in the early 21st century, that our leaders are operating on a principle of anti-utility, seeking the greatest happiness of the numerical few. The Washington establishment would dispute the truth of this claim, but then, as three examples will suggest, elites answer to a separate reality. To paraphrase Scott Fitzgerald, let me tell you about the very rich. Their facts are different from yours and mine.

The C-Suite and Main Street
Earlier this month, March job figures coughed up a slim volume of 85,000 new jobs, and the unemployment rate ticked down to 7.6 percent from 7.7 percent in February. As happens every month in this comical pantomime, the facts are shotgunned into the public consciousness by venerable propagandists like *The New York Times* and *Washington Post*, and the semi-articulate cable networks. The State Department then steps forward to impart a few rosy sentiments, although providing the necessary cautionary language lest our optimism overwhelm us.

The positivity of the official interpretation of the jobs report was belied by the 663,000 more citizen-consumers who slipped behind the black curtain of idle despair (47 percent of them women), not even bothering to seek work. According to Mike Gimbel, an analyst for socialist weekly *Workers World*, adding the decrease in the active labor force to the number of workers with insufficient part-time work, the unemployment rates skyrockets north of 20 percent. Nearly 90 million American adults are now out of the labor market, a new threshold of despair. (That's nine times the number of unemployed at the height of the Great Depression, when there were only 123 million people in the country.) The jobs report complemented the specter of the sequester or a grand bargain still swirling overhead, promising to slice four trillion dollars from the economy over the next decade.

Yet a recent *Financial Times* survey of 400 global senior executives reports new optimism among business leaders, who project economic and industry improvements in the next six months. This peculiar optimism of corporate

172

leadership, even amid the collapsing scenery of American society, is revealing on two levels. First, it evinces the degree to which Fortune 500s have uncoupled themselves from the American consumer market. The United States may be sliding toward Third World conditions, but expanding segments of Brazil and China are racing toward First World abundance. These markets, not ours, have laid claim to the attentions of corporate profiteers. What does it matter to the multinational if median income in the U.S. has climbed a mere $59 since 1966, when Brazil's per capita income has nearly doubled since 1999? One salient example: Nearly seventy percent of Coca-Cola's revenue comes from outside the U.S. In the first quarter of 2013, its international sales volume grew three times as fast as its American volume. Over the next five years, Coke plans to spend $30 billion on international expansion in China, India, Russian, and the Middle East. So long as one continent is in the ascendant, the fall of another is of little interest.

Second, the survey elicits the degree to which Wall Street financial markets have untethered themselves from Main Street industry. Industrial manufacturing has been in heavy decline as a percentage of American GDP, from a peak of 34 percent in the fifties to about 11 percent now. Perhaps as corollary, the GDP share held by the financial sector is on a steady uptick, now over eight percent and rising, while the total turnover of financial markets is many times our GDP. Derivatives, exempted from tepid Dodd Frank controls, are being purchased in bulk every month by the Fed, which is also holding interest rates at zero, ensuring banks can borrow for nothing, swivel on a dime and fleece credit card desperados at 18% a month. Why should corporate leaders care that it is slowly gaining a huge reserve army of American labor, to use Karl Marx's term, which it can one day play off against some arriviste working class in a BRIC country?

Madison Ave and the 90 Million
Much like the heady delirium in the boardroom, these shadow facts too infrequently penetrate the optimistic consciousness of our vast marketing industry. As oil pipelines hemorrhage and radioactive waters sieve into the soil, we are admonished by a new nationally broadcast ad for the Acura RXL: "You wake up in your luxury bed and slide out of your luxury sheets. You get into your luxury shower and dry off with your luxury towel. You put on your luxury suit and your luxury watch. You grab your luxury coffee from your luxury coffee maker, and add some luxury sugar. You step out of your luxury house and step into your luxury car…which makes everything else seem ordinary." Another class of commercials trots out sonorous-voiced actors like Tommy Lee Jones to lean on farm fences and talk about retirement planning, while Matt Damon's soothing voice reminds how "common sense" is all we need to build a halcyon tomorrow. It always seems a healthy number of the wide-grinned retirees portrayed zooming down the California coast are minorities, often the African-Americans who lost half their wealth during the housing collapse.

What must the mass unemployed think as the television drones forth with this condescending drivel? *The Boston Globe* reports on a study by the Urban Institute that claims Generation X and Y—the two generations following the Boomers—have saved less than their parents did in their early adulthood: "Stagnant wages, diminishing job opportunities, and lost home values are behind the issue and have kept young Americans from saving even as the economy doubled from the early 1980s, the study found."

The drear state of the economy is compound by what the young do to counteract it—take out loans. *The Globe* story notes, "'People in my generation are of the opinion that it's OK to take out tens of thousands of dollars in student loans,'' said Young, who graduated in May 2012. "That puts them in debt right away.''' The article concludes that, with no savings, Gen X and Y will rely more on the social safety net, the very programs millionaires Barack Obama and John Boehner are so anxious to cut. But millionaires can afford to be utopian, hence the blandishments about the road to a stronger America.

If the actor in the Acura commercial were a genuine luxury guy living a genuine luxury life, and his address were placed on a title screen at the end of the ad, I suspect a large mob drawn from the 90 million unemployed would soon descend on his luxury house. As Obama rather imperiously told a frightened assembly of derivatives kingpins during the collapse, "I'm the only thing standing between you and the pitchforks." Of course, the commercial is just another tawdry piece of condescension foisted on the masses from Madison Avenue, but it artlessly demonstrates the second disconnect in our storyline—between the media and the masses. The Acura RXL lists at $48,450. Average per capita debt is $47,500.

The White House and the Poor House
It was Freud who said that if you wanted to know human nature, simply reverse its clearest moral injunctions. If we are forbidden to steal, it is because we are thieves. If adultery is verboten, it is because we are covetous. By that measure, perhaps we can discern the aims of Washington by reversing the desires of the American public. (Much like we can find countries that receive the most American aid by seeking out the nations with the most egregious human rights abuses.)

Testing Freud's formula bears some interesting results. According to relentlessly consistent polling numbers, we oppose cuts to social spending such as education and Social Security and favor national health insurance provided by the government. Yet the policies we receive from either wing of the Business Party are healthcare reform that will leave millions still uninsured (but usefully fined), higher defense spending, lower education spending, and aggressive interventions across the planet. Far less than half of Americans want to prioritize immigration and gun control, but these topics dominate media coverage. We want jobs and a strong economy before a level deficit. Yet we get an austerity package designed to slow the economy and job growth. Even though our paychecks have flatlined for forty years, and our schools are growing poorer and our prescriptions dearer. Even though sixty percent of the jobs created by the stimulus were part time, and the piddling median wage in 2011 was $26,965.

At a macro level, the Freudian formula works the same. The Journal of the Academy of Arts & Sciences recently reported on the disparity between public opinion and policy. In polling, large majorities have favored federal policies to cut greenhouse emissions, even supporting tax breaks for corporations that reduce emissions—a stance that reflects global consensus on the reality of climate change and the need to do something about it. In fact, 118 countries have set national targets for renewable energy (RET). As the formula predicts, the U.S. has no national renewable energy target, placing it on the regressive right of the global political spectrum.

While nearly <u>two thirds</u> of Americans favorable developing renewables over oil, gas, and coal, we churn ahead with oil, gas, and coal exploration and encourage states to draft their own environmental targets. Extraction is keeping the federal government too busy to deal with such peripheral concerns. Substitute your own favorite federal failing and watch the formula work for you. Rather than prosperity, austerity. Rather than due process, solitary confinement. Instead of higher wages for Main Street, higher earnings for Wall Street. In lieu of jobs, offshoring. Instead of substance, rhetoric.

Here lies our third disconnect, between government and the people. Like the Wall Street and Madison Avenue realities, individuals in the highest echelons of federal power are wildly prosperous, moving seamlessly between the precincts of the state and the serene towers of global enterprise. They are showered with the patronage of both while employed by either, such that the distinctions between the two become opaque and nominal. The goals are common—dominion. The profits are shared—the costs socialized. And the media continually rehabilitates the profile of power like the Soviets rehabbed victims of the gulag—*ex post facto*. The facts of life for the obscenely rich are not like the facts for the majority. They are doing fabulously. Witness the outpouring of mawkishness in the wake of Margaret Thatcher's death. In her first decade in power, she cut taxes on the wealthy by half while the income of the poor <u>plummeted</u> by forty percent. Who penned those lavish encomiums to sit atop Thatcher's grave? Who but the survivors?

Interesting that the quote from Fitzgerald, about the rich being different from the rest of us, was from a set of short stories called *All the Sad Young Men*, largely about the rich and the shimmering anomie of the world they inhabited. Yet if the surveys, media, and policies on offer are any indication, all the sad young men have shed their survivor's guilt and moved on. Life is a fairy tale waiting to be bought. Darker realities, like the distant wail of an ambulance, hardly register anymore.

(*CounterPunch*, April 30, 2013)

Forward to Fascism
Rhetoric and Reality

The Orwellian concept of doublethink, and its synonyms 'doublespeak' and 'doubletalk', are relatively recent euphemisms for political deceit, but they have a classical analogue in the Roman Empire. Janus was the Roman god of transitions, principally between war and peace. As such, he hovered in spirit over doors and passageways and gates, was celebrated during harvests and weddings and births. As depicted on Roman coinage, he boasted two heads, which allowed him to look forward and backward. Hence, the term "Janus-faced", which is now almost universally synonymous with hypocrisy, even though the god was not initially a symbol of mendacity. Perhaps Janus' primary claim to fame—aside from being a phenomenally apt metaphor for every American politician—is that he is a uniquely Roman creation. The Greeks had no corollary. If you've read any Gibbon, you'll instantly see why the Romans required a two-faced personage to preside over their society. Augustus, to pluck one name from the imperial genealogy, cleverly bought off the Senate, ostensibly restoring them but subtly disempowering them, assuming for himself all the essential authorities of state. His behavior naturally belied his rhetoric.

Some things never change. Last Sunday Glenn Greenwald, the tireless Guardian journalist and defender of civil liberties, got word his boyfriend David Miranda was detained, harassed, and needlessly interrogated for nine hours at Heathrow Airport in London. On Wednesday, Miranda "won" a British court decision that claimed his seized assets could not be used in criminal investigation, but only to track terrorist connections. While discrediting the criminal investigation of Miranda launched by London's Metropolitan police, the judgment does little to prevent harassment of journalists or those around them.

Similarly to David Miranda, in July Bolivian President Evo Morales was blocked by France, Portugal, and Italy from passing through their sacred "airspace" for fears he was smuggling Edward Snowden to asylum in South America. (One conjures visions of symbologist Tom Hanks and Jesus' lineal descendent, Audrey Tautou, being secretly squired to Rome on their manic "grail quest" in Dan Brown's *Da Vinci Code*). In a related and equally contemptible incident, the British police ransacked offices of *The Guardian*, destroying hardware containing Snowden's leaked files. Surely these events happened at the behest of the American government, which is the implicated party in the files and which has targeted the fugitive contractor since his revelations. Now the United States is extending its scope to include intimidation not simply of journalists, but also of those who assist them (much like double-tap drone strikes target suspects and those who try to rescue them).

Both of these international fiascos also happened in transit, the rightful territory of our twin-faced Roman deity. Miranda was even held by the British under the Terrorism Act 2000 act, which applies only in areas of transit: borders, ports, and airports. Snowden himself spent a month huddled in the "transit zone" of Moscow's Sheremetyevo airport. This is all apposite since these behaviors not only occurred in transitory spaces, but also because they indicate a regressive program of intimidation, sponsored by the White House, but that curiously is nowhere to be found in its progressive posturing about liberty.

Janus' unmistakable modern approximation is Barack Obama, who has made sickeningly disingenuous statements in the wake of the Spygate eruption, namely that "we don't have a domestic spying program" (that *The Atlantic* called, "Obama's Bill Clinton moment"). But Obama also said that he wants to set up a "national conversation" about NSA spying and that it's "right to ask questions about surveillance." As if, without the Snowden leak, he would've hosted a town hall meeting on CNN—moderated by the venerable Candy Crowley—to discuss the overblown global surveillance networks entrenched in our digital infrastructure. Perhaps asking a question about surveillance is all right, but one must then accept, with all the obtuse credulity of a born patriot, whatever sophomoric answers the spy state offers. That's not a conversation; it's a prefabricated Q&A. It's Jay Leno pretending to be a journalist and Charlie Rose fashioning a rhetorical landing strip for the Dissembler in Chief. Tilt your head back and swallow the blue pill offered by our serene Morpheus.

How he pacifies us with his calmly imparted but utterly casuistic prescriptions. We'll add an independent voice to the FISA court review—a privacy ombudsman representing…god only knows what. The interests of the populace? Wasn't the FISA court supposed to do that? This is beginning to resemble a regression argument in which each justification requires its own justification. But who will supervise the ombudsman after he is bought off by Northrop Grumman or intimidated by Homeland Security or converted to the Tea Party? Beside, as Obama silkily explained to Rose, he is already looking after our interests (while scrupulously balancing them with our desire for freedom). In an almost surreal disclosure Wednesday, the administration is developing (via outsourcing, naturally) a Federal Cloud Credential Exchange (FCCX) that will allow citizens to safely access federal websites and services using a single password. The cloud-based authentication network will secure sensitive personal data from everyone except—the government! It's all part of the President's now-comically named "National Strategy for Trusted Identities in Cyberspace" (NSTIC).

But this is just one of the many ways in which the administration will soothe our civil anxieties. As Obama tells it, we won't simply appoint a feckless scarecrow to watch as the crows (and hawks) ravage our privacy. We'll hold closed-door meetings with lapdog Fortune 500 companies, industry lobbyists in cash-lined suits, and privacy activists (one small step removed from 'domestic extremists'). We'll reform Section 215 of the Patriot Act to create a new lexical puzzle for the DOJ to swiftly solve (like a six-year old savant with a Rubik's Cube). And, the *piece de resistance*, we'll launch a brand new website disclosing intelligence activities to the nation, easily accessed with your new FCCX password, courtesy of NSTIC. All of this stands in disfigured contrast to the needless harrowing of Morales and Miranda, and the easily forgotten fact that all of these programs—from PRISM to XKEYSCORE—are all active and haven't been restrained in the least.

The world is splitting down sharp ideological lines over the surveillance revelations. The line runs between the smoldering resentment of Latin American leaders, who were disgusted both by the Morales grounding and the NSA spying on South American governments, and the obsequious European governments who surely prostrated themselves before requests from Washington to interdict Morales. One region looks forward to a future of expanded rights and participatory governments. The other looks back to the cloistered fascisms of history, where the dictums of state were sacrosanct, and meant to be thoughtlessly ingested by a scorned and marginalized body politic.

In Roman antiquity, the gates to Janus' numerous sanctuaries were traditionally left open in times of war so that he might intervene when appropriate. They were closed during peacetime. They now look to remain open for a long time to come. Our surveillance apparatus is premised on the fear of the other, the terrifying enemy who lurks in the shadows and silhouettes of our own backyards, but so rarely shows himself. The purveyors of 9/11 are dead, but their namesakes are metastasizing in distant lands thanks to our own clever efforts to produce largely via signature strikes, sanctions, and shock-and-awe—an enemy worthy of our totalitarian dreams. Our imperial president seems intent on masking the master plan, but the destination is clear. As George Orwell slyly warned, a society transitions to totalitarianism when its ruling class retains power by dint of either "Force or Fraud," which in our case is both: a fist for the foreigner and a façade for the free. We live in a land of in-betweens, but we are tipping forward into fascism, and away from anything resembling republicanism. Not to worry, though. Like Janus, we can always look the other way.

(*CounterPunch*, August 23, 2013)

Laissez Unfair

Free market zealots have long been on the wrong side of history.

As the new atheists have tirelessly rehearsed over the past half-decade, religion poisons everything and should be replaced by some sort of secular credo. Well, perhaps they haven't noticed, but we've already got one. As grim and myopic as your rural madrassa or suburban altar-and-steeple, neoliberalism is a cult as superstitious and baseless as any church of the holy rood, any baptistery of the blood. Believers heed its monotheistic calls for ideological fidelity, ignoring damning case studies and shrugging off blaspheming economists. Its creed was forged in a pin factory, and its first ancestor was named Adam. Its most fanatical adherents don't understand its first principles, its high priests don't believe them.

Yet this cult of the abacus has spent the last forty years dinning into our ears the sanctified glories of the free market, so now millions of adults believe that a thoroughly deregulated economy and its companion fetish—a gutted federal government—is the highest calling of mankind. Those who dissent are swiftly buried under an avalanche of cliché. Namely, that the market works in mysterious ways—an utterance generally followed by an improvised homily on the vastness of market knowledge and the paltriness of our own. The combinatorial effect of the former with the latter is intended to render us in a state of mute stupefaction, humble sheep awaiting the beckoning call of the Good Salesman. Empirical evidence need not be summoned, for we take these truths to be self-evident. Hence the need not to test them in reality.

Over the centuries, our *laissez faire* cult has enjoyed an upward trajectory (a veritable ascension!). Only occasionally has it been beset by blind regulatory tribes. But these foolish marauders have been swiftly dispatched, allowing the moorings of capital controls and tariffs to slip the surly bonds of earth, setting us adrift on oceans of liquidity. Those on Wall Street, and in the hallowed halls of beltway think tanks, are today trembling with anticipation. Like Voltaire's Dr. Pangloss in *Candide*, they believe that "all is for the best". And as Fed billions flood their coffers every month, they wonder if they are indeed living in "the best of all possible worlds". But what of the millions slipping beneath the quicksand of a jobless recovery? Take heed, ye doubting liberal, croons the glassy eyed convert. Higher powers are in play. Soon all will be revealed.

What has been revealed over several hundred years is that the champions of *laissez faire* have been frequently on the wrong side of history. For centuries now, the forces of reason and the forces of blind faith have fought tooth and nail to define the shape of modern civilization. Some battles were won by the defenders of fairness. Others by the advocates of market fundamentalism. The rest are still being contested. The mortgage meltdown of 2008 was a consequence of rampant financial securitization and overleveraged insurance swaps, the kinds of financial 'innovations' that are the hallmarks of deregulation. The Occupy Movement was at root a challenge to the deregulated economics that has sent America spiraling into the depths of inequality. The recent Bangladeshi protests over collapsing factories on fire are directly related to the march of unfettered global capital. The austerity protests in European capitals were aimed at the dictates of a neoliberal market model. All over the world, voices are rising in unison against a common target.

But history is a good barometer of the validity of an idea. Let's turn to five arguments from neoclassical history that should lay plain the quality of thought behind the *laissez faire* doctrine, and help us understand why it is so despised today. I've also described the little-known monuments to these lost wars that free market diehards have built to commemorate them.

Five Arguments of Laissez Faire economics (and the monuments they inspired)

1) **The Argument for Slavery** is commemorated by a statue cast in stainless steel and called *The Invisible Hand*, which exhibits an exhausted slave hovering over a gigantic GMO cotton plant on the crest of the Texas Hill Country. Pro-slavers of the 19th century like George Fitzhugh and William Joseph Harper believed that the abolition of slavery was a violation of free market principles. After all, shouldn't a man have the right to sell himself at auction? After abolition, all he was able to do was rent himself for a fee. Naturally, this contractual relationship was intrinsically uncertain, whereas a final sale delivered a peace of mind to the man being bought that no temporary contract could provide. Not only that, but slave owners would naturally keep their permanent 'possessions' in a finer fettle than they would rented labor. As such, Fitzhugh argued for universal slavery, suggesting that all men had an "inalienable" right to be slaves.

2) **The Argument for Child Labor** is memorialized a clever statue carved in coal, which exhibits a small, soot-faced consumptive child bringing his weekly wages home to his deadbeat parents. Nicknamed *Black Lung*, this statue represents the battle to subject unwitting children to the impenetrable wisdom of the market. Its argument essentially stated that labor ought to be free to do what it likes, whether that be selling one's soul to the devil or plantation owner, or permitting one's children to gainfully employ themselves at the corner sweatshop. An 1819 British Parliament bill to regulate child labor—banning those under 10 from working and those between 10 and 16 to limit their hours to a shameful 12 a day—caused an uproar. To gainsayers, the regulatory scheme undermined the sanctity of the contract and prevented a perfectly natural market transaction between illiterate children and base industrial kingpins.

181

3) **The Argument for Opium** is canonized in a famous bronze, called *Rational Self Interest*, which features a stupefied Chinese man lying prone in a den of iniquity, eyes closed and a weak grin on his face. While anyone who has ever been anaesthetized with morphine may lend a sympathetic ear to this argument, it tends to discredit itself when its object is the biochemical enslavement of an entire population. *Laissez Faire* theology was deployed during the days of the British Empire to defend the sale of opium to the Chinese as a free market right. Or, from the reverse perspective, it was asked what right the British East India Company—and their faithful Bengali field laborers—had to deny surging consumer demand? Clearly, there were plenty of people in Canton clamoring for opiates of every kind. The market was going to be filled one way or another, argued leading British opium importers Matheson Jardine, so they might as well turn a profit for empire instead of ceding it to unscrupulous types. The Opium War of 1839 was launched to demolish a Chinese attempt to outlaw the drug. Lord Palmerston, the British Foreign Minister, famously rationalized the war as a defense of free trade, to the nodding assent of parliament's scurfy backbenchers.

4) **The Argument for Pollution** is sanctified by an enormous installation, called *Externalities*, which features a giant lead cumulus cloud spewing toxic rain on a crowd of Congressional lawmakers. This monument commemorates the heroic struggle of market fundamentalists to protect their right to pollute the earth. More than 60 lawsuits have been filed since the 2007 Supreme Court ruling granting the Environmental Protection Agency (EPA) the right to regulate greenhouse emissions if they were found to be dangerous to the public good. Launched by a paranoid President Nixon in 1970 to pacify rabid earth-firsters, the EPA has suffered nothing but abuse ever since, serving as a perennial target for anti-government fundamentalists. The EPA took a beating from free market fanatics in the 2012 Republican primaries, with Michelle Bachmann calling for its repeal and Mitt Romney accusing it of driving up energy prices. A meeting of the Texas Public Policy Foundation earlier this year issued a "bill of particulars" against the EPA, claiming that total and complete inaction on climate change would be in the best interests of the environment, since "the most successful environmental policies emanate from liberty."

5) **The Argument for Low Wages** is memorialized by a glass monument depicting a zigzagging graph of stock prices ascending into the sky. Christened *By Stocks and Bounds*, the minimum wage argument insists that, if water is permitted to find its level, wages too should be afforded the same natural right. After all, the market works by universal law just like gravity, and may be proved so by Miltonian physics. History is rife with neoclassical theories why raising wages by any amount will instantly obliterate growth. Some like to conjure the ghost of Benjamin Franklin when claiming that the cost of higher wages will automatically be passed on to the consumer by moguls anxious to optimize margins. Higher costs will depress demand, which will depress investment, which will depress

employment, which will lower wages, which will ultimately profit penurious moguls once again awash in a sea of cheap labor. In other words, raising wages will lower them slightly less then not raising them at all. But even the slightest of margins must be vigilantly defended. Still, it is hard to see what the problem is here, other than a few pointless empirical studies.

Atlas Drugged

As the above examples lay plain, the religion of the free market is heady stuff. It belongs alongside autographed L. Ron Hubbard tomes in the pantheon of human credulity. The banging of the bell at the stock exchange ought to be installed in a Smithsonian casement next to the most elaborate Haitian voodoo rituals. They are much the same. As Gordon Gekko noted in Wall Street: Money Never Sleeps, "Bulls make money. Bears make money. Pigs? They get slaughtered."

Today, the cathedrals of capital are attended by financial fleecing crews in their Sunday best. Instead of incense, they burn Camels and Winston's until the final bell. The ashes are strewn along Wall Street's splattered pavements. And if you simply laud and applaud the god of the market, fight off any impediments to his unfettered whimsy, you too might find yourself singing hosannas to the highest, perched like Dr. Pangloss over an earthquake zone declaiming a paradise on earth. Only in your case, you'll be surrounded by fellow believers, waving flags of freedom amid the collapsing scenery of American society. Most likely, you'll be in a state of high fever. Such are the workings of the invisible hand. As such, you probably won't notice your children stumbling forth from the fairy palaces, their faces as sooty as their lungs. You won't notice your black brethren staggering whiplashed back to their airless pens. Or your Asian friends keeling over in fits of giggling inanity, penniless and drug addicted. Nor will you see the forbidding skies overhead, full of smoke and carbon and unfiltered ultraviolet, performing their toxic photosynthesis on your kin. Ah, but surely this is the best of all possible worlds. Amen, brothers Milton and Tom. Verily, it takes a Friedman to understand the virtues of liberty.

(*CounterPunch*, June 28, 2013)

Obama's Downward Spiral

Four freedoms have always formed the bedrock of American liberty. The freedom of speech, the freedom of assembly, the rights to privacy and to a fair trial, largely covered in the first, fourth, and sixth Amendments. It is astonishing that a single president has so thoroughly undermined all four. With the conviction of Bradley Manning Tuesday on 20 criminal charges carrying a potential sentence of 136 years in prison, the verdict on the muckraking aspect of free speech is clear—state crimes must be hidden, and those who expose them must be destroyed. That the Obama administration so vigorously pursued this outcome raises once more the question of whether America will finally see through the ruse of the modern Democratic Party and its now thoroughly disgraced leader—or will it continue, against all evidence to the contrary, to cling to that party's threadbare mandate, now reduced to the shameful claim of being "the lesser evil." If by chance, the American majority recognizes our Machiavelli for what he is, let this be an epitaph for the headstone of a dead mythology.

Falling for Faust

From a supposedly stirring speech at the Democratic National Convention into 2004 to the weepy confirmation in Chicago four years on, millions fell for the mystique of Barack Obama. Ignoring the realities of power—his vetting by corporate leadership, his subservience to institutional wealth, his massive funding by finance, insurance, and real estate conglomerates—they bought hook, line, and sinker the vacuous idea of "Change We Can Believe In." This portmanteau served as an idealist's suitcase into which desiccated liberals packed all their disappearing dreams. Once their man was elected, they were pacified with little more than some high-flown rhetoric and a few tawdry policy proposals destined for the Congressional guillotine. Then they could wash their hands of it and get back to the business of making money, conscience intact. Welcome to liberal politics in the 21st century.

Had anyone been following activist and author Paul Street, for instance, they would have been quickly freed from their illusions. Or at least exposed to the truth about Obama. As evolutionary psychologist Robert Trivers has laid out extensively in his book *The Folly of Fools*, people with a desire to believe a particular story are often impervious to facts that contradict it. There are strong evolutionary incentives for people to sustain false historical narratives in their quest to achieve survival or reproductive advantage. You can see the ease with which these farcical storylines caused millions to leap so credulously into the arms of a vitiated Democratic Party. It's also a testament to our paucity of choice that millions of marginally deflated liberals decided to vote again for Obama in 2012, salving their consciences with the daft 'lesser of two evils' analogy, by which they were able to dispense with the harder questions about an electoral system that only offered two evils. No longer able to sustain their narrative of

184

incremental change and lesser evilism, they are now left with nowhere else to go, a politically displaced people, the latest refugees of the franchise.

So here we are, five years in, and we find that our messiah-scholar is a Savonarola of apocalyptic proportions. With a world for a stage, he capers from role to role. As an imperialist, he wields power like a Borgia. As a paranoiac, he resembles a police state Napoleon. As a militant, he disregards borders like Teddy Roosevelt. As a gunrunner and friend of stateless jihad, he mimics Reagan. Our freedoms lie in spangled tatters at his feet.

Speaking Freely...

As for the particular freedom of speech, Obama has taken steps to drastically circumscribe the free exchange of ideas. By grossly expanding the scope and reach of NSA surveillance and seizing the private communications of mainstream media outlets, he has sent a chill rippling through the country. Programs like PRISM and Boundless Informant—or possibly the broadest program of them all, XKeyscore—capture our private thoughts and inscribe our digital ethnographies in clandestine data silos. No doubt we'll all think twice next time we think to speak our mind.

What about the freedom of assembly? Well, the freedom to gather in peaceful protest of government policy is dutifully enshrined in our constitution. It may not be the anointed scripture that old school right-wingers think it is, but it is the closest thing we have to a ten commandments. Obama is desecrating the tablets. By literally cordoning off the commons, we have shuttled protestors and petitioners into pens of expression that more resemble the foreyards of an abattoir than a public space. Witness the diminished strike zones of Con Edison workers last year and the truncated cobblestones of Wall Street during the Occupy protests, the rebel-swept grounds of Zuccotti Park.

But police efforts to deny protest will soon be augmented by a helpful partner. In June, an expansion of military laws granted the military explicit power to intervene in public spaces to "quell…civil disturbances." Naturally, as breaking news about sitcom stars dominated the airwaves, this expansion of martial policy went unnoticed. The Pentagon is developing a troop force to deal with "domestic catastrophes." You can easily imagine that useless phrase being tossed aside and substituted with "civil disturbances" caused by "domestic extremists," formerly known as peaceful protestors. Entrapment is now a legitimate tool of police work. The Department of Homeland Security (DHS) is now prepared to surveil your peaceable marches, infiltrate your gatherings, and sow dissent among your ranks. In so doing, the DHS can hopefully incite you to violence—at which point you cross the threshold from deranged anti-corporatist to domestic extremist (the NSA's foreground of terrorism) and can be usefully detained and deposited in a tent prison on the periphery of your crumbling metropolis.

Fair Enough?

Due process, you say? Guantanamo prisoners, if they still had the strength to, would laugh in the face of a patriot pronouncing this blessed creed. Your indefinite imprisonment is authorized by the NDAA. As is your trumped-up trial before a military tribunal, should a show trial be necessary in your case. And so is your liquidation should anonymous authorities deem you not worth the trouble of detaining. It's no wonder Obama signed the NDAA under cover of darkness on New Year's Eve. A satanic verse is best inscribed in Cimmerian conclave.

How arrogant is this administration? It believes it has the right to reinterpret any judicial ruling, like the one by a brave judge prohibiting indefinite detention of Americans. Or perhaps the point is cast in sharper relief by the fact that—under the President's guiding hand—the CIA conducts "signature strikes" on hapless villagers in countries across the Middle East—a population of people with no rights. Their crime: looking like trouble. Perhaps youngish, male, disgruntled at a pandemic lack of work, irritated by the perpetual droning in the sky, frightened by the frequent explosions in nearby villages. Hard to imagine anyone in such a climate of fear wouldn't bear the signature of a terrorist. The 'double-tap' hits are equally cruel, as they obliterate first responders to an attack (by first eliciting a tragedy to which they are bound to respond). Note how the CIA here imagines that the first to respond will be nefarious terror suspects. They are not like us. We are guilty by the falsest of associations; they by the most intimate. The enemies, in these strikes, are people defending their own homes, moving to rescue mortally wounded relatives, otherwise known as 'insurgents'. One in fifty killed are known militants. The euphemisms of mayhem drone on. How they reach a fever pitch before the shot is fired—by remote control from a benign bunker outside Sin City.

An Actor Unmasked

I'm afraid that our constitutional scholar and ethnically mixed prodigy has proven himself a shapeshifter. From friend of the downtrodden and community activist, he became the conscience of a liberal nation, the messianic voice of an oppressed minority, the hope of a guilt-ridden bourgeois. From there, amid the collapsing scenery of American society, he swiftly turned his back on his people, his adopted communities of color, and embraced the starched collars of global finance. FIRE's favorite lackey has handed trillions to his pals in pinstripes. His rhetorical palinodes were myriad and predictable. You could do the pantomime yourself. You need only learn the maxims of cool-headed centrism, and the master the footwork of retreating promises. For every war denounced and terminated, conjure a new conflict. For every faux terrorist entrapped, draw true jihadists from the signature of a drone strike. Match each miniscule jobs program with a momentous trade agreement that offshores millions. With every reference to American exceptionalism, wiretap a citizen-suspect. Instead of dragging America

186

off to hydrocarbon detox, launch a saturnalia of fracking. Rather than champion the underclass, spy for the ruling class.

That is the crux of it, class war. As president, you know your true constituency—it's Ed Herman's "unelected dictatorship of money." The job description doesn't mince words: befriend the rich, and defraud the poor. Chastise the whining billionaire in public, and then cut a deal behind closed doors. Lay a soft palm on the shoulder of a prole for the press, and then teach him to vote against his interests. One market, self-regulating. One people, self-censoring. One empire, self-interested. One enemy, psychopathic.

There you have it. A presidency in a nutshell. Obama has not shied away from redefining the office, although he is history's progeny. He has consolidated the excesses and failings of his most famous predecessors. From the grave, Nixon blushes at our unblushing surveillance state. From his imperial crypt, Reagan sees his strategic stamp on arms back-channeled to Sunni contras. Clinton sees all the hallmarks of a corporate sellout in his public platitudes and private fundraisers. Bush finds his signing statements appended to every legal sheaf. They croon with envy, our presidents emeritus. The centrist for Obama's ability to boycott conviction. The neocon for the temerity of his overreach. Chameleon, fascist, Iago, Faust. Is there a term of betrayal that won't suit this maestro of appearances? Apparently not.

(*Dissident Voice*, August 3, 2013)

Obama's Empty Gesture
President Cavalier

Sometimes you get the feeling that President Obama is just mailing it in. That he has wearied of his stewardship of the American empire and has little energy left to vigorously maintain the pretense of Democratic virtues that he was originally paid to espouse. Such was the case last week, when he offered up, like a token souvenir to departing tourists, a half-hearted defense of NSA spy programs. The propaganda, the spin, the lip service to civil liberties, all rang hollow in the mouth of this increasingly disengaged Commander in Chief.

After a brief and futile attempt to justify surveillance by situating it in the context of American history, he moved onto the endlessly rehearsed, tiresome pantomime of 'hard choices'. Obama and his armies of wiretappers and data baggers, would have us believe that they, like so many other political charlatans and counterfeits, conscientiously work to strike that oh-so delicate balance between liberty and security, making "important decisions" with our best interests in mind.

Could any argument be less persuasive, not least for its overuse? Picture the moral professionalism of the NSA drone—sleeves rolled, bent over the digital troves, assiduously conducting batch keyword searches, combing the data for threat signals. How he so selflessly "labor(s) in obscurity," to use the President's own phrase. How he pines to protect our families of four, our green lawns and double-car garages, our porches with their patriot's flags hanging still in the warm August air.

So Incremental as to be Meaningless
The picture sketched, Obama moved on to the so-called changes. Out of fortysomething recommendations, the President marginally addressed three or four. Notably the bizarre and pointless decision to store illegally collected phone metadata off-site, so to speak. Was this an ironic attempt to privatize more government activity? Or was it what it so transparently appeared to be at first glance—an attempt to deflect attention from the illegality of the practice by emphasizing changes in the process by which it happens. We'll still hoover up your records, but we'll outsource their storage to private companies (who, by the way, will charge us a premium, which we'll happily pay by siphoning off more tax dollars to corporate interests. Surely, one asks, if there was ever an opportunity for a bulk discount...).

This feckless tweaking of an odious violation of the Fourth Amendment was meant to be the signal action by which the Obama administration assured us that it was guarding our liberties. Even as it guaranteed our security from a threat four times less imminent than a lightning bolt to the brain. Epic fail.

188

This fatuity was swiftly seconded by another. From now on, intoned our Spymaster in Chief, the NSA shall be required to obtain court approval. This 'reform' hardly merits the label, even parenthetically. Why? Because the F.I.S.A. court that has been issuing blanket approvals to the phone records program has denied NSA requests 0.03 percent of the time. It will now simply have to rubber-stamp its craven acquiescence more frequently (given that our phone records are scraped daily). Naturally, as with all Obama legislation or reform, a loophole has been added, this one for "emergency" situations. Forgive me, but I thought every terror threat was an emergency? Are we thus to conclude that the emergency clause will be permanently invoked?

Also, National Security Letters, delivered by the F.B.I. to businesses demanding they turn over their customer records, will—wait for it—not be altered or subjected to court sanction (explicitly rejected by Obama). However, gag orders on petitioned businesses will be shortened in length, permitting those companies to complain that their hands were tied, not five years after the fact, but perhaps three?

Then, in a reform that truly deserved its own press conference: Angela Merkel's phone will not be tapped. Now Europe's first lady can safely resume destroying the European economy.

A panel of advocates would also be created to represent the privacy interests of the public. This nominal attempt to balance privacy interests with security concerns, on investigation, is revealed as another public relations sham. These latter-day tribunes, as it were, will have zero visibility into the F.I.S.A. caseload, and only be permitted to weigh in on privacy concerns when invited into the room by F.I.S.A. itself.

Nothing of note was mentioned in regards to the PRISM program, which sifts Internet data for signs of terrorist intent (as opposed to the phone data collection program, this one appears to focus more on computer web traffic, although the two are increasingly indistinguishable).

An Enforced Consensus
Of course, it would be remiss to close without commenting on the impact of mass surveillance on the public—the very reasons unreasonable searches and seizures were banned in the rosy-fingered dawn of the republic. A recent survey by the venerable PEN organization reported that one in six respondent authors had seriously considered or actually constrained their speech, whether written or spoken, due to fears of NSA spying.

This is precisely the effect revelations of the Edward Snowden kind can be predicted to produce. Surveillance itself has a two-fold character: first, to externally monitor a population; second, to make the population internally monitor itself. The goal of both is censure. Whether police state censorship or the self-censorship of an apprehensive and disquieted conscience, it comes to the same—everyone sticks to the official narrative.

A decreed consensus, in other words. Interestingly, by my count, President Obama used the word "debate" nine times in his speech. How the President takes such comfort in that word. So often in public venues he'll concede the very thing he is enabling or preventing: a multiplication of inequality, the offshoring of jobs, the right to privacy. It seems for him enough to believe that he is raising the issue in public—that acknowledgment is tantamount to reform. But it isn't.

There is not debate happening between the government and the public. Obama noted that, "we shouldn't expect this to be the last time America has this debate." Perhaps America is having this debate—he called it a "public debate" at least three times. But it is the public debating privacy and spying amongst itself. The government is sitting this one out. These cynical and bootless alterations give the lie to the government's intransigence, its fundamental disinterest in change, and to the administration's obsequiousness in enabling system injustices to proceed apace.

The Circle of Censorship
Noam Chomsky has countless times referred to the democracy deficit, that fundamental gap between public wishes and the policies they receive. Obama's fraudulent notion of debate lays this gap in plain sight. Since the government is no longer meaningfully responsive—beyond calculated PR gestures—to public interests, the next step in the dismantling of democracy is to bring the population into alignment with elite rule. Surveillance is the tool; self-censorship is the desired outcome.

Jeremy Bentham, the famous social theorist, devised the ingenious prison system known as the Panopticon, which later formed a key lens in Michel Foucault's examination of discipline. The Panopticon was designed to physically realize the totalitarian dream of perpetual surveillance. In Bentham's mind, the prison would form a complete circle, with an open yard in the middle. At the center of the yard would be a guard tower. From there, guards could peer through shuttered shades at any and all prisoners, whose cells all faced the open yard and the forbidding tower. Evidently, authorities saw fit to realize Bentham's cracked concept in, at the very least, the Illinois penal system and in the Netherlands.

Unlike those brickwork replicas of Bentham's sketch, we have realized a far more pervasive system through digital means—one that spies on our physical whereabouts, but also inhabits the spaces where we think and form our views. The digital Panopticon not as visible as Foucault would have expected—you can't see it except as tiny roving eyes atop traffic lights. But it perfectly satisfies one of Foucault's other criteria for "panopticism", that of unverifiability. By being suspected but never verified, the system instills self-censorship in the minds of men. We act differently if we think we're being watched, even if we aren't. Often, we hew to the nominal values of the society we believe is watching us. We internalize the ethics of power.

As President Obama demonstrated with his easy casuistry last Friday, the administration is nothing if not cavalier about intrusion into the private lives of its citizenry. Its apparent—if not stated—goal is to circumscribe how the population thinks, and what it feels permitted to think about, enforceable by clandestine agencies, and wrapped in the fulsome banner of security, by which we are made to feel less secure.

(*CounterPunch*, January 28, 2014)

Promises, Promises
Obama's Propaganda Presidency

The American propaganda machine rolls on, superior to the paltry efforts of past American, British, and German public relations machinery. Then, it was enough to sketch terrifying cartoons of Huns or Jews or other ethnicities and fulminate nonsensically about racial purity. No more. We have evolved. Now the deception of the tirelessly distracted masses requires dissimulations of far greater sophistication.

Take, for instance, the recent news that, once again, for the umpteenth month in a row, the unemployment rate has <u>dropped</u>. This happy turn of events was accompanied by the heart-warming news that President Obama has <u>launched</u> "Promise Zones" in five cities that his economic policies have helped "fast track" to destitution. Thus, a cursory glance at the headlines—all anyone has time for these days, right?—is enough to instill the garden-variety commuter with enough cautious optimism to plough through another day of alienating work. One imagines the *Man in the Grey Flannel Suit* cruising down the pavements of Manhattan, stupendous grin across his face, *Times* tucked under his arm, chest swollen with American pride. Or—perhaps I've mistakenly lifted a phenotype from another time. Perhaps today we should substitute the *Man in the Coarse Cotton Hoodie*, striding broadly down the gum-spackled sidewalks of Gotham, a crumpled *Post* beneath his elbow, a suspicious glare scanning the street for crazies. Nevertheless...

Water cooler chatter notes the rising employment numbers, then quickly turns to important development on *The Walking Dead*, before the drones dispatch themselves back to their cubicles to eyeball the Excel grids surging across their monitors. Alas, all is seemingly well in America, if not ideal.

Meanwhile, Obama progressives and White House inner circle congratulate each other on another PR coup, snowing the public for one more week. (One thought does occur: that the administration believes its own rhetoric, a chilling notion, but one not without its theoretical basis: evolutionary biologists have posited that the best liars are those who believe their own lies. It makes them more convincing since—according to their inner voice—there's nothing to hide.)

A deeper dive, or even a shallow dive, into the nuance of the unemployment numbers reveal what authors like Paul Craig Roberts have been railing about for years—that the figures are a sham. The 6.7% unemployment ignores long-term unemployed, who comprise an ever-expanding percentage of the population. Nor does the unemployment number recognize the underemployed—both underpaid and part-timers. You know these people. They serve up your McWhoppers with an absent look in their eyes; they ask if you're a Barnes & Noble member and if you'd like to become one; they sullenly drag your discount DVD purchase across the face of the scanner at Best Buy. They work fewer hours than they need and earn fewer dollars than they should. They are the mass underclass, and the administration's monthly jobs report shoves them aside. Job creation is mostly seasonal, part-time, or low-wage. Third World jobs, in other words. None of these facts would bolster the optimism of our disaffected youth, aimless middle-agers or frightened retirees. Better to stick to the saccharine fibbery that produces happier outlooks.

You are likewise saddened to find that the "Promise Zones" too are a canard. Lifted from the Clinton playbook, it seems—recall the Economic Empowerment Zones that set a lovely precedent of urban tax shelters for booming businesses—on closer inspection we discover that Promise Zones are intended to help children escape the curse of their ZIP codes by dint "of her work ethic and the scope of her dreams." (Note the use of the female gender, doubtless designed by some diligent PR flack to "optimize" empathy.) How will the industrious Obama administration help "her" do this? Not, of course, by offering anything useful, like money. God, no. Remember, Obama is a "free-market guy." Better to "aid in cutting through red tape" that will help immiserated communities access existing resources. One could be forgiven for asking if the lack of existing resources wasn't part of the problem in the first place. But no matter. This is a forgotten detail of an otherwise hopeful, gracious, and sympathetic act of government, notably its Democrat wing.

One other piece of news fairly startles the jaundiced reader. Namely, that the administration has actually assembled a group to recommend ways to regulate the National Security Agency (NSA). And that the President is actually mulling over their proposals. Given the efficiency of the White House dissimulation engine, it's fair to withhold final judgment on this story. It is a standard political technique to organize committees to simulate progress, to erect a hologram of reform that looks good but is nothing more than a rhetorical cipher. And perhaps part of the subterfuge is to generate the appearance of partisan and interagency gridlock, such that the proposals will never be implemented, and the President can throw his hands in the air and decry the feckless partisanship of Democratic governance. To that end, new FBI chief James B. Comey publically <u>vented</u> his displeasure with one of the review group's better ideas: to require court review of "National Security Letters" (N.S.L.s) before they were sent to companies demanding that they hand over all customer data.

"What worries me about their suggestion that we impose a judicial procedure on N.S.L.'s is that it would actually make it harder for us to do national security investigations than bank fraud investigations," Mr. Comey said. He noted that the N.S.L.s are "a very important tool that is essential to the work we do." Comey adds this last fatuity while providing neither evidence as to how it secures the populace nor how mass privacy invasions meet the probable cause criterion of the Fourth Amendment.

Democratic Representative Adam Schiff chimed in with the idea that the crucial question, "is if the program has some value, how is that weighed against the cost of collecting millions and millions of domestic call records of the American people?"

Note how Schiff cleverly smuggles in the same assumption that Comey bluntly stated—that the program is useful. This claim was denied by the review group itself when it quite openly announced that the NSA's bulk data collection, "was not essential to preventing attacks and could readily have been obtained in a timely manner" using more traditional—*and legal*—methods.

The note of disagreement—or partisanship, in the idiom of the beltway—will likely lead to the ever-prudent and conciliatory Commander in Chief rejecting this useful level of review. He is presumed to be favoring a couple of toothless "proposals" that will cost millions and change nothing, except perhaps the perception that he has moved to address the public's outrage over illegal spying. The two programs to which the President has evidently given "penetrating and searching thought" (of the kind no mere citizen might be capable) include assembling all telecommunications data in a single silo not owned by the federal government, as well as appointing a kind of Roman tribune, or "public advocate" whose express mandate would be to argue against the government when it assails telecom companies with its histrionic N.S.L.s. Neither appears, on the face of it, to offer much in the way of resistance. It's quite likely national security agencies, now numbering in the dozens, will simply steamroll past the bootless civil liberty complaints of the tribune straight into the data mines of AT&T, Verizon, and the rest. What good is it to store the data elsewhere than on government property when they can access it any time they like on any pretext they like?

This too fails the legitimacy test. Obama's review board, like his Promise Zones and BLS reports, are transparent attempts to mollify public fears and assuage popular anger. None have as their object the needs of the majority. But rather like a father patronizing a child with slapdash answers to ontologically astute questions ("Why do we exist, Dad?"), the White House continues to siphon off what's left of the Bill of Rights and the government's mandate as guarantor of our "liberty" and "pursuit of happiness." And therein lies the obvious contempt with which elite Americans perceive their lessers.

(*Dissident Voice*, January 12, 2014)

Ten Myths about Obama and the Democrats

As we head into The Chosen One's second term, it might be useful to explode a few of the chronic myths that cling to the man more tightly than his shadow. Myths that have helped liberal intelligentsia justify its enthusiastic support for this lesser of two evils. Here are the myths as articulated by a young, imaginary, and starry-eyed Obama progressive, momentarily detached from the stampeding liberal herd, just long enough to have a conversation with a leftist on the political fringe...

Myth 1. Now look, Obama wants nothing more than global peace, but Iran is a nation of madcap mullahs looking to nuke Tel Aviv. We have to do something.

Obama is definitely not a peace advocate—unless by peace you mean: peace on our terms. That means a disarmed, defanged, and docile Iran with mullahs in exile and puppet doyen in ascendancy. We take with Iran the same line that Israel takes with the Palestinians. Sure, we want peace—on our terms. Meaning the less Arabs in Jerusalem the better. Meaning a Bantustan province with notional national status. A series of tidy little prison camps strung together by gauntlets of IDF troops. So peaceful at night you can hear the safety switches at the security checks clicking off.

The administration's posture on Iran has already violated international law—using open threats and coding a few others. (Everybody knows what "all options are on the table" means.) Our sanctions amount to economic warfare visited on little children who can't define the word sanction. Iran has done nothing wrong. They are within their IAEA rights. There isn't a shred of evidence they are using nuclear for anything outside the purposes of civilian power. Yet the U.S. and Israel are nuclear states, signatories and serial violators of the Non Proliferation Treaty. Israel has 200 nukes. We have more. Iran has none and they know they would be instantly vaporized if they bombed either Israel or us. They don't have a death wish. But we are openly threatening to bomb them. We have already carried out acts of war within Iran, including cyber-warfare and assassinations. If Iran had done either inside the United States we would have invaded them instantly and reduced Tehran to rubble. Palestine is so bad there's not enough space to get into it. And on a side note, we're rapidly surrounding China militarily, and we've infuriated Russia by building a defense shield on its doorstep. There are two kinds of people that claim to crave peace. Those that want peace and those that want peace on their terms. Obama is the latter.

Myth 2. You seem to forget that Obama decided to end the Iraq war and brought all our troops home.

Actually, George Bush did. The man we know as Dubya actually pushed through and signed the SOFA agreement that called for the troop removal. He actually tied off his own war. In fact, Obama pushed hard for a revised agreement that would allow troops to stay on in Iraq, but the Iraqis rejected his efforts. So he's taking credit for something he didn't do; he wanted to do the opposite. But we are still leaving tens of thousands of military contractors—mercenaries paid for by our government—behind just to reassure the Iraqi people of our benign intentions. What country wouldn't want the illustrious Blackwater roaming its streets in blacked-out SUVs, cigar-chomping sociopaths from Texas at the wheel? And don't forget the Green Zone, that billion-dollar, taxpayer-funded Fortress-on-the-Tigris. Hard to miss from a satellite.

Myth 3. But he ended torture, rendition, and closed Guantanamo!

Regarding Guantanamo, it is still open for business. Obama supposedly didn't close it because of Congressional resistance and the legal issues involved with bringing 'enemy combatants' into the states. I guess even the Department of Justice sometimes stumbles on its own nebulous doublespeak. Rendition is still an active program, although it is being—ahem—more closely monitored to avoid prisoner abuses. (I almost used the not-so-laughable euphemism 'detainee' by accident.) But that is really beside the point since we've created a mirror image of Guantanamo at Bagram in Afghanistan, except that it is larger. Sixty thousand square feet of detention dementia in the heart of opium country.

Myth 4. Let's not forget that he liberated Libya and wholeheartedly supported the Arab Spring?

He bombed Libya into the dark ages, much like Bush did in Iraq, all in the name of democracy. Since Congress wasn't awakened from its dogmatic slumbers long enough to rubber stamp the attack, the action violated the War Powers Act of 1973. But no matter, the bombing helped remove the inimitable Colonel Gaddafi. But Libya is now more dangerous than it was under Gaddafi, and is turning into a bloodbath that would make Quentin Tarantino rush out the door with a Super 8. As for Egypt, a look back at the record will confirm that the administration supported Mubarak for years up until the very moment when the tide turned and it became clear he was going to be ousted. Then we took the position of the people and hailed a new democracy. That is not our preference, however, in the Middle East. In country after country, both Democrats and Republicans have supported and continue to support repressive regimes. As well in Latin America and Asia. There is actually a study by Edward Herman that shows a clear correlation between an increase in human rights violations and an increase in American aid.

Myth 5. Besides, Obama must know something we don't, so we probably shouldn't question the war on terror.

196

I think this argument, that the government may know something we don't, so he gets the benefit of the doubt, has always been a Republican response to liberal criticism of illegal wars. It's a dangerous position to take. There's an international protocol, within the UN and NATO, for situations of unavoidable state violence. We don't follow it. We act with impunity when we violate the sovereignty of other nations on a regular basis in Pakistan, Libya, Afghanistan, Yemen, Iran, and Syria. We do as we please because might makes right. A good way to think about it is to ask yourself whether you would be okay with Iraq bombing Washington to take out a terrorist we were harboring? We harbor plenty, including Bush, who has been convicted in a war crimes court, and to whom Obama has granted immunity by ending torture investigations. There was a moral standard set at the Nuremberg Trials called the principle of universality, that you should apply to yourself the same principles you apply to criminals. That's the moral foundation for all our international conventions. But we don't follow it.

Myth 6. Obama just can't get anything done because the Republicans won't let him!

The argument that Obama doesn't do more because the Republicans won't let him is unconvincing and doesn't fit the facts. The Democrats had four years of Congressional majorities where they controlled the budgets, including two years under Obama. Their budgets reflected the neoliberal consensus—heavy war spending, small-scale social spending or regressive social policy. He could have pushed through so many progressive measures with budgets and executive orders, and if he were truly progressive, he would have. As many diehard liberals claim, he may be progressive at heart, but that doesn't matter much if his policies are firmly neoliberal. In fact, they always have been, as was laid bare before his 2008 election by authors like Paul Street. Also, budgets can't be filibustered.

Myth 7. But he means well.

The evidence that I've seen—his actions—overwhelmingly shows that the Obama administration is on balance moving us in the wrong direction. If you want to roll in arguments about improvements in the racial mood and self-belief of the country, there may be truth in that, but those are intangible factors that can't be measured. The actual policies are a different story altogether. Neoliberal economics and imperial foreign policies are a radically regressive force in the world—studies of nation after nation show their negative effects. See Naomi Klein's *Shock Doctrine* and Chalmers Johnson's *Sorrows of Empire* for a nice recap. Not content to be one or the other, Obama has proven to be a neoliberal imperialist, as opposed to your garden-variety fascist. It's not really a question of opinion, unless you introduce intangibles, which I'm not discounting because I do believe the fact of a black president matters, and is in itself positive, despite the

197

kind of pandering Obama had to do to make himself acceptable to our moneyed and pale-cheeked elites.

Myth 8. Poor people support him. He must be doing something right!

He did well in the election with African-Americans and Hispanics, minorities often facing brutal economic realities. It is a shame he won their vote again, because their interests are not being served. The thirty-year trend in this country of declining wages and offshoring of jobs continues apace. His jobs bill at best addressed 1/24th of the unemployed. One twenty-fourth. His housing help was about as bad. He even rejected McCain's request to release $300 billion in funds to help underwater homeowners. Even as he took $13 trillion in toxic mortgages onto government books as part of a bailout of about $24 trillion to banks. If that doesn't convince you where his loyalties lie, nothing will. In any case, the jobs that have vanished—through either offshoring or the meltdown—have not come back. Many were good middle class jobs. What jobs are being created, if any? Low-income jobs. Most pay between $7 and $13 dollars an hour. Not even a living wage. The only real jobs being created are those that can't be exported. Service industry jobs: waiters and bartenders or social service people who help care for the elderly. Cashiers at Best Buy. Servers at Ruby Tuesday. So the stimulus of $700 billion, although woefully inadequate by design, was better than nothing, but can't be said to be the right decision when so much more was—and is—needed.

Myth 9. Still, things are getting better.

The fact is, half of all Americans—half of us—are now either low income or poor, according to the Census office. Forty million people rely on food stamps. Those numbers are increasing, not decreasing.

The government—at the behest of its finance patrons—is deliberately creating a large, low-income labor pool. Exactly what capital wants in a neoliberal system. Cheap labor. Macroeconomic policy used to aim at full employment. Neoliberal economics instead demands a focus on controlling inflation—largely to protect finance capital. Again, you can see who is being protected at whose expense. So when Obama stimulates 10,000 new manufacturing jobs, it provides positive press that helps him get re-elected, but it doesn't begin to stem the tide of millions of better jobs that have flown out the door. And when you export production, you often find that product development and production design work follows in short order. Like Bob Dylan sardonically sings, "They say low wages are a reality/if we want to compete abroad." A false storyline peddled to millions by *The New York Times'* Tom Friedman and his ilk, that roving clan of Panglossian optimists. It's surprisingly easy to be a globalization triumphalist when you sit atop a media empire, your telescope trained on exotic Asia, and your handlers feeding you juice

198

and nuts while you dictate your latest bestseller. By the way, unemployment stats are skewed. They no longer count you if you're out of work and haven't looked for a job in four weeks. A terrific little perversion of reality that one might call 'Friedmanesque.'

Obamacare won't help, either. Low-income debt slaves won't be able to afford it and, even if they could, they wouldn't want to pay for a policy that doesn't provide adequate coverage. They will be taxed instead, which they won't pay because they don't have the money. So they will be government debtors, which will then have the right to garnish their wages and unemployment checks. There are sadly no serious cost constraints in the Affordable Care Act. Instead, it hands $447 billion to the insurance companies that are the actual cause of spiraling costs. When Bill Clinton said during the Democratic Convention speech that he was so lauded for, that healthcare costs were dropping, he was diddling the numbers. Healthcare costs always drop during a recession, as do other costs. So he used the lousy economy to argue that Obamacare was working. Kind of Orwellian, if you pause to think about, which you probably shouldn't. Watch what happens if the economy recovers.

Myth 10. Well, if we could just get rid of the Tea Party fanatics and other Republican radicals, things would return to normal.

The further radicalization of Republicans is more symptom than cause. At a macro level, I think we're seeing a war of finance capital against labor and industry. Capital—in the neoliberal model—pushes hard for deregulation, privatization, and downsizing. It's been implemented for 30 years in the third world by the International Monetary Fund (IMF) and World Bank through austerity bailouts, all with disastrous consequences (although not for American finance and multinationals). Now the model is being applied in the first world for the first time. It was only a matter of time. The Democrats and Republicans have jointly adopted its prototypical narrative—of cutting public spending and reducing government. Another false narrative. The deficits went up when the economy went down, as they always do. They'll go down again when the economy goes up. We can and should be deficit spending our way out of this recession, but the administration sticks to the required talking points about the fiscal cliff and the horrors of debt. As if the American public needs to be reminded.

The real goal is to eliminate the social safety net. So, finance capital moves aggressively against labor with the goal of erasing the New Deal and Great Society. With those onerous programs gone and healthcare shifted onto the back of the individual courtesy of Obamacare, big business can truly earn the kind of astronomical profits it fantasizes about. To help, the Democrats can soften the harsh edge of austerity in a way Republicans can't. That's their doctrinal role now that they've been bought by finance. And they can always count on the votes of the unions and the poor because, as Clinton famously put it, "They have nowhere else to go."

(*CounterPunch*, November 13, 2012)

The Dawn of Austerity in America
Distinctions of Little Difference

Since the rosy-fingered dawn of austerity in America, the liberal media have consistently proclaimed that the Republicans are a deluded gang of filibustering rejectionists. By contrast, they make the rather more strident claim that, for all their faults, Democrats at least believe, as *The New York Times* columnist Paul Krugman puts it, "in letting its policy views be shaped by facts; the other believes in suppressing the facts if they contradict its fixed beliefs." But is this true? Are Democrats a clear-eyed party of well-meaning centrists, and are conservatives a frothing admixture of venal Congressional lifers and mob-backed junior legislators, both taking their talking points from a dim confection of scripture and grainy clips of "Free to Choose"?

The Right—Delusional and Demented?
First, liberals seem to believe that the Republicans who push for austerity are ignorant knaves, a seething clan of badly misguided ideologues who whitewash their realities with the worst theoretical models to emerge from the Chicago School of Economics. For his part, Krugman has nobly piled fact upon fact in his columns and blogs, outlining the harshly regressive outcomes associated with spending cuts during economic downturns. Exhaustively argued, scrupulously referenced, Krugman is an economic champion of the liberal class. Even so, in articles like, "The Ignorance Caucus," "Sequester of Fools," and "Friends of Fraud," Krugman asks, in a state of jaded disbelief, how could it be that, "Republicans are deep in denial about what actually happened to our financial system and economy."

He's not alone in this regard. Leslie Savan in *The Nation* also chalks up the deficit obsessions to the pitfalls of "groupthink," a kind of innocent self-delusion that encourages "the punditocracy to repeat, despite incontrovertible evidence to the contrary, that austerity will pave the toward economic growth." Robert Reich, who regularly and expertly denounces austerity, also seems baffled by the apparent inability of Congress to look facts in the eye. Columnist Ezra Klein touts studies that confirm the myopia of GOP legislators.

But the facts suggest that conservatives foresee austerity's aftermath quite clearly, but are simply disinterested. To put it bluntly, Republicans and their backers know precisely what they're doing. They aren't mathematically-challenged stooges fumbling away the American dream. They're conniving dogmatists bent on real social change—for the worse. A recent joint investigation by Democracy Now! and the Center for Media and Democracy is rapidly exposing the fraudulent claims of the Fix the Debt gang, a group of at least 127 corporate CEOs led by billionaire Pete Peterson. Like their Congressional shills, the Fix the Debt thugs claim they want to salvage America's economy from being wrecked by debt. But what lies just beneath the surface of this thinly veiled publicity campaign is a desire by corporate interests to decimate the New Deal and Great Society initiatives.

Why? For a couple of reasons. First, because this faction of plutocrats and their confederates genuinely believe in the radical individualism they espouse: tax is theft, welfare is the path to dependency, and poverty is the rightful destiny of the dilatory and thriftless. And here's the crucial verdict: if preserving the sanctity of individualism means America becomes a sea of indigence, so be it. If each of us controls our fate, and if our fate has led us to ruin, who's to blame but ourselves? In this sense, we are witnessing the rise of a kind of secular Calvinism in which our destinies reveal our character.

Second, eviscerating the safety net is a good bottom-line bargain. A dramatically enervated and sickly state, bereft of its capacity to regulate, stripped of its assets, and shorn of its social mandate, is a state deterred from taxation for want of cause, and too enfeebled to counter the rapacity of monopoly capital. Capital is thus freed to cannibalize labor. Like a mining colony in a jungle with natives swept aside, the drills won't cease until every fluid drop and mineral grain of profit is safely nestled on a northbound container vessel. Anything to stave off a declining rate of profit.

The related claim that our half-sighted multinationals needs to recognize that if American incomes continue to slide, the populace will no longer be able to purchase the products they peddle, is neither important nor novel for elite interests. Renewed lending and debt accumulation can falsely inflate another housing market, generating a freshet of new derivative plunder. But the larger point is that America is no longer corporate America's primary growth market. China is. India is. Latin America is. The United States already looms large in the rear view mirror, diminishing by the day.

The Left—Decency Denied?
If conservatives are Machiavellis incarnate, what about those malleable Democrats? That glum tribe forever beset by weak temperaments, constitutionally incapable of taking a hard line, handicapped, perhaps, by their bottomless empathy. Along these lines, liberals are happy to claim that President Obama is simply being stonewalled by his Republican colleagues, who have capitalized on his naïve faith in human decency to press their savage austerity agenda on the population.

The President, exhausted by ceaseless good-faith attempts to reason with pathologically irrational extremists, finally capitulates. "Alas," writes Krugman, fawning with forgiveness, "Mr. Obama did not stand firm." The intimation is that the President is a paragon of progressive values, an emblem of liberalism clad in multi-cultural cloth. In fact, the multi-cultural is running interference for the multi-national.

But looking past Obama's hypnotic rhetoric, one finds a political graph marked by one artificial crisis after another, perpetrated by Democrats and Republicans alike. The debt ceiling, the fiscal cliff, sequestration. Afghanistan, Iraq, Iran. Every one a politically manufactured, fear-mongered crisis. Every one carrying a trillion-dollar price tag. Every one a bipartisan swindle. It's Disaster Capitalism par excellence, as Naomi Klein laid out in her bestseller *The Shock Doctrine*, which popularized how crises are manipulated to justify the introduction of fiscal austerity.

While Republican intransigence—cemented by a record filibusters in the last two years—has muddled the president's efforts to add some progressive sops to legislation, an obsession with conservative obstructionism obscures the bipartisan foundation of the deficit debate. From the earliest days of his presidency, Obama signaled that "entitlement reform" was a central plank in his agenda, offering up these sacrificial lambs marinated in talk of "bitter pills" and "reasonable" spending cuts. Not only did Obama appoint Alan Simpson and Erskine Bowles to head his deficit commission, knowing they were deficit hawks of the highest order, but Peterson's Fix the Debt gang grandly supported Simpson-Bowles precisely because it advocated the dramatic spending cuts both parties favor. Yet former *New York Times* editor Bill Keller recently claimed that Obama has not embraced the commission's wisdom.

Obama's own 2011 plan—different from the commission's version in that its tax revenues were at least mildly progressive—also aimed at $4 trillion in deficit reduction, with all three social programs included for euphemistic "reforms." Sequestration itself was hatched in the White House, a trigger mechanism that creates the illusion that Congress is at the mercy of a higher law and, of course, conservative hordes brandishing wildly underlined copies of *Atlas Shrugged*. Likewise, the notion that the Senate can only pass a bill with a super-majority of sixty is a technicality that can be dispatched by a simple Democratic majority. But the decorum of tradition trumps the exigencies of an anonymous populace. In the end, the policy prescriptions of both parties are overwhelmingly austere.

When the administration does differ from its conservative counterparts, largely in the desire to impose a degree of taxation to polish its progressive credentials, the onus falls largely on the working class. Obama's much-celebrated tax on the wealthy is a clever sleight of hand: the tax hits a couple of million Americans whose incomes exceed $450,000, but the tax only applies to income *over* $450,000 and only by the smallest of marginal increases. Cobbled together with slight increases in capital gains taxes, new Obamacare taxes, and fewer deductions for the wealthy, the 1 percent will cede an extra $62 billion a year. By contrast, the media-slighted payroll tax will sift <u>$95 billion</u> in 2013 alone from the pockets of the working class. Although initially and intelligently proposed by Democrats as a stimulative measure in 2010, the payroll tax was allowed to expire with the consent of both parties. Treasury Secretary Timothy Geithner said he saw no reason to extend it. (Granted, it is hard to discern the smoking ruin through the cloud bank.) Nor did Obama bother to include it in his 2013 budget. Yet the tax penalizes 160 million working class Americans with a 50 percent increase in what amounts to a nationwide wage cut, wiping out the wage gains of 2012.

If it's not austerity, it's elitism. Both are now beltway consensus; the notion of handcuffed liberal do-gooders has worn thin, exposing the Janus face of progressive Washington—rhetorically populist, practically bought.

The Media—Paying the Price of Inclusion?
As crass and crude an image as it may seem, the Oval Office is little more than a luxury suite being peddled to palm-greasing plutocrats, their lobbyists, and the venal sophists whose pockets they ply with cash. The political hue is never red or blue—but always green. It is ever Spring in Washington. But this truth, that both parties are consciously visiting hardship on a defenseless populace—is unspeakable. That Obama knows he's favoring wealth at paucity's expense—unmentionable. That conservatives know austerity will crush vast majorities—unprintable. And to coin a lie of this magnitude and continue to employ it as ideological currency requires you to simply elide sizeable sections of reality from your worldview.

Perhaps the price of writing for a mainstream paper like the *Times*, then, is silence on this point and substituting for it the fallacy that our leaders have honorable intentions. That purity of motive is part of our American exceptionalism, our ahistorical singularity. But even if it were so, and by our well-intentioned deeds we were unwittingly paving a highway to hell, how would this be any more ethically commendable than the brainwashed suicide bomber who believes liked a blind Bush that his actions are pure? Both are tragedies of delusion. Yet evidence abounds as counterpoint. The powers that be know exactly what they're doing and attempts to render their Machiavellianism more palatable by obtruding it from sight, is itself a form of complicity. As Noam Chomsky once noted, there isn't much value in speaking truth to power; they already know it.

(*CounterPunch*, March 6, 2013)

The Language of Neoliberalism
On the Calming Idiom of Social Violence

Outsource. Streamline. Downsize. Liberalize. Flexibilise. Get lean. Offshore. Lay off.

If you use the Google Ngram Viewer to research the use of any of these words in American or British English publications over the last fifty years, you'll see a sudden spike in their use in the early to mid nineteen eighties. Why? Probably because some of the words were invented or untombed fairly recently, in order to accompany the trajectory of neoliberal economics. Likewise, the advent of offshoring and a corollary collapse of the American economy took control of the C-suite at about the same time. Neoliberalism has for its primary tenets 'downsizing', which means firing; along with the benign 'privatize', which in the free market vernacular means the private theft of common wealth; and the innocuous 'deregulate,' which means to remove laws or, in its particular application, to make lawless.

What is behind the rise in the use of these terms? Why not instead use those like 'fire' and 'dislocate' and 'steal' and other more lucid descriptions of the cold-blooded work of corporate chieftains to fire millions of American workers and replace them with Asians at a pittance wage in unregulated environments? Doesn't their use suggest that the people who use them are uncomfortable with more candid descriptions of what is happening? Why has *The New York Times*, for years now, used "enhanced interrogation techniques" instead of "torture"? Why has "shell shock" been replaced by progressively more obscure terminology, such as, "war fatigue" and "combat stress reaction" and "post traumatic stress disorder," now rendered as simply "PTSD"? (How much verbal unpacking is necessary before the nucleus of that temporizing acronym is discovered?)

Is this lexicon not the herald of a people deeply troubled by their reality? Or is it simply the unconscious response of the human mind to a horror of its own making? Is it our fumbling attempts to tolerate the intolerable? To mask terror, cloak slaughter, and refabricate misery in a slightly more palatable tongue—with expressions that ask little more from us than a sonorous groan as we reach for the steaming cup of Earl Grey on the breakfast table? So that, in time, we can forget the epoch entirely, dismissing it as one of the countless misfortunes of history, which is, after all, we tell our dinner guests with tolerant gazes, simply the story of a fallible species striving to improve itself. Naturally mistakes will be made, however regrettable. Nods all around. But this opaque language—much like "traffic calming" street furniture slows the pace of traffic—becalms the public mind by disguising the ferocity of social violence it putatively describes.

It is accompanied by a macro ideology that also assuages public outrage by shifting guilt away from individuals onto a faceless superstructure. Author Gilad

Atzmon, in a recent article on the 2012 movie, "Hannah Arendt", relates how the Jewish establishment slandered Arendt after she covered the Adolf Eichmann trial for *The New Yorker*. What Arendt had reported was the infamous "banality of evil", by which she appeared to mean the way immoral behavior becomes institutionalized, its purveyors reduced to necessary cogs is a machinery of oppression, and in which actors are blandly executing the bureaucratic tasks of a state whose ambitions they are committed to by dint of nationality if not patriotism. The Jewish community, like many others, wanted a figurehead of evil to emerge from the Eichmann trial, a sharply sketched image of horror—the profile of Savonarola comes to mind—against which victim populations could aim and vent their fury.

Needless to say, caricatures help fulminating victims unburden themselves of some of their ire. Targets are always produced. Epithets hurled. Maxims inscribed. But Arendt had undermined this process by suggesting that Eichmann was little more than an apparatchik of an evil system, not its distilled representation. This is a sinister concept for some, since it removes, in a recondite sense, responsibility from the individual and places it on the system. Thus the crime is depersonalized, thinned out over a systemic architecture the outlines of which are mind-boggling to unwind. The clarity of blame is lost in the fog of bureaucracy, much like fury loses its force when its focus is diffused. Although Arendt did insist on the actor's moral choice, and his subsequent culpability in his crime, she said Eichmann was not a monster, which is what the masses craved.

The need for scapegoats, on the one hand, and the need to deflect blame, on the other, continues to haunt us. Part of the failure of Occupy Wall Street to galvanize a broader population of restive citizens might be traced to its unwillingness to furnish recognizable targets of popular outrage. A list of public enemies, for instance, composed of CEOs behind the mortgage meltdown, might have inspired far more indignation that the somewhat vague symbol of Wall Street, which conjures less an image of traitorous behavior than a cinematic wash of numbers, a tickertape, bespoke suits, Ivy League hubris, and emptied martini glasses. Eventually you throw your hands in the air. What can be done? What was perhaps feared in Arendt's insight, was just this loss of focused culpability, and its companion fury, which might, over time, instance another Holocaust. The swapping of individual targets for institutional ones can sometimes summon a feeling of helplessness, of being overmatched or ranged against a corporate Cyclops. The result is often resignation and—as we've seen along the liberal spectrum—a retreat into dangerously comfortable mythologies.

There's a hint of the same in the liberal response to Barack Obama. Many liberal defenders of Obamacare characterized it as the best that was possible under the circumstances, despite the fact that Obama never pursued single payer even backed by stupendous popular support and a pliant Congress (even after Scott

Brown was sworn in, since reconciliation might have been used to pass single payer as it was to pass Obamacare). This argument, that Obama was blocked by the irrational bellicosity of the right, unburdens the progressive folk hero of his hypocrisy and flings it onto the broad shoulders of "the system," for which no one is ultimately responsible and which was dropped in our laps by our misguided forbears. We just inherited the system. Behold our ill-shaped bequeath. Best to settle for incremental wins.

This might be part of the descriptive difference between leftists and liberals—one primarily blames the human being, the other the system. (Even if the left is clear-eyed about the system and liberals concede the moral failings of the individual.) And it shows. Liberals are far more forgiving of Obama's failure to live up to his promises. They hustle the imperfections of democracy to the foreground of the conversation, where they elicit shrugs and concessions that defuse the conflict. He was handcuffed. He was stonewalled. Is this true, or is this an elaborate conflict-avoidance strategy, the subtlest of methodologies by which we assure the mainstream of our complicity while maintaining a veneer of principle? The conscientious reformer's middle ground: Sure, we want single-payer healthcare, but we have to be pragmatic. This is probably why so much mention is made about whether or not Obama means well. In the "imperfect world" ideology, motive is all. He tried. He failed. Give the guy a break. Here the conciliatory debater shifts the guilt from human to history, from individual to infrastructure. But, the leftist replies, he didn't try. He never meant to try. He meant to advance the interests of capital and placate the masses with his populist rhetoric. Veneer. Façade. Whitewash. The vocabulary of hypocrisy is rich; choose your label. Here the leftist tries to bring the guilt back to the man, the crime back to the criminal.

Language is critical to this process of calming the anger of the people. In the detail it obfuscates; in the macro, it depersonalizes. Words like "PTSD" and "outsourcing" remove the clarity and even the human element from the description, serving—at a granular level—the same purpose as the "imperfect world" rhetoric serves at a macro level. Where we assign the blame—and the idiom we use to apply it—is decisive in the character of our politics.

This is a central reason why thirty years of offshoring was so effortlessly conducted in the public space. The language softened the appearance of the violent reality, and the systemic nature of the process decriminalized the actions of the outsourcer. How little protest emerged when Jack Welch and his ilk were lionized in the pages of the *USA Today* as our admirable captains of industry. Even as they were shredding the American working class, and the middle class in its wake. Thanks in part to the nuance of neoliberal prose, to the blandishments of a nonthreatening corporate vocabulary, it all passed largely without comment. Times change. We must accept the harsh realities of global competition. The knowledge economy will manifest itself soon enough. Just hang on. A few fairy tales were enough to disarm a population of three hundred million. Nobody blinked when shareholder value was elevated above stakeholder value. Nor when corporate health was prioritized over human health. We swallowed it with our morning joe. This is the impetus of the idea that the pen is mightier than the sword. Rather it is the rationalizer of the sword, the court historian and profiler of the sword. Orwell warned of this and mapped its outline in his fiction. Even Confucius declared that any form of social reclamation must begin by "rectifying the language."

When will we rectify ours? When will Kissinger be tried as a Machiavelli? When will "former U.S. President George Bush" be replaced with "fugitive war criminal George Bush" and the welfare-reforming friend-of-the-poor Bill Clinton be unmasked as a welfare-destroying foe-of-the-poor? Not any time soon, if we can judge by our thesaurus of common usage.

(*CounterPunch*, October 25, 2013)

The March of Capital: From Chicago to Dhaka

On a Friday evening, as a summer twilight falls across Manhattan, you can see the slow but steady streams of consumers filing in and out of Hennes & Maurtiz (H&M). Perhaps a healthy number of them have heard the story of the European retailer's hazy association with the tragedies in Bangladesh. Some are vaguely aware of a factory collapsing, but can't quite recall if 100 people died or 1,000. Fewer still recall the furious fire in the same garment district of Dhaka in November, or that 112 died then. And few know that for months now, tens of thousands of garment workers have poured into the streets of Dhaka's Ashulia industrial area, protesting the scandalous wages, deathly conditions, and the union-blocking legal code that help keep one of the world's largest textile communities enslaved by savage corporate profiteering, led by retailers H&M, Wal-Mart, Gap, Calvin Klein, Nautica, and others.

Along H&M's blazingly lit racks and shelves, nobody mentions the Bangladeshi government's attack on protestors May 20th, gunning down fiftysomething citizens with rubber bullets, a painful but tiny wound on a twenty-thousand member contingent blocking access to the Ashulia district, where 300 factories churn out the goods that line the shimmering shelves of the western world. Stacks of cheap but stylishly designed clothing appeal to young New Yorkers anxious to resemble the city's youthful urbanites, striding purposely through the Manhattan sun in form-fitting blazers, thin neckties, and cuffed skinny jeans, and at night downing local ales in scruffy Williamsburg bars in plaid flannels while thumbing glinting iPhone 5s and Samsung Galaxies. Nobody notices that Karl Johan Persson, the thirtysomething inheritor of the H&M multinational, has announced with the *sangfroid* of an aloof and incurious capitalist, that in response to the collapse of the Rana factory in Bangladesh, he is considering shifting production to Africa. From the pan into the fire, one supposes. Persson also noted that South and Central America were also on the company's radar for future factories. Naturally, this announcement comes on the heels of the company's celebrated endorsement of fire and building safety measures in Bangladesh.

Business as Usual
This is par for the course. Corporate multi-nationals relocated much of their textile production to Bangladesh after Chinese workers began to demand higher salaries and wages began to rise. Chinese workers—who could pocket a staggering $150 a month stitching and sewing western wear—have been swiftly replaced with largely illiterate Bangladeshis for a more reasonable $38 a month. (Imagine the feverish CPA bent over his abacus calculating the cost savings.) Rather than concede a few percentage points off their stupendous margins, clothing conglomerates looked for cheaper shores. Bangladeshi garment production leaped 20 percent in 2009, while Chinese garment production slipped five percent. Of course, when multinationals go in search of low-wage production,

they implicitly understand what that means—slight if any wage provisions, few occupational safeguards, and a dearth of benefits. Shareholder value is the byword of capitalism; any conditions that create it will suffice. This is what makes after-the-fact *mea culpas* seem so disingenuous; it is only the exposure of the crime that conditions change. In this case, capital and production flight.

These meager pay scales are a consequence of the labor arbitrage that is the bane of global labor and the unions that attempt to represent it. As has forever been the case with industrial capitalism, capital is always one step ahead of labor, shifting production around the globe just an arm's length out of reach of provincial unions, legal advocacy groups and hazy fraternities of environmentalists. But even the presence of those perennial champions of the underclass and the defenseless earth are no guarantee against exploitation.

Back to the Future
Perhaps collapsing nine-story buildings and furious garment fires are largely confined to the miserly conditions in Bangladeshi production zones, but some manifestation of sweatshops are still an issue in the first world, too. The New York City District Council of Carpenters was recently embroiled in a dispute with pension fund giant Teachers Insurance and Annuity Association-College Retirement Equities Fund (TIAA-CREF) over its funding of a residential building in Queens. As so often happens, the developers hired non-union labor and refused to pay it "Area Standard Wages" nor health or pension benefits. Facing repeated protest from the NYCDCC, the fund eventually sold off its interest in the project. Now the NYCDCC is fighting the same battle with the EMC Corporation because its divisions hire sub-contractors to evade union workers. The Area Standard Wage concept dates from the Hoover administration, when there was a state-led attempt to ensure out-of-state bid contractors paid the "prevailing wages" of the geographic region, not cheaper wages that might have prevailed in their home states. Since many states lack prevailing wage rules, these battles are still being 'waged' across the country.

On Wednesday, May 22nd, reports surfaced of the collapse of two garment factories in Cambodia. Representatives for H&M affected surprise on learning that its clothes were being manufactured at one of these buildings. Ironically, the H&M spokesperson blamed the dearth of supply chain control on the vile practice of unapproved sub-contracting.

Yet just over a hundred years ago, Urban Sinclair was documenting conditions in Chicago's meatpacking district that resembled the heedless practices we see today in Bangladesh and Cambodia, and the same sort of underhanded methods we see in New York. Decades of unceasing protest, including the use of general strikes, led to whatever wage standards and safeguards American workers enjoy today. Yet as American labor costs rose throughout the 20th century, corporations got nostalgic for the old days, when profits topped seventy percent and laborers were a fragmented mass of immigrants, platoons of desperadoes with scant language skills and American dreams, all too willing to sign onto any project that paid. There were few confederates or leagues or unions in play. No covenants between capital and labor, when the nation was a good seventy years shy of an Occupational Safety and Health Administration (OSHA). Corporate America soon founds its Shangri-La on the cluttered shores of the Pearl River Delta and densely packed Dhaka garment zones, where it was Chicago's Packingtown and England's Manchester all over again. What luck! You could pay 19th century wages and charge 21st century prices.

Naturally, today the shelves of H&M are cleared on credit. Incomes have stagnated or fallen, depending on your metric, since the late sixties. The credit card bubble, more than $800 billion and counting, is surpassed only by the college debt of the cardholders. When these bubbles burst, a great leveling will follow, as the quality of life in America will slide inexorably toward the Third World, while hundreds of millions of arriviste middle class in Asia will discover H&M for themselves, as shops filter down to lower-tier cities. Its products might be denominated in Yuan, but they'll be shilled with the same carrot of social cache, iridescent anchor stores, and images of callow ingénues lingering under the shade of palms—just in Macau, not Malibu. The point being, for any middle class to emerge into the modern age and take up the baton of mass consumption, there must be a fledgling populous of wage slaves emerging in parallel, a couple of centuries and countless injustices behind. As Asian wages rise and America's fall, it will economic sense to bring offshored jobs back home to escape pesky unionized Mandarin and Thai and Bangladeshi labor. Back to the deflated cities and beggared communities of North America, where the war for a fair share can begin afresh.

(*Dissident Voice*, May 29, 2013)

The Middle Children of History
The not so subtle demise of the American Dream

Gore Vidal once said, "History is the story of the migration of tribes." No surprise, since the concept of migration typically conjures images of huge congeries of peoples moving across the plains of some remote developing state, generally in piecemeal fashion, trickle rather than flood, until the character of that region is fundamentally remade. Think of Republican fear of America soon assuming a Hispanic complexion. Think of European fears that the EU will soon assume an Arab or North African complexion. But these are perhaps historical shifts, slow-motion migrations that cannot be brooked by fragile legislation.

But there are other kinds of migration. Like geographer David Harvey evolved his discipline into a broader study of the social geography of capitalism, migrations occur on planes other than topographies. America is in the midst of one that may be irreversible. We are on a glide path from the high peak of peerless economic and military might to the low plain of a hypermilitarized deindustrialized backwater. It is a kind of historical and economic migration that may one day be memorialized by a latter-day Gibbon.

FDR gave us a New Deal. LBJ gave us the Great Society. Reagan gave us trickle down. Clinton felt our pain. Bush gave us mission accomplished. Obama gave us hope we could believe in. All that, and look where we are now.

A recent Demos study shows that the top 10 percent of families own 75 percent of America's wealth. The bottom half own one percent. Within this wealth picture, Demos further found that white families own 90 percent of the nation's wealth. Blacks and Hispanics? Two percent each. The other five percent is owned by a mishmash of ethnicities.

The White House and the Bureau of Labor Statistics (BLS) place extraordinary emphasis on the unemployment rate as one of a couple of measures by which we can say—with scientific certainty—that the economy is recovering, however tepidly. But the unemployment rate trumpeted by the White House and the Bureau of Labor Statistics (BLS) naturally fudges the data by not counting people who have stopped looking for work. Some are in school, some are retired, and some are discouraged by the persistent absence of viable employment.

The other preferred White House metric is the total number of jobs created each month. The BLS jobs report is treated with near religious reverence on a monthly basis. Although it takes close to 100,000 new jobs just to keep pace with population inflation, this is a largely forgotten qualifier of the sunny coverage that the media lavishes on any BLS report that shows the slightest uptick in jobs.

But there are numerous other metrics that belie this rosy hologram.

Let's look at some 160 million adults who are in the work force. The Freelancers Union and Elance-oDesk recently reported that a third of American workers are now "freelancers". Or temps, to use the less flattering term. The shifting of workers from permanent to a contingency basis is no surprise and seems to follow in the wake of the longstanding trend in offshoring—both committed to making labor costs a smaller share of overhead. Likewise, many of the jobs created during Barack Obama's "recovery" have been low-wage service sector jobs, many of them part-time or temporary. Yet academic studies suggest that it is full-time work—and only full-time work—that produces economic growth.

Then take a look at the rate of labor participation, which excludes retired, mentally ill, and discouraged workers. This is a 30-year low. Not a good sign. Despite the administration's triumphalism, more would-be working adults are out of the labor force than at any time since the early eighties.

Not surprising then that economist Richard Wolff notes that one in seven American families are now coping with food insecurity. He has said this figure, which exploded after the mortgage meltdown, has not appreciably declined since, hovering in the 14 percent range. So one in seven people are struggling to fill the family belly. Plenty more pulling doubles at your local fake Irish pub. Plenty more are ghosts that flit from temp job to temp job, bereft of benefits and the cash or confidence to make long-term investments.

Which means, to make ends meet, people are taking on yet more debt. The U.S. credit market debt has reached $57 trillion. No surprise there. But the only solution to the debt is either default or, as the market seems to think, the exponential expansion of credit. Which is what led to the mortgage collapse in 2008. People couldn't pay their bills. You might suggest that people simply pay their debts, but the reason consumer debt is skyrocketing in the first place is because our bereft citizenry can't afford to pay the bills they already have on the salaries they already earn. Incomes that have been on a glide path to subsistence wages, even as inflation creeps higher.

Which is why retailers are flat-lining. And remember, a retail sale includes dodgy propositions like buying on a no-money down installment plan. No payments until Doomsday. Zero interest until the Apocalypse. Given the institutional bias against economic reform, credit expansion seems the only acceptable solution. (Note the swelling subprime auto-loan market.) But more credit at the consumer level means adding new bills to cover the ones you couldn't pay in the first place—at interest. Wal-Mart, Target, McDonald's and even Whole Foods are struggling. These are lynchpins of American consumption.

Rather than create new jobs, the plan seems to be to reinflate the housing market and allow owners to borrow against their rising equity—just like before. The National Association of Home Builders (NAHB) and a hefty share of the mainstream media (MSM) are waxing optimistic about our economic prospects. Economic observer Wolf Richter trots out the phrases that roll off the media tongue: "historically low rates," "affordable prices," and "pent-up demand."

It's true that home prices have risen since last year, a *prima facie* cause for optimism. But the rise in prices isn't matched by new sales. Across the board, it seems, home prices have been rising in particular at the top end, even as home sales collapse. Seems a $500,000 McMansion is a decimal too far for your garden-variety server at TGI Friday's. And yet homebuilders are sustaining their optimism even as foot traffic fades and inventory climbs. The debt solution seems unworkable. People don't have the resources to buy the home in the first place, before even thinking about borrowing against its equity.

What's the upshot? You could do worse than conclude that Democrats and Republicans alike offer little to nothing for the working class—and the increasing unworking class. That we live in an disinterested oligarchy rather than a much-trumpeted democracy has been laid plain by none other than Princeton. Another ineluctable conclusion is that we're headed for another meltdown.

The main authors and editors at Zero Hedge publishes under the name "Tyler Durden", which was Brad Pitt's memorable character from 1999's *Fight Club*. He sums things up nicely: "In other words, the economy doesn't really recover but remains in a depressing and durable state lingering between shallow contraction and [the] absence of that."

This is a fact hidden by the beltway de-emphasis on quality of jobs being created and a tunnel-visioned focus on simple quantitative figures. A faint note of hope was rung by Yves Smith at Naked Capitalism, where he suggests that some policymakers are beginning to understand that massive inequality actually affects growth, namely by placing what should be self-evident in bold headlines: there won't be much consumer demand from an economy that keeps around a quarter of the work force unemployed, a third swimming from gig to gig in a "flexible" labor market, and many of the rest racking up debt in part-time jobs that pay a pittance.

It was Marx who argued that capital doesn't particularly want full employment. Instead, it prefers that "flexibilised" labor market with a huge army of reserve labor, pooled in an economic stew of mortgage, credit, and college debt. An army of desperados help capitalists keep wage growth down and profits up. If anything, this insight lends weight to the idea that this slow glide into a developing economy profile is all part of the larger strategy conceived and executed by

214

globalized elite capital. Maybe one day wages will come on par with China and they'll start onshoring production in order to cut delivery costs. Unless of course by then China is the consumer market worth courting. At that point they might just leave production where it is.

In any event, the average liberal American with a steady job and bright career prospects will likely be content to digest the administration's two-point summary of the jobs market, commit the stats to memory, and deploy them as a rationale to stump for Hillary in 2016, who will trot out those same figures, stump on a foundation of faux recovery policies like a vague "jobs program" and "onshoring more manufacturing" and helping debt peons to tread water for another four years.

Fight Club was one of the first and last Hollywood films to actually challenge the cult of consumerism and its various discontents. Midway through the movie, Durden preaches to his underground crew of social misfits. "I see all this potential. And I see it squandered. An entire generation pumping gas, waiting tables, slaves with white collars. Advertising has us chasing cars and clothes, working jobs we hate so we can buy shit we don't need. We're the middle children of history, man. No purpose. No place. We have no Great War. No Great Depression. Our Great War is a spiritual war. Our Great Depression is our lives."

Fifteen years later, this feels slightly prophetic. Are we the middle children of American history, caught between a post-war boom and Third World status? Sightseers of decline and fall? From a populace with more material wealth, higher incomes, and a seemingly stable set of relations between capital and labor, to a nation mired in stagnation, declining wages, and emptied factories in which that delicate balance of constituencies has been upset? In the grand marriage of democracy and capitalism, it appears capitalism has bought democracy and become an oligarchy. The rich live high above the street, immunized against the quotidian blight. The rest subsist far below, wandering aimlessly among the ruins of a lost idealism.

(*State of Nature*, October 6, 2014)

The Poverty Party
The neoliberal elite envision the end of poverty—with great fanfare.

The backslapping one-percent threw themselves another party last week. An air of accomplishment and self-regard hung in the air. The stewards of progress donned their Sunday best. The paladins of global growth mounted their white steeds. And together they announced that they had, under the rippling banner of free market capitalism, dragged a billion peasants from the forests of deprivation into the elysian fields of a buck twenty five a day. A self-congratulatory bacchanalia ensued.

The cover of *The Economist* told the story. At the bottom of a crudely drawn hill, a silhouetted man raced gleefully toward prosperity. Beyond him a pictogrammed child leapt in the air, thrilled to be on the cusp of subsistence wages. In business class air space across the globe, corporate jetsetters sipped their silent cocktails, sniffed the air for the filets being prepared in the forward cabin, and leafed through the "End of Poverty" issue. As they scanned the numbers, they felt a vague uplift at being part of a system that promised to put an end to human misery.

The occasion was an upcoming meeting at the United Nations, where the international community would be tasked with replacing the soon-to-expire Millennium Development Goals (MDG) with a fresh tranche of well-intentioned targets. The magazine leader set the scene. In the last two decades, a billion people have crossed the dollar twenty five a day threshold, supposedly a brilliant marker of our collective progress. Plenty of reassurances were on offer: all figures had been properly adjusted for inflation; there was no legerdemain at work here.

Further down, amid the clinking glasses and triumphant boasts, we discover that three quarters of these billion lucky souls are Chinese. This disposable fact—an intellectual party favor for the swooning neoliberal crowd—is quickly bypassed as a fresh sub-head exults, "Capitalism, take a bow!"" Gratitude is lavished on the responsible parties: "Most of the credit, however, must go to capitalism and free trade…" and later, after a rubbishing of subsidies for the middle class, the anonymous author notes that "the biggest poverty-reduction measure of all is liberalizing markets to let poor people get richer." And the party was on.

The Magic of Metrics
Before addressing these claims, we should briefly note what the leader and subsequent briefing left out. (Much of the following is drawn from the inestimable globalissues.org, run by editor Anup Shah.) First, all of these claims are based on World Bank statistics that attentive economists have derided (see Sanjay Reddy and Thomas Pogge's "How Not to Count the Poor") and a majority of others have met with an opaque silence, evidence either of disinterest or

arithmetical inattention, or likely a combination of both. The numbers—big surprise—focus narrowly on incomes, and aren't holistic in that they don't factor in malnutrition or under-nutrition, water access, sanitation, heath care, education, literacy, or a range of important quality-of-life indicators beyond the almighty Yuan.

Such indicators are especially important when you consider that, though a majority of the world's extreme poor dwell in rural areas, millions are hustling into the cities, where the expansion of urban slums are <u>outpacing</u> urban growth, according to the MDG. One in three city dwellers are slum dwellers. Slum conditions have their issues, too. Lots of ghetto residents fuel their fires with animal dung, which does wonders for indoor air quality, more fatal even than malaria or tuberculosis. But in conditions of collapsing makeshift shelters and open defecation, these may be lesser concerns. By the way, unlike earlier estimates, only a "proportion" of households using pit latrines are now counted as slum residences.

Sans China
Consider other overlooked facts from the *Economist*'s chest-thumping paean to market fundamentalism. Let's remove China from the equation. It is a unique case to which we'll return. Aside from the Mandarin Miracle, what does the world look like? Well, poverty <u>doubled</u> in Africa between 1981 and 2005, roughly the timespan the World Bank has used for its estimates. What's more, the total numbers of global poor have remained steady over the same period, excluding China, at just over a billion. This suggests that the percentage of extreme poor have dropped, but not the number of extreme poor. The misery is static. This is an important point about neoliberal economics we've been laboring under for about forty years, since it refutes the free-market claims produced in the leader. This, too, is a point worth repeating: we're talking about the *extreme* poor, not the poor or low income. *The Economist* routinely ignores this fine distinction when, in various headlines and sentences, it simply uses "poverty" instead of its more fatal variety.

So let's broaden this picture just a bit. By the World Bank's own questionably optimistic methods, half the population of the earth lives on $2.50 or less a day. A mere 80 percent of us live on $10 or less a day. Including China. These numbers have held steady since the eighties. So thanks to the Chinese economy a hefty chunk is rising out of extreme poverty, but the rest of the low-income world is on a treadmill going nowhere. No surprise, as Reddy's report challenges the idea that $1.25 is enough to supply basic necessities or enough to fuel attempts to escape poverty. It may be just enough to slow the down escalator to disease, misery, and death. Perhaps the champagne elites overlooked this mite-sized factoid. If you are reading this on a cross-Atlantic jet, you may want to summon that second cocktail.

The poorest 40 percent of the world bring in about five percent of its income. Seventy-five percent accrues to the top 20 percent. The 2007 United Nations Human Development Report suggested that for the vast majority, these gaps are growing. These inequality figures belie the congratulatory tone of *The Economist* article, but one can plausibly assume that the authors have never stepped foot in a Mumbai slum or spent their formative years foraging for food in a Dhaka ghetto. After all, the billion or so that have can't read or write. Nor can they count on adequate access to water, or basic sanitation, which can lead to the health problems mentioned earlier. A steady mix of stunted growth, sickness, and missed schooling is no path to the staff of *The Economist*. Rather than meditating over the sacred texts of Austrian economists, millions of developing-world women spend hours a day gathering water supplies for their families. First things first.

Many of these poor are children. With about two billion kids in the world, half are impoverished. Most of these billion children struggle to find adequate shelter, safe water, and minimum healthcare. Like their parents. Not a recipe for optimism about the future. However, the magazine remains sanguine about our prospects. The thumping party tunes at the home office help, like the libations at cruising altitude.

State Secrets
A passerby might note the underlying tenor of sarcasm in my prose, and might ask, "Well, didn't those Chinese billion do better under capitalism?" No doubt they did. But the subtle lie at work here is what kind of capitalism put that extra penny in the pockets of the urban migrant. *The Economist* staff would have you believe neoliberal prescriptions are responsible for lifting those grateful billion from the pit of economic despair. The recipe is familiar: starve the state, unwind the regulatory regime, corporatize the commons. But this tired and discredited storyline holds less water than the clay pot on the head of a Ghanaian woman. Six hundred and eighty million Chinese didn't emerge from the bogs of indigence by dint of the invisible hand. No, no. The hand was quite visible, and it belonged to the Chinese state. A semi-socialist state at that. (Note the mild turbulence at ten thousand feet.).

Anyone watching for the past decade should know that China's boom has happened thanks to massive state intervention in the economy. You remember the bylines. Bridges to nowhere. Cities from scratch. Monolithic dams designed to divert entire water tables. You name it, Beijing had a hand in funding it.

The Chinese government, led by former President Hu Jintao and current Premier Wen Jiabao, took a conscious left-turn from free market policies in the early 2000s. They funneled monies into state companies and initiatives and exerted a variety of federal controls over utility prices and major productive capacities.

218

State-owned companies, for instance, largely dominate Chinese telecommunications and the energy industry. In *The New York Times* article linked above, Jiabao even extolled the organizational advantages of the socialist system. (A few scoffing grunts can be heard in business class—those Communist dinosaurs just don't get it.)

Yet socialism isn't necessarily the key issue here—it's Keynesian capitalism. By exerting the power of the state, China was more or less following the Keynesian growth strategy that Britain and the United States used to transform themselves into global empires. And which protected fledgling domestic industry for a century before embracing the 'free market'—once it had competitive advantages with which to demolish foreign competition. This is the antithesis of the "market liberalization" *The Economist* credits with the reduction of poverty.

The Flip Side
But not all is socialist sunshine and light. The free market does deserve a little credit. In fact, those Chinese factory workers collecting their pittance have *laissez faire* to thank for their sprawling factory zones and spuming industrial chimneys. When all the Bretton Woods capital controls came down in the 1970s—as the sages of deregulation had campaigned for—a curious thing happened. Corporate chieftains immediately began to scour the globe for rock-bottom labor. Imagine how Jack Welch's eyes lit up at the thought of building engines in Asia for a fraction of what he paid the spoiled American line-worker. Can you envision Phil Knight's grin when he recognized the cost savings of erecting a few unregulated factories in some tropical South Asian jungle? Or when Steve Jobs—fresh off another Vegas-style product announcement—was approached by the venerable capitalists of Foxconn? They found their Shangri La in the Pearl River Delta. In the last twenty years, we've hemorrhaged millions of jobs to China, generating pittance wages for millions of rural migrants lured into urban slums by the promise of Western standards of living. (Remember that the issue isn't simply the poverty wages, but the slight percentage of the surplus value created by production that these workers receive.)

So where does that leave America? Clearly not in the same destitution of developing world's ghettos. But not in a flush of prosperity either. Consider this: One in six Americans is living in poverty. If you put extreme indigence, general poverty, and low-income conditions together, you find that about half of America is low income or worse. Nearly a third of urban African-American kids are facing food insecurity. A million American students are homeless. Hard to do your homework when you can't figure out where to sleep at night. Or what to eat. In the 1970s, one in 50 Americans used food stamps. Today it is one in six, for a grand total of fifty nine million citizens.

This is the flip side. Despite neoclassical dreams of uncapped growth, in what author and professor Geoff Mann calls, "actually existing capitalism", when jobs appear in one location, they've often been shipped from another location. China's rise is our demise. At least in actually existing globalization. It doesn't have to be this way. An import-substitution economy, with firms owned or funded by the state, could easily maintain American prosperity even as China grew by the same approach. But that wouldn't deliver the astonishing profits that corporate captains earn form shareholders and themselves by playing global labor arbitrage.

That's the crux of it—greed. The Gap and Wal-Mart have refused to sign onto the Bangladeshi Accord for Fire and Building Safety in the wake of the factory fires and collapse in Dhaka. According to the International Labor Rights Forum, upgrading the facilities would cost Wal-Mart, "two-tenths of 1% of the company's profit last year, and just 1% of the dividends paid out last year to the Walton family heirs" and "…at most, 0.8% of the [Gap] company's profits last year, and just 1.5% of the net wealth of Gap's founder Doris Fisher". If this isn't greed, what is it? A judicious responsibility to shareholder value? Corporate profits in America have reached levels unseen since the 1960s, and still CEOs balk at the smallest outlay for worker protections. That's the neoliberal model— privatize your assets so they can be monetized for the benefit of the few instead of the many, deregulate your industries to reduce overheads like wages and benefits, and downsize your government so it can't enforce what hasn't already been deregulated.

For a system of wealth creation as wondrous as *laissez faire* capitalism—at least according to the high priests at *The Economist*—it is strange to see so much social unrest around the world. Can't these grating hordes have a little patience and wait for the invisible hand to sprinkle a few pennies on their benighted heads? Why all the outrage in Istanbul and Ankara, Sao Paulo, Rio, and Belo Horizonte, Chicago and Dhaka and Kunming?

Attention, world. Turbulence ahead. The captain has just signaled we might be in for a spot of bother. Even in business class.

(*State of Nature*, July 1, 2013)

The Trans-Pacific Sellout
Guaranteed profits—at any price

Last Tuesday, President Barack Obama told beltway bullhorn Chris Matthews that Senator Elizabeth Warren was "wrong" about the Trans-Pacific Partnership (TPP), the largest trade deal in American history, linking United States and Australia, Brunei, Canada, Chile, Japan, Malaysia, Mexico, New Zealand, Peru, Singapore and Vietnam in a pervasive and binding treaty. The president was referring to Warren's claim that the trade treaty will license corporations to sue governments, and her contention that this was, to put it mildly, a bad idea.

Warren isn't wrong, Obama is. And he knows it. The entire TPP, as understood, is based on a single overarching idea: that regulation must not hinder profiteering. This is a fundamentally anti-democratic concept that—if implemented—would effectively eliminate the power of a demos to make its own law. The final authority on any law's validity would rest elsewhere, beyond the reach of popular sovereignty. From the TPP point-of-view, democracy is just another barrier to trade, and the corporate forces behind the draft treaty are intent on removing that barrier. Simple as that.

That's why the entire deal has been negotiated in conclave, deliberately beyond the public purview, since the president and his trade representatives know that exposing the deal to the unforgiving light of popular scrutiny would doom it to failure. That's why the president, like his mentor President Clinton, has lobbied hard for Trade Promotion Authority, or Fast Track, which reduce the Congressional role in the passage of the bill to a 'yea' or 'nay.'

Cracks have begun to show in the formidable cloak behind which the deal has been structured. A coalition of advocacy groups advanced on the U.S. Trade Representive's office this week. Wikileaks has obtained and released chapters from the draft document. Senator Harry Reid declared his position to Fast Track as, "…not only no, but hell no." Warren has proved to be a persistent thorn in the side of White House efforts to smooth over troubling issues with the deal. But the monied interests that rule the beltway have all pressed for passage. And as a Fast Track draft makes its way through Congress, stakes are high. The TPP is, in the apt estimation of political activist Jim Hightower, a "corporate coup d'état."

Not for the first time, the president and his Republican enemies are yoked by the bipartisan appeal of privilege against this faltering fence of protest. The marriage of convenience was described in last Friday's sub-head to a *New York Times* article on TPP: "G.O.P. Is Allied With President Against His Own Party."

All The Usual Suspects

Who else supports the TPP? Aside from this odd confection of neoliberals, the corporations that rule the beltway feverishly back the TPP. From the leak of Sony digital data we learn that it and its media peers have enthusiastically pressed for the passage of the deal. Sony is joined by major agricultural beneficiaries (Monsanto), mining companies like Infinito Gold, currently suing Costa Rica to keep an ecology-harming mine pit active, as well as pharmaceutical coalitions negotiating stiff intellectual property rights unpopular even in Congress, and various other technology and consumer goods groups. And don't forget nicotine kingpins like Philip Morris.

Obama reinforces the corporate line: "We have the opportunity to open even more new markets to goods and services backed by three proud words: Made in America." Perhaps he isn't aware that our leading export is the workforce that once took pride in that moniker. We've exported five million manufacturing jobs since 1994, largely thanks to NAFTA, the model on which the TPP is built. The TPP will only continue that sad trend. The only jobs not being offshored are the ones that can't be: bartenders and waitresses and health care assistants. That's the Obama economy: a surfeit of low-wage service jobs filled by debt-saddled degree holders. As Paul Craig Roberts argued in *The Failure of Laissez Faire Capitalism*, between 2007 and 2014, some eight million students would graduate from American universities and likely seek jobs in the United States. A mere one million degree-requiring jobs would await them. The irony of Obama's statement is that the TPP would actually move to strip the use of labels like, "Buy American," since they unduly advocate for local goods.

In truth, the authors of the treaty already know all this. The bill concedes as much, with Democrats building in some throwaway provisions of unspecified aid to workers whose jobs have been offshored, and a tax credit to ostensibly help those ex-workers purchase health insurance. Cold comfort for the jobless, as they are exhorted by the gutless paladins of globalization to 'toughen up' and deal with the harsh realities of a globalized economy. As neoliberal stooge Thomas Friedman has said, companies in the glorious global marketplace never hire before they ask, "Can this person add value every hour, every day — more than a worker in India, a robot or a computer?" Of course, the answer is invariably no, so the job goes to Bangladesh or a robot. No moral equation ever enters the picture. Just market discipline for the vulnerable and ingenious efforts by a captive state to shelter capital from the market dynamics it would force on others.

The Investment Chapter
Despite Obama's disingenuous clichés about "…fully enforceable protections for workers' rights, the environment and a free and open Internet," the trade deal makes it clear that labor law and environmental law are both barriers to profitability. We know this thanks to Wikileaks, which once again proved its inestimable value by acquiring and releasing another chapter from the cloak-and-

dagger negotiations. This time it was the investment chapter, in which so much of the treaty's *raison d'etre* is expressed.

As Public Citizen points out in its lengthy analysis of the chapter, any domestic policy that infringes on an investor's "right" to a regulatory framework that conforms to their "expectations," is grounds for a suit. Namely, the suit may be pressed to "the extent to which the government action interferes with distinct, reasonable investment-backed expectations."

Here's what the TPP says about such legislation as it relates to investor expectations: "For greater certainty, whether an investor's investment-backed expectations are reasonable depends, to the extent relevant, on factors such as whether the government provided the investor with binding written assurances and the nature and extent of governmental regulation or the potential for government regulation in the relevant sector."

Try putting that tax on financial transactions. Forget it. Barrier to a reasonable return. Don't believe it? Just read the TPP investment protocols that would ban capital controls, which is what a financial tax is considered to be by TPP proponents. Try passing that environmental legislation. Not a chance. Hindrance to maximum shareholder value. Just ask Germany how it felt when a Swiss company sued it for shutting down its nuclear industry after Fukushima. Try enacting that youth safety law banning tobacco advertising. Sorry. Needless barrier to profits. Just ask Australia, which is being sued by Philip Morris for trying to protect kids from tar and nicotine.

Public Citizen has tabulated that, "The TPP would newly empower about 9,000 foreign-owned firms in the United States to launch ISDS cases against the U.S. government, while empowering more than 18,000 additional U.S.-owned firms to launch ISDS cases against other signatory governments." It found that "foreign investors launched at least 50 ISDS claims each year from 2011 through 2013, and another 42 claims in 2014." If these numbers seem small, recall that for a crucial piece of labor legislation to be struck down, only one firm need win in arbitration in order to financially hamstring a government and set a precedent that would likely ice the reformist urge of future legislatures.

As noted earlier, the text also appears to suggest to ban the practice of promoting domestic goods over foreign—another hurdle to shareholder value. This would effectively prohibit a country from implementing an import-substitution economy without threat of being sued. Governments would be relieved of tools, like tariffs, historically used to protect fledgling native industries. This is exactly what IMF prescriptions often produce—agricultural reforms, for instance, that wipe out native crop production and substitute for it the production of, say, cheap Arabica coffee beans, for export to the global north. Meanwhile, that producer nation must then accept costly IMF loans to pay to import food it might have grown itself.

Naturally, its not considered meet to mention that protectionism is how the United States and Britain both built their industrial economies. Or that removing competitor market protections is how they've exploited developing economies ever since. The TPP would effectively lock in globalization. It's a wedge that forces markets open to foreign trade—the textual equivalent of Commodore Perry sailing his gunships into Tokyo Harbor.

ISDS Tribunals
The bill's backers point to language in which natural resources, human and animal life, and public welfare are all dutifully addressed in the document. The leaked chapter explicitly says that it is not intended to prevent laws relating to these core concerns from being implemented. So then, what's the problem? The problem is that these tepid inclusions lack the teeth of sanctions or punitive fines. They are mere rhetorical asides designed to help corporate Democrats rationalize their support of the TPP. If lawmakers really cared about the public welfare, they'd move to strip the treaty of its various qualifiers that privilege trade over domestic law. By all means, implement your labor protection, but just ensure "…that such measures are not applied in an arbitrary or unjustifiable manner, or do not constitute a disguised restriction on international trade or investment."

If lawmakers cared about national sovereignty, they wouldn't outsource dispute settlement to unelected arbitration panels, more fittingly referred to as, "tribunals." (Think of scrofulous democracy hunched in the dock, peppered with unanswerable legalese by a corporate lawyer, a surreal twist on the Nuremberg Trials.) Just have a glance at Section B of the investment chapter. Suits will be handled using the Investor-State Dispute Settlement (ISDS) model, itself predicated on the tribunal precedent. And in the event a government lost a suit or settled one, legal costs would be picked up by taxpayers, having been fleeced by an unelected committee whose laws it has no recourse to challenge.

Perhaps investor protections like ISDS were once intended to encourage cross-border investment by affording companies a modicum of reassurance that their investments would be safeguarded by international trade law. But the ISDS has been used for far more than that. The ISDS tribunals have a lovely track record of success (first implemented in a treaty between Germany and Pakistan in 1959). Here's Public Citizen: "Under U.S. "free trade" agreements (FTAs) alone, foreign firms have already pocketed more than $440 million in taxpayer money via investor-state cases. This includes cases against natural resource policies, environmental protections, health and safety measures and more. ISDS tribunals have ordered more than $3.6 billion in compensation to investors under all U.S. FTAs and Bilateral Investment Treaties (BITs). More than $38 billion remains in pending ISDS claims under these pacts, nearly all of which relate to environmental, energy, financial regulation, public health, land use and transportation policies."

New Era, New Priorities
Now the ISDS is a chisel being used to destroy the regulatory function of governments. All of this is being negotiated by corporate trade representatives and their government lackeys, which appear to have no qualms about the deleterious effects the TPP will have on the general population. But then the corporations these suits represent have long since discarded any sense of patriotic duty to their native nation-states, and with it any obligation to regulate their activities to protect vulnerable citizenries. That loyalty has been replaced by a pitiless commitment to profits. In America, there may have been a time when "what was good for Ford was good for America," as memorably put by Henry Ford. But not anymore. Now what's good for shareholders is good for Ford. This was best articulated a couple of years ago by former Exxon CEO Lee Raymond, who bluntly reminded an interviewer, "I'm not a U.S. company, and I don't make decisions based on what's good for the U.S." Those decisions usually include offshoring, liberalizing the labor market, practicing labor arbitrage, relocating production to "business friendly climates" with lax regulatory structures, the most vulpine forms of tax evasion, and so on—all practices that ultimately harm the American worker.

Apple says it feels no obligation to solve America's problems nor, one would assume, any gratitude to the U.S. taxpayer for funding essential research that Apple brilliantly combined in the iPod and iPhone. Former Labor Secretary Robert Reich finally admits corporations don't want Americans to make higher wages. The U.S. Chamber of Commerce encourages shipping American jobs abroad. World Bank chiefs point to the economic logic of sending toxic waste to developing nations. Wherever you look, there seems to be little if any concern for citizenry.

The Financial Times refers to ISDS as, "investor protection." But what it really is, is a profitability guarantee, a legal bulwark against democracy expressed as regulation. Forgive me for thinking that navigating a fluid legislative environment was a standard investment risk. Evidently the champions of free trade can't be bothered to practice it. Still the White House says it has our best interests at heart. If that were true, it would release the full text, launch public charettes to debate its finer points, or perhaps just stage a referendum asking the American people to forfeit their hard-won sovereignty. No such thing will ever happen, of course.

As it turns out, democracy is the price of corporate plunder. After all, the greatest risk of all is that the mob might vote the wrong way. And, as the language of the

TPP makes explicitly obvious, there are some risks that should be avoided at all costs.

(*Dissident Voice*, April 26, 2015)

The Not-So-Small Voice of American Socialism
Wolff in the henhouse

It's instructive listening to a born-again Socialist like Dr. Richard Wolff, Marxian economist and author of *Capitalism Hits the Fan*, which more or less tells you what he thinks of our present economic system. He had been delivering monthly "updates" at the Brecht Forum in New York, but now that venerable institution of the left community has shuttered its doors thanks to a dramatic spike in the greed of local landlords. A couple of years ago, the Forum was still in Manhattan, but had relocated after Hurricane Sandy. One self-identified employee claimed the landlord rescinded the Forum's $5,000 a month rent and replaced it with a $30,000 a month rent. The Brechters promptly decamped for Brooklyn.

And this is just the kind of thing Dr. Wolff preaches about: the unjust power a few people wield over the many. This is at the very heart of his critique of capitalism: the means of production and distribution owned by a few—versus a system in which production and distribution were owned by the many. In his monthly lectures, which seem to have relocated to the New School, the good doctor delivers the truth with unerring simplicity, threading together all the hidden and not-so-hidden injustices of capitalism into a powerful bill of indictments of the capitalist model itself—all with the passion of a political firebrand. Wolff is a confirmed radical in society of apathetic conformists. He wants to talk about America's great taboo topic, class struggle. Thanks to the Great Recession, the shameless bailouts, and the unrepentant thievery of Wall Street, Wolff now has an audience. Books like Tomas Piketty's *Capitalism in the Twenty-First Century* have helped, although Wolff is nonplussed by Piketty's thesis.

Tinkering at the Margins
What irritates him most is the underlying con of Piketty's analysis. After piling up an Egyptian pyramid of data demonstrating capitalism's proclivity to produce ever-greater inequalities, Piketty suggests the rather tame solution of a wealth tax. This, Wolff intones, is little more than was suggested by John Maynard Keynes decades ago, when he promoted greater government intervention to stabilize the economic crises that capitalism ineluctably visits on every society in which it is practiced. (All the more so in societies where the reigning ideology has morphed into a theology, such as ours.) The flaw in the balm applied by these well intentioned but timid architects of reform is that they resolve a symptom but not the system.

For Wolff, it is the system of capitalism that must be radically overthrown if we want to truly rectify the injustices of a construct that privileges elite capital with the majority of the surplus produced by workers, with the freedom to accrue wealth untaxed, and with the discretionary monies with which to buy a venal political class and ensure that the construct never changes. Piketty, like Keynes before him, would tinker at the edges of the system, a bland reformist content to administer a gentle reproof to a greed-consumed elite order.

Perhaps a few tepid reforms would be enacted after years of bitter struggle by an activated proletariat. An alarmed administration might reluctantly skim a sliver of the gains of elite capital and redistribute it to the indigent minions. But as with Keynesian economics, rollback would swiftly ensue. Because by simply taking a wrench to the engine without rebuilding it, one leaves in place the very cause of the original injustice—a capitalist class whose cupidity is not sated, a consumer class whose wallets grow vanishingly small while prices grow oppressively large, and the same cabal of influence peddlers whose swinish behavior brooks no ethic than cannot be reversed for pennies.

The Vitiated Masses
Wolff deploys graphic illustrations of the divide between the rights of the wealthy and the poor, between American democracy and justice. He cites an alarmingly large prison system that functions less as a rehability institution and more as a low-wage labor pool for corporations. Even as crime declines, incarceration rates rise. Even as unemployment surges, providing plenty of inexpensive labor for capital, businesses would often rather enjoy the low-cost benefits of employing indentured slaves (aka prisoners) to handle less palatable industrial work, sometimes for as little as a quarter an hour. What a perverse incentive for incarceration, but what a clever and profitable scheme for unscrupulous multinationals. Just think of it. Corporations looking to stimulate a stagnant bottom line make lavish contributions to ruling parties, who in turn promise to expand the War on Drugs. In so doing, police find fragile minority communities where drugs are trafficked as perhaps the only reliable revenue stream. Find the "perps", incarcerate them, strip them of their rights—especially the right to vote—and send them to the clinker. Presto, you've now ethnically cleansed your cities, denied them the franchise, and produced an insanely profitable business model to boot.

Naturally, it is largely less affluent minority communities that are targeted for arrest for fatuous "crimes" such as holding micro-doses of "contraband" such as marijuana. On a parallel track, upper-echelon white communities in financial industries are finding their far more harmful behavior decriminalized. Wall Street's derivative trades, the lack of position limits, securitization, all march on, shredding the vellum skein of Dodd-Frank as they go. Since most fair-wage American jobs now reside in low-wage Asia, profits are up. Since the Federal Reserve inflates the financial sector with monthly cash injections, stocks are up. All good news for the decriminalized financial class—from which few if any of the perpetrators of the mortgage meltdown are behind bars.

But notice the consequence of this behavior. None of this new money created by fiat is being used to offset the hardships being endured by those who have lost their jobs and have seen their social supports dwindle. Thus it comes as no surprise that Americans are ransacking their 401Ks at record rates. Or that many millions have reached in desperation for the reverse mortgage trap, which exhausts family wealth and leaves despairing progeny with a debt burden rather than a helpful bequeath. No matter—you can work it off behind bars.

History's Legacy
And still none but the few rise in protest. Are we simply too vitiated as a people to care? Too softened by creature comforts? Too bloated by indulgent meals and wearied by the endless entertainments of the distracted class? Drudgery by day, burlesque by night. Who has time to storm the Bastille? Maybe so. But why?

Dr. Wolff points to history. He points back to the days of the New Deal. He notes how, in the wake of FDR's unprecedented activism at the behest of left-wing pressure groups, that one by one the elements of the American Left were isolated, demonized, and demolished. First, the Communists. Easily accomplished through the Cold War and its handmaiden, the McCarthy Era. Next up were the Socialists, whose unique faith was easily conflated with that of Communism. And finally, the workers. Trade unions were tarred with the same Communist brush, said to be harmful to growth and dramatically undermined. Private sector union membership is now below 7 percent.

Yet only by demanding, insisting, importuning, and discomfiting power, and then persisting in that behavior, is real change ever achieved. Wolff seems somewhat optimistic that a groundswell is coming; he sees large turnouts for his talks in places like Nebraska and Kansas City. He sees swelling frustration in the deflationary politics of the times. Perhaps he is onto something, is himself driving something. The forces arrayed against *his ilk*, as the facile MSM might paint him, are formidable, amoral, and monomaniacal in their pursuit of wealth. But Wolff often recites an apocryphal tale from the Bolshevik Revolution that illustrates a puissance far beyond that of any police state or surveillance apparatus. One that might outflank both.

Lenin, Stalin, and Trotsky sit together in the Winter Palace in the aftermath of Red October, flush with the shock and optimism of their sudden triumph. As they converse, a comrade enters the room to tell them the state police records are on their way. They arrive, a pile of papers documenting the informants of the state. As they page through the stack, their faces darken. They are each astonished by the number of their comrades who were secret informants of the government. Quislings, traitors, and turncoats among their inner circle. They gaze at each other in disbelief. The room quiets. The mirthful mood of the day vanishes beneath the bleak recognition that their solidarity was naïve. Then Lenin leans back in his chair and smiles. Stalin and Trotsky frown at him—nothing is funny about deceit. But Lenin brightens and says, "Don't you see? It doesn't matter that the government had infiltrated our ranks. When the tide of history is upon you, resistance is futile."

(*CounterPunch*, July 1, 2014)

Part Three
Media Analysis: Sins of Omission

"The most effectual engines for pacifying a nation are the public papers... A despotic government always keeps a kind of standing army of news-writers who, without any regard to truth or to what should be like truth, invent and put into the papers whatever might serve the ministers. This suffices with the mass of the people who have no means of distinguishing the false from the true paragraphs of a newspaper."

Thomas Jefferson

Secretary Kerry Weighs In
Peddling myths to a credulous public

Just last week, the pagliacci at the head of America's Department of State, John Kerry, gave an interview on the much-esteemed house organ of domestic propaganda, the "PBS NewsHour". The entire interview was a farce of human reason, yet was mindlessly absorbed by millions of armchair Americans, 41 percent of whom cannot name the Vice President of the United States. If they cannot perform this simple act of civic sentience, how can they be expected to cut through the thick fog of propaganda that blankets American consciousness on a nightly basis?

They can't. They can't be expected to laugh uproariously when Secretary Kerry points a condemnatory finger at Tehran, blaming them for the mysterious instability in Yemen, and saying, with not the slightest trace of irony, that, "...*the United States is not going to stand by while the region is destabilized* (italics mine)." Nor can they be expected to choke with incredulity when, in his next breath, Kerry says, "...or while people engage in overt warfare across lines — international boundaries of other countries."

No, this is all too much to digest. We are blind to the irony. Blinkered by the hypocrisy. After all, the CIA has been arming al-Qaeda thugs in plain sight for several years now in Syria and Iraq, under the myopic eye of the American public, with hardly a murmur of protest. How compelling must be the White House spokespersons that tell us we are only arming "moderates." We nod sagely from our couches: it is far better to be deposed and slaughtered by moderates than genuine radicals.

No, our blank faces register nary a twitch when Kerry accuses Iran of destabilizing its own neighborhood when it is the United States that has turned the entire region into a confused pastiche of tattered borders, despoiled sovereignties, roving refugees, makeshift graves, and tribal compounds. Evidently, in Kerry's twisted beltway perspective, only the U.S. is authorized to ruin the region—a region where it doesn't belong but has refused to vacate since the collapse of the Ottoman Empire. From the arrogant diktats of British imperialists to the cynical coups and free-market experiments of imperial America, the Middle East has suffered ceaseless depredations at the hands of the West. One wonders how countries like Iran are even capable of sitting at the negotiating table and facing our cabal of inveterate cheats. Maybe they don't read history. We certainly don't.

History As Myth
For Kerry and his State Department lemmings, history is a blank slate on which future historians will pen a chronicle of plaudits to American power. We will be

232

lauded as peacekeepers or, as President Obama noted in 2009, the exceptional nation that "...has underwritten global security for over six decades."

Presently, the U.S. is stepping up weapons shipments to Saudi Arabia and establishing a "joint coordination planning cell" with Riyadh to help in the destruction of Yemeni rebels seeking redress for religious oppression and other injustices inflicted upon Yemenis by pro-Western governments in the capital of Sana (such as idly permitting unrelenting drone attacks by the U.S.). This is Obama's, and by default, Kerry's, idea of global security. To hurry arms to a brutal authoritarian dictatorship that wishes to violate the sovereignty of a neighboring nation in order to install a pro-Western government that mirrors its own regime. Thus far it has met with little success, destroying only civilian infrastructure, murdering just 500 civilians and uncounted Houthi rebels (soldiers are unpeople, duly fit for slaughter), but doing little to impede radiating Houthi control over the country.

This is quite surprising considering that Nobel Peace Prize winner Obama awarded the protest-crushing, female-silencing, citizen-beheading Saudi royals the largest weapons deal in the sordid history of U.S arms sales in 2010. Not to mention a colossal shipment of banned cluster munitions two years ago. Why exactly, one wants to ask, do the Saudis need more guns? Haven't we supplied a sufficient arsenal with which to thwart populist uprisings and annihilate Shia calls for justice in the flashpoints of self-determination that dot the peninsula? One would think. But then there is always the possibility that the Kingdom might unspool itself back into the array of fiefdoms from which it first emerged.

The NPT Community
Later, deeply concerned interlocutor Judy Woodruff (a modest improvement on unblinking zombie Jim Lehrer) suggested the Iran deal was really about just delaying Tehran's acquisition of a nuclear weapon. This question itself is so profuse with false assumptions that it would require an entire seminar to unpack. But Kerry breezily dismissed the query with his own priceless riposte, claiming that the deal represents "...a guarantee that for the next 15 to 20 years [Iran] won't possibly be able to advance that program and then, *when they become a more legitimate member of the non-proliferation community and subject to lifetime inspections* and investigation, we will have accountability (italics mine)."

As a member of the Non-Proliferation Treaty (NPT), Iran was determined to have concluded its nuclear weapons program in 2003, subsequently subjecting itself to the most rigorous and unnecessary inspection regime in the history of the IAEA. It was hectored and harrowed into this regime by the two leading nuclear threats to world peace: the United States and Israel. The former has openly violated the NPT by distributing nuclear formulas to India, both a non-signatory and serial provocateur in Kashmir, the lush territory it disputes with arch-rival Pakistan, another nuclear power that has the U.S. to thank for its status. The latter, America's deputized aggressor Israel, is another non-signatory of the NPT and currently holds the dubious honor of being the single member of the Middle East opposed to the creation of a Nuclear Weapons-Free Zone, such as exists in Latin America and other saner parts of the planet.

Woodruff, masterfully emulating a paranoid neoconservative, continued to ask misinformed questions, one of which prompted the pagliacci to reply, "They have agreed to abide by what is called the additional protocol of the nonproliferation treaty. That protocol requires participating states to adhere to a higher standard and if they don't, Judy, then the sanctions can, and will, come back."

Interesting that the aforementioned U.S., violator of the NPT and the only country to actually use nuclear weapons, has refused to abide by the additional protocols it desperately wants applied to any nation it deems a regional rival.

In 2004 the U.S. adopted the Model Additional Protocol in a good-faith attempt to bring other NPT members on board. But they were of little consequence to the U.S. as it is a Nuclear Weapons State (NWS) and thus held to less stringent standards than Non-Nuclear Weapons States (NNWS). Nuclear states don't have to comprehensively apply the safeguards to all of their sites. They can even except sites for reasons of national security. Non-Nuclear states have to make practically all of their facilities—even non-nuclear energy sites with the additional protocol—eligible for NPT safeguards.

But that's not all. As soon as it pretended to adopt the protocols, the U.S. added two addendums to its adoption, a corollary of the NPT's exemption for NWS members, called by the U.S. a National Security Exemption (NSE). The NSE lets the U.S. permit access to sites, activities, information, and additional locations, *at its own discretion*. A second addition limits the use of environmental sampling and the number of inspectors who can access a site.

Before Congress ratified this feckless edition of the additional protocol, it added a letter from the Senate Foreign Relations Committee that stipulated that the NSE would be used with, ahem, some regularity. It also insisted that the President ensure that security and counterintelligence training will have been completed by the time any sites are declared to the IAEA.

Were Iran to attempt anything of the sort, the Lausanne negotiations would have instantly collapsed, additional sanctions would have been hysterically imposed, and both the U.S. and Israel would have begun issuing veiled threats (violating, in the process, both the NPT and the UN Charter). As it is, Iran has dealt with demands to "anytime, anywhere" access, air reconnaissance, access to military bases, and other invasive measures. Remember, when the U.S. was turning the vice grip on Iraq before attacking it more than a decade ago, it even requested unfettered access to Saddam Hussein's presidential palace, which it later inhabited. Most of this while Hussein was frantically trying to negotiate a peace via any go-between he could find—including Syria, France, Egypt, Russia, and Germany. Aside from Iraq, it is also useful to contrast U.S. hyper-vigilant posture toward Iran with its laissez faire attitude toward Israel's absurd "policy of deliberate ambiguity" regarding its WMD stockpile. Of course, it isn't as though the Israeli arsenal is manned by some rabid paranoiac.

Buying Friends, Abetting Allies

Woodruff, at this point, has descended into a frothing neocon huff. She announces that cutting a deal to limit Iran's nuclear program is fraught with concerns (as opposed to the alternative, perhaps, of annihilating Iran's nuclear sites and rendering swathes of Persia uninhabitable thanks to the not-so sanitary act of dropping thousand pound bombs on nuclear reactors). She clamors, "The U.S. is going to have to increasingly show its support for those in the region who fear Iran." Kerry attempted a dignified and fulsome response, mumbling some well-rehearsed stock clichés about defending "friends and allies." He might have simply shouted into Woodruff's ear that the United States delivers $3B annually to Tel Aviv for its bi-annual slaughter of defenseless Palestinians. He might have hammered the table and reminded the world that he personally mails Egypt's criminal President Abdul Fattah al-Sisi some $1.3B a year to fund mass trials of dissidents, fulfill numberless death sentences, and slaughter protestors. He might have flung his hands in the air and recalled the bombastic $10B deal the U.S. cut in 2013 with Israel, the Saudis, and the United Arab Emirates, providing even more aircraft, missiles and transport vehicles to these terribly fraught apartheid states and fanatical theocracies teetering on the edge of civilization. Finally, calming himself, he might have softly reiterated the $60B record-setting deal with the Saudis, the munitions of which are proving themselves admirably in their ability to liquidate both human quarry and entire municipalities across Yemen.

Finally, our lantern-jawed secretary closed the interview with a fatuity, claiming that Iran was flying supplies to the Houthis "every single week", despite the fact that the Saudis have imposed a no-fly zone over the country that would have prevented this. No matter, there is little time to resolve contradictions when there are so many raging fires to extinguish on the ground across the oil-rich Middle East.

Perhaps Kerry should have ended the show by stating the obvious: we are executing a global campaign to disarm every potential rival via the effete and infinitely manipulable constructs of international law. As part of this campaign, Iraq was combed by inspectors and bombed by Western aircraft on a regular basis for more than a decade before having its defense systems torpedoed and its entire army disbanded. All this as a deliberate prelude to permitting the artificial nation-state to sink into anarchy. Syria had its chemical weapons stockpile destroyed on the farcical premise that it used them against citizens just as international observers entered the country. Libya had to have its air force vaporized, its government toppled, and its left-leaning president brutally murdered. And then— the coup de grace—Iran has had its 20 percent enriched uranium destroyed, its civilian nuclear program rolled back, and its nation set to by IAEA inspectors eyeballing every nuclear facility in search of the slightest discrepancy. Clearly, that 1979 revolution still burns brightly in the minds of Pentagon hardliners.

Fear not, Mrs. Woodruff, for it won't be long before there aren't any countries left in the Middle East capable of defending themselves. That is, aside from the vitiated autocrats and trigger-happy settlement builders we have authorized to arbitrate the bloodletting in the world's most brutalized region.

(*CounterPunch*, April 15, 2015)

Whitewashing the Middle East
Removing America from the picture

It bears repeating what George Orwell said about propaganda, that what is left out is often more telling than what is left in. To take a sampling of two recent mainstream articles on Syria, it's painfully obvious that Orwell had a point. A piece for CNN by Geneive Abdo, a fellow at the Brookings Institute and Middle East specialist, called, "Why Sunni-Shia conflict is worsening"; and an article for *The New York Times* by Robin Wright of the U.S. Institute of Peace and the Wilson Center, entitled, "Imagining a Remapped Middle East."

You'd think, reading essays from two "distinguished" regional experts, all your bases would be covered. You'd imagine these specialists would delineate the various sources of conflict in the region. But then you'd be wrong.

Abdo trots out Sunni Egyptian cleric Yusuf al Qaradawi, whose ideology-cramped visage broadcasts his Sunni theology to millions across the Arab world. Over the summer, Qaradawi launched some vehement broadsides against Shias and Alawites, both sunk in the quicksand of Syria's civil, sectarian, ethnic, and proxy war. Qaradawi wants more disgruntled Sunnis to flood across the Syrian border and help destroy the al-Assad government. Given Qaradawi's recent penchant for spray-painting the non-Sunni world as a bacterial swamp of infidel faiths, one can only imagine the Sharia Elysium he envisions for the post-Assad Levant.

Against Qaradawi, Abdo poses Hezbollah's Hassan Nasrallah, who has led Hezbollah fighters into Syria to defend Assad against their eternal Sunni nemeses. Nasrallah, too, says Abdo, has enflamed sectarian divide between the two strains of Islam. Then there is Iraq's Nuri Kamal al Maliki, branding the Sunnis terrorists and marginalizing them at the federal level.

So there we have it, the impetus of the factionalism across the region. Even the astute reader is left to wonder why these turbaned clans can't pull themselves together and live in republican amity like we in the West. The astute reader then turns the page, reads with a kind of dumb fascination about the government shutdown, though never drawing a parallel between the two cultures riven by sects.

But here's the kicker: Abdo says nothing about America's role in any of the conflicts she spotlights—not Syria, not Palestine, not Iraq. It's as if the United States is some partial observer, gazing judiciously across the wide gulf of cultural superiority that separate us from them. No article claiming to explain the source of rising Sunni-Shia infighting can exempt American antagonism from its explanation without losing credibility.

Yet no reader without the imperial backstory will know this. What is more likely to happen is that the liberal page-turner drops into Starbucks the next morning to sip a steaming latte and peruse the heady journalism of the *Times*. There he or she encounters another article about the regional chaos, this by another "distinguished" scholar, Robin Wright. Quickly confirming that this is not Robin Wright, the actress and star of the imperishable *Princess Bride*, our reader naively imbibes Wright's whole-born narrative. Surely, this byline has the ring of authenticity. Wright namedrops historical events like Tea Partiers namedrop Founding Fathers.

Within a few paragraphs everything is clear. It was the European colonial powers a century ago that lit the fuse. Visions are conjured of Sykes and Picot wielding their long knives and "carving up" the flayed carcass of the Ottoman Empire. Hence the Syrian, Iraqi, Libyan, and Yemeni chaos. One has the feeling of reading from the vantage point of post-history, as if we've buried our errant colonial impulses, and moved forward into a well-lit world of democratic liberalism, where we gently impart our values to the benighted nations of the East who, in Dutch politician Pym Fortune's memorable phrase, "haven't yet been through the Laundromat of the Enlightenment."

Wright then maps out—with the help of a *Times* cartographer at his elbow—a new Middle East composed, essentially, of several fascinating new nations, including Sunnistan, Shiitestan, Kurdistan, a Mediterranean Alawistan, and an African Tripolistan and Cyrenaicastan. You have to concede—in the best Sykes-Picot tradition—that this new map seems to make some sense. After all, all the nations are aligned along tribal or ethnic lines. One could see it working out. And yet this evidently easy-to-achieve remodeling of the colonial architecture fails to note even in passing the influence of the arch neo-colonialist currently plaguing the region—the United States. It's as if Wright, like Abdo, suffer from a historical blind spot, into which plummet cruel sanctions, forgotten incendiary interventions, imperial occupations, and the incessant floggings-by-drone of the entire region.

Neither Wright nor Abdo once mention that America brutalized Iraq for twenty years, and turned Sunni against Shia in a nation in which the sects had lived in amicable proximity, albeit under the Baathist Saddam Hussein regime. Neither notes that but for American arms, training, and cash—plus the help of its local proxies—the Syrian rebellion, such as it was before metastasizing with foreign infusions, would by now have been put down by the Syrian government. Nor is NATO's pernicious role in the destabilization of Libya given the slightest column width. Forget the drone strikes in Yemen—another dustbinned piece of nonhistory.

Of course, Wright and Abdo are constricted by the unspoken taboos of their publishers—two centrist pillars of the mainstream media (MSM). They likely would've faced rejection or redaction had they scrutinized the U.S. role with even the slightest disapproval. Even so, our reader is left to conclude something on the order of believing that our noble attempts to bring a semblance of humanitarian calm to the region is a futile endeavor. That we (with our ahistorical impatience) will never pacify the enmities that enflame these obscure sectarian tribes. The reader shakes his head despairingly, swigs the last of his spiced latte, and exits into the bright day of his brand-saturated cityscape. In America, the reader ponders, we have consumer tribes, harmless in their affectations, gentle in their fangless rivalries: Apple versus PC, Coke versus Pepsi, Target versus Wal-Mart. Capitalism, he thinks, is such a benign thing. If only we could better export it to peoples abroad, how much better off they'd be. Yet it is this same capitalism that underlies the xenophobic uproar of the Middle East. Not its first cause, to be sure, but its latest irritant. And if our own scholars are the agents of our geopolitical blindness, what hope do we have of ever awakening to the omissions at its core?

(*Dissident Voice*, November 1, 2013)

Responsibility to Inflict
How the U.S. perverts the language of conflict

You wouldn't expect a comedian to deliver an insight into the American doctrinal system, but George Carlin once did. During a memorable stand-up performance, he talked how the American military manipulates the nomenclature of war to shield the public from the grisly effects of the battlefield. He noted how, after World War I, soldiers returned to the States having been "shell shocked." After World War II, those vacant stares, concussed reasoning, and horrible headaches were refashioned as, "combat fatigue". A lexical summit was reached following the Vietnam War, when psychiatrists hit upon the bland and innocuous, "Post-Traumatic Stress Disorder", a benign term more suggestive of the clinical aftermath than the living hell.

As our Gulf Wars unfurled before us on CNN, the phrase was truncated to "PTSD", satisfying the all-new 24-hour news cycle. Once mentioned, it was swiftly buried beneath an avalanche of mystifying military terms, such as the F-15, the scud, SA-3s, WMDs, projectile munitions, ABMs, incendiaries, UAVs, bunker busters, APCs, Kevlar vests, DMZs and IEDs, among others. No surprise that the viewer would often fall into a catatonic state as the on-screen army lieutenant waved a magic wand at a topography of bombardment.

Carlin's expert description of this nuanced progression from clarity to anguished abstraction is still relevant, as the Pentagon busily redefines every new term generated by feckless international bodies hoping to place constraints on its reckless imperialism. Even as I write, three such terms are helping to freshly disarm the conscience of the American public for wars with Syria and Iran, a process now codified into three simple steps, no more difficult to learn than a Caribbean salsa.

Falsifying a Legitimate Framework: RTP
America has for some time been intervening abroad under the flimsy pretext of "humanitarian intervention." Since Bill Clinton's Eastern European exploits made a travesty of this well-intentioned term, and George Bush's Iraqi quagmire helped cement its fate, it became obvious to the sage arbiters of empire that our ham-fisted use of such a delicate euphemism had delegitimized it. Hence the more recent "Responsibility to Protect" (RTP), which makes imperial interference feel a bit more consequential if not sufficiently messianic. The RTP protocol was defined and passed as a resolution by the United Nations General Assembly in 2005, the latest in a long line of ethical protocols designed to restrain state terror, but whose ironic fate is to be used by states to justify the very acts they were meant to deter.

As Noam Chomsky recently related, another version of RTP has been commonly invoked by the West, namely that of *The Report of the International Commission on Intervention and State Sovereignty on Responsibility to Protect*, by an extempore Canadian commission headed by Gareth Evans, former Australian Prime Minister and "intellectual father" of RTP. It authorizes "action within an area of jurisdiction by regional organizations subject to their seeking subsequent authorization from the Security Council." Note how this version makes the Security Council's sanction a requirement—*ex post facto*. The U.N. version requires not only a Security Council resolution in advance of action, but also real attempts at mediation, sanction regimes, and other non-military means as a necessary impediment to rash unilateral interventions. By including an option for states to act beyond the purview of the U.N., the Evans version simply elides the very protocol that gave the RTP its heft. States are thus morally compelled, when faced with a temporizing Security Council, to act unilaterally to address "conscience shocking situations crying out for action." This hyperbolic moral injunction was conjured, in spirit if not name, by George Bush in 2003 just moments after conjuring WMDs out of thin air. The right often rails against the idea of diluting our sky-clear moral vision in the amoral bogs of the U.N. General Assembly, where worldwide pariahs like Iran and Iraq and Venezuela have a say in the decision-making process. But the alternative—leaving decisions about interventions up to the jaundiced and self-interested judgment of imperial states—is far worse.

Summoning the Mushroom Cloud: WMDs
With the shabby justifications of a reworked RTP at the ready, the fear of "conscience-shocking" events must be made to "cry out for action." This spring and summer, the always-useful Weapons of Mass Destruction (WMD) rationale is being re-commissioned as the falling domino that invokes RTP in the Syrian conflict.

In contrast to PTSD, which is what our soldiers suffer, and is thus designed to disguise the evidence of real anguish, the term WMD is what the enemy possesses, and is thusly calibrated for maximum fearmongering. So far it is a brilliant acronym for stirring up hostile sentiment. The signal for intervention used to be given by a mushroom cloud, the fear of which had mid-century Americans frantically digging absurd bomb shelters in their backyards. Today, the mushroom cloud is a low fog. Chemical weapons are the trending WMD and clear "red line" across which dire consequences await the perpetrator. On Tuesday *The New York Times* noted that the Obama administration has concluded "with some degree of varying confidence," that the Assad regime has slain rebels with chemicals. This despite concessions that the sarin chain of custody is hazy. The issue is thus settled. Evidence is no longer a prerequisite for conviction. A dose of speculation from the *Times* and a grave look from John Kerry will do. (See the annexation of Texas and Gulf of Tonkin as useful precedents in this regard.)

Thus President Obama will be free to step forward, unencumbered by needless legal restraints, to invoke his fuzzy math: WMD + RTP = NATO. Later a few groggy journalists, hung over from the festival of premeditated bloodlust, will hazily recall that key evidence for the use of chemical weapons is by the rebels themselves. But the story will be drowned in the din of gurgling marine fuel as aircraft carriers speed toward Syrian shores.

War By Another Name: NFZ
If WMDs are the smoking gun, the vaunted "No Fly Zone" has become the default mechanism by which we actually implement RTP. As witheringly outlined by Conor Friedersdorf of *The Atlantic*, the imposition of a no-fly zone is an act of war. Imposing one means laying waste not only to a country's air force, but also its caches of anti-aircraft missiles. Warmongering zealots like Arizona Congressman John McCain, who persistently calls for a no-fly zone in Syria and anywhere else bombs can helpfully fall, often fail to note—as even U.S. military officials have—that just 10 percent of the casualties in the Syrian conflict are victims of President Bashar al-Assad's air power. Doesn't this call the no-fly strategy into question? Not if your objective is regime change. Any pretext will suffice.

It is instructive to note the disinterest with which the U.S. treats another less scintillating strategic option: diplomacy. Proposed talks between Syrian stakeholders and Russia, the United States, and Iran have been kneecapped by America's petulant insistence that Iran be excluded. After all, the larger point of the conflict is to expose Tehran. Having them usefully negotiating a cease fire would only undermine that objective's critical dependency: deposing Assad. Comically, the Syrian National Council (SNC) has lifted a page from America's negotiating playbook by refusing to participate unless Assad's removal is agreed to in advance. This is asking that one's demands be met as a pre-condition of negotiations. If Assad were to concede this, what would be point of the talks? Could not the SNC simply fax a timetable to the bunkered regime?

This petulant demand by the SNC belies its hubris. The SNC knows that the West is salivating at the prospect of replacing Assad with a pliant Sunni proxy. But even this is naïve. Can we be sure that the SNC itself is not a front for a bought-and-paid-for mix of Salafist mercenaries, motivated, armed, and backed by Western intelligence?

Victimized, Ignored
In any event, foreign populations aren't much interested in our brotherly assistance. Perhaps because it so often results in greater bloodshed than was originally anticipated by state action, as was the case with the NATO bombing of Serbia in 1999, when massive ethnic cleansing was hysterically conducted under

the chaos of the bombing raids. In just the last dozen years, our unquenchable thirst for petro-resources has led, directly or indirectly, to hundreds of thousands of deaths across the Middle East, beginning in Iraq and continuing through the Syrian conflict today, with rubble-strewn Libyan towns and Afghan villages littered in between. And that's leaving aside the many thousands of dismembered, otherwise maimed, exiled or internally displaced citizens.

It was precisely this fear that caused the RTP to draw fire at a 2009 General Assembly debate. All of the usual suspects objected. Iran complained of the lack of a normative framework for the application of RTP. Venezuela stressed the possibility that the concept could be manipulated for the exploitation of weaker states. Syria complained that a critical clause on the protection of the population had been mysteriously elided from the Secretary-General's report on implementation of RTP. But their misgivings fell on deaf ears. We're now witnessing the consequences, as the Syrian plot unfolds with an Iranian showdown brimming on the horizon. Is it any wonder that the U.S. and Israel were notably silent during those proceedings? Would their insipid platitudes have inspired anything but contempt?

Almost anywhere American foreign policy is at work, there are tragedies afoot. Drones filter through the depleted ozone over lands still smoldering with depleted uranium. The most heinous deformities now appear in the birth population of Fallujah, where the U.S. deployed white phosphorous against Iraqi 'insurgents.' At the State Department, bizarre blueprints dating from the neocon era still promise to refashion the Middle East as a deregulated free market paradise—or at worst, an plundered ghetto good for renditions and other imperial habits that require a touch of inhumanity.

Flags of Freedom
Whether the rationale is RTP or WMD or a flight-free sky, the images that will soon swarm your television set will serve up the prefabricated triumph of might in the service of higher moralities. You already know the script. Our benevolent but militant emissaries will plant our spangled flags alongside foreign oil derricks. They'll prop up a makeshift government infused with uncomprehending exiles and unfeeling sociopaths. Then they'll attempt to pacify the vanquished with the maxims of a threadbare paternalism—and the great gift of a phantom democracy. The storyline has become so tawdry and discredited in recent years, it is a wonder that our government even bothers to defend its actions. Better to drop the pretense altogether, embrace the dark side, and proclaim our lofty vision for the planet: One world, under surveillance, with indignity and injustice for all. All rights reserved.

(*CounterPunch*, June 14, 2013)

The Department of Justice v. the Fourth Estate
Under Normal Circumstances

On Tuesday the *New York Times* revealed that the Justice Department had seized without notice caches of Associated Press phone records. Not simply work phone logs, but home and mobile phone records of A.P. journalists as well, from the agency's bureaus in New York, Washington, and Hartford, Connecticut, and the House of Representatives itself. How kind of them to finally break the news to the A.P. We don't exactly when the DOJ seized the records. Initially, their response to that query was a limp, "sometime this year," according to the *Times*. Later in the day, Attorney General Eric Holder got marginally more specific, conceding the records were taken in April and May. We may not know just when the AP's private audio correspondence was taken, but we know why.

Last June, AG Holder launched two investigations to discover the sources of two leaked stories: one, information on the Central Intelligence Agency's foiling of a Yemeni bomb plot, broken by an A.P. journalist; and second, the Stuxnet cyber-attacks on Iran, broken by the *Times*. It's hard to imagine Holder's actions as anything other than an extension of President Obama's nationwide dragnet on whistleblowers, or as the Commander-in-Chief might say, snitches. Six federal officials have been indicted for leaks under Obama.

Notable among Obama's domestic targets is soldier Bradley Manning, whose release of files to WikiLeaks may conceivably have led to the Iraqi rejection of the American Status of Forces Agreement (SOFA) that then Secretary of Defense Leon Panetta was attempting to ram through Baghdad's puppet parliament. A mightily armed, billion-dollar embassy at the heart of the country evidently does little to assuage American alarm over precious Arab oil possibly falling into the wrong hands—hence the persistent request to keep tens of thousands of troops in-country on a semi-permanent basis, legally immune from prosecution. If Manning's actions help derail this imperial arm-twisting, should he not be lauded among both Iraqis and liberty loving Americans? Perhaps, but instead Manning has enjoyed the dank and dreary half-life of solitary confinement—for the better of two years. Such is Obama's regard for truthdiggers. Like a Mafia don ordering hits over his nightly repast, Obama too is anxious to seal the vaults of empire from pesky gadflies. What iniquities may lurk behind those sealed doors—which are ironically less secure than Manning's own concrete block?

The Times then notes, "Under normal circumstances, regulations call for notice and negotiations, giving the news organization a chance to challenge the subpoena in court." That's right. The Justice Department is supposedly beholden to the law, which stipulates it must subpoena records—like ordinary mortals—and then only as a last resort. A spokesman for the U.S. attorney of the District of Columbia (notice how far down the tree we've tumbled from the Oval Office; Holder was forced into the spotlight later on Tuesday) said that the DOJ must notify the affronted party in advance *unless*—and here comes the clichéd caveat that renders meaningless everything that goes before—unless that notification jeopardizes the investigation, or as the spokesman put it, "poses a substantial threat" to the inquiry. Note here that the threat is not to national security, but to the investigation into the leaking of information related to an investigation of a potential threat to national security. Rather quickly, the vocabulary of fear is extended into the abstract, where complicity soon becomes the subject of supposition.

What *The Times* fails to notice, although it might when it discovers half its journalists have been wiretapped, is that "normal circumstances" have been banished to the netherworld (where lurk our naïve, pre-McCarthy ancestors). The war on terror has transformed the entire globe into a potential flashpoint or field of fire. Notably the online world. The offline world is already swarming with Homeland Security agents, baiting Arabs into basements to plot crimes against the state. The DHS is stockpiling weapons at a frantic pace, clearly anticipating a domestic Armageddon. But it's the online world from which we have the most to fear. Far easier to craft the appearance of complicity from a few transaction records and cell transcripts than by suckering unwitting immigrants into bomb-making workshops.

Obama's contempt for the rule of law is now legendary. Already his wake is strewn with the tatters of discarded precedent—due process, *habeas corpus*, assassination (which his former heroes Lincoln and Reagan outlawed in writing), not to mention the shredding of fragile international conventions on torture and acts of aggression. Think of the consequences. Will journalists now think twice before breaking a controversial story that casts the administration in a dubious light? Will they think again before interviewing a source that might have contacts in terrorist cells? How easily, with phone records in hand, could the DOJ assemble a slapdash case against an official or a journalist for having delivered, via the media, "material support" to the enemy, who, as mentioned before, is everywhere. The White House definition of the enemy now assumes the character of the ancient definition of God, "a circle whose center is everywhere and circumference nowhere." There are simply no boundaries left for innocents to cross. We are suspect by the mere fact of our being. This is a crucial point of *Darkness at Noon*, Arthur Koestler's magisterial depiction of the cannibalistic nature of the Communist purges. The authoritarian state always internalizes its conception of evil—it looks within for targets, those it suspects of undermining its grip on power. And if that power is wantonly held, as it invariably is, the state becomes paranoid and suspects everyone. So, as Koestler's Rubashov notes time and again, one's actual innocence is of little regard to the state. What matters is sustaining the national narrative and silencing dissenters (those who would offer an alternative account). Which is precisely the point of these DOJ investigations.

Obama is anxious to put the proverbial kibosh on leaks, constitutional hurdles notwithstanding.

And all of it—from indefinite detention to the destruction of whistleblowers—is sanctified under the banner of keeping you safe. Your security is paramount, thus your liberty is required. We have dispensed with finite campaigns such as actual and cold wars, where the enemy is a state, and opted for a campaign far more catholic in its embrace, a campaign against a tactic—war without end. It is this narrative, so tirelessly rehearsed yet so tiresome and trite, that still needs to be relentlessly discredited. Until it is, normal circumstances will remain a legal fiction, as removed from reality as so many of the conjured threats themselves.

(*CounterPunch*, May 16, 2013)

The Illusion of Debate
Consensus for the people that matter

A recent article in FAIR reviewed the findings of its latest study on the quality of political "debate" being aired on the mainstream networks. It studied the run-up to the military interventions in both Iraq and Syria. Perhaps the arbiters of the study intended to illustrate what we've learned since the fraudulent Iraq War of 2003. Well, it appears we've learned nothing.

FAIR spent hours painfully absorbing the misinformation peddled by such soporific Sunday shows as CNN's State of the Union, CBS's Face the Nation, NBC's Meet the Press, and ABC's This Week, plus some of the more popular weekly political programming including ADHD-inducing CNN's Situation Room, Fox News Channel's Special Report, the venerable sedative PBS NewsHour, and MSNBC's Hardball. You know the cast of characters: glib George Stephanopoulos, forthright Candy Crowly, harrowing Wolf Blitzer, and stentorian Chris Matthews. Images of their barking maws are seared into the national hippocampus.

Overall, 205 mostly government mouthpieces were invited to air their cleverly crafted talking points for public edification. Of them, a staggering sum of three voiced opposition to military action in Syria and Iraq. A mere 125 stated their support for aggressive action.

Confining its data to the Sunday shows, 89 guests were handsomely paid to educate our benighted couch-potato populace. One suggested not going to war. It stands to reason that considered legal arguments against these interventions got the short shrift, too.

The media consensus on Syria and Iraq isn't an isolated instance of groupthink. Far from it. It conforms to a consistent pattern, one that has at its core a deliberate disregard for international law and efforts to strengthen transnational treaties and norms regarding military action. (Although transnational law regulating trade is highly favored, for obvious reasons.)

Here the *New York Times* uncritically repeats Israel casualty figures from the recent attack on Gaza. The journalist, Jodi Rudoren, gives equal legitimacy to sparsely defended claims from Tel Aviv and "painstakingly compiled research by the United Nations, and independent Palestinian human rights organizations in Gaza." She adopts a baseless Israeli definition of "combatant", ignoring broad international consensus that contradicts it. She dubiously conflates minors with adults, and under-reports the number of children killed. And so on. All in the service of the pro-Israel position of the paper.

In 2010 Israel assaulted an aid flotilla trying to relieve Palestinians under the Gaza blockade. Author and political analyst Anthony DiMaggio conducted Lexis Nexus searches that demonstrate how U.S. media and the NYT in particular scrupulously avoid the topic of international law when discussing Israeli actions. In one analysis of *Times* and *Washington Post* articles on Israel between May 31st and June 2nd, just five out of 48 articles referenced international law relating to either the flotilla raid or the blockade. DiMaggio dissects several of the methods by which Israel flaunts the United Nations Charter. He adds that Israel has violated more than 90 Security Council resolutions relating to its occupation. You don't get this story in the American mainstream. But this is typical. U.S. media reflexively privileges the Israeli narrative over Arab points of view, and barely acknowledges the existence of dozens of United Nations resolutions condemning criminal actions by Israel.

It's the same with Iran. For years now, Washington has been theatrically warning the world that Iran wants to build a bomb and menace the Middle East with it. That would be suicidal. It is common knowledge among American intelligence agencies, and any others that have been paying attention, that Iran's foreign policy is deterrence. But this doesn't stop the MSM from portraying Tehran as a hornet's nest of frothing Islamists.

Kevin Young has done a telling survey of articles on nuclear negotiations between the U.S. and Iran. Some 40 editorials written by the *Times* and the *Post* were vetted. Precisely zero editorials acknowledged international legal implications of U.S. public threats and various subversions led by Israel, such as assassinating scientists and conducting cyber-attacks, both innovations on standard violations of sovereignty. However, 34 of the pieces "said or implied" that Iran was seeking a nuclear weapon. Forget that 16 American intelligence agencies stated that Iran had no active nuclear weapons program. These papers of record prefer to trade in innuendo and hearsay, despite assessments to the contrary. More than 80% of the articles supported the crippling U.S. sanctions that are justified by the supposed merit of the bomb-building claim.

Prior to Young's work, Edward Hermann and David Peterson looked at 276 articles on Iran's nuclear program between 2003 and 2009. The number itself is staggering, more so when stacked against the number of articles written over the same period about Israel's nuclear program: a mighty three.

This is interesting considering the posture of both countries in relation to international treaties. Israel freely stockpiles nuclear weapons and maintains a "policy of deliberate ambiguity" about its nuclear weapons capacities, despite frequent efforts by Arab states to persuade it to declare its arsenal (which is estimated by some to be in the hundreds). Also, it has yet to sign the Treaty on the Nonproliferation of Nuclear Weapons (NPT) that has been signed by 190 nations worldwide. This intransigent stance has marooned the broadly embraced idea of working to establish a nuclear weapons free zone in the region.

Contrast Israel's behavior with that of Iran itself, which has permitted extensive inspections of its nuclear facilities. The *Times* recently noted the country's main nuclear facilities were "crawling with inspectors." Iran is also a party to the NPT and is a full member of the IAEA. It continues to try to work toward a reasonable solution with the West despite debilitating sanctions levied on it by the United States. America has unduly pressured the IAEA to adopt additional protocols that would require prohibitively stringent demands on Iran, rendering the possibility of a negotiated solution comfortably remote from an American standpoint. (These additional demands reportedly include drone surveillance, tracking the origin and destination of every centrifuge produced anywhere in the country, and searches of the presidential palace. All of this passes without comment from our deeply objective journalist class.)

Coverage of Iraq is no different, particularly in advance of periodic illegal war of aggression against it. Former U.N. Special Rapporteur on Palestine Richard Falk and author Howard Friel conducted a survey in 2004 assessing the *New York Times'* pre-war coverage of Iraq in 2003. In more than 70 articles on Iraq, the *Times* never mentioned "UN Charter" or "international law." The study also found "No space was accorded to the broad array of international law and world-order arguments opposing the war." But such arguments only exist outside of Western corridors of power in Washington, London, Paris, and Tel Aviv.

This isn't debate. Real debate is pre-empted by internal bi-partisan consensus on some basic issues: maintain a giant garrison state, shrink the state everywhere else, preference corporations over populations, restrict civil liberties to secure status quo power structures. So when it comes to Iran, Iraq, Syria and the like, the question isn't whether to go to war, but what kind of war to fight. Hawks want bombs. Doves want sanctions. Publicans want Marines. Dems want a proxy army of jihadis. They both want Academi mercenaries. (Obama hired out the gang formerly known as Blackwater to the CIA for a cool $250 million.) And when we've finished off ISIS, the question won't be about an exit strategy, but whether to head west to Damascus or east to Tehran.

The question isn't whether to cut aid to Israel given its serial criminality in Gaza and the West Bank, but how fast settlements can annex the Jordan Valley without attracting more international opprobrium. (International law, again, set aside.)

On the domestic front, the question isn't whether to have single payer or private healthcare, but whether citizens should be forced to purchase private schemes or simply admonished to do so. The question isn't whether or not to keep or strengthen New Deal entitlements, but how swiftly they can be eviscerated. The question isn't whether or not to surveil the body politic, but where to store the data, and whether or not to harvest two-hop or three-hop metadata. The question isn't whether or not to hold authors of torture programs accountable, but how much of the damning torture report to redact so as to leave them unprosecutable. The question isn't whether or not to regulate Wall Street but, as slimy oil industry lawyer Bennett Holiday put it in *Syriana*, to create "the illusion of due diligence."

All this is not to say the MSM isn't aware of alternative viewpoints. It is, but it only acknowledges them when they can be used to justify a foregone conclusion. In the past year, the MSM has nearly become infatuated with international law. Friel has tracked the paper of record's response to the Ukrainian fiasco. What did he find? When Russia annexed Crimea, the *Times* inveighed against the bloodless "invasion" as a gross violation of international law. Eight different editorials over the next few months hyperventilated about global security, castigating Russian President Vladimir Putin for his "illegal" violation and his "contempt for," "flouting," "blatant transgression," and "breach" of international law. Calls were sounded to "protect" against such cynical disregard of global consensus. Western allies needed to busy themselves "reasserting international law" and exacting heavy penalties on Russia for "riding roughshod" over such sacred precepts as "Ukrainian sovereignty."

Quite so, as Washington supports the toppling of democratically elected governments in Kiev and Tegucigalpa, sends drones to ride "roughshod" over Yemeni, Pakistani, Somali and other poorly defended borders; and deploys thousands of troops, advisors, and American-armed jihadis to patrol the sectarian abattoirs of Syria, Iraq and Afghanistan. But better to exonerate ourselves on those counts and chalk it up to the fog of war. After all, we follow the law of exceptionalism, clearly defined by Richard Falk as, "Accountability for the weak and vulnerable, discretion for the strong and mighty."

(*CounterPunch*, December 2, 2014)

All the News Fit to Omit

The New York Times published a thought-provoking <u>exchange</u> last week between its former editor Bill Keller and journalist Glenn Greenwald, expositor of the infamous Snowden files. The dialogue was highly entertaining and articulate, with veiled nastiness simmering just beneath the surface. Keller played his typical hand, that of the coolly dispassionate paladin of journalism, while Greenwald was his usual feisty self, unapologetically so. The tete-a-tete revolved around the question of whether there was or could be or should be objective journalism. Keller, representing the fatally corrupted establishment, suggested it was the shining ideal to which all journalists should aspire. Greenwald said that every journalist had an opinion, which was better disclosed than masked. It is hard to imagine anyone eluding the grip of bias. Doesn't conviction quietly shade every sentence, each minute construction, every essay? If nobody is objective, why not reveal one's stance in advance? But Keller hews to his position, one that I believe is belied by a look at *The Times* coverage in practice.

Keller then claims that when journalists—or activists, to use the pejorative— reveal their actual views, it "becomes tempting to omit or minimize facts, or frame the argument, in ways that support your declared viewpoint", or undeclared views, as it were. This is, of course, what *The New York Times* excels at— minimizing facts. And as Greenwald later points out, why does revealing one's views make it more tempting to shade the argument than if one disguises one's views? In fact, the latter provides more "latitude" to deceive. Keller later claims the opposite, that the self-declared partisan has put his pride on the line, and thus has greater incentives to deceive. This definitely may be true, but it cuts both ways. There is more pronounced pressure on the partisan to recognize and deal with facts contrary to his argument. The closet partisan can simply omit or overlook uncomfortable facts without feeling his publically visible personal ideology is at stake.

Rather, the relevant distinction is between those journalists who try to reveal all the facts, and those who deliberately conceal half of them. Or, in some cases, deliberately falsify them. As Orwell said, the power of propaganda is in what it conceals, not what it reveals. That is indeed the power of *The New York Times* in its capacity to win the faith of millions of liberal readers who, without the least apprehension, finds it even-tempered journalism entirely trustworthy. Even as *The Times*, usually in its political pages, presents half the facts. For instance, to take the recent case of Syria, *The Times* deliver the facts of the chemical weapons attack in Damascus suburb. All very well and good. Then they offer the stated opinion of the State Department that these attacks were carried out by the al-Assad government. *The Times* does not usually include the consensus of myriad nations that contest the State Department line, or the findings of U.N. investigators that offer evidence that contradicts the U.S. position. If these contrary opinions are noted, it is infrequently and with significantly fewer column inches than is devoted to the official White House position. Never is the U.S. opinion critiqued for its truthfulness. Never is the veracity of the U.S. claim established. Journalism is by definition an attempt to find and report facts; since *The Times* fails to pursue and report facts in instances like this, it is here abdicating its journalistic ethos and rather practicing an elaborate form of stenography. This is tantamount to being the official press service of the White House.

Even so, Keller claims his paper succeeds by, "telling them (readers) what they needed to know to decide for themselves". He uses waterboarding as an example. And in this instance, he has a point. The waterboarding facts were laid plain in the paper, as far as I know. In this instance he defends the substitution of "enhanced interrogation techniques" for the word "torture", rejecting the argument that to do so is a failure of courage. And yet—to use an unbracketed phrase such as, "enhanced interrogation techniques" is tantamount to an endorsement, is it not? Words are sanctioned by their use.

Recognizing a need to deal with omitted stories, which include the paper's advance knowledge of illegal wiretapping prior to the 2004 elections, Keller argues that the real test for journalists is judging whether to withhold information because it may jeopardize lives. He points to a decision in the late nineties to not publish information on unsecure enriched uranium in the Caucasus. Smart move by *The Times* that probably did save lives. But against this single instance one might counterpoise countless stories of biased reportage that certainly helped lose lives. The case for the Iraq war being foremost among them. World opinion, informed research and conclusions by people like former UNSCOM investigator Scott Ritter, were laid aside, and the unproven and unsubstantiated word of the State Department and White House were afforded complete credibility. If this isn't an instance of minimizing facts, framing an argument, concealing one's opinion, failing a test of courage, and endangering lives through institutional bias, then what is?

This model of half-truth reporting is the standard operating procedure of *The Times*. We've seen it on countless occasions. Noam Chomsky first documented it for the masses in his writing on *The Times* lack of coverage of the East Timor massacres in the seventies by the Indonesian military. *The Times*, as mouthpiece of the establishment, had a direct conflict of interest in reporting fully on the slaughter—the United States had engineered the rise of Indonesian ruler and perpetrator Suharto. Carl Bernstein reported in the late seventies on the paper's relationship with the CIA, which including crafting and planting stories on behalf of the CIA. We saw the half-truth model practiced par excellence throughout the rule of Hugo Chavez of Venezuela. Fact after fact was deposited into the aural canal of readers about high crime in Venezuela, about the rate of inflation, about Chavez' effort to extend his presidency through constitutional amendment. All of these gloomy facts, while certainly valid, amounted to an unmistakably negative portrayal of the South American leader.

What was absent from *The Times* criticism was a trove of facts about his presidency that didn't fit the darker narrative *The Times* was developing. Namely, facts about the reduction in hunger, the expansion of healthcare, the eradication of illiteracy, the country's independence from controversial international lending regimes, and the considerable reduction of poverty. Nor were certain conditions, like crime and inflation and debt, contextualized through comparisons with other Latin nations, or with American or European countries. To have done that would have dramatically altered the perception of the Venezuela under Chavez. But to have done so would have also undermined the official U.S. position, which demonized Chavez because he had dared to defy American dominion in their "backyard".

Moreover, when the U.S. position is offered and its counterpoint—often the position of the rest of the world—is not, the former is reinforced with editorial articles on the opinion pages that subjectively justify the American stance. A recent article by scholar Robin Wright discussed the potential for the fragmentation of the Middle East, its causes, and possible outcomes. Wright pointed to British colonialism and the dismantling of the Ottoman Empire as root causes of sectarian conflict. Beyond that, Wright rather typically points to the, "rival beliefs, tribes, and ethnicities—empowered by the unintended consequences of the Arab Spring" for the fraying bonds of Middle Eastern states.

Again—all of these are fair facts and Wright is right to cite them. He then discusses variously the regional conflicts.

Wright then moves into murkier territory. Each point begs a larger question. He talks of Iraq's volatile factionalism. He says Syria, "set the match to itself." Did it? He points to tribal enmities as a spark of the overthrow of Libya's Muammar el-Qaddafi. But were these enmities the decisive factor in his overthrow? He says hope lies in "good governance, decent services and security, fair justice, jobs and equitably shared resources", but concludes those "factors" are a distant hope for the region. Is tribalism the real reason the region lacks these foundational goods?

Nowhere in the article, nor in the capricious redrawing of the Middle East (perhaps channeling the spirit of Sykes-Picot) appended to it, does Wright note the influence of the United States. Its invasion and occupation of Iraq, its backing of Israeli action against Lebanon, its efforts through NATO to overthrow Qaddafi, or its supply of arms to dubious "Syrian rebels". These are incredibly important factors in the sectarian conflicts of the Middle East. There was little factionalism in Iraq before the invasion. Qaddafi would not have fallen to sectarian forces without NATO. Likewise, the so-called Syrian revolution would likely be over but for American arms, training, and money—and targeted strikes from our regional ally Israel. Given these facts, a reader might reasonably conclude that the United States is the primary recent cause of the sectarian strife, and not the incessantly repeated, and racially tinged, "tribal" conflicts.

To cast the absurdity of this kind of non-journalism in stark relief, consider the following hypothetical situation: Imagine if the American South rose up and decided to secede from the Union. As the rebellion was about to be put down, suppose Russia and China chose to back it with small and heavy arms, logistical support, and infusions of cash. At this point, the tide turns and secession seems likely. Then imagine reading an article in the *South China Morning Post* that blamed the dissolution of the country on the fiery and uncontrollable "tribal" disputes among Caucasians—from centuries of hatred between Northerners and Southerners to the unfathomable enmities between Democrats and Republicans, and among fringe radicals on both ends of the political spectrum. Imagine the article never once mentioning the decisive involvement of the Russia-China alliance that was ensuring secession happened. Would the informed reader find this evasion or oversight strange and unjustified? Would she see it as an

254

indication of bias, or at the least shoddy journalism? Or would she see it as a thoroughly reasonable exclusion for the staff at the SCMP to make?

The New York Times greatest sin is one of omission. Presenting half the facts is not journalism, it's partisanship—the very thing former NYT editor Bill Keller claims journalists like Greenwald are practicing. Much like the government of Oceania in Orwell's *1984*, which claims that "war is peace", Keller gets it backward. By design, perhaps?

(*Dissident Voice*, November 7, 2013)

Sins of Omission

The New York Times coverage of Hugo Chavez' death was a bunker buster of misinformation.

The world got word last Tuesday evening that Hugo Chavez had died. Felled by chronic cancer, the 58-year old transformed Venezuela in his 14 years at its helm. He lifted masses of his countrymen from the depths of poverty, from the ignorance of illiteracy, and out of the penury of medical neglect. He reclaimed Venezuela's oil resources for the benefit of the majority, and rallied Latin nations under a banner of common interest, anti-imperialism, and self-determination.

Little to none of this, of course, was mentioned in *The New York Times* ungenerous lead on the demise of the Venezuelan leader. Already, our leading propaganda daily has begun its historical revision of Chavez' legacy. Its prejudiced coverage of the *El Commandante's* death was remarkable only it what it elided from view—namely any of the progressive transformations the Bolivarian socialist engendered. Regarding the state of the nation, only a few conditions were noted. While vague mention was made that Chavez had "empowered and energized" millions of poor people, the print edition headline said Venezuela was a nation in "deep turmoil." The digital edition brusquely mentioned, "high inflation and soaring crime," as well as, "soaring prices and escalating shortages of basic goods." While there is some truth to these claims—particularly in relation to crime—none of Chavez' achievements were noted, an astonishing array of programmatic successes that have dwarfed the failures of his tenure.

But before adding anything else, let's briefly look at the indictments delivered by the *Times*:

- After devaluing its currency in 2010, pundits predicted massive inflation. Instead, inflation declined for two years, while economic growth topped four percent both years. Nor do critics note Venezuela's spiraling rate of inflation before Chavez took office—or that he has actually significantly reduced it. While prices rise with inflation, the government offers subsidi zed goods through weekly *Mercal* and also regularly adjusts minimum w age to match or exceed inflation, which increases consumer purchasing p ower, which itself has increased 18 percent in Chavez' first decade in off ice.

- In stark contrast to improving economic numbers, Venezuela's murder ra te increased threefold during Chavez' three terms in office, now third hig hest in the Americas, calling into question the effectiveness of police trai ning. A new training program was launched in 2009, but has yet to produ

ce results. The Bolivarian National Police, also launched in 2009, has lo
wered rates where it is active, but chronic problems continue to plague th
e country, particularly Caracas, including police corruption, biased judici
aries, the likelihood of not being prosecuted, the presence of millions of
weapons, and the fact that Venezuela is a main thoroughfare for illegal d
rugs on their way to the United States.

- Food shortages are also present, another surprising condition in a country
  of declining poverty. Western critics naturally point to price controls as t
  he cause, providing a typically ideological explanation for a problem that
  appears to have a more nuanced answer. Food consumption in Venezuela
  has exploded since Chavez took office in 1999. The population consume
  d 26 million tons of food in 2012, double the 13 million tons they consu
  med in 1999. The government suggests the shortages are a consequence
  of rapidly increasing consumption. Food production is up 71 percent sinc
  e Chavez took office, but consumption is up 94 percent.

Claims without Context

A day later, the *Times* decided that its stinting initial coverage was too generous:
it had merely listed the flaws in Venezuelan society. What it had failed to do was
pepper the pot with a heavy dose of falsification. It then released a factless
catalogue of misinformation that, when it wasn't quoting louche academics, was
irrigating the column with toxic dogma. It began, in its home page tout, with a
headline about "Debating Chavez's Legacy," by author William Neuman. The
sub-line anxiously opened the festivities with an elephantine distortion:
"Venezuela had one of the lowest rates of economic growth in the region during
the 14 years that Hugo Chavez was president."

Well, after that opener, why bother writing a column? The case has already been
made. Best to have the tout lead to a broken link, or redirect to Thomas Friedman
hyperventilating about the glories of globalization on display in Indonesian
sweatshops. But no, the *Times* were out for blood. This was no ordinary socialist.
Chavez deserved a double-barreled dose of disinformation.

Regarding its initial claim that Venezuela had one of the "lowest rates of
economic growth in the region during the 14 years that Hugo Chavez was
president." This statistic is taken from the World Bank. It is true. What it fails to
mention is the nosedive the Venezuelan economy fell into when U.S.-backed,
right-wing elites overthrew the democratically-elected Chavez in 2002. The
economy fell at nine percent into 2003. Then there were devastating oil
production shutdowns engineered by the same cadre of oppositionists when
Chavez moved to nationalize the oil industry.

Despite this and other opposition attempts to sabotage the economy through food hoarding, price speculation, and other noble measures, the *Times* neither bothers to contextualize their claim nor balance it against the significant achievements of the Bolivarian government. If elements of socialism actually work, don't the *Times* readers deserve to know about them? Evidently not, according to the editors, who see it as their duty to shelter their gullible readership from the facts. But consider these facts about Venezuela's socialist experiment:

- Per capita GDP in Venezuela is up 50 percent since the coup.
- The Venezuelan economy was among the fastest growing Latin nations in 2012.
- Its economy has grown steadily for nine consecutive quarters.
- Inflation has been cut nearly in half since Chavez took office, when it was spiraling out of control thanks to the ever-efficient neoliberal private sector leadership.

A Legacy Belittled
The article then claims that Chavez' massively attended funeral was "a tribute to the drawing power of the charismatic leftist leader, although perhaps not to the lasting influence of his socialist-inspired policies." This line nicely inverts the obvious truth—the masses turned out precisely because of Chavez' socialist-inspired policies. The policies the paper had given an unfair drubbing in the opening tout have driven consistent growth in society's most impoverished sectors. Poverty has been reduced by 70 percent since Chavez won the presidency. Nutritional measures among the poor are up across the board, while strengthened pension programs, freely available healthcare, and an inflation-linked minimum wage are helping produce a viable workforce with growing purchasing power—a prerequisite of demand and economic expansion.

The paper then says Chavez' revolution "remains more limited than he would have liked," a spurious attempt to cast the Bolivarian revolution as a failure, when in fact, against most significant social and economic metrics, the socialist experiment exceeded itself. To reinforce this portrait of another foreclosed attempt to establish a socialist state, the Times trots out Alejandro Toledo, a former president of Peru. Toledo replaced the Peruvian strongman Alberto Fujimori, and was so unpopular—even though he succeeded one of the continent's most vile authoritarians—that his approval rating dropped to six percent in 2004, when street rioting briefly paused to permit the survey. Here is Toledo:

"The important thing is that Mexico has not followed his example, Chile has not followed his example, Peru has not followed his example, Colombia has not followed his example, Brazil has not followed his example. I'm talking about big countries with large, sustained economic growth."

258

Toledo, like the paper, obviates Chavez' stunning impact on continental politics, an influence that has encouraged similar leftist triumphs in Ecuador, Argentina, Paraguay, Guatemala, Nicaragua, and others. Chavez convinced many of his regional colleagues of the dangers of forging discrete trade agreements with the United States—with NAFTA as the *ne plus ultra* in the category—and then promoted regional agreements among his Latin counterparts. Chavez worked to expand Mercosur into a continental trade platform, not simply that of South America's southern cone. Then he established such inter-continental co-operatives as Telesur, PetroCaribe, and Petrosur, as well as the Bolivarian Alliance for the Americas (ALBA).

Sidelining Socialism

With little left to criticize, and plenty of column width to fill, the author resorts to repetition and veiled attacks on socialism. The claim about Venezuela's low rates of growth is repeated. Then the social flaws from the previous day's coverage are hurried back into commission: high inflation, shortages of basic goods. High crime, bitter political divisions.

Then, in a turn both sour and childish, the *Times* concedes that "poverty went down significantly," but quickly adds that, "other countries…made progress in reducing poverty while following paths very different from that of Mr. Chavez."

A Brazilian academic then claims that governments in countries like Brazil have "a more balanced position" and that unnamed left-leaning governments are looking to its model and not Venezuela's for guidance.

No evidence is offered for this claim. Nor does the Carioca academic mention what precisely is "balanced" about a Brazilian society in which the household income of the top one percent is equal to that of the bottom 50 percent of society.

After a short series of additional points—including the passing notation that masses of citizens marched for hours alongside Chavez' casket—much is made of Chavez' use of oil resources to build relations with other South American governments. The unstated claim: that Chavez bought his friends. An "energy fellow" at the Council on Foreign Relations, notes rather peevishly that "Venezuela's influence in Latin America was built on the back of oil exports," as if it is somehow bad form to play one's cards in international affairs. And as if the United States hadn't been bribing its way across the Middle East for the last decade.

Disarming Protest

There you have it: the disingenuous reality of *The New York Times*, a paper that disguises its bias behind a thin veneer of cool detachment and a studied use of non-inflammatory language, much like the paper's bedmate in neoliberal apologetics, *The Economist*. The lengths to which the paper will go to discredit the creditable would be laughable if the paper weren't so popular among self-proclaimed progressives. It is a powerful tool by which corporate power softens the blunt edges of austerity and disarms mainstream liberals with soothing messaging about good intentions and "balanced" approaches to economic development.

By rehearsing the standard refrains of American exceptionalism—a love of democracy, an abiding concern for the voiceless inhabitants of the developing world and the scourge of tyrants that seem forever to afflict them, and a noble need to extend our love of freedom to points south as well as the backward caliphates of the East—the *Times* tranquilizes would-be progressive protestors with the gentle rationalizations of corporate life—the ultimate virtue of which is the appearance of even-handedness. The kind of professorial restraint best represented by Obama, a façade the opposite of which—the dangerous passions of the oppressed—is frowned upon as "counterproductive" and known to be the bane of respectable men. And by respectable one may read fatally compromised.

(*NYTimes eXaminer*, March 21, 2013)

Manipulate and Disseminate: Massaging the Narrative
How liberal media shape reality to fit a preferred narrative

Few groups can massage a dubious forecast into a decidedly optimistic one more readily than liberal Democrats, whose role in the American doctrinal system is to play the lesser of two dire and terminal evils. This banal, tepid, pulseless kind of faux-activism is perfectly suited to the habitués of this giant demographic, many of who exhausted their political passions cheering civil rights and picketing Vietnam in the Sixties. But they inhabit a curious and inviting place along the register of U.S. politics. Liberals know they will always be marginally better than the Republican right, which is caught in a nasty, unresolvable ménage a trois between conservatives, neoconservatives, and Tea Party libertarians. And they can rightly ignore that rabidly socialist left that has slipped outside of the party's embrace, and thus out of earshot of anyone that matters. Aside from even that, a sizeable number of voters simply want to believe America is improving, that the American Dream is still alive, and that their children will benefit by the promises of the platitude-mouthing candidate they just elected.

Within liberal punditry, or any punditry for that matter, few doctrinal methodologies more persuasive than the use of simple imagery. Pie charts, bar charts, column, bubble, scatter plot, the X-Y axis—take your pick. They all exist for the garden-variety propagandist to employ to distill, twist, turn, slice and slenderize into elementary, self-evident and easily-digested data graphics. The better to edify and convince the average American. For an exhausted population tired from the quotidian slog, which increasingly includes the search for work, there's little appetite for complicated graphics or, worse, deep and thought-provoking reportage on the signal issues of the day. Better to provide calming palliatives that soothe and reassure, and offer emotional safe harbors where citizens can park their political faith until the next "quadrennial extravaganza," to use Noam Chomsky's phrase.

Case in point: an episode of Thom Hartman's RT show The Big Picture, featuring his usual "Politics Panel." This is not to say that Hartmann doesn't often provide some incisive commentary on the travails of the American experiment, but this edition offered a template for persuasion-by-pie-chart punditry. The assembled panel jovially discussed Hillary Clinton's derisive comments about President Obama's foreign policy, eventually smoothed over with a quick White House summons. Clinton said the administration's failure to get more involved in Syria led to the rise of ISIS. (Of course, Clinton failed to note that it was our involvement in Syria and Iraq that have deposited a huge arsenal of guns and artillery in ISIS' lap, the better to overrun every vestige of democratic sentiment in the region.) She also added that "don't do stupid stuff" is not a strategy, as if that was the pinnacle of the administration's sophistication. That aside, one can hardly recall strong leadership emerging from the State Department during

261

Clinton's reign, nor does the former First Lady instill confidence—of any kind. She looks rather fatigued, sounds disinterested, and frequently conveys the impression that she is being dragged into a campaign she'd rather dodge by her megalomaniacal consort, lurking like Polonius behind the nearest drape. And yet—an alarming percentage of Americans <u>seem</u> to fancy her as a woman-of-the-people.

What Hartman's show did was outline Clinton as the budding neoconservative and attempt to separate her from Barack Obama, who it then proceeded to paint as a net positive for the American public. As the Politics Panel revved up, Hartman <u>trotted</u> out several charts to justify his mystified response to Republican critics of the president.

The first was a simplistic chart drawn from the federal budget department. It contained a single line representing government spending through the Bush and Obama eras. Dutifully dichotomized in traditional red and blue, the chart depicted spending surging mightily during the Bush era and then, in Hartmann's words, showing how it has "plateaued" since. Hartmann presents this as indisputably clear evidence of Obama's prudence as a commander-in-chief.

While perhaps commentators like myself don't often credit the president for stabilizing the debt inflation of the Bush era, it's usually because of the way he's done it. Obama opportunistically seized on the morbid "Fix the Debt" mantra echoing from the halls of Koch Mansion early in his presidency. It was the perfect rationale: he could claim, as a representative of the people's party, to want to expand the safety net, create middle-class jobs, and strengthen education just as perhaps FDR and LBJ had in times of crises past. Yet—the crucial caveat emerges—because of the Bush wars our debts have grown so menacing that the only prudent path was to tackle the deficit (much like his exemplar and presidential prototype, Bill Clinton). My hands are thus tied, he seemed to say. This tactic permitted a temperamentally cautious president—and unsurprisingly wary black president—to skirt the kinds of radical change he had conjured in the minds of the voting public (quite deliberately, of course). But as forgiving voters never seem to forget, it's the thought that counts.

From that starting point, Obama announced he was amenable to cutting social programs in an effort to address the spending spiral. Hence the <u>deal</u> he cut with Republicans that trimmed a trillion dollars from discretionary social spending, plus another trillion enacted by the "sequester". He <u>proposed</u> real cuts to unemployment benefits, Medicaid, Medicare, and a more stringent formula for Social Security (though some of these were actually rejected by Republicans). These domestic cuts were implemented in the wake of an economic collapse that bore the dirty prints of a venal Democratic Party that had auctioned off Washington's regulatory role to the highest bidders. Even as cuts took hold, the defense budget was protected, largely through the chicanery of appearing to publicly enact and then quietly annul sequester cuts. The 2015 budget has defense spending cresting at $648 billion dollars.

Aside from the source of the spending cuts, the context of budgetary decisions, unexplained by the simplistic graph, is crucial. Bush spending skyrocketed in the wake of 9/11, when he sought, as any president likely would have, to use an atrocity as a pretext to further his political agenda. By the time Obama came into office, both wars—Afghanistan and Iraq—were lost causes destined to be ignominiously wound down. Obama's job along the continuum of U.S. power was to exit those quagmires,
both of which have long since staggered past the $700 billion mark. Obama polished his warmonger credentials by effecting a brief surge in Afghanistan before moving forward with the inevitable retreat. Much of his tasks consisted of couching defeat in triumphal terms. Rhetorical flights aside, the Taliban are resurgent in Afghanistan and an even more virulent strain of Islamic radicalism is dismembering Iraq.

After a comparable chart on the deficit depicting similarly steep spikes and stunning descents, another chart nobly provides a Bush-and-Obama-era timeline on employment. Columns above a horizontal line are net job gains, below are net job losses. Both show plummeting losses across both administrations before the $700 billion stimulus, a plausibly effective check on the economic slide for which Obama deserves the credit. After that, as the chart depicts, it's been all positive gains. Not much, but consistent gains that marginally outpace population growth—a factor not mentioned by Hartmann or included in the chart.

(As a sop to the Bermuda Triangle of conservatives, neocons and Tea Partiers, the chart cleverly limits Bush's job statistics to his final year in office, as the Great Recession opened its gaping maw and sucked the life out of the American economy. None of the fairly typical job growth from the first seven years of his presidency are anywhere in evidence.)

Aside from the lost population insight, the chart does note that it only reflects private employment, not public. This is largely because Obama has been shedding public sector jobs since he took office at a "violent" pace unmatched in recent memory.

Perhaps most alarmingly, Hartmann's chosen chart offers no assessment of the quality of jobs created or lost under Obama. It runs through May 2014, and correctly shows the month-by-month uptick in job creation. Yet what happened this June is indicative of the kind of quality shifts that have taken hold since the Great Recession and so-called recovery began. In June, the U.S. lost some 500,000 full-time jobs and replaced them with 800,000 part-time jobs. Although the half-million full-timers erased from the inventory were more than usual, the trend of exchanging high-wage, full-time jobs for low-wage, part-time jobs has been rollicking along since we began offshoring work in earnest in the 1980s.

After spotlighting their irrefutable facts on the set's giant flat screen, Hartmann turns from the charts to face his panel of critics with a shrug and a supercilious gaze. Who could argue with a line chart? The facts are clear. The verdict is in. Obama is good for America. A more nuanced perspective would have served viewers far better than the bickering panel of politicos debating whether Hillary was right to savage her former boss. But a dialogue with more depth would have run the risk of depositing pundits and viewers alike in a kind of ideological wasteland, where none of the present alternatives offer the slightest hope for the kind of political metamorphosis America so desperately needs, but finds so despairingly remote.

(*Dissident Voice*, August 15, 2014)

How to Make Friends and Influence Plutocrats
A Primer on Political Careerism

Super Bowl weekend is upon us. The ultimate distraction in a nation of five-minute attention spans. More of us will likely spend more time dissecting the San Francisco 49ers and the Baltimore Ravens than we will unpacking the debt ceiling debate. If so, then we'll get what our political ignorance deserves. Citizens are supposed to make informed decisions in a democracy. We have millions of citizens, but so few of us are informed. We spend our free hours—understandably in many cases—planted in front of the tube, decompressing after another long slog through the working day. We're too tired to dig for alternative political sources on the Internet—we'd rather ingest our politics at the fetid troughs of Fox News and CNN and *The New York Times*. But corporate media feeds us a steady diet of business-friendly (and labor-hostile) opinions designed to elicit unthinking support for state policies—which reflect the interests of the businesses who paid for them. So, with a population unwilling to rise in defense of its own interests, we naturally get a raft of venal politicians willing to accept the bribes of big business to do their bidding in government. For the enterprising and unscrupulous, is there a more attractive career path?

A Proven Formula for Political Fraud
For Congressional hopefuls with dreams of national fame, it is such a simple formula to follow: run on a populist platform, promise to fight for democratic reform, pledge to battle vested interests and to create a new kind of government—one that listens to its people. Then, once you've been elected, reverse course. For every time you mentioned 'the American people,' take a dollar to work against them. For every time you denounced a war of foreign aggression, vote to fund a foreign war under the guise of 'supporting our troops.' For every time you claimed that the planks of the New Deal were non-negotiable, agree to de-link one plank from inflation in the interests of 'deficit reduction.' Hire a few fledglings to craft some tepid legislation denouncing some egregious piece of elite corruption, champion it on the floor of the House, get it ratified, and then bury it.

This formula accomplishes two things: first, it establishes relationships with all the fat cats in Washington and in your district. You signal your willingness to work for the betterment of big business, and that your campaign promises were just a series of populist stump speeches the better to be ignored by the financiers of your re-election. Your vacuity is depthless, your cupidity—endless. Fill me, you say, with the special interest of your choice. Second, the formula inures you from serious criticism in the next election. After all, you'll have a couple of comical laws or censures to hold aloft as you remind the threadbare populace how you labored tirelessly on their behalf. The corporate media, purveyor of the status quo, will trumpet your meager achievements with thoroughly disproportionate glee. The rest, the flotilla of ways in which you sacrificed people and principle for short-term profits—annoyingly summoned by gadfly idealists and imperial gainsayers—can be gently brushed aside as part of the compromise of politics. Sacrifice is necessary, you tell Americans, especially theirs.

A Time-Honored Tradition
This is the pantomime of democracy, the little puppet show that has us all transfixed. Obama is simply its latest avatar, a master of the form, like his heroes Ronald Reagan and Bill Clinton before him, who pioneered the tradition of hostility toward poor minorities. We can't really know why Obama admires Reagan and Clinton. Perhaps for their subterfuge. But we can at least say what they did. Reagan launched a racist war against African-Americans called the 'War on Drugs.' Drugs were harshly criminalized and since its inception in the 1980s millions of minorities have been incarcerated. When you think about it, criminalizing marijuana is just outlawing a liberal lifestyle choice. If you want to throw a bunch of unsavory types into prison, don't wait for them to commit a crime—criminalize what they're already doing. So you can't smoke a mind-expanding drug, even though it doesn't lead to violence, and actually calms people down and helps with pain. Of course, Reagan claimed he was saving people from drug addiction, claimed to be helping the very people he was attacking. But we are no closer to eradicating drug use than we were thirty years ago. Either Reagan launched one of the most foolhardy campaigns in the history of police work, or he wanted to attack poor blacks in a socially acceptable way. I say the latter.

Clinton, the New Democrat, also attacked the poor under the guise of helping them. He smartly split indigent Americans into two groups. First, the miniscule clan of the legitimately unlucky—for them he created a program called From Welfare to Work, which sounds like a noble effort to help those who would help themselves. Naturally, it was nothing of the sort. All it did was restrict government assistance and 'transition' millions off the welfare rolls. This allowed the program to trumpet fewer welfare recipients, ostensibly a positive development based on the assumption that people no longer needed help as they helped themselves to jobs, which of course were nonexistent. The second group of Clinton poor were the ones Reagan had called 'welfare queens,' the thriftless black woman who kept having kids so she could fleece the government of more funds, and arrived to pick up her welfare checks in a limousine. In order to create a pair of stereotypes with which to bookend this bipartisan racism, Clinton created the term, 'deadbeat dads,' to stigmatize irresponsible black fathers. So queens and deadbeats were arrested for smoking by Reagan and punished for their poverty by Clinton.

But why would Obama, who's half-black, admire that kind of behavior? Might as well ask why Christians launched bloodthirsty crusades when their savior was a known pacifist? In politics and war, everything gets twisted into its opposite. In

266

Orwell's 1984, war was peace, freedom was slavery, and ignorance was strength. For Republicans today, war is regime change. For Democrats, imperial conquest becomes humanitarian intervention. Your terrorist is my freedom fighter. Sigmund Freud said that if you really want to know the true nature of humanity, just invert society's most important moral injunctions. Seems the same rule can be applied to our government. We all genuflect before the god of peace, but we pursue policies of violence. We repeat platitudes about self-determination and sovereignty, but work to imprison our neighbors. We rail against intellectual piracy after having built an empire on theft. So if we relentlessly extol democracy, does that mean we secretly hate it? And, to my earlier point, is there some kind of deep-seated self-hatred in Obama that makes him want to cut assistance to the poor—to leave Social Security and Medicare and Medicaid open to reductions—so many of whom are minorities?

The False Doctrine of Personal Responsibility

Maybe there is. Or maybe he has swallowed their propaganda of personal responsibility: If you're down and out, it's your fault. If you're unemployed, it's for lack of industry. If you're in debt, it's for lack of thrift. If you're sick, it's for lack of self-care. You need to take responsibility for your life and pull yourself up by the bootstraps—as impossible to do as the metaphor suggests. If you're taking government money, you're a heedless parasite who needs to be starved. That was Reagan's phrase for destroying the New Deal. He called it, 'starving the beast.' The beast is government, not people. 'People' are usefully abstracted into a fearsome image of a bloodsucking bureaucracy, which of course everybody hates.

But that's just half the story of personal responsibility. There's the upper class narrative, too. The tale of the one percent. They're the ones who have actually 'taken responsibility' for themselves. If you're a millionaire, it's thanks to your innate industry. It's got nothing to do with your natural advantages—a rich father, an educated family, private schooling, an inheritance, the countless benefits of being born into a civilization with paved roads, functioning hospitals, policed neighborhoods, secure borders, and instant access to hard-won human knowledge of every kind. In the narrative of personal responsibility, none of this amounts to the slightest obligation to society. Your success is wholly your own. It's John Donne's apothegm inverted: 'Every man is an island unto himself.'

And that's why we need to starve the beast, to ensure that we are not our brother's keeper. To make people go without help—unless it's a bowl of soup from a church or a cheap tourniquet from the ER. In America, you're on your own. That is likely Obama's true position—judging from his actions. It is also the legacy that Obama hopes to fulfill—starving the beast. From Ronnie to Willie to Barack, the beat goes on. By using Republican stonewalling as cover, Obama can enact cuts to the social safety net and blame conservatives for it. Reality, he'll tell us, is a series of compromises. Change is incremental. Progress comes slowly. For every tiny tax we gain on a few thousand elites, there are billions in senior benefits we must sacrifice. So let's suffer the pain of others with equanimity and be sure not to make the perfect the enemy of the good. If all goes well, Obama will leave the White House having restricted our freedoms, reduced our benefits, endangered our planet, and retarded democracy, all while being carried from office on a carpet of plaudits that lionize him for being a champion of progressive values and democratic change. Quite a feat. But don't forget, if it makes you do a double take, it might be doublethink.

(*Dissident Voice*, July 2, 2013)

The Business of Manufacturing Opinion

Are you a fledgling journalist trying to plot a path to prosperity? Do you find yourself torn between high-minded activism and straight-news reportage? Between Michael Moore's florid exposes and Britt Hume's studied gravitas? Are you confused by mainstream media efforts to discredit *The Guardian's* Glenn Greenwald when he scooped the *The New York Times* and other establishment media on the Edward Snowden revelations? Do you wonder if Greenwald is a journalist or just a partisan pundit engineering nefarious disclosures that threaten our troops? Should you simply trust in the defamatory columns by Thomas Friedman and other respectable men with meaningful moustaches and Pulitzers in safe deposit boxes? To help you cut through the fog of modern media, here's a short primer on the options that await you, and how to get ahead in the cutthroat business of manufacturing opinion, the last American industry not to be offshored.

Choose Wisely

You may have witnessed plutocratic pundit David Gregory, in a televised interview with Greenwald, seemed not to recognize the latter's right to the conventional protections of a journalist—leaving open the question whether mainstreamers saw Greenwald as a journalist at all. You may have read David Carr, in a recent NYT essay, where he wrote with a bit more tact about whether journalism was compatible with activism. It began rather decently by conceding that Greenwald was both, but ended by questioning whether the combination was a good idea, seeding your mind with doubt. Let's clarify.

Almost all journalists are activists in some sense of the word. Ann Robertson and Bill Leumer nicely contextualized Carr's editorial by noting the fact that the question isn't whether to be a journalist or an activist, but whether journalist-activists are serving existing power structures or majoritarian causes. The duo pointed out that there are really only two kinds of journalists. The first works to maintain the status quo, the second to overthrow it. They suggest both are activists, however, and call the first a "kind of activism" that aims at "refraining from changing" society.

Functionally, Greenwald is the latter species: a muckraker with a cause, a latter day Upton Sinclair with a sharp pen and fire in the belly. Think I.F. Stone, William Grieder, and Chris Hedges. This is a dodgy business for any young journalist to enter. As backers of progressive agendas, your role will be offensive—you will be the minority voice tirelessly seeking out systemic injustice. You may make a name for yourself by exposing safety violations in the meatpacking district or chronicling the sudden liquidation of wedding parties in Waziristan, but you'll likely become a social pariah, perpetually under attack from smug and complacent establishment types. Google "David Brooks" to see your bête noire. You also might have to live in another country, as your personal correspondence will no doubt be tracked, collected, analyzed, distributed and stored, should you need to be blackmailed, slandered, or detained in the near future. Let's face it, nobody likes a gadfly.

Carr is typical of the former species: the establishment journalist who has internalized the values of power and seeks to discredit threats to their legitimacy. Think Fareed Zakaria, Joe Klein and Thomas Friedman, among others. As supporters of the status quo, your job will be defensive in nature. You'll be required to further the cause of the free market and security state above all—its maintenance, justification, and promulgation—with a fervency equal to Greenwald's. Having already absorbed the value system of Social Darwinism, this will come easily to you. You will also be allowed to camouflage your ideological prescriptions with cheap conceptual siding borrowed from various whitepaper clearinghouses, also known as think tanks. Useful concepts may include Charles Krauthammer's 'Democratic Realism', a version of our supposedly noble mandate to bring liberal democracy to the benighted developing world, whether they want it or not. This is, for instance, a useful justification for both military intervention and the imposition of prefabricated market economies (with a decided emphasis on foreign direct investment, of course).

The best advantage of using hackneyed updates on American Exceptionalism is that your prose won't sound like the unhinged proselytizing of the far left or right. You will simply be espousing a consensus view that, because of its ubiquity, doesn't sound like evangelism to the average reader. It sounds like normal. The fiery oratory of the cause crusader, by contrast, stands in stark relief to our complacent consumer society. It will sound like madness to the unaccustomed ear. Like an Old Testament prophet carrying a message of imminent doom to a community of happy sodomites, yours will not be a welcome storyline. That's why Carr's piece ends by smuggling a seed a doubt into the public mind. *Maybe activism and journalism just aren't a good fit?* This is a false dichotomy the acceptance of which only harms Greenwald, but not Carr.

Manufacture an Air of Impartiality

A second difference between the types is in the manner of their appeal, the form their proselytizing or polemics take. Greenwald writes with passion. You can feel the animus simmering beneath the prose. He doesn't bother to mask his outrage, doesn't care to craft a veneer of impartiality.

Defending a status quo rife with injustice requires a different tack. If there's little to recommend your position intellectually, its best to camouflage it behind a freshet of dispassionate prose, a vocabulary of enervated clichés. This is the modest lexicon of the conscientious reformer: cautious, hopeful, trusting, and above all, patient. The reformer has enough ballast in his gut to weather the most turbulent of storms with aplomb. Even amid calls for gallows and guillotines, his message will soothe frayed nerves: *Everything in its time. We must remember, change is incremental. Let's not do anything hasty here. Let's not do anything rash.*

Unlike Greenwald's alarming displays of rational thought, this tonality plays extremely well among the skittish bourgeois with too much skin in the game to stomach a revolution. Reform is the perfect palliative. It cauterizes the raw feelings of the mob by delivering nominal support for populist agendas, but crucially ensures that white-collar wealth will never be jeopardized during this lifetime.

In the newsroom, reasonable rules apply. Policy prescriptions should always be introduced with subjunctive verbs, the better to promote the policymaker's spin than to call its motives into question. *The administration policy would aim to reduce dependency on federal aid*...Noble intentions are axiomatic. Journalist I.F. Stone once wrote that war planning required one to believe the best about technology and the worst about man. It's the other way around with establishment journalism: Every public servant always deserves the benefit of the doubt, while the technical aspects of bureaucracy deserve merely our contempt.

Beltway leadership, for instance, instead of being revealed as pampered Roman senators disfigured by bribery, should always be portrayed as conscientious men-of-the-people, sleeves rolled and workmanlike paws wringing sensible policies from the demotic fen. *As the Congressional committee wrestles with how to regulate the industry without stifling innovation...*

When police and military battalions beat up their own populations, be sure to cast this as a violent exchange between opposing forces, one legitimized by the imprimatur of the state, the other an unruly mob descending into madness. *Protestors and police clashed again on Thursday...* Naturally, these aren't clashes; they're instances of illegitimate state violence. But there's no need to needlessly impugn riot forces if you don't have to. Also, blur the focus on the increasingly callous nature of technologized state violence, such as liquidating distant villagers along darkened roads lit by thermal imaging cameras from 30,000 feet—achieved with a mouse click in a Nevada bunker. And be sure to spend considerable time criticizing the mob for not producing clearly outlined policy positions (they so rarely do). These are the hallmarks of the invisible activism of establishment reportage.

Abdicate the Role of the Fourth Estate by Avoiding Tough Questions
Another character trait of the establishment journalist worth adopting is an almost universal reluctance to ask hard questions. It would be uncharitable to call this

indifference. As supporters of power structures, establishment media accepts the statements that issue from federal institutions such as the White House, State Department, Bureau of Labor, and so on, not from indolence, but from a simple faith in the purity of Washington's motives. Asking hard questions leads to what Greenwald sees as the value of journalism: "to serve as a check on power". But if you are servicing power, why would you seek to check it? That would be self-negating, and self-sacrifice is best left to environmentalists and right-to-life fanatics.

Perhaps rather cheaply, Truman Capote once said of Jack Kerouac's work, "That's not writing. That's typing." We might say the same of the NYT and its peers, minus the petty envy. For all we know, the staff may print the oracular statements of the government verbatim. It certainly feels that way. If you do rewrite, practice an overweening respect for power, make fastidious efforts to project a mannered impartiality in your prose, and enforce an absence of journalistic skepticism. This will add an air of credibility to the dictums of state. No, that's not journalism. That's stenography. But the paychecks are better.

What You Will Accomplish
When your story is chiseled, dusted off, and lifted to its full height, the effect will be tremendous. You will influence millions. You'll also find yourself assuming some fairly astonishing positions. You might support empty accusations of WMDs against a secular Arab state America once supplied with WMDs. You might feel the need to heap calumny and defamation on a dying socialist president that you have long reviled as a serial falsifier. You may have to invoke the arts of obfuscation to characterize a peaceable Muslim nation as a bomb-obsessed existential threat to bomb-obsessed Israel. By contrast, it will be easy to support White House (false) outrage over (false) claims that an Arab government has deployed (false) chemical weapons against its own (false) citizens. Despite these indefensible positions, you will be lauded for your even-handed review of the facts on offer—except on the left fringe, where the nonstop fact-strewn fusillades will continue, but happily amount to nothing.

You will be widely read. That glistering star on the horizon? A Pulitzer for the mantelpiece. That email in the inbox? An invitation to join the lucrative lecture circuit.
It won't be all sunshine and light, though. You'll have to defend wars that turn sideways, policies that imperil the peace, and economic models that defy arithmetic. But this is the burden of the public intellectual—laboring to advance unpopular causes in the face of the 'bewildered herd', as PR godfather Walter Lippmann liked to call it.

But the educated classes will embrace you. For those of us with a degree, your paper is the gate-key to our ruling class pretensions. How we love to settle down

272

in our sunlit living room on a Sunday morning to sip coffee and leaf through *The Times*, feeling the frisson of liberal respectability. We'll swallow your politics along with the masterly literary and cultural reportage, and not think twice.

But be warned, this state of affairs may not endure. It has become difficult for average Americans to sustain the threadbare illusion that they are Middle Class. According to Paul Craig Roberts in his scrupulously researched *The Failure of Laissez Faire Capitalism*, about 16 million smart, naïve and mostly entitled college graduates will have fired forth from our universities between 2007 and 2014. They will find just over a million jobs waiting for them that require a degree. Either they will launch a Facebook campaign to force fast casual restaurants to require PhDs to 'build' a naked burrito, or they will burn their papers of record, if not their degrees, in the nearest bonfire. There should be plenty to choose from.

(*Dissident Voice*, July 13, 2013)

From *Squawk Box* to CSPAN—Cutting Through the Beltway Bubble & Democracy Gap

Failed ideas, infighting, and glimmers of hope. I found myself watching CNBC's Squawk Box the other morning and an Ohio Republican named Ron Portman was on. He was being beamed in from the Russell Rotunda in Washington, with its columned grandeur and air of gravitas. What a lovely backdrop for the savaging of America. Portman is the Republican prototype. Innocent eyes. Puritan earnestness. Flour white face. Bland coat and tie. As part of that long-running hit, the GOP Weekly Address, Portman announced a seven-point plan to create American jobs. He said his program would spark an economic recovery, a whip that political hacks never tire of using to flog the presses. Here are his seven sterling steps to the next big boom:

1. Adopt "Common Sense" Healthcare Solutions
Portman didn't go into much depth on this one, but a majority of Americans would agree. Although Portman and the people might fall into a bit of a quibble over what exactly "common sense" meant. For Portman and his colleagues, common sense healthcare means leaving it to the market, where the all-important profit margin invariably dictates stingy coverage and unaffordable premiums. For many Americans, health is a sacred human right that ought not to be subjected to human greed. More to come on that front…

2. Power America's Economy
Note the pun in this one? Clever. This is mostly about fracking, faster permitting, and exporting liquid natural gas (LNG). None of which are the slightest bit helpful from a climate change standpoint (See Gasland and this fast-track special for more on that). As the powers that become ever more enthralled by "energy independence" and the wondrous profits it promises our billion-dollar petro giants, the work of committed anti-frackers may be increasingly marginalized by the enormous financial incentives to fracture the bedrock of the earth, no matter how many poisoned aquifers result.

3. Begin Living Within Our Means
This is more fearmongering around the Koch brothers' deficit reduction campaign, a bipartisan con if there ever was one. Without mentioning the elephants in the room—the military budget and the periodic trillion-dollar bailouts of corrupt mega-banks—Portman wants to slash the deficit in other ways. Gee, I wonder where those cuts will come from? Perhaps "reform to entitlement programs"? Republicans like nothing more than anything that will "encourage personal responsibility," a perpetual refrain of Senatorial millionaires. Perhaps Goldman Sachs' Jamie Dimon can be brought in to help make this case to Main Street.

4. Reform Tax Code to Spur Economic Growth

This is especially farcical coming right after the harangue about cutting debt. It must be acknowledged that cutting taxes cuts government revenue, which pays for programs that must otherwise be sustained with loans or—as the GOP prefers—not sustained at all, but rather demolished altogether. Yet "reform tax code" is itself code for lowering taxes on corporations and individuals, with particular callouts for cutting taxes on the rich. It's not as though taxes are already pretty low by historical standards, and when you begin factoring in deductions, you soon arrive at globally competitive corporate rates, and occasionally discover that your multinational owes no tax at all. In any case, this concept is based on the fallacy of trickle down economics, that the more money you put into the pockets of rich people, the more they will spend creating jobs for poor people.

Perhaps Portman and his rabid neoclassical colleagues have been napping since 2008 and missed the mortgage meltdown, the too-big-to-fail bailouts, and the aftermath, when banks sat on more than a trillion dollars in government money since they had what is sometimes referred to as a "liquidity preference." As political economist Alan Nasser has noted, nobody likes to invest in a crappy economy. Hence the need for Keynesian stimulus. But that would require government intervention, a terrifying scourge at which we'll soon arrive. Even Obama seems to believe jobs can only come from the private sector, as he famously touted in 2009. But set reality aside, and let's embrace failed economic theories in the hopes that uneducated workers will fall for the ruse of tax cuts one more time. Viva a falsidade!

5. Unburden the Economy from DC Regulations

This is perhaps the most comical point, especially when Portman tosses around terms like, "regulatory relief" as though American business is simply hamstrung by the myopic interference of our frothing socialist government. It's not as though the lack of regulation, happy encouraged all through the Clinton years, led directly to the mortgage meltdown and the subsequent horror show, thanks to savings and investment bank mergers, lax lending standards, unregulated derivatives and commodities markets, and toothless criminal regulation of premeditated mortgage fraud, pension theft, and so on. And it's not as though the history of British, American, and German, not to mention Korean, Japanese, and Chinese industrialization was dependent precisely on regulation in the form of protectionist measures such as import tariffs and currency and price controls.

6. Create Competitive Workforce

This is another laugher. As if Barack Obama isn't already fast-tracking America labor toward Third World status. Have any Republicans been paying attention to the jobs being produced by the Obama-conomy? Part-time, low-wage, low-skill, high-turnover, nontradeable service positions. In other words, bartenders, wait staff, and bedpan emptiers. Or, to put it another way, we're only creating jobs that can't be exported. A Chinese laborer in Shanghai can't bring a beer to your table in Des Moines, no matter how cheaply he can be had.

Of course, Portman's bullet points on the workforce ignores the need to generate good jobs, and instead offers a fog of rhetoric about consolidating job training programs, consolidation being a synonym for cutting programs, as is the call to defer decisions on how to allocate training monies to states, where Republicans control the majority of legislatures. There is some logic to this: why train people for nonexistent jobs? Portman's colleagues also smuggled education beneath the banner of a competitive workforce—another strange inclusion. Why waste money educating the population? But the purpose of mentioning education is, as always, the desire to enervate the Department of Education and empower the privatization of education, primarily by creating more charter schools.

7. Increase Exports to Create More American Jobs
Perhaps the only way to do this on a mass scale would be to drive wages down far enough for America to be competitive with Bangladesh and other nations were factories routinely collapse on top of their employees. Of course, ten buildings have collapsed in Harlem in just the last five years, so perhaps the analogy isn't so apt. If this is indeed the goal—and the president does frequently harp on exports—this may be as much of an admission as point six that the bipartisan objective of our government is to pauperize America. Then feudal conditions can be implemented. Fiefdoms overseen by CEOs instead of Lords. We vassals can trade our labor for subsistence, never wondering where the surplus goes (who reads Marx anymore?). And perhaps then we will proudly become the world's sweatshop, filling shipping containers with the plastics craved by Indian parvenus and Chinese arrivistes. It has been suggested that in a few years a Detroit autoworker will be competitive with his Chinese cohort. Should we rue the day, or accept our reduced privileges, even as our corporate moguls, untethered from their employees by labor arbitrage, soar above us in private sky fleets, while their state minions monitor our hoods from hovering drone helicopters, awaiting the advent of a tepid protest?

Hope Springs Infernal
But then you see Senator Dianne Feinstein making a speech before Congress that accuses the CIA of spying on the Senate. This is mighty surprising coming from one of Edward Snowden's biggest haters on Capitol Hill. I suppose so long as the spying is done on low-wage, low-profile Americans, it's fine. But once the surveillance community turns its wanton eye to Congress and its bevy of millionaire influence peddlers, the ethics take a sharp U-turn. Feinstein was plenty irate at the thought of Obama's paramilitary "agency" impeding her committee's investigation into its torture habits after 9/11. Anxious to further impair its public

276

reputation, the CIA has accused the Senate of criminal activity and asked the DOJ to investigate. Nothing like getting out in front of a scandal, right?

But there's always a harsh rebuke in store for a freethinker. This one comes in the form of CIA Director James Brennan, who openly scoffs at Feinstein's accusations. A bemused Brennan claimed that illegal, clandestine activity is far below the ethical code of the CI—but wait, isn't illegal, clandestine activity the heart of the CIA's mission statement? You hear him tell a CSPAN staffer that Congress ought to be careful not to inflate its description of what the CIA has done. Yes, Mr. Brennan, because prudence has long been the byword of the Central Intelligence Agency. We all remember how careful it was in assessing the threat of Iraqi WMDs—it's not as if it played fast and loose with the facts in the lead up to the Second Iraq Oil War.

What is occasionally mind-boggling is just how close these federal agencies actually come to seeing the truth—and even stating it. The Quadrennial Defense Review, or QDR, released last week, provided a summary of international threats. The authors were remarkably clear-eyed in noting that Al-Qaeda has vastly expanded its influence across the Middle East. Then, in a staggering admission, they conceded that destabilizing events in the region, such as wars in Syria and Iraq, were the leading causes of Al-Qaeda's resurgence. It's only the smallest of leaps from here to the question, "Why is the Middle East unstable?" Answering this question would lead our brave military leaders to the nearest mirror. But the leap is never made, the question left unasked, and the dark visage never glimpsed. This habitual lack of self-incrimination is increasingly a device employed by the White House.

Few presidents have spoken the truth with more regularity than Barack Obama. He has talked about the uninsured, income inequality, the trouble with surveillance, the need to reboot American manufacturing, and on and on. It's clear, in some compartment of his brain, he knows what's wrong with America, but is incapable of acting to fix it. It's as though, in his incrementalist philosophy of political change, merely stating the truth is an innovation worthy of the name 'progress.' He might feel differently if his most secret conversations were being openly compiled by the dismissive Mr. Brennan.

The Subversive Breakout Session
Thankfully, there are pockets of sunlight, blades of brightness that slice through the dark cloud of ignorance that darkens the beltway day. A couple weeks ago, the irrepressible Senator Bernie Sanders hosted a hearing on healthcare, an event expressly designed to cast scorn on Obama's Affordable Care Act (ACA). Sanders assembled a Benetton ad of healthcare experts from around the world— Taiwan, Canada, Denmark, Australia, and one dismayed and defensive defender of the ACA. This paladin of corporate interest increasingly retreated to some

fortuitous study on infant mortality, only to see it quickly discredited by a bored academic seated along that dire row of socialists.

One after another, goaded by Sanders, the guests dispassionately extolled the virtues of free publicly funded healthcare—taking time, as one Canadian did, to disparage elements of their system (prescription drugs) foolishly left to the private sector. From lower costs to higher outcomes, the case was made. Eventually, the sole guest defender of the ACA and a couple of Republican Congressmen—condescendingly bemused by this minor specter of socialized medicine—argued that all of these Benetton nations were simply benefiting from America's prodigious research budgets and thus able to offer free care. The implication being that only private industry was driving the medical innovation that saved lives. Nobody bothered to mention that vast funding for R&D comes from the government itself via taxpayer dollars. In any event, Sanders soon closed the proceedings and the foreign guests were sent packing, while the transcript of the festivities were hurled down Orwell's memory hole. But trust me, this actually happened.

The Continental Divide
While there's plenty of media coverage now—thanks to Occupy—about the gross inequalities of American incomes, very little coverage is given to another gap: the democracy gap. Or, to frame it otherwise, the gap between what Americans say they want and what American politicians give them. An abyss has opened between our desires and our policies. A majority want universal health care. We get the ACA. A majority want us out of other countries. We get clandestine coups. A majority want more spending on education. We get bigger Pentagon budgets. If polls like those of Pew or Gallup are to be believed, Americans generally don't get what they want. Examining some of the debates underway in the beltway bubble is enough to illuminate you to this fact—you needn't poll anyone. The story of our anti-democratic drift also occasionally surfaces, like a bubble from a gaseous swamp, amid the general miasma of mainstream media. The stray left-wing blogger. A labor union old-timer scribbling in a socialist rag. The curious senator with a bottomless ire for injustice. If only there were some force multiplier by which we could clone and amplify their voices. But then, something like that would have to be called democracy.

(*Media Roots*, March 30, 2014)

278

Hit Him Hard, Please

Leafing through *The Economist* can be a disorienting journey for the garden-variety leftist. As you enter the sanctified space of the week's leaders, you are confronted with a pastiche of fulminant one-pagers by anonymous staffers exasperated with either the Western world's reluctance to bomb somebody, or the Eastern world's reluctance to immediately relinquish all forms of economic protectionism. This week's spotlight was devoted to the former. But first, a word from our sponsor. Across the two-page spread from the leader is an image of Liam Neeson, the tenured international actor who has lately reinvented himself rather convincingly as a brutal killer in a string of Hollywood action flicks. The header beneath his tasteful pose—turtlenecked against the reddish slats of what appears to be a New England barn—proclaims, "He's a fan." A fan of the Mandarin Oriental, a luxury hotel chain which profits by a steady traffic of neoliberal jetsetters, who settle into their lavish suites from Guangzhou to Prague.

It is in environments like these, and at luxuriant G20 dinners, that the doyens of geopolitics debate whether to remove this regime or that as they refashion the character of continents in the interest of institutional wealth. Once you have been soothed by Neeson's muscular health and cajoled into believing you, too, might be part of that globetrotting set of enlightened modernists, you turn to the lead. It's crude header, "Hit him hard" is a tad unsettling. But this is what we've come to, two decades after the fall of the Soviet Union removed all constraints to the hubris of American empire and its parasitic breed of economists, profiteering philanthropists, and arms lobbyists—steady subscribers of *The Economist*.

Punishment Before Proof

As the leader opens, we are instantly transported from the realm of healthy skepticism into the land of impatient humanitarianism. The author, protected from scrutiny by the clever editorial policy of removing bylines (like the absence of last names on certain team jerseys in an effort to erase individualism from the collective sporting mind). The subhead offers this petulant opening: "Present the proof, deliver an ultimatum and punish Bashar Assad for his use of chemical weapons." Rather quickly we are beset by contradictions, namely the rush to judgment about a claim that has not been proven. The existence of evidence is assumed and the journalistic lens trained on the punishment, which the article them proceeds to debate.

In order to annex the moral authority required to insist on bombing the innocent, it is claimed that the "grim spectacle of suffering in Syria...will haunt the world for a long time." Nice writing, to be sure. Yet I doubt this is true. It will haunt the families of the dead, and the Assad loyalists who yearn to return to glory days of Hafez Assad, Bashar's father. The rest of the world will move on to the next flashpoint in the march of militarized hegemony across the planet. As Paul Craig

Roberts notes, we are about to launch our seventh war in 12 years, an unprecedented scale of activity for American imperialism. Syria will soon be forgotten, at least for a few years until, as with Afghanistan, the natives are blamed for not getting their act together and taking over the capitalist Elysium the West has fashioned for them (as conflicts rage among the seething militias). After all, our troops are needed elsewhere—other Mesopotamian capitals are now on fire.

The article bashes President Obama for being slow-footed. He is blamed for not bombing Assad more than a year ago, "when this newspaper argued for military intervention" (one of my all-time favorite journalistic clichés, endlessly trotted out with righteous indignation). Surprisingly, the word "apparent" is added before "use of chemical weapons." But this admission of the lack of confirming evidence is swiftly set aside.

A Menu of Mayhem
Three options are presented: do nothing, stage a full-scale intervention, or strike Assad "grievously," all as "punishment for his use of weapons of mass destruction (WMD)," a claim earlier conceded to be unproven. The potential for mass casualties is conceded, but this is rationalized beneath the subhead "No option is perfect." Sacrifices must be made, the author thinks as he sips his aperitif at London's Mandarin Oriental hotel bar. There's nothing quite so heady as a posture of moral rectitude.

The possibility of retaliation is then broached. It is noted that Assad has friends, including Iran, Hezbollah, Russia, and others. A regional conflagration may ensue. But then no option is perfect. Among Assad's friends, no mention is made of the majority of the population that supports him. Rule One of power politics: the fate of the mob must not be left to the mob. Hezbollah is mentioned with a shuddering nod to the "dark arts of international terror" and which "threatens Israel with 50,000 rockets and missiles." No mention is made of Israel threatening Lebanon with 200 nuclear warheads, or its perpetual warmongering behavior around the immediate region, including not infrequent invasions of Lebanon. The author then shiveringly wonders what would happen if chemical weapons wound up in the hands of militants close to al-Qaeda. No note is made of the fact that much of the circumstantial evidence on hand points to the likelihood that "militants close to al-Qaeda" already have chemical weapons, and have used them twice on the Syrian people. One understands why this troubling possibility is omitted, as it would quickly lead to a disorienting conclusion: that if the United States wanted to be consistent, it should first bomb the rebels who used the WMDs, and then attack itself for associating with al-Qaeda. Clearly, this won't do.

Red lines. North Korea. Credibility. The author stirs up the usual fen of counterfactual drivel. The conclusion is then made that option three, a limited but "grievous" war crime, would be best. Hesitatingly, the author worries that he didn't select the more destructive option two—the thoroughly satisfying notion of a full-scale war of aggression that used "the pretext of the chemical strike to pursue...regime change." Sometimes the imperial press momentarily forgets to uphold its faith in empire's ethical justifications for war. Sometimes it simply admits that the moral arguments are merely a pretext, as all but the most ardent and purblind imperialists already know.

The "limited" crime of aggression is advocated to ensure that "Mr. Assad is deterred from ever using WMD again." Again, the premise of guilt is assumed, the conclusion assured in advance. Excellent advice is then offered by the militarily savvy *Economist*: don't bomb the chemical weapons stores themselves, as that might lead to more chemically induced deaths. No mention is made of the likely deaths that will result from the American use of depleted uranium, and perhaps white phosphorous or napalm. Still, this is welcome advice. The authors—I'm now of the opinion that it required several *Economist* staffers to cobble together this gem—call for a week of bunker busting, demolishing "command-and-control centres, including his palaces." I must disagree with this latter recommendation. If palaces are leveled, where will our latter-day Paul Bremer be housed, to lift his jackbooted feet onto the imperial desk as he peers through his Cimmerian shades across the Barada River, a "golden stream" now polluted with uranium wastes?

International Law Dismissed
The article has little to say about engaging international diplomacy to scale back the threat of violence in the region. America has refused to engage Iran, Hezbollah, or the Arab League in an effort to bring Assad to the table. Surely, this should be the first option on the table? Not if your goal is to refashion the Middle East after your own image.

Nor do the authors appear cognizant of the fact that there is no legal basis for a flagrant war of aggression by the United States. One must be under imminent threat or have suffered an attack, as is spelled out in the United Nations charter, to which the U.S. is a party, which makes it the law of the land in America. But these marginal matters merit no mention in *The Economist*. Perhaps because they are unknown.

Finally, just to launch one last falsehood into the media sphere, the "newspaper" insists that "Syria's refusal to let the UN's team of inspectors visit the poison-gas sites for five days after the attack was tantamount to the admission of guilt." This is sheer falsehood. Syria agreed to allow access to the site of the chemical "attack" one day after the U.N. request was made. Naturally, two other lies are smuggled into the debate under cover of this one, namely the question of whether there was an "attack" at all. There is no such proof, only proof that chemical weapons had contaminated the suburb of Ghouta. Residents claim weapons may have been mishandled by rebels. Secondly, the area where the attack occurred was under government control, suggesting the regime attacked itself. Another counterintuitive feature of the White House storyline, which seems to assign blame to an actor that has no motive, but rather antithetical motives.

Thankfully, the authors begin to come to their senses in the final paragraph, suggesting Obama provide one last opportunity for Syria to hand over its chemical stores. As it happens, it was "increasingly hostile" Russia that proposed this sensible solution. Obama, seeing an opportunity to climb down from his warmongering perch, seemed to initially agree. Should this apparent breakthrough succeed, it will be a decided triumph for the power of internationalism and global skepticism in the wake of the Iraq War. But it will be no thanks to hawkish magazines like *The Economist*. But then, it is just as George Orwell said, "It is the same in all wars; the soldiers do the fighting, the journalists do the shouting, and no true patriot ever gets near a front line trench."

(*Dissident Voice*, September 11, 2013)

The Empire's Shill
The Real Mission of the New York Times

A cursory glance at *The New York Times* is enough to unsettle an otherwise tepid Tuesday. One recalls the story of Noam Chomsky's doctor telling him he ground his teeth, which Chomsky explained might have come from reading the *Times* each morning. Clearly not a prescription for low blood pressure. Unless, that is, you are an uncritical adherent of America's adopted rhetoric—the unceasing recitation of "The White Man's Burden," Rudyard Kipling's antiquated piece of racist condescension from centuries past and grim ideological accessory to our War on Terror. Over the last hundred years the complexion of the protagonists has changed. Our current imperial caretaker is of mixed race, but it seems to make little difference to the dynamics of power. The engine of empire roars on, with the *Times* as its mouthpiece of imperial rectitude.

Postcards from Pyongyang
The headline of the digital edition opens with a photo of Kim Jong-un, North Korea's pudgy scion, and the title, "North Korea Confirms It Conducted 3rd Nuclear Test." The article quickly summons the necessary note of trepidation—this test was far more advanced than past tests by the cultish Koreans. Experts are hastily assembled to discuss kilotons, and President Obama rushes to a White House microphone to declare this distant test a "provocative act," unlike our own mindless production of weaponry, which of course is defensive in nature and benign in intent.

The Great Transformation
With headline histrionics out of the way, a "Washington Memo" talks in dulcet and reasonable tones about whether Obama will prove a more aggressively liberal president in his second term, now that he no longer has to worry about his re-election. The authors murmur excitedly about an agenda of true progressive policies in advance of the President's State of the Union address. Still the shimmering façade dazzles. No mention is made of Obama's obsequious submission to power, an intellectual abdication made decades ago in the misty dawn of our false prophet's ascendency. Yet how the faithful pine.

Doing Africa
Having successfully portrayed the President as liberty's judicious steward and not simply empire's latest janitor, the paper moves on to another unquestioned assumption: that our military has a rightful stake in the African continent. The article is titled, "Militant Threats Test Role of a Pentagon Command in Africa." Is this a newsworthy insight? Why wouldn't there be "militant" threats to yet another imperial intrusion? Yet without once questioning our involvement in a land still reeling from the effects of colonialism and struggling to elude the shackles of the IMF, the paper reflexively states, "Created to train African forces

and build social, political and economic programs, the Pentagon's Africa Command..."

Two observations come to mind—one the fatuous notion that the Pentagon is or should ever be engaged in building social, political, or economic programs, and second that the imposed entity is artlessly named "Africa Command." First, isn't the Pentagon's sole purpose to reduce said social programs into a flaming rubbish heap? Particularly in instances in which "militant threats" cannot be otherwise distinguished from their social peers, who may have—*how can we ever know*— provided "material support" to the enemy? What, then, is this new and novel humanitarian gesture—laying aside arms and forging ploughshares? Or perhaps this is just another piece of State Department drivel. And secondly, regarding the name of our outpost, what better way to signal one's intentions than to simply state them in your nomenclature? *Africa Command.* Forgive me if I have it wrong, but doesn't that mean, "to command Africa?" As the Roman's often remarked, "Nomen est omen."

Persian Goodbyes
An Western commonplace follows: another timeless tale of a desert people's bungling attempts to civilize themselves. In this latest installment, a "Budding Generation" of "Afghan Strivers" face "Fears of the Future." As an unthinking imbiber of doublethink, one wonders why these aspiring Persians would fear their glittering democratic future? Has their distant nation, surely not an American concern, been harmed in some way, perhaps trampled underfoot by a nomadic, oil-thirsty hyper-power? Hard to say. In any case, the *Times* suggests that "thousands of Afghans" who have built careers on international aid, now comprise a "budding" Afghan Middle Class. Later the authors tepidly note that, "the norm is still grinding poverty." That aside, the new Middle Class of thousands now fears that, as America beats a hasty retreat from yet another smoking battlefield, Pentagon dollars will go with it, sinking the Washington-funded bubble economy on which young Kabulites shaped a false future.

Cultural Kitsch and Mad Mullahs
Various other unrelated but necessary articles swiftly follow: an even-handed review of Pope Benedict XVI's short-lived reign, conducted with the preternatural sangfroid only *Times* editors can bring to the world's foremost pedophile amnesty program; a passing mention of a random shooting on an American campus; the requisite corruption inquiry; and a grave look at the fate of Olympic wrestling; and, finally, a discussion of Iranian nuclear activities, this time a nervous about-face from previous articles in which the Iranians were largely viewed as a nation of seething mullahs and other bearded radicals racing toward a nuclear bomb. Now, it seems the Iranians have foolishly converted enriched uranium to reactor fuel, making it harder to build the bomb they so desperately crave—oh, but for the

incompetence of terrorists—but that does make the creation of civilian nuclear energy—their stated aim—easier to achieve.

Shouldering the Burden

It might be instructive to ask exactly which nations these obvious rogues North Korea and Iran have actually invaded in the last fifty years. Since we are pathologically obsessed with their every footfall, there must be some historic precedent for our fears? In fact, neither nation has invaded another country since 1950, when North Korea attacked South Korea. It shouldn't be overlooked, though, that North Korea has skirmished with South Korea, allegedly sinking one of it's warships, and Iran has funneled arms and cash to various regional parties like Hezbollah in Lebanon and Hamas in Gaza. Evidently this is sufficient cause for the U.S. to brand both nations as global pariahs and to launch economic and cyber offensives against them. If our criteria for vilification is aiding and abetting, we might ask, has noble America invaded any countries in the past half century? According to William Blum, no less than 70 just through 2000. Naturally, all of these were humanitarian necessities, but such is the thankless task of empires. When it doubt, simply recall Rudyard Kipling's imperishable verse, delivered to Theodore Roosevelt as he contemplated the colonization of the Philippines,

Take up the White Man's burden—
Send forth the best ye breed—
Go bind your sons to exile
To serve your captives' need;
To wait in heavy harness,
On fluttered folk and wild—
Your new-caught, sullen peoples,
Half-devil and half-child.

On Tuesday night the President paid homage to these themes, noting the need to help an array of nations, "provide for their own security," and to train Afghan forces so the country "does not again slip into chaos." He also sounded the house organ of noble virtues, and the American exceptionalism that render our actions just. Ah, the benevolence of kings. This hubristic fatuity is exceeded only by the distant sound and fury of myopic economist Paul Krugman, raving in fulminant sprays of spittle at Republican "ignorance" of the economic "facts," as the *Times'* venerable masthead hovers above him like a forbidding drone.

(*NYTimes eXaminer*, February 14, 2013)

Condemned in Advance
The Times paints a bleak picture of Venezuela's future.

If you went to *The New York Times* for even-handed coverage of the Venezuelan election this past Sunday, you were out of luck. Rather than an impartial summary of events, readers of the *Times* were made privy to the petulant internal narrative of an imperial power that can't countenance its loss of stature in Latin America.

To give the *Times* some credit, the initial paragraphs of its front-page story were largely accurate. The state-sponsored storyline could wait a few paragraphs. The article concisely related the victory of Nicholas Maduro—Hugo Chavez' preferred nominee—over opposition candidate Henrique Caprilles, who has now lost two general elections in six months. Trounced by Chavez in November, Caprilles could not muster a victory even against Maduro, the charmless former union organizer and foreign minister who has been pushed prematurely into the limelight, the hopes of millions of *Chavistas* now hung like an albatross around his untested neck. Caprilles was typically ungenerous in defeat, instantly claiming fraud and refusing to recognize the vote, despite Venezuela's reputation for electoral fairness.

In its opening, the *Times* only mustered a few oblique swipes at Maduro, claiming the race had been "unexpectedly close" and signaled "an emboldened political opposition" that would "complicate" the task of governing for the longtime Bolivarian foot soldier. The idea that the opposition has been emboldened in defeat seems wistful, as the right has been little more than a tattered constituency that has limped along in Chavez' shadow for the last 14 years, and has now lost six more years to the socialist project. Think of the self-hating Tories during the Blair tenure. Interestingly, the *Times* saw Maduro's thin margin of victory (50.7 percent of the vote to 49.1 for Caprilles) as an indication of societal division and unrest. By contrast, when Barack Obama defeated Mitt Romney with a smaller percentage of votes (50.4 percent), even Fox News said he had "soundly defeated" Mitt Romney, while Huffington Post claimed Obama "rolled to reelection." In 2004, the *Times* itself referred to the reelection of George Bush— with the same 50.7 percent and a very slightly wider margin—as "decisive."

Useful Omissions
Finished with the facts of the election, the authors' crank up the mystification machine as they turn to Chavez legacy. According to the *Times*, Chavez "built his political career on flaying the United States and its traditional allies in the Venezuela establishment." No doubt a galvanizing factor in *El Comandante's* rise, the claim is left in a narrative vacuum. No mention is made either of the merit of his critique of the United States or any of his radically people-centric solutions, with which he countered the structural adjustment prescriptions of the

286

International Monetary Fund and World Bank and which in point of fact established his popularity as the majority poor saw their lives improve.

An anonymous U.S. State Department official is then quoted as saying Maduro's "harsh rhetoric had made the possibility of improved relations more difficult." Presumably the "harsh" rhetoric included condemnations for foreign interference in Venezuela's internal affairs, notably the millions of dollars the United States shamelessly pours into the country to subvert any socialist-leaning party. Would Congress tolerate the direct funding of third-party candidates by, say, Iran? Nor is it mentioned whether explicit U.S. support for the failed 2002 coup against Chavez had also made "improved relations more difficult."

It is then rather gloomily noted that Maduro will likely attempt to continue Bolivarian leftist policies and efforts to free the continent from dependence on international lenders. In an effort to enliven the proceedings, the authors decide to disparage Maduro's capacities as a leader. Notable flaws include his lack of charisma and his inability to muster the respect Chavez had enjoyed with the military. A small halo of hope emerges over the mind of the anti-*Chavista*.

A retired Venezuelan military admiral—and stout Caprilles supporter—is then introduced. (One can only imagine where this crusty old suzerain was unearthed.) The admiral darkly claims the country would become more "polarized" by the bitter feuds of the campaign. Probably an accurate statement, insofar as class war will intensify in Chavez' absence, but again only the negative possibilities of the election are mentioned, and not that a majority of the impressive 78 percent voter turnout elected to continue a radical socialist restructuring of society. The admiral's glum forecast is followed by three paragraphs describing nearly every major social and economic problem in Venezuela, and none of its strengths. High inflation, shortages of goods, predictions of slowed economic growth, fears of recession, "stagnant" oil production, frequent blackouts, and a surge in violent crime rattle forth.

There are clearly plenty of problems in Venezuela, notably the violence. Venezuela's murder rate is the highest on the continent, while firearms in circulation are estimated at between nine and 15 million—in a nation of 29 million. The Bolivar slid significantly against the dollar in recent years. And four times during his tenure, Chavez was troublingly granted power of decree by parliament to push through socialist measures. The creeping fear of authoritarianism was warranted, regardless of one's position on the general program. The use of Presidential fiat has an unfortunate history in Venezuela.

A Lack of Context
Yet for a paper that styles itself as an objective news organization, should the *Times* not balance the administration's failings with a sampling of the myriad

triumphs of the Bolivarian project? Sprinkle the partisan critique with a few crumbs of impartiality? In addition to outlining the challenges Maduro faces, should the paper not also signal the successes he is charged with upholding?

Evidently not. No mention is made of the halving of poverty or cutting deep poverty by 70 percent. No space is spared for the erasure of illiteracy (by UNESCO standards). No note is taken of the vast expansion of healthcare and pensions. Nor are any of Chavez' robust regional coalitions given the slightest column width. But these omissions are decisive in shaping public opinion. If this is neutral journalism, it is a universe that admits of no shading, second opinions, or departure from received wisdom. A mediascape not unlike that of the Cold War, where the enemy was so starkly outlined against the spotless goodwill of the homeland.

Aside from these extraordinary achievements—accomplished in the teeth of bitter opposition from a regional hegemon—some context ought to have been given to the state of the country prior to the birth of the Bolivarian program. After all, this is largely the programmatic platform that Caprilles would reinstall. Unemployment was soaring—Chavez cut it in half. Per capita GDP was less than $5,000—Chavez doubled it. Monthly inflation rates reached 100 percent in the years before Chavez—his government reduced it while improving incomes. In the 20 years prior poverty had skyrocketed from 17 percent to 50 percent—Chavez again halved it. And as Renaud Lambert noted in *Le Monde Diplomatique*, the hemispheric situation was little better. Mexico was conducted a fire sale of state-owned companies and the Clinton administration was trying to push through NAFTA's South American sibling, the Free Trade Area of the Americas (FTAA). The region was rife with neoliberalism. Then came 1998.

Of course, in the delusional narrative of Washington—where the *Times* receives its talking points—these are non-facts, consigned to the dustbin of non-history—the black conscience and bête noire of every imperial project. Synonyms like "strongman," "demagogue," "dictator," and "totalitarianism" will no doubt be rushed back into service for use in the demonization of Maduro. The lexicon of evil was nearly exhausted during Chavez' radical run of power. Had he endured, a new vocabulary of hate might have been necessary to freshen the syndicated slander of the American press. In any case, he is gone and his replacement is a frail substitute, a fact that has put wind in the sails of American foreign policy. Intrigue springs eternal. And at the *Times*, opinions are precast in the ideology of the state, which in its anxiety of influence perceives the slightest spark of independence as a threat to its Latin hegemony.

(*NYTimes eXaminer*, April 17, 2013)

PBS Mask of Respectability Sells Iran Nuclear Propaganda

There are few things more harmful to the public discourse than the cloak of false r espectability – especially on a nationally or globally disseminated news network. When corporate media broadcasts propaganda, a benighted public is duped into be lieving the twaddle of stark raving mad political ideologues as though they were t he very words of Socrates by satellite. The mainstream's reach and influence is st aggering, and when unchallenged, fatal. Take, for instance, the estimable Republi can Representative Mike Rogers of Michigan. Let's consider for a moment the au ra of respectability that enveloped, like a hot towel on a transatlantic flight, the mi ndless bluster Rogers so thoughtfully aired for the nation last month on <u>The Charl ie Rose Show</u>.

PBS' Charlie Rose commands a high station in the china shop of American respec tability, somewhere above the delicate porcelain of Frontline and slightly beneath the glittering chandelier of *The New York Times*. Rose has an impressive array of i nterviewees on his lengthy resume, which doubtless adds to the gravitas of the ma n, as he peers across an oaken table at his terrified guest, his long and rugged face and watery eyes outlined against a pitiless backdrop of black.

Beyond the matchless imprimatur of Charlie Rose, Rogers is preceded by his own titles, which unfurl like royal insignia across the screen: Rep. [R] Mich. Chairman of the Permanent Select Committee. Most of us haven't the slightest notion of the "Permanent Select Committee" is, or what is does. Nor does anyone on air explai n its significance. We know only that it has the ring of authority to it (it is in fact a committee tasked with providing oversight of the intelligence community).

Next is Rogers' personal demeanor, which itself suggests everything fine and dec ent about the state of Michigan. He is white, middle-aged, modestly overfed. His hair pleases with its bland and faded side parting, and he assumes a look of kindly and good-humored politesse.

Rogers is beamed in from the beltway, where all things of significance occur. He i s said to be in the "Russell Rotunda". He stands or sits, flanked by a few impressi ve Dorian columns, which signify decorum and justice and tradition, of which, pr esumably, Rogers humbly partakes. On the other side of the camera sits Rose, his left hand, like a satyr's mangled claw, carving new grooves into his line-saturated brow. Charlie is distraught over something. What might it be? After expressing hi s consternation visually, Rose stammers himself toward a coherent question: Wha t do you make of this deal with Iran?

Cut to Rogers, his manly, Midwestern, and homely smile, for a moment untrouble d, suddenly drops off his face as the most fearsome four letters in the idiom surge through his earpiece. Inside Washington, the phrase, "Iran" serves like a Pavlovia n on-switch for beltway fearmongerers. Rogers begins to drone through his talkin g points: Iran has gotten everything it wanted from this deal, namely the ability to continue enriching uranium; America did not get what it wanted, namely the etern al cessation of all Iranian nuclear activities; Rogers himself is "worried" and "con cerned" and clearly afraid for the fine people of Michigan that Iran will continue i ts "nuclear weapons program".

Rose, picking up that Rogers is more or less savaging the Obama administration i n his drubbing of the temporary pact with Iran, breaks in and forces Rogers to ad mit that the cessation of fuel-related work at the Arak facility is a good thing, sinc e it will prevent Iran from pursuing a bomb via plutonium, as against its supposed present pursuit via uranium. Briefly derailed, Rogers recovers and paints a few m ore worrisome images for the edification of the trusting viewer, namely an "arms r ace in the Middle East". In this he parrots Shimon Peres, who touts the idea that Ir an achieving a nuclear bomb would cause all other Middle Eastern countries to cr ave one. Rose, his visage now curdling into a painful clutch of arched wrinkles, at tempts to interrupt, but Rogers cuts him off three times (with all the forcefulness o f Peter denying Christ). Finally, with the utmost decorum and courtesy, Rose bids Rogers adieu, thanking him for gracing the American public with his matchless sa gacity.

Rose then breaks for commercial, presumably a horrifically tepid message from A rthur Daniels Midland Company, one of the world's leading food monopolies, mu ch to the chagrin of numberless third world subsistence farmers; or perhaps a thou ghtful piece of mendacity from BP, one of the world's leading thieves of Iraqi oil, much to the bootless anxiety of the Iraqi people.

Sins of Omission
Millions of viewers were exposed to this dialogue, and millions more will see it in syndication. As they watch, few will be aware of some damning omissions.

First, Iran is fully within its rights under the Nuclear Non-Proliferation Treaty (N PT) and its agreements with the International Atomic Energy Commission (IAEA). It has the right, as do all signatories, to develop peaceful nuclear energy (as cont rasted with non-peaceful nuclear energy of the kind being perpetually pursued by the United States).

Second, there isn't a shred of evidence that suggests Iran is trying to develop a nu clear warhead. Not if you believe successive National Intelligence Estimates of th e United States. Perhaps Rogers has overlooked these fine reports. After all, he re peatedly misrepresents Iran's civilian nuclear energy program, calling it a "nuclea r weapons program". He would deserve censure for this, were not his voice drown ed in the din of his Republican and Democratic colleagues rehearsing the same lie .

Third, Iran made concessions in this agreement. It agreed to limit its uranium enri chment to five percent, a level from which, perhaps, a dirty bomb might be cobble d together, were Iranian leadership of a mind to pursue collective suicide by buildi ng and using one. It also agreed to halt fuel production at the Arak site. An additio nal facility would likely have to be built there to reprocess spent fuel into plutoniu m, like enriched uranium a fissile material usable in a nuclear weapon. It also agre ed to convert all its existing 20 percent enriched uranium into unusable formulae. Lastly, it agreed to grant the IAEA regular access to its enrichment facilities. For t his, a mere four billion of its rightful monies was unfrozen by the U.S. and its alli es. The remaining tens of billions in sanctions on the Iranian economy and money tied up in foreign banks have been left in place, frozen, and untouched. No matter that these sanctions have had devastating effects on the Iranian economy and soci ety.

Fourth, the United States' attempt to sharply curtail Iran's nuclear program is hyp ocritical, to put it mildly. Not only did the U.S. support civilian nuclear energy in Iran during the Shah's reign decades ago, but America can hardly be regarded seri ously when it suggests that other nations don't have the right to pursue nuclear we apons. The United States possesses thousands of nuclear weapons, and its viciousl y aggressive and perennially aggrieved Middle Eastern proxy Israel has an additio nal 80 nuclear weapons—and a total monopoly of weaponized uranium in the Mid dle East. Rogers seems to think Iran has an interest in not only pursuing a weapon , but in launching a pointless and suicidal arms race against the two most powerfu l nuclear states in the world. Not to mention his conjuring of a certifiable former I sraeli prime minister whose own histrionic notions—that Iran would instantly bo mb Israel if only it could—has been contradicted by saner members of the Israeli military who have admitted that Iran poses no "existential threat" to its statehood, including former defense minister Ehud Barak.

Thanks to Charlie Rose, Rogers' ceaseless fatuities have been aired and absorbed by countless Americans, while none of his lies have been challenged, countered, o r discredited. We only got to witness Rose and Rogers exchanging pleasantries at the conclusion of the dialogue, as though they had just finished a highly erudite te te a tete on the Higgs Boson particle.

Now, when the viewer turns to CNN or FOX News, he or she will sooner or later be served images of some Arab Imam (perhaps Hezbollah's Hassan Nasrallah) fro thing with fury, his trembling turbaned head and well-fingered beard striking fear into the heart of clean-shaven, well-meaning Americans, who prefer the easy deco rum of the Rose-Rogers dialogue to the visceral anger of an aggrieved party. Wha t they won't see or hear is what Nasrallah may be saying, possibly condemning A merican interference in Syria—not an unreasonable critique.

Having heard gentlemanly Mike Rogers, and having seen Nasrallah, they might re
adily conclude that one is sane and reasonable and the other a madman of historic
proportions. This invidious conclusion, equal parts ignorance, misinformation, an
d xenophobia, is what you get when you treat the unreasonable as respectable and
the unfamiliar as threatening. On its face, the mainstream media seems rather inco
nsequential, with its grim-faced interlocutors soft-peddling questions to tendentio
us Congressional lightweights. But as Hannah Arendt once said, even evil can be
banal.

(*Media Roots*, February 1, 2014)

Anatomy of a Perversion
Empires rely on the studious manipulation of facts to maintain a pristine image

One of the simplest ways to pervert the facts of a story is to take them out of context. Isolated, facts can be made to support nearly any prefabricated ideology. This technique is usefully employed by fanatics of various faiths, from Christianity to Islam, as well as their no-less zealous opponents. But ideologies cut across every spectrum of social discourse. Religion is an obvious example, but it is equaled in American society by political ideology—not of Democrats or Republicans, but of the U.S. state itself.

The context-free technique is largely how the world's leading propaganda paper, *The New York Times*, adheres to the doctrinal system of the American state. That doctrine fundamentally demands that the United States be portrayed as a 'force for good' in the world, actively seeking to defend liberty and human rights wherever they are threatened by amoral actors who themselves have been perverted by false ideologies such as Islam, Communism, Socialism, or Totalitarianism. This concept has always been colorfully expressed in the broadcast advertising of the armed forces, as bright-eyed, innocent American youth are transformed into grease-faced warriors emerging from swamps in their waterproof fatigues, M16s leveled at some anonymous shoreline. Here, the narrator enthuses, troops are fighting for peace. The Navy has even adopted the line, "A Global Force for Good" as its marketing tagline.

Sometimes, though, this activist portrait isn't useful as a frame through which a particular geopolitical scenario can be reshaped. In such instances, the objective shifts. The goal is then to present the United States as an innocent bystander in the international arena, a passive entity confronted with regrettable violations of international law or norms. The U.S. is then depicted as being forced to act— often ruefully and with deep reservations—by virtue of the noble values it is constitutionally made to uphold, wherever they are in peril.

A Decent and Disinterested Onlooker
This latter profile—of freedom's reluctant defender—has lately been used to characterize the United States in relation to the events in the Ukraine. (Note that when I say, "United States" I'm largely referring to the U.S. government, not its people.) A perfect embodiment of this portrait was cleverly sketched in Saturday's *Times*. Front page, right rail, headline, "U.S. and Russians will hold talks in Ukraine crisis."

The article is ostensibly reporting on Vladimir Putin's "surprise step" in calling President Barack Obama to "discuss ideas about how to peacefully resolve the international standoff over Ukraine." This comes as a surprise to Western ideologues because until then, in their view, Russia had positioned itself on "the

293

brink of an escalated confrontation that has put Europe and much of the world on edge." The article continues, noting that Russia has spent weeks committing "provocative moves punctuated by a menacing buildup of troops on Ukraine's borders."

These facts are debatably accurate if a bit theatrical: First, Russia has theoretically violated the U.N. Charter by annexing Crimea, notably by first violating the 1997 accord with Ukraine to station a fleet on the Black Sea. By scrambling troops beyond the ambit of that agreement without Kiev's authorization, it opens itself to charges of aggression under the U.N. Charter. Second, the Crimean vote to secede violates the Geneva Conventions on the illegality of secessionist decisions taken under occupation by foreign powers. Since Russia had broken its military accord with Ukraine, it could be said to be occupying Crimea. But there are other points of view to consider. Russian authorities have displayed an invitation from then sitting President Viktor Yanukovych asking for its military intervention. This might then invalidate the foregoing arguments. Still others suggest that the regional Crimean authorities were absolutely within their rights under the U.N. Charter articles on self-determination, regardless of the presence of Russian troops, which, they might argue, were a welcome deterrent to a illegitimate new nationalist regime that had already moved provocatively against Crimean interests by scrapping a language law vital to ethnic minorities. Also cited in this line of defense is the Kosovo precedent, in which Kosovo unilaterally declared its autonomy from Serbia, a decision later confirmed by the U.N. general assembly. The sheer ambiguity of international law on the issue of autonomy and annexation should surely be acknowledged. The U.N. seems at odds with its own track record on this topic.

The larger point to note, however, about America's leading newspaper is this: in less than two paragraphs, the *Times* has succeeded in characterizing Russia as an aggressive and "menacing" actor in Eastern Europe. It has evidently acted in an unprovoked and wildly aggressive manner. Note, by contrast, the absence of any actions attributed to the United States. Nothing aside from Barack Obama lifting the receiver of his Oval Office phone, a sign of the President's quintessentially American capacity to open-mindedly engage troubled foreign leaders. A textbook example of the 'innocent bystander' motif.

The article goes on to further characterize the U.S. as a skeptical observer. It is "uncertain whether Mr. Putin was seriously interested in a resolution." The shorthand is decades old: Russia is not to be trusted. Putin may in fact surreptitiously be seeking "diplomatic advantage" given that Russia is "isolated internationally." For once, this last addition is accurate. The United Nations passed a widely supported resolution in its general assembly condemning the annexation as illegal. More than 100 nations voted in favor, only 11 against.

294

Finally, we find a hint of a deeper narrative. Putin is said to have complained to Obama about "extremists" in Ukraine. This is simply deposited in the third paragraph with no explanation. Why? Because the explanation is a Pandora's Box which would instantly add unwanted context to the situation. And, as noted above, the lack of context is required in order to sustain the building narrative of Russia as rogue and America as disinterested mediator.

Since the question of extremists has been noted only in passing with no clarification, the article's goal has been achieved: the garden variety reader will have firmly concluded that Russia is in the wrong—again—and that America is simply hoping to defuse a situation it wishes had never emerged.

Forgetting Half the Facts
What is omitted? Only a few important chapters in the story (aside from the legal ambiguities mentioned earlier). Here are a few of them:

The American-Backed Coup – First, we should consider the spark that lit this prairie fire: the American-engineered fascist coup. This has been elided from the narrative: namely, the fact that the United States unarguably provided billions of dollars in support to anti-government elements within Ukraine, leading directly to the putsch by violent neo-Nazi factions in Kiev. American support included funnel monies through false NGOs such as the National Endowment for Democracy and CANVAS to supporters of right-wing elements such as the Ukrainian Svoboda party. A recent European Parliament report highlighted the party's xenophobia and racist proclivities. Their leader Oleh Tyahnybok has claimed that "organized Jewry" controlled the Ukrainian government. It was this U.S.-backed coup by these Nazi sympathizers that led directly to the Crimean 'yes' vote join the Russian federation.

NATO Expansion – Nor should we omit the fact of continuous Western military provocations since Mikhail Gorbachev's unrequited efforts to thaw the Cold War (troop reductions, weapons reductions, submitting to the reunification of Germany, etc.). In agreeing to these steps, he was assured by George H.W. Bush that NATO would not move to fill the military void created in Eastern Europe by the withdrawal of Soviet forces and the dissolution of the Warsaw Pact. Since then, NATO has moved aggressively East, swallowing up Poland, the Czech Republic, Hungary, Estonia, Latvia, Lithuania, Slovakia, Slovenia, Bulgaria, Romania, Croatia and Albania as part of a widely recognized plan to envelop Russia militarily. It now enjoys military access to both the Baltic and the Black Seas. Yet when Russia moves troops to the Ukrainian border, fully within the scope of its international agreements, it is demonized as a "menacing" expansionist power. Neither the mendacity of the West in reneging on its word nor the hypocritical double standard applied by Western media is given the slightest mention. But why would it?

Historic Western Aggression – Why would it, indeed, since the *Times* also conveniently overlooked the historic fact of fascist and imperial aggression against Russia from the West. The post-Bolshevik invasion by four Western nations, including attacks from the Black Sea. Likewise, the Nazi invasion of the Soviet Union cost millions of Russian lives. Russia bore the brunt of the cost of the Allied victory over the Axis powers. This history cannot be ignored in light of the fact that Western-backed fascists in the ideological lineage of Hitler and Mussolini have taken power in a Russian border state, threatening to throw open its doors to a hostile and duplicitous NATO as well as attempt to eject Russia's Black Sea fleet from Sevastopol.

The Black Sea Prize – The *Times* also overlooked the gargantuan fact that the Ukraine sits alongside the resource-rich Black Sea with its tremendous fossil fuel stores—a coveted geostrategic prize by numerous world powers.

Neoliberal Expansion – Nor did the *Times* note that democratically elected but now deposed Ukrainian President Viktor Yanukovych suffered his ouster when he turned down an austerity-conditioned multi-billion dollar IMF loan in favor of a less strictly conditioned offer from Moscow.

This deliberate absence of context and the elision of inconvenient facts demonstrate the glaring bias of the *Times* and the American intelligentsia that both informs it and shapes much of beltway thought on foreign policy. It likewise reinforces the doctrinal view of the United States as a benign bystander shoved into action by the rascality of rogue states. This dramatically perverts the picture; the truth is that the U.S. was the 'first mover' in this crisis, backing and enabling a coup that set off a chain of events. Given the wider context, American readers would likely form a strikingly different opinion of both Russia and the government that acts in its name. But so long as this myopic and nationalistic perspective persists, Americans have little hope of escaping the dragnet it has cast over the population, generating prejudice in even the most apolitical of citizens.

(*NYTimes eXaminer*, April 5, 2014)

Accepting the Narrative of Power
The Nation buckles beneath the propaganda onslaught

One of the cardinal sins of political critique is accepting without challenge the presumptive narrative of state power. Last week *The Nation* did just that. Michael T. Klare's article, "Why the Deal With Iran Is Worth Fighting For," swallows whole the poison storyline of the Obama administration regarding the Iran negotiations.

The official storyline goes something like this: Since the Islamic Revolution in 1979, Iran has been a festering swamp of fundamentalism, and a happy supplier of ready-made takfiri who proceed to wreak havoc on the Middle East. Even the one positive to do with Iran is a negative: it hasn't got a bomb yet. But it feverishly wants one. Only heavy, economy crippling sanctions imposed by more civilized and peaceable Western nations have prevented the mad clerics in the Marble Palace from acquiring a nuclear weapons capacity, which in the hands of a trigger-happy Shia theocracy is the knee-trembler of all terrorist threats. Sanctions have brought them to the negotiating table. John Kerry's lantern-jawed resolve (which has no equal in the Orient) has brought them to their knees. Iran has agreed to surrender the majority of their centrifuges, most of its enriched uranium, and their (potentially) plutonium producing Arak reactor. Plus Tehran has submitted, at the West's behest, to ceaseless inspections by IAEA technical minions who may or may not be Western spies. As Barack Obama regularly touts (impotently to the warmongering Republican right, which cannot hear Obama's importunate cries above the din of their threat alerts) that Iran is the most inspected country in the world.

The last bit of this storyline, about what Iran surrendered in negotiations, is true. The rest, to put it mildly, is bullshit. There are sheaves of documented proofs that this entire tinsel-town plotline is a fabrication, an elaborate falsification designed to make witless American consumers pull the ballot levers for whichever neoconservative party tells the most frightening version of the story. According to what we know, Iran is not looking to build a nuclear weapon; is tired of the sanctions ruining its economy; is sickened by the West's cynical manipulation of oil prices to much the same effect; assumes and has always assumed a defensive military posture; is worried principally about Western aggression, which it understands would be triggered should it be found to be pursuing a WMD. In fact, Iran has joined with the rest of the region in supporting for a Nuclear Free Middle East.

Sorry to say, none of the above facts fit the administration's farcical tale. Thus are they elided from view. Nor are corollary conclusions admitted. For instance, that Israel is the largest obstacle to a peace and a nuclear weapons free ME, as a non-signatory of the Nuclear Non-Proliferation Treaty (NPT), the only ME country with a large inventory of nuclear weapons, and an unwillingness to even document its stockpile. By extension America is also at fault. As Israel's patron— to the tune of $3 billion a year in military assistance—the United States allows Tel Aviv to continue its asinine policy of "deliberate ambiguity" regarding its nuclear stockpile. It is said to have hundreds of weapons, but this has never been confirmed. The U.S. has also allowed the rabid bellicosity of Israeli Prime Minister Benjamin Netanyahu to flourish. The pugnacious Zionist radical has kept up a steady drumbeat of demonization the entire <u>length</u> of this century, convincing Israelis, Europeans, and Americans that a bomb-bearing Iran would spell apocalypse.

None of this is helpful for those interested in putting out the numerous sectarian bushfires that now scorch the entire region. Neither is it helpful for supposedly progressive magazines like *The Nation* to lazily endorse the Democratic line.

Klare opens his piece by citing the opinions of Barack Obama, the conservative right, APAC and its clients, and phantom leftists who evidently fear a deal with Iran will inflate military aid to Egypt and Israel. Of course, we know this last will not occur unless those nations demonstrate newfound methods of trampling human rights—always the signal precursor to generous American aid packages.

But note what Klare has done here. He's done what all well-taught propagandists do—limit the spectrum of debate. He cites only those opinions that fit the state narrative. Some think the deal will duly constrict Iranian nuclear ambitions. Some think the shifty mullahs will circumvent it. Nowhere is it mentioned that there is no reason to fear Iran. That there is no bomb. That there is no bomb on the way. That there is no reason to believe—that even if it had one—Iran would use it. Sixteen national intelligences agencies in the United States have repeatedly affirmed this <u>view</u>. Iran quit its research into weaponization technology more than a decade ago. And it has repeatedly made peaceful overtures to the United States during that time, hoping to move itself out of the bull's eye of Western contempt. But this view cannot be entertained lest it be endorsed.

The article then argues for the negotiations because their failure "will almost certainly result in heightened tensions and a very real risk of war." Tensions would only rise if the U.S. wanted them to, which it presently would. That lays the onus on Washington, not Iran. Yet Klare is here arguing by extension that Iran should forego its energy rights in order to prevent the American empire and its Israeli proxy from committing acts of aggression against it. Reasonable enough, in a pacifist sense, but without the context of the negotiations--launched on a campaign of false pretext, shoddy evidence, and steady vilification--it is impossible to understand how Iran is making an enormous concession to a fatuity. After all, the treaty is not based an authentic threat, but on a concerted and

298

relentless desire by the U.S. to disarm all of the West's perceived enemies, enemies being defined as those that reject U.S. hegemony.

Once disarmed, there will be little deterrent for the West to indulge its pillaging instincts wherever it sees fit. This eventuality is never discussed. It is also interesting to hear Western pundits on the left argue that Iran surrender a degree of its sovereignty to avoid the whiplash of imperial warfare, while trumpeting the Palestinian right to resist. This is not to say an agreement may not delay a conflict. It will. But treaties built on false foundations soon expose their flaws. The piece then notes the process of removing the sanctions, but never so much as hints that they are thoroughly baseless and based on conjecture provided principally by Israel and the U.S. to create a basis for illegal actions that have none.

Then, because he feels obliged, as all Western authors do, Klare adds the possibility that "Iran will cheat." James Clapper, the head of the 16 National Intelligence Agencies (all insufficiently warlike according to beltway neocons), rather wearily pointed out before Congress the fact that undermines this oft-repeated fear. Namely, that if Iran somehow eluded the anthills of inspectors crawling the country's nuclear facilities, and began madly enriching uranium toward 90 percent purity, and flicked on a hidden reactor and began furiously working to make plutonium, the United States would see it happening. Satellite detection. How swiftly would our missile-wielding drones get airborne? Nor has anyone bothered to explain why the Islamic Republic would have a death wish in the first place.

Klare then pauses to note that, in dealing with ally requests for more guns to fend off phantom Persian bomb squads, Obama "should be cautioned against taking any steps whose net effect would be to exacerbate regional tensions." This is a nice milquetoast aside, tossed off to softly admonish a President who has done little but exacerbate regional tensions since arriving in the Oval Office. Droning Yemen. Destroying Libya. Destabilizing Syria. Reentering Iraq. Plunging more aid than to any other nation ($89B in fiscal 2014) into the aid sinkhole of Kabul.

The article again warns of the "likelihood of crisis and war" if the provisional agreement falters. One wants to ask the author why, if he is so worried of provoking regional conflict in a region already brimming with it, why not propose the one step that could reign in the most belligerent country in the Middle East? Namely, threating to cut off foreign aid to Israel until it quits occupying and settling Palestinian land, discloses its nuclear arsenal, signs the NPT and opens a path to reduction. The answer would undoubtedly be that such a demand is untenable in today's "political climate." But why? Because there is no public uproar demanding it. This is not unlike voters who continue to vote the lesser evil while arguing that no third-party candidate can win. But that is only so because lesser evil voters refuse to begin building a third party by voting for one.

The article wraps up by reminding us that negotiations produced "concessions on all sides." It doesn't bother to name the Western concessions. It may mean to say the lifting of the sanctions, but what precisely are we losing by ending them? Nothing. In fact, we're opening up new revenue streams for Western multinationals, including a new energy source for Europe that doesn't include Russian energy—long a goal of the administration, which has hoped to split Russia from the EU. Not to mention, once more, that the sanctions are groundless, gratuitous, and hurtful to Iranians.

In sum, what the article has left out are facts that would damn the Obama administration's entire narrative about Iran, undermine the wholly illegal sanctions regime it has established, and expose the entirely unjust and cretinous nature of the negotiations themselves. That Iran has come to the table, obliquely validating the Western fairy tale, is little more than an exhibition of American power. As Iran acutely understands from watching the bonfire of its neighbors at Western hands, the U.S. can wreck your economy, assassinate your scientists, divide your allies, obliterate your cultural patrimony, topple your government, steal your most cherished resources, and leave you for dead. One can understand taking steps to avoid this fate, if they leave one's sovereignty partially in tact and one's borders untrammeled. What is harder to comprehend is the insatiable desire to visit these terrors on others. But that is the enigma of power, and why it turns narratives of peace into the sanguinary nightmares we so often see.

(*CounterPunch*, May 15, 2015)

Acknowledgements

When I was 18 years old I voted for George H.W. Bush for President, largely because I believed he was "strong on defense." That was the depth of my political knowledge. The first time I read anything that contradicted the clichéd mainstream view that Democrats were socially conscious and Republicans security conscious, I was astonished. I think it was an interview with Noam Chomsky in *Rolling Stone* circa 1992. From that point forward, I was immensely interested in this alternative point of view, an underground narrative that claimed to be the true story of the United States. I've been reading and digging ever since.

Among the many sources of knowledge, truth, and inspiration that I've been lucky enough to come across are, principally, the incomparable Noam Chomsky for his big picture understanding of "the new world order"; Paul Street for his grasp of the neoliberal system; Robert Fisk for his superb knowledge of the Middle East; Naomi Klein for her brilliant synthesis of the neoliberal doctrine; David Harvey for his deep explorations of capitalism; Alexander Cockburn for his fearless muckraking and scintillating prose; Jeffrey St. Clair for publishing my first essay and for producing such incisive political critiques; Gore Vidal for his incomparable wit, cynicism, and style; Arundhati Roy and Christopher Hitchens for demonstrating that writing about politics could be artful as well as impassioned; and numberless others I admire, including William Blum, Michel Chossudovsky, Mike Whitney, Tariq Ali, Glen Ford of the Black Agenda Report, Howard Zinn, Edward Herman, Ralph Nader, Mark Weisbrot and Dean Baker of the Center for Economic and Policy Research, Richard Wolff, Patrick Cockburn, Dan Glazebrook, Andrew Gavin Marshall, Michael Hudson, Eva Golinger, Glen Greenwald, Jeremy Scahill, Pepe Escobar, Chris Hedges, Stephen Lendman, Jason Ditz, Thom Hartmann, Abby Martin, Peter Lavelle and the *CrossTalk* crew, and many more. And thanks to Soheila Ghodsi of Press TV, Algerian journalist Mohsen Abdelmoumen, and Iranian journalist Kourosh Ziabari for their efforts to bring truth to the world.

What's interesting is that I've only personally met or corresponded with a handful of these people listed here, but their passion and insights have helped shape my thinking about the world we live in. That I've stumbled across so many good sources is a testament to the power of the Internet, and also to long hours browsing the local bookstores, where they still exist. Not least among them Twice Sold Tales in Seattle, The Strand in New York City, and A Cappella in Atlanta. Anyone who reads any of the above authors or peruses the political science sections of any of these bookstores will come away with new and probably stunning information about imperial America and its march of folly. I highly recommend doing both.

About the Author

Jason Hirthler is a writer, political commentator, and veteran of the digital media industry. His work has appeared in CounterPunch, Dissident Voice, Asia Times and many other progressive publications. He has also appeared on RT's *CrossTalk*, St. Petersburg's Channel 5, and Press TV, among other media.

Made in the USA
San Bernardino, CA
15 October 2015